International Perspectives on Teaching Excellence in Higher Education

What makes a university teacher 'excellent'? How might we best promote the growth of teaching excellence in higher education? And is current policy supporting such growth? These are some of the questions considered in this first international collection on teaching excellence in higher education.

With contributions from leading writers in the field, *International Perspectives on Teaching Excellence in Higher Education* adopts a critical approach in analysing pedagogical policy and practice. It explores conceptual, practical and strategic challenges faced by the 'worldwide excellence movement' and examines recent developments in a range of different countries such as Australia, Canada, Japan, New Zealand, South Africa, the UK and the US.

Split into three parts: conceptual challenges; policy and discourse; and development initiatives, *International Perspectives on Teaching Excellence in Higher Education*:

*   challenges the myth that the excellence movement is a monolithic enterprise;
*   offers perspectives that critically engage with current orthodoxies;
*   suggests that international learning about teaching excellence can only take place through learning from difference and contemplating a range of alternative future possibilities;
*   considers how we can move beyond elitist and relativist notions of teaching excellence;
*   interrogates a range of recent high-profile initiatives such as the Centres of Excellence in Teaching and Learning (CETL) programme in the UK.

This innovative book provides a guide for all those supporting, promoting and trying to achieve teaching excellence in higher education, and sets the scene for teaching excellence as a field for serious investigation and critical enquiry.

Alan Skelton is Senior Lecturer in the School of Education, University of Sheffield, UK. He undertakes critical research investigations into higher education pedagogy and is the author of *Understanding Teaching Excellence in Higher Education*, published by Routledge in 2005.

This book makes a very valuable contribution to extending people's understanding of the concept of teaching excellence in higher education. I warmly recommend it to anyone who is in the least bit interested in thinking seriously about this important topic.

Professor Roger Murphy, Director, Institute for Research into Learning and Teaching, University of Nottingham

What, if anything does 'teaching excellence' mean? Alan Skelton challenges common sense notions of excellence, but rejects the view that we should simply ignore it and hope it will go away. Instead he opens up a much needed and more sustained critique. The book draws upon research from a wide range of contributors who really care about the ways in which the changing context of higher education is shaping our understanding of teaching and learning. Through their writing ideas of excellence in teaching are given substance which is founded upon educational insight rather than bureaucratic rhetoric.

Professor Stephen Rowland, Centre for the Advancement of Learning and Teaching, UCL

International Perspectives on Teaching Excellence in Higher Education

Improving knowledge and practice

Edited by Alan Skelton

Routledge
Taylor & Francis Group

LONDON AND NEW YORK

First published 2007
by Routledge
2 Park Square, Milton Park, Abingdon, Oxon, OX14 4RN

Simultaneously published in the USA and Canada
by Routledge
270 Madison Ave, New York NY 10016

Routledge is an imprint of the Taylor & Francis Group, an informa business

Transferred to Digital Printing 2008

Typeset in Times by Wearset Ltd, Boldon, Tyne and Wear

British Library Cataloguing in Publication Data
A catalogue record for this book is available from the British
Library

Library of Congress Cataloging in Publication Data
A catalog record for this book has been requested

ISBN10: 0-415-40362-6 (hbk)
ISBN10: 0-203-93937-9 (ebk)

ISBN13: 978-0-415-40362-7 (hbk)
ISBN13: 978-0-203-93937-6 (ebk)

Contents

Contributors

Angela Brew is Associate Professor in the Institute for Teaching and Learning at the University of Sydney. She is internationally renowned as a researcher and speaker and has worked in the UK and in Australia in the area of higher education. Her research on the nature of research and human knowing and its relationship to teaching has been published widely. Her books include: *The Nature of Research: Inquiry in Academic Contexts* and, most recently, *Research and Teaching: Beyond the Divide*, published by Palgrave Macmillan (June 2006). From 1999–2003 she was President of the Higher Education Research and Development Society of Australasia (HERDSA) and she is co-editor of the *International Journal for Academic Development*.

Sue Clegg is Professor of Higher Educational Research at Leeds Metropolitan University. Her publications span close-to-practice research, often in collaboration with practitioners, to theoretical interventions for example in her work on the social and pedagogical significance of the gendering of information technology and her critique of the debate about the nature of 'evidence-based' practice. She has written about the importance of critical distance and work which scrutinises higher education as well as serving it. In her recent work she has taken seemingly mundane pedagogical practices, such as those involved in personal development planning, and explored how these are understood by staff and students and the ways in which they are reframed in policy discourse. She has also taken a critical look at institutional practices designed to improve teaching, analysing the rhetorical repertoire of learning and teaching strategies and exploring how these strategies are mediated in practice. She is editor of *Teaching in Higher Education* and is a regular contributor at higher education conferences.

Vaneeta-marie D'Andrea is currently Director of Academic Affairs and Operations and Professor of Sociology of Education at Central Saint Martins College of Art and Design, University of the Arts London. In addition, at this time she is involved with carrying out consultancy projects in the Gulf States, Russia and Northern Ireland for the British Council on a variety of topics related to higher education policy developments. She has received numerous awards for her work as an educator, and in 2000 she was selected as a Carnegie Scholar. Her primary research and teaching interests include: quality enhancement of teaching and learning, scholarship of teaching and learning (SoTL), higher education policy, educational development and issues of gender and ethnicity.

Hugo Dobson is Senior Lecturer in Japan's international relations in the National Institute of Japanese Studies and School of East Asian Studies, University of Sheffield. His teaching and research interests are in Japan's role in the world, global governance and the G8. He is the author of *Japan and the G7/8, 1975–2002* (RoutledgeCurzon, 2004), *The Group of 7/8* (Routledge, 2007) and co-author of *Japan's International Relations: Politics, Economics and Security* (RoutledgeCurzon, 2005, 2nd edition).

Joëlle Fanghanel is Acting Director of the Educational Development Centre at City University, London. She is involved in educational development at national and international level. She has published on teaching in higher education, educational development, higher education policy and professional practice.

Richard A. Gale is a Senior Scholar at The Carnegie Foundation for the Advancement of Teaching, a centre for educational research and policy studies in Stanford, California, where he serves as Director for The Carnegie Academy for the Scholarship of Teaching and Learning (CASTL) Higher Education Program.

David Gosling taught philosophy and education before becoming Head of Educational Development at the University of East London. He is now an independent consultant and Visiting Research Fellow at the University of Plymouth. His publications include work in applied philosophy, higher education policy and educational development. Current research projects include the Centres for Excellence in Teaching and Learning and an international study of academic development centres.

Andrew Hannan is Professor of Education at the University of Plymouth. His recent research has been concerned with such topics as innovating in higher education (including the impact of the CETL initiative), external examining, the student experience of widening participation and comparing the undergraduate student experience in the UK and China.

Mick Healey is Professor of Geography at University of Gloucestershire. He is the Director of the Geography Discipline Network (GDN) and Senior Adviser for Geography to the Higher Education Academy's Subject Centre for Geography Earth and Environmental Sciences. He is Co-Director of the Centre for Active Learning in Geography Environment and Related Disciplines. In 2000 he was awarded a National Teaching Fellowship. He has written and presented extensively about the research-teaching linkage and has advised The Higher Education Academy, HEFCE and the Canadian Federal Government about enhancing the linkage. He co-wrote with Alan Jenkins *Institutional Strategies to Link Teaching and Research* (York: The Higher Education Academy, 2005).

Alan Jenkins long taught and researched geography and was founding co-editor of the *Journal of Geography in Higher Education*. He is now an educational developer, researcher and Emeritus Professor at Oxford Brookes University UK, a Reinvention Fellow for the Reinvention Centre for Undergraduate Research at Oxford Brookes and Warwick, consultant on teaching/research relations for the Higher Education Academy and visiting Professor at Staffordshire University.

Joce Jesson is a Principal Lecturer in Social and Policy Studies at the University of Auckland in New Zealand. Her research interests are in the fields of educational policy, sociology of education and the sociology of unions. She is a member of the editorial board of the *New Zealand Journal of Teachers' Work* and has published in a number of national and international journals including the *New Zealand Journal of Educational Studies, ACCESS: Critical Perspectives on Communication, Cultural and Policy Studies* and the *Journal of Education Policy*. She recently co-edited a book on the Performance-Based Research Fund with Richard Smith (2005).

Carolin Kreber is Professor of Teaching and Learning in Higher Education and the Director of the Centre for Teaching, Learning and Assessment at the University of Edinburgh as well as Adjunct Professor at the University of Alberta, Canada, where she was associate professor of higher education from 1997–2005. From 1993 to 1996 she was an educational development consultant and lecturer at Brock University in Ontario. Her PhD is from the University of Toronto.

Philippa Levy is Academic Director of CILASS, the Centre for Inquiry-based Learning in the Arts and Social Sciences, and Senior Lecturer in the Department of Information Studies, at the University of Sheffield. She holds a University of Sheffield Senate Award for Excellence in Learning and Teaching (2002). Her research is in the areas of inquiry-based learning, networked learning and networked learner support, and she has a special interest in participatory and practitioner-led forms of educational inquiry. She is the co-editor of a recent book entitled *Developing the New Learning Environment: The Changing Role of the Academic Librarian* (Facet, 2005).

Bruce Macfarlane is Professor of Education and Director of the Centre for Research in Tertiary Education at Thames Valley University, UK. The nature of academic ethics and professional identity form the main focus of his research interests. His most recent publications include: *Teaching with Integrity* (RoutledgeFalmer, 2004); and *The Academic Citizen* (Routledge, 2006).

Sioux McKenna will shortly become Senior Lecturer in Higher Education at the University of KwaZulu-Natal. In her doctoral research study Sioux considered the ways in which academic literacies are constructed in higher education and the implications of this for a transforming society. She has published on a variety of policy and practice issues related to higher education teaching and learning.

Janice Malcolm is a Senior Lecturer at the University of Kent. She has researched and written extensively on the ways in which pedagogic identity in further and higher education is constructed through workplace practices, disciplinary communities and policy discourses, as well as through formal teacher education practices.

Yukako Mori was a Research Associate working at Nagoya University in Japan until March 2007. Through her former experience as an administrator, she became interested in national policies of higher education. After graduating with an MA in Education Policy and Practice at the University of Sheffield, she assumed her aforementioned position which involved promoting the internationalisation of universities. Her research concentrates on higher education policy, staff development and standards of professionalism within both academic and administrative university departments.

Jon Nixon, Professor of Educational Studies, University of Sheffield, has previously held chairs at Canterbury Christ Church University and at the University of Stirling. Until recently he was Head of the School of Education at Sheffield. He now plays a central role in the development of home and overseas research degree programmes. His recent research has focused on the institutional management of education, the values underpinning academic practice and the role of the public educator. The central theme of his work is the democratic renewal of educational institutions through a reorientation of professional practice and purpose. He has worked closely with Stewart Ranson on a number of projects relating to this theme.

Ruth Searle is currently Director for the Centre for Higher Education Studies at the University of KwaZulu-Natal. As a member of the Centre she and her colleagues are responsible for both formal and non-formal academic professional development. Her areas of interest are in teaching and learning, institutional development and postgraduate supervision.

Alan Skelton is a Senior Lecturer at the School of Education, University of Sheffield, Director of the M.Ed in Teaching and Learning for University Lecturers course and a member of the Research Centre for Higher Education and Lifelong Learning. He conducted an Economic and Social Research Council-funded study of the National Teaching Fellowship Scheme between 2002–2003 which formed the empirical basis of a recent book entitled *Understanding Teaching Excellence in Higher Education: Towards a Critical*

Approach, published by Routledge. Alan is a member of the Executive Board of the journal *Teaching in Higher Education* and publishes within the field of higher education pedagogy.

Richard Smith is a Senior Lecturer at the School of Education, AUT University, in Auckland, New Zealand. His research interests are in the fields of educational policy, sociology of education and educational leadership. He is a member of the editorial boards of the *New Zealand Journal of Educational Leadership, ACCESS: Critical Perspectives on Communication, Cultural and Policy Studies* and *Policy Futures in Education* and, more recently, *Teaching in Higher Education*. He has written for a number of national publications including the *New Zealand Journal of Educational Studies, New Zealand Journal of Educational Leadership, New Zealand Journal of Teachers' Work* and *SET: Information for Teachers*. Richard is currently the Vice President of the New Zealand Association for Research in Education.

Miriam Zukas is Professor of Adult Education and Director of the Lifelong Learning Institute at the University of Leeds. She is also the current editor of *Studies in the Education of Adults*. Her research interests include pedagogic and disciplinary identities and pedagogic learning in adult, further, higher and workplace contexts.

Acknowledgements

I would like to thank all the contributors to this book who have devoted considerable time and energy to this shared enterprise; I have gained great insights from working with you and from your different perspectives on teaching excellence.

I would also like to thank Jon Nixon, Bruce Macfarlane and Elizabeth Kovacs in particular for offering support and comments on specific chapters; and Kirsty Smy at Routledge for dealing with my practical concerns and questions. Finally, I would like to acknowledge a conference paper that informs Chapter 9 of this book: Jesson, J. and Smith, R. (2006) 'Tertiary teaching matters: yeah right! The evolution of TE policy on "quality" tertiary teaching', paper presented to the annual conference of the New Zealand Association for Research in Education, December, Rotorua, New Zealand.

Introduction

Alan Skelton
(University of Sheffield, UK)

The need for new understandings of teaching excellence

The 'worldwide excellence movement' marches on – affecting education in not only developed countries but also in nations with different forms of government and economic circumstances (Iannaccone, 1989; McDonald, 1990; Fritzberg, 2000). This movement is closely associated with educational reform processes sweeping the globe, informed by managerialist, market-driven and performative policies and discourses (Ball, 2003). Excellence is so potent because it brings together a range of neo-conservative and neo-liberal interests. It offers a way in which the seemingly contradictory goals of expansion, efficiency, choice, the maintenance of standards, economic relevance and meeting individual needs through specialization can all be brought together under a common banner. It also provides a way in which the move to mass and 'universal' systems of higher education can be managed under conditions of reduced funding, since excellence shifts responsibility away from the state to enthusiastic and self-regulating individuals, teams and institutions.

Within this context 'teaching excellence' has taken on particular meanings and become part of the everyday language and practice of higher education. It is now a significant object of policy reform and mechanisms to promote it have proliferated and intensified, operating at different levels (e.g. individual, institution and subject discipline) to create 'synergistic' impact. Avoiding teaching excellence is therefore becoming increasingly difficult – it regularly features as part of institutional rhetoric and self-presentation, and academics are frequently invited to take part in and contribute to teaching excellence initiatives. Those involved in teaching increasingly have to monitor performance and provide evidence of excellence to satisfy managers and external stakeholders. Whilst there is a possibility that over time such performative processes may change the way academics think about teaching and what they hold to be of educational value, a more sophisticated understanding of different ways we might talk about teaching to different audiences may be taking root. As Deem (2004: 291) notes, in commenting on the impact of globalization on higher education more generally:

, Public service workers may thus retain their existing values about the importance of the services they provide, whilst accepting the necessity of talking about markets, performance indicators and other business metaphors in certain settings.

In an effort to make teaching excellence explicit and to subject it to public scrutiny, I recently outlined four 'ideal type' understandings, calling these: traditional; performative; psychologized and critical (see Skelton, 2005: 21–37). Empirical research that informed this work showed that performative and psychologized understandings currently dominate the way we think about teaching excellence whereas traditional understandings are under attack and critical understandings banished to the margins. A performative teaching excellence is attractive to policymakers and institutional managers given its emphasis on the three 'E's of economy, efficiency and effectiveness (see Morley, 1997). Performative understandings emphasize a type of teaching that is relevant to commerce and industry; one that is successful in attracting students on to courses which compete globally; and one which allows teaching itself to be regulated by the state to maximize individual, institutional and system performance. It is becoming increasingly clear that this view of teaching excellence is limited for three main reasons. First, 'to be relevant to the economy' is not a sufficient ontological project for the university. This is merely a defensive reaction to contemporary economic pressures rather than a proactive expression of its identity and potential contribution to society. Second, there is a fundamental conflict between the principles of education (and a teaching excellence that flows from this) and market models of provision. Put simply education cannot be reduced to a problem-free object of consumption (McMurtry, 1991). Finally, academic staff are becoming increasingly disillusioned by an excellence that is obsessed with monitoring and measurement. An exclusive focus on technical-practical matters and an overemphasis on operational concerns does not sit easily with the intellectual culture of higher education (Rowland, 2000).

A psychologized understanding of teaching excellence concentrates on the transaction between individual teacher and student. It is underpinned by psychological constructions of the teacher/learner and seeks to establish universal procedures for teaching and learning, their successful implementation in practice and the achievement of specified outcomes. One of the attractions of viewing teaching excellence in this way is that it appears to offer a means of predicting and controlling what will be learnt and how. Psychology's scientific paradigm – which suggests that it is possible to undertake objective and reliable studies of teaching techniques and processes of learning – provides an approach which allows behaviour to be understood and categorized, and for practice to be subsequently improved (Malcolm and Zukas, 2001: 35). The problem with this view of teaching excellence is that it fails to recognize the complexity and context-specificity of learning situations. It also assumes that teaching takes place in a social vacuum – that transactions between individuals are not mediated by the social and political circumstances of the time.

For the reasons expressed above, it is now becoming apparent that performative and psychologized understandings of teaching excellence are neither adequate nor desirable. If teaching excellence is to become a meaningful concept in our lives it has to look beyond current preoccupations with the economy, efficiency and effectiveness – in common parlance 'what works'. It also has to look beyond interpersonal relations to examine the broader purposes it might serve as higher education seeks to make a full and valued contribution to wider society. We need to put teaching excellence on to firmer ground in order to do this – to treat it as a matter of serious intellectual investigation. This book offers a range of international perspectives on teaching excellence in order to provoke debate and encourage future action.

Taken-for-granted assumptions

In one sense the normalization of teaching excellence in the academy has had a positive impact in terms of raising the status of teaching relative to research. It has put teaching on the agenda and ensured that some academics put more time and energy into thinking about pedagogical processes. As high quality teaching becomes an expectation within our working lives, the efforts of people who wish to concentrate on this aspect of their practice has also been affirmed, even within 'research-intensive' institutions (Skelton, 2004). A variety of awards for teaching have supported this process, comprising traditional prizes, teaching fellowship schemes, educational development grants and promotion/bonus initiatives (see Warren and Plumb, 1999: 246–249). Having won awards for teaching excellence, some academic staff are giving up their substantive research interests and actively pursuing new identities as educational specialists within a particular discipline (see Leon, 2002). This is consistent with the vision of Ernest Boyer, who identified the 'scholarship of teaching' as a legitimate pursuit for academics carrying equal value to research or the 'scholarship of discovery' (see Boyer, 1990). Teaching excellence therefore has the potential to raise fundamental questions about the teaching–research relationship and to support an academic professionalism that unifies high quality research, teaching and scholarship. Looked at in this way teaching excellence can be a progressive force, something which clearly has the potential to enhance the student experience.

On the other hand, a teaching excellence that has become part of our everyday language and practice also runs the risk of becoming taken for granted. With the rush to put teaching excellence on the agenda and to embed it within institutions through a variety of development mechanisms, a range of 'common sense' and problematic understandings about it have emerged. With the intensification of higher education work and the constant calls for information (some of which are to do with teaching), there is little time to question these understandings. We are encouraged to enter into performative and psychologized discourses and further circulate their meanings and assumptions through endless form filling and other regulatory practices to do with monitoring and evaluation. This can undermine critical faculties and de-energize people from questioning the way in which teaching excellence is being constructed.

It has been argued that within the context of new regulatory regimes, entrants to the profession may find it difficult to think outside dominant discourses of teaching in higher education (Zukas and Malcolm, 2002b). However, there is evidence to suggest that even those people who appear to be advocates of teaching excellence initiatives retain some private reservations about them (Gosling and Hannan, Chapter 10, this volume; Skelton, 2005: 51–52). It is important therefore to identify commonly held assumptions about teaching excellence in order to subject them to public scrutiny. We need a teaching excellence that is resilient and fit for the long term. Current common sense about teaching excellence is built on the following problematic assumptions:

- *Teaching excellence is a 'good thing'*: here the assumption is that it is both natural and desirable to want to improve our teaching and reach the very highest standards. Who would not want to sign up to the virtuous project of teaching excellence? From this perspective, teaching excellence is a 'hurrah concept' – it is associated with the meritocratic ideals of fulfilling individual potential and sustaining human progress – this is why it is so difficult to argue against it. The assumed goodness of teaching excellence prevents us from looking at its 'dark side'; for example, how it can foster divisiveness and how mechanisms designed to promote teaching excellence may have negative or unintended effects.
- *Teaching excellence is value free and non-ideological*: this assumes that teaching is essentially a technical-practical act which involves passing on culturally approved knowledge, skills and attitudes to the next generation. Teaching is a neutral and objective affair – information is communicated impartially with respect for the facts. This view fails to take into consideration the ideological character of higher education teaching, for example, the way in which values inform decisions about the selection, transmission and assessment of knowledge (Young, 1971). Explicating these values and recognizing that constructions of teaching excellence are inevitably socially and historically contingent, demonstrates that ideology is alive and well within the academy (Barnett, 2003). Recent moves to make higher education teaching more relevant to commerce and industry show quite clearly how ideology can influence the way we think and practice.
- *All teachers can become excellent through continuous improvement*: now that teaching excellence has shaken off its elitist shackles, there is an assumption that everyone can become excellent with appropriate effort and sustained reflection. This assumption denies the inequalities that exist between staff (both within and across institutions) in our increasingly stratified higher education system (Nixon *et al.*, 2001: 232). Higher education

workers are fragmented with uneven resources to commit to excellence. This will inevitably influence the time they can give to sustained reflection on their own practice.

- *Students want a teaching excellence that is responsive to their needs*: this assumes that students as consumers within the market are driving the push for teaching excellence and that excellence involves providing greater choice. There is little empirical evidence to support these assumptions and research tends to collapse student opinion into one homogenous voice (rather than explore qualitative differences in perspective). Student evaluation data are often derived from surveys which make questionable assumptions about teaching and learning (for example, how effective a member of staff is in 'delivering' a lecture).

- *All institutions can provide teaching excellence; different forms can coexist and have equal value*: here the assumption is that we can move towards a mass system of higher education without a decline in academic standards. Institutional differentiation is pursued as a policy goal to cater for different student needs and aspirations. Different types of institution can offer a particular type of teaching excellence in keeping with their history, mission and identity. Multiple forms of teaching excellence can emerge; competition between institutions will drive up standards; different expressions of teaching excellence will have equal value. This assumption about how teaching excellence can be 'democratized' (offered to more people and in a variety of forms) fails to take into consideration the differential status accorded to different institutions within stratified systems and the funding streams that perpetuate such systems. Different types of teaching excellence may evolve, therefore, but unless significant policy and funding changes are made, it is unlikely that they will have equal status and weight.

- *Teaching excellence is necessary for economic competitiveness*: there is an assumption – underpinned by human capital theories – that university teaching can give national economies a competitive edge in the global marketplace. Excellence here means not only high quality teaching but also one that is more relevant to the needs of commerce and industry. Some have expressed doubts about the long term application of a teaching that is geared to what is economically relevant today. According to this view, a competitive edge in the future may require qualities associated more with 'traditional' university education such as critical thinking and originality of thought (Barnett, 1997). A teaching excellence that is increasingly linked to economic relevance also discourages us from thinking about the range of aims and purposes higher education might have in contemporary society (see Skelton, 2005: 21–22).

- *Teaching excellence helps to promote teaching generally and lessens the teaching/research divide*: here the assumption is that teaching excellence helps to drive up general standards of teaching (through a 'trickle down' effect) and reduces the status differential between teaching and research. An emphasis on a common language of 'excellence' and the creation of new funding streams to promote teaching excellence attempt to redress the balance between teaching and research and prevent the former from remaining the 'poor relation' of the two. As yet we have little empirical evidence on which to make judgements about the extent to which the promotion of teaching excellence has driven up general standards of higher education teaching. What evidence we do have presents a somewhat disappointing picture. For example, research into the NTFS in the UK casts doubts on its ability to impact on the sector as a whole (Skelton, 2004; HEFCE, 2005: 40–45), a finding which has led to the scheme being radically revised for 2006 (see Skelton, Chapter 14, this volume). Whilst teaching excellence initiatives may have raised the status of teaching in higher education, they have reinforced the separation between teaching and research which is limiting in terms of developing a unified view of academic work (based on teaching, research and scholarship). Separate policies and funding streams for teaching and research also maintain a distance between them. There is also evidence to suggest that policies devoted to research and teaching are contradictory; they work against each other to obstruct positive change (Trowler *et al.*, 2005).

- *Teaching can only be excellent if it serves learning*: a dominant view seems to be emerging that teaching is only as good as the learning it fosters. According to this view, the proof of excellent teaching can be found only in what learning outcomes are achieved. This new found sovereignty of learning is demonstrated in the names given to national organizations (for example, the Institute for Learning and Teaching in the UK) and also in how 'didactic teaching' and any notions of 'teaching as a performance' have almost become demonized (see Skelton, 2005: 36). Moral panics about the quality of teaching have led politicians and managers to place their faith in structures, resources and technology as a basis for improvement rather than teachers themselves. The emphasis has been on creating systems and standardised approaches to teaching that are 'teacher-proof': capable of replication across time and space. This attempt to de-professionalize teachers shifts our attention from thinking about teaching as value-laden, creative and embodied; something which cannot be reduced to a technical act. The joint emphasis on standardization and learning outcomes also plays down the importance of context in teaching. Is a teaching excellence that takes place in poor conditions with 'non-traditional' learners the same as one which can rely on privileged resources and students?

Some would argue that given these deeply entrenched common sense assumptions, we should have nothing to do with teaching excellence. We should try and ignore it, hoping that it will go away. According to this view, teaching excellence has always been a problematic concept. First it was an elitist concept associated with privilege. Now it is a technical and bureaucratic notion which lacks any substance (Readings, 1996). From this position it is difficult to see any potential good in teaching excellence. This is not the view taken in this book. Adopting a 'critical approach' discussed at length elsewhere (Skelton, 2005: 10–14), this book seeks to engage seriously with teaching excellence – to treat it as a matter worthy of serious intellectual exploration. This exploration questions current assumptions about teaching excellence with the intent of shifting common sense into more 'critical directions' (Apple, 2004: 24).

International perspectives

International perspectives on teaching excellence are an important part of a critical investigation. They support comparative analysis which helps to contextualize, locate and situate particular understandings of teaching excellence that are geographically bound. The latent power of the worldwide excellence movement rests on the myth that it is a monolithic enterprise: consensual, coherent and uniform. Looking at developments in different countries, however, allows us to uncover similarities and differences in the way teaching excellence is being expressed. Such differences remind us of the importance of the local context and raise important 'questions about the universal effects of globalising tendencies' (Deem, 2004: 295). For example, a recent comparison of the Canadian 3M awards, the Australian Awards for University Teaching, the US Professors of the Year Program and the National Teaching Fellowship Scheme for England and Northern Ireland revealed differences in the nature, locus and emphasis of national level award schemes (see Skelton, 2005: 43–44). Such comparative analyses allow inter-national learning about teaching excellence to take place: to learn from difference and to anticipate future possibilities.

Of course the charge could be made that a book on international perspectives promulgates the discourse of teaching excellence – legitimizing it, pushing it further in terms of global reach. On the other hand, comparative perspectives offer an opportunity to see the world anew, to consider alternatives and to shake up taken for granted ideas. An important part of a critical approach is recognising that existing ways of understanding and realizing teaching excellence could be different and indeed *better* (Skelton, 2005: 12): the comparative analysis afforded by international perspectives helps us to develop reflexive and robust interpretations of teaching excellence – those that will allow it to become a valuable concept in our lives.

The approach taken by the book is therefore positive and hopeful. Teaching excellence arouses our curiosity since it raises fundamental issues to do with the role of higher education in contemporary society. The book features four forms of writing that attempt collectively to shift common sense about teaching excellence into more critical directions:

- Work that attempts to 're-appropriate' teaching excellence for the good of higher education, to set in train a 'reverse discourse' that is more meaningful and positive;

- critiques of teaching excellence that directly challenge taken-for-granted assumptions and values;
- accounts that look at the contradictions in policies and practices designed to promote excellence, identifying progressive and regressive elements;
- comparative analyses which consider the way teaching excellence is expressed and promoted in different countries. This work seeks to learn from difference and to suggest possibilities for the future.

Structure of the book

The book comprises three main parts. Part I consists of Chapters 1–5 and is called 'Conceptual challenges'. It considers some of the key conceptual challenges facing teaching excellence: for example, what form(s) might it take? How does it connect with the broader aims and purposes of higher education in contemporary society? And what significant issues emerge as we begin to think seriously about it (for example, debates about whether excellence can be democratized and, if so, how this can be achieved). This part of the book seeks to encourage a critical debate about teaching excellence that has been absent to date (see Skelton, 2005: 167–170). It aims to address fundamental questions that have been sidelined given the emphasis on practical initiatives to promote teaching excellence.

Part II of the book comprises Chapters 6–10 and is called 'Policy and discourse'. It aims to address serious questions about higher education policy and discourse relating to teaching excellence and their impact on practice. This part of the book examines policy processes and considers how discourses of excellence relate to broader social goals and aspirations. It examines how academic staff at 'grassroots' level respond to 'rational-purposive' policies (Trowler, 2002) and what opportunities they have for resisting dominant discourses or re-appropriating them to serve valued ends. Part II includes: critical reviews of policy; investigations into the relationship between policy and practice; detailed interrogations of policy processes; searching examinations of discourses of teaching excellence within policy texts and critical suggestions for future policy.

Chapters 11–16 comprise Part III of the book, which is called 'Development initiatives'. It offers a series of critical investigations into current initiatives designed to promote teaching excellence. However, unlike a lot of previous work which has focused on the operational impact of such initiatives, these chapters provide a broader perspective which is balanced, reflective and questioning in style.

Contents of chapters

Part I: conceptual challenges

In the first chapter, Jon Nixon makes a strong case for excellence as a moral endeavour that unifies different aspects of academic practice. He explores how we can transcend elitist and relativist notions and offers us a new language to think about excellence: one characterized by truthfulness, respect and authenticity. Jon argues that it is possible to democratize teaching excellence but if different forms – related to the particular strengths of different institutions – are to be afforded equal status and value, then we must fund higher education accordingly. Otherwise, the 'widening participation' agenda has little real meaning – students will only have access to unequal forms of provision. The chapter maintains that a teaching excellence underpinned by truthfulness, respect and authenticity is difficult to achieve in the current stratified system of higher education. Jon argues that 'If the appeal to excellence is to mean anything at all, that meaning must be sought in conditions that are shot through with alienation and inequality'.

In Chapter 2, Richard Gale makes reference to the work of a number of teachers who display the sorts of dispositions referred to in the previous chapter. Through these illustrative examples, Richard presents a view of teaching excellence as 'braided practice' which involves integrating disciplinary knowledge, pedagogical expertise and scholarly inquiry. The chapter maintains that scholarly inquiry, in particular, has transformatory potential within this trilogy of practice. Richard outlines what is required to support such inquiry as a basis for an evidence-based approach to teaching in higher education.

In Chapter 3, Bruce Macfarlane explores what we mean by the *teaching* in 'teaching excellence'. He argues that teaching excellence initiatives tend to only recognize that teaching which is associated with performance (e.g. lecturing) and able to be captured by performative measurement (e.g. through peer observation and student evaluation questionnaires). This is part of a broader process of 'unbundling' the teacher's role in higher education into constituent elements, thereby reducing numbers of 'core' staff and leading to a situation of 'teacher de-skilling'. The chapter offers a more holistic reconceptualization of teaching which recognizes what happens 'off stage'; for example, the often painstaking and ill-rewarded tasks of supporting students through tutorials, advising, giving feedback and pastoral support. Bruce argues that contributing to these sorts of activities is not only vital to student development but part of the infrastructure and moral foundations of higher education teaching; in short, part of a broader view of the teacher acting in the capacity of an 'academic citizen'.

Miriam Zukas and Janice Malcolm further develop the line of exploration pursued in the previous chapter. In Chapter 4 they locate 'teaching' within a broader notion of *pedagogy* which situates teaching practice within a cultural, institutional and historical context. They distance themselves from a view of teaching as simply method and argue that pedagogy unfolds within 'disciplinary and vocational practices; personal and political values and beliefs; national and institutional issues such as quality assurance … the purposes of teaching, and the relationships between teaching and teachers, and learning and learners'. From this standpoint on pedagogy, the authors explore what impact existing disciplinary communities and other established actor networks have had on recent attempts to define and promote teaching excellence. They conclude that if we use the metaphor of a net to think about higher education, teaching excellence discourses and initiatives can be seen as an attempt to patch up areas of perceived weakness in the net (poor teaching; raising the status of teaching relative to research etc.). However, they suggest that the problem with such an approach is that the complex nature of the existing net (and the smaller 'net-works' that constitute it) has not been apprehended – and this will inevitably lead to the patching being unsuccessful.

In the final chapter of Part I, Angela Brew proposes a view of teaching excellence based on the formation of inclusive knowledge building communities. Drawing on examples from the Australian context, she shows how such a conception of excellence challenges orthodox perspectives on the research-teaching nexus, knowledge production, curriculum processes and academic staff and student relationships.

Part II: policy and discourse

In Chapter 6, Sue Clegg identifies excellence as the latest in a series of change management strategies aimed at improving organizational quality. She considers the implications of the discursive migration of excellence from commerce and industry into higher education. Sue argues that higher education cannot be viewed as just another generic organization given the craft-like nature of teaching which has historically involved practitioners making judgements about quality based on their extensive training and interiorized notion of standards. Even if excellence is imposed by fiat, therefore, accompanied by 'brute sanity' and fierce resolve, there is likely to be a mismatch between what professionals think about excellent teaching and the views held by governments, managers and policymakers. Sue suggests that it is always possible for teachers to 'write themselves back' into excellence discourses in ways that are affirming. She concludes, however, that many contemporary texts devoted to promoting teaching excellence offer little scope for teachers to maintain a practice based on critical engagement, pedagogical love and pleasure.

Ruth Searle and Sioux McKenna critically examine discourses of teaching excellence that are present in key policy documents about higher education in a rapidly changing South Africa. In Chapter 7 they show that competing understandings of teaching excellence are evident in these policy documents which opens up different possibilities for future direction and change. The authors raise concerns that social justice concerns are being eclipsed by performative understandings of teaching and learning which focus on South Africa's positioning in the global economy. As with the previous chapter they consider the potential impact of teaching excellence discourses on practitioners and identify the implications of an emerging 'compliance culture'.

Alan Jenkins and Mick Healey propose in Chapter 8 that any notion of teaching excellence needs to be situated clearly within the research–teaching nexus.

They argue that under contemporary conditions of 'supercomplexity', all students should be 'taught' in and through a research culture and the higher education curriculum should foster and be informed by inquiry-based learning. Institutions may express a teaching excellence of this kind in different ways, depending on their identity and resources. The authors argue, however, that current higher education policy separates out teaching and research and is based on a selective mis-reading of the evidence on the research–teaching relationship. Recommendations for future policy change are made requiring the retention of core activities across the sector supplemented by particular ways of supporting inquiry in research-intensive and research-informed institutions.

In Chapter 9, Joce Jesson and Richard Smith critically unpack the policy process in the development of a National Centre for Tertiary Teaching Excellence in New Zealand, showing how any real deliberation around the meaning of excellence became sidelined in disputes over constitution and governance. They argue that a university model of teaching is being valorized through awards for teaching excellence and raise concerns about whether the new National Centre will take on regulatory functions in the future (e.g. accreditation of professional development courses for lecturers).

In the final chapter of Part II, David Gosling and Andy Hannan show how a major policy initiative – the CETL programme in the UK – was interpreted by individuals and institutions and how its initial ideology (rewarding best practice) shifted to a more developmental focus. They suggest that this focus opened up possibilities for the democratization of teaching excellence but conclude that the CETL programme is unlikely to lead to a re-stratification of the higher education system given the larger amounts of funding available for research.

Part III: development initiatives

In Chapter 11, Vaneeta-marie D'Andrea undertakes a comparative analysis of national-level development initiatives for supporting teaching excellence in six different countries – Australia, Canada, New Zealand, Sweden, the UK and the US. Given the significant investment into these initiatives, Vaneeta argues that we should expect more from them in terms of return. She identifies a range of meta level criteria for making judgements about the quality of teaching excellence initiatives at the national level, including: the extent to which they draw on existing research into teaching excellence; how valid and motivating they are perceived to be; whether they are underpinned by an explicit set of purposes and values; and the degree to which such initiatives impact on the quality of teaching and learning in the higher education sector as a whole.

In the following chapter, Hugo Dobson and Yukako Mori focus on teaching excellence within a specific non-western but developed country – Japan. They locate their discussion within a historical context of higher education in Japan and recent educational reform. Recent development initiatives to promote teaching excellence are considered and the authors demonstrate how these are meeting with resistance from individual academics. Despite this resistance, Hugo and Yukako argue that recent initiatives have done a lot to shake up the traditional emphasis found in Japanese higher education which privileges research over teaching.

In Chapter 13, Joelle Fanghanel adopts a socio-cultural perspective on teaching excellence. She argues that understandings of teaching excellence are inevitably shaped not only by disciplinary and institutional contexts but by personal and educational values and beliefs. From this perspective she examines recent quality initiatives in the UK, focusing, in particular, on the Teaching Quality Enhancement Fund. Joelle concludes that these initiatives have met with limited success since they do not adequately take into account the highly context-dependent nature of teaching and the need for sophisticated understandings of educational change.

The individual level of the Teaching Quality Enhancement Fund was called the National Teaching Fellowship Scheme which is the subject of Chapter 14. Alan Skelton reviews the NTFS during the period 2000–2006 and argues that recent changes to the scheme – in particular the separation of past achievement from future development – have undermined its radical potential. In the light of a critique of these changes, Alan advocates a view of teaching excellence which integrates accumulated wisdom with a commitment to ongoing inquiry.

In Chapter 15, Carolin Kreber offers an interesting comparison of the situation in the UK compared with that of Canada. She explores initiatives to promote teaching excellence in both settings and finds far less development activity taking place in Canada. She sees this as both a strength and a weakness – there is less regulation and standardization of teaching but at the same time fewer opportunities are available for teachers who want to develop their practice. Recognizing Canada as an emergent context for teaching excellence she draws upon the work of Habermas to consider the very different ways in which higher education pedagogy might develop in the future (for example, driven by technical, practical or emancipatory interests and goals).

In the final chapter Philippa Levy offers an 'insider' perspective on the CETL programme in the UK. As Director of the Centre for Inquiry-based Learning in the Arts and Social Sciences at the University of Sheffield, she makes the case for a view of teaching excellence informed by inquiry-based learning. Philippa outlines systematic mechanisms for embedding this view within her institution and its practices. She argues that a teaching excellence based on inquiry can challenge performative understandings and offers a space for the development of a critical community of scholars that includes both teachers and students.

Part I

Conceptual challenges

Chapter 1

Excellence and the good society

Jon Nixon
(University of Sheffield, UK)

'Excellence' is rapidly becoming the watchword of the University, and to understand the University as a contemporary institution requires some reflection on what the appeal to excellence may, or may not, mean.

(Readings, 1996: 21)

The rapid expansion of higher education has necessitated a reconsideration of what is meant by 'excellence'. Policies relating to that expansion tend to assume that excellence should be judged according to the different ends and purposes of higher education. This is a convenient mantra for those with responsibility for funding an increasingly stratified sector, since it allows for differentiated funding while at the same time allowing policymakers to argue that everyone can, and should, have access to excellence. Diversity is assumed to be a good thing, because it allows for greater choice; excellence is assumed to be essential, because it ensures that whatever is chosen is as good as anything else.

Within the dominant rhetoric, choice and excellence are yoked together as the twin principles underlying an increasingly competitive and market driven system of higher education. Institutional diversification, and the funding differentials that drive it, must be a good thing, because they allow everyone access to the excellence of their choice. The rhetoric works precisely because it privileges two supposedly incontrovertible, but arguably incompatible, goods: consumer choice *and* academic excellence. Everyone can now buy into the excellence of their own choice – or so the argument runs.

A counter argument is premised on the view that excellence is the kind of thing that, if spread around, necessarily loses its distinctive quality: excellence, by definition, is not something that can be 'diluted'. This viewpoint presupposes academic excellence as the preserve of the few, and that presupposition is often cited in attempts to discredit those, who, on very different grounds, express grave misgivings regarding current policies relating to higher education. At the outset, therefore, it is important to point out that the argument of this chapter does not adopt that stance. It is possible to move towards a notion of 'excellence for all' without buying into neo-liberal consumerism and signing up to its credo of the primacy of individual choice. The idea of the good life presupposes an attempt to achieve excellence; and the idea of the good society presupposes that we organise our being together in such a way that we can all aspire to the good life.

An alternative counter argument is based on the assumption that excellence is at best an unhelpful and at worst a mystifying term. Excellence, so the argument goes, implies a scale and there is no longer a privileged position from which to construct such scales, or, indeed, from which to make authoritative judgements of specific cases in respect of such scales. Again, that is not the argument of this chapter. Excellence is a supremely important notion, but one which, I argue, should be conceptualised in terms, not of private choice, but of the public good. Individual choice, as the indispensable currency of the competitive market and its culture of consumerism, is the enemy of quality. What matters is the refusal to compromise on the personal and public cost of creating a society within which all citizens might aspire to some form of excellence.

My argument is that the dominant discourse of excellence, and attempts to resist that discourse by recourse to either elitist or relativist notions of excellence, are inadequate to that task. We require a different way of thinking and talking about excellence; a way of thinking and talking which recognises excellence as a moral category. The purpose of this chapter is to explore what it might mean to define excellence in this way.

Stratification, fractionalisation and atomisation

> Castes or classes are universal, and the measure of harmony that prevails within a society is everywhere dependent upon the degree to which stratification is sanctioned by its code of morality.
>
> (Young, 1961: 152)

Any analysis of the dominant discourse of excellence should, I believe, begin from an understanding of what the current pattern of institutional differentiation across the higher education sector means in practice. There is a vast international literature which helps us map the new hierarchies and exclusion zones, the new castes and classes, that have stratified, fractionalised and atomised the higher education workplace. If the appeal to excellence means anything at all, that meaning must be sought in conditions that are shot through with alienation and inequality.

Gamson (1998: 103–104) highlights what she calls 'tremendous inequalities in the academy on almost any measure we might want to use'. She points to the fact that, within the USA, 'among four-year institutions, only 8 per cent of private colleges and universities and 3 per cent of public universities are very selective. All the rest, both public and private, are less selective or totally unselective, with the largest percentage concentrated at the bottom'. Within the small proportion of 'very selective schools' the average income of students 'is three to four times that of students in the least selective schools'. Moreover, 'faculty in private research universities earn almost twice as much as faculty in liberal arts colleges'. When total income, including consulting income, royalties, and other institutional income, is factored in, 'faculty in private research universities are by far the highest paid, earning two and a half times more than liberal arts college faculty'. A similar ratio applies with regard to expenditure: 'expenditures per student in private universities are more than twice those in liberal arts colleges and more than three times those in community colleges'. Within the UK the disparities are less pronounced, but the increasing demand by the older, elite universities to set their own fees is likely in the future to reproduce the multiple inequalities highlighted by Gamson. Moreover, the existing mechanisms whereby research funds are allocated through a rigorous selectivity exercise (such that medium and low 'rated' institutions receive little or no research funding) further increase the disparities between institutions.

Kerr's (2001) fifth edition of his classic text, *The Uses of the University*, contains a new chapter in which its author reflects upon the university of the twenty-first century. Less sure than in his original 1963 edition, in which he outlined the development of the American university in the second half of the twentieth century, Kerr restricts himself to possible 'scenarios' and acknowledges his own uncertainties regarding the future. Nevertheless, one of those 'scenarios', which he terms 'the fractionalization of the academic guild', would already seem to be shifting from the realms of possibility to those of actuality. The key characteristics of this 'scenario', he argues, are that 'subject matter specialization increases, breaking knowledge into tinier and tinier topics'; that fractionalisation also increases in the battle over academic merit versus social justice in treatment of students – 'whether it should be treated as equality of opportunity or as equality of results'; and, finally, that 'conflict may occur over models of the university itself' (p. 26). Writing from the UK context, Barnett (2000a) paints a similar picture of what he terms 'the Western University' faced with 'supercomplexity', in which institutions risk fractionalisation as their frames of understanding, action and self-identity are continually challenged. Both Kerr (2001) and Barnett (2000a) make the point that the university with its traditional moorings in philosophy has been cast adrift both morally and epistemologically. This moral and epistemological uncertainty, as Kerr (2001: 206) points out, drastically foreshortens the time horizon for planning: 'in the 1960s we were confident of progress in higher education. We made plans for twenty, thirty, forty years ahead, certain of their realization. Now the time horizon for planning is three or five or ten years'. Fractionalisation is both synchronic and diachronic in its impact.

Alongside the increasing stratification and fractionalisation of the university, are profound changes in the conditions of academic work. As early as the mid-1990s a report sponsored by the Organisation for Economic Co-operation and Development (OECD) argued that 'it is no longer sensible to speak of a single academic profession' and that 'a caste distinction is emerging between "have" and "have-not" groups'. The latter, it went on to argue, constitute 'an underclass

... with limited prospects for advancement or employment stability'. At the same time increased differentials and tensions are apparent among what the report calls 'top-level academics' who are under pressure to produce high profile research and to develop and market new and appealing courses. (Kogan *et al.*, 1994: 62–65). Rhoades and Slaughter (1998: 36) argue a similar case for the situation within the USA, where, they claim, 'the number of part-time faculty has increased to 43 percent of the total faculty workforce'. Moreover the percentages vary by subject, with those subjects (and subject-specific institutions) teaching the largest numbers of undergraduates having the highest percentages of part-time academic staff. 'The inequalities in people's material existence in higher education are', they argue, 'vast and expanding'. The result is an atomised profession, which is not only increasingly part-time but also increasingly managed by new cadres of administrators and non-academic managers.

There is not much in this overall picture of systemic stratification, institutional fractionalisation and professional atomisation which would lead us to a sense of optimism regarding the primacy of choice, for either academics or students, within the higher education sector. Archer (2003: 128–130) provides further evidence to support this bleak view in her discussion of the impact of what she calls the 'hierarchy of universities' on the choices and opportunities open to students. Students, according to her analysis, are all too aware of how their choice of university involved adaptations to the contextual constraints operating upon them. Her respondents were also keenly aware of how those adaptations 'would prejudice their later chances of getting a job' (p. 130).

The general message to be taken from the literature is that of the closing down of options and the increasing difficulty of achieving excellence across a highly divided, and divisive, system. As Considine (2006: 258) argues, that closure has occasioned an 'emergency' of both professional and institutional identity:

> From being places where one could think about anything, universities have evidently become sites where everyone must at some point think about everything ... Scholarly domains are now infused with managerial values and goals, pedagogical actions are now dominated by organizational imperatives, and the life of the student is increasingly intersected by the priorities of work, finance, and future returns. The new 'everything' that must be included in academic thought is not simply the new forms of knowledge erupting inside and between disciplines; it is also expressed in multiple, non-intellectual projects ... These include ways to raise national export earnings, metrics for status competition, avenues for the expression of personal or sociological identity, and methods for poaching and transporting Nobel Prize winners from one part of the globe to another.

Against this backdrop, it is hardly surprising that Readings (1996: 39) concluded, in his last words on the matter, that, within the North American context, 'the appeal to excellence marks the fact that there is no longer any idea of the University, or rather that the idea has now lost all content'. He goes on to argue that 'excellence marks nothing more than the moment of technology's self-reflection. All the system requires is for activity to take place, and the empty notion of excellence refers to nothing other than the optimal input/output ratio in matters of information'.

Hartley (2006: 4) makes a similar point with regard to the UK context when he argues that 'over the past ten years excellence, efficiency and effectiveness have been joined by equity to form the e-litany of contemporary education policy in England'. He continues: 'The easy alliterative appeal of the terms gives the appearance of a seamless affinity among them. Excellence, efficiency and effectiveness are associated with the national need to compete globally'. So conceived, excellence becomes the new currency of the higher education market place.

Excellence as a moral category

> Let us assert, then, that any kind of excellence renders that of which it is the excellence *good*, and makes it perform its function *well*. For example, the excellence of the eye makes both the eye and its function good (because it is through the excellence of the eye that we see well). Similarly the excellence of a horse makes him both a fine horse and good at running and carrying his rider and facing the enemy.
>
> (Aristotle, *Nichomachean Ethics*, I, 5)

The new marketplace of higher education is not entirely malign. Universities undoubtedly contribute to wealth creation and the economic regeneration of the regions within which they are located. They provide skills and understandings, without which an advanced society could not hope to compete within the global market. They are key partners in economic regeneration schemes that benefit regions and help locate those regions within a broader frame of economic competition. They are part of the complex infrastructure of global capitalism, which relies increasingly on the recognition of knowledge transfer as a key component of economic well-being. Their trade is knowledge; and they have undoubtedly become increasingly successful in this entrepreneurial endeavour. Some universities, at least, have grown up and got wise to the economic reality of late capitalism; and the more grown up and wised up they have become, the greater their competitive edge.

Nevertheless, economic growth is not the prime purpose of the university. Universities exist to hold a mirror up to society and, in so doing, ask it to examine its assumptions and underlying logic. This is not necessarily an either/or. Sometimes, happily, the university and society can have it both ways. But when the chips are down, hard decisions have to be taken. Then the question of what universities are for resurfaces and has to be addressed. Sometimes, in the interests of learning, universities have to take a stand against what is seen to constitute progress or growth (as when, for example, the imposition of managerialist structures threatens the very practice of learning). Because of this possible eventuality, universities have to sustain their underlying purposefulness as a resource for an indeterminate future. The university must be a repository of these other, sometimes oppositional, ways of thinking about why we do what we do and what it is we are doing when we judge ourselves to be doing it well. Viewed in this light, excellence is the condition practitioners aspire to in acquiring those dispositions that can only be achieved in, and through, practice; and whose acquisition sustains and nurtures that practice.

Excellence, Aristotle reminds us, is less a matter of efficiency and effectiveness, than of the virtuous dispositions that, as academic practitioners, we acquire through our professional work as teachers, researchers, scholars and colleagues. I focus specifically on the intellectual virtues of truthfulness, respect and authenticity. This is by no means an exhaustive list of the virtues implicit in academic practice. Nor am I suggesting that universities have a monopoly on truthfulness, respect and authenticity. That is clearly not the case. All I am seeking to do is highlight the obvious point that to be a good academic one has to go on learning about what it means to be accurate and sincere, attentive and honest, and courageous and compassionate. That is the only way to become better; the only way to aspire to excellence (see Nixon, 2004b).

Williams (2002) reminded us, in the last book of his published during his lifetime, of the importance of the notion of *truthfulness* in any attempt to carry learning forward. Truthfulness, he argues, relies crucially upon a commitment to *accuracy* in respect of belief and *sincerity* in respect of professing those beliefs that we hold to be accurate. Learning how to learn is in large part a matter of acquiring those dispositions that make such a commitment possible. Truthfulness does not presuppose an ultimate truth; it aspires towards a set of practices that limit the potential violence of untruth. Truthful people may sometimes deceive, tell lies; but they acknowledge the troubling and disabling impact of their deceptions and lies both on their own lives and on the well-being of others. To seek to be accurate in respect of the beliefs one holds and sincere with regard to professing those beliefs is intrinsic to becoming a good academic practitioner. In that sense we might say that accuracy and sincerity are the virtuous dispositions associated with the urge towards truthfulness that is implicit in academic practice and that is a defining feature of whatever academic excellence might mean.

In the current context of managed misinformation and 'spin' it is hardly necessary to emphasise the importance of developing a citizenry capable of distinguishing between beliefs that are fuelled by self-interest and wish-fulfilment and beliefs that are grounded in how things are (regardless of how shaky and contested that ground may be). To probe the accuracy of our own and others' beliefs is at times a matter of sheer survival: if not for us, then certainly for others. Had, for example, more academics insisted on the requirements of accuracy and sincerity (of truthfulness) in assessing the evidence that was presented to the public by way of justifying the invasion of Iraq, then the decisions and actions that were taken might in retrospect have a little more moral clarity. Indeed, the actions and decisions taken might have been rather different. The inaccuracy and insincerity of the public reportage by government to the citizens of the UK and the US were, as Marquand (2006: 46) puts it, 'not detected because we radical intellectuals (I include myself in the indictment) did not want to detect them' (see also, Pillar, 2006).

Learning presupposes, in its emphasis on truthfulness, *respect* for the other. Sennett (2003) reminds us that respect necessarily takes as its starting point a deep *attentiveness* to difference. That attentiveness involves identification through sympathy and empathy, but must move beyond those sentiments to an *honesty* regarding the difficulty of practising respect within a deeply unequal world. We cannot collapse the self into the other. There is, Sennett goes on to argue, a kind of phasing into respect through identification and then through recognition. What might then emerge is respectful distance: the respect accorded to those we know to be different, but have learnt are part of whatever 'care for the world' (Arendt, 1998, recurring phrase) might mean. Living life purposefully for the betterment of an imagined good society is a matter of entertaining openness to difference while maintaining one's own integrity and sense of moral agency. Sometimes, of course, that involves agreeing to differ on matters that are significant but potentially divisive. The dispositions of accuracy and honesty implicit in the traditions of teaching, learning and scholarly activity are crucial means by which, as academic practitioners, we set about that task and, in so doing, aspire to excellence.

Again, within the current context, which poses unprecedented problems regarding the recognition of incommensurable difference, the need for attentiveness cannot be overemphasised: the capacity for receptiveness to other positions and the historical and cultural location of those positions has become a condition for human survival. Academic excellence, as I am defining it, is centrally concerned with acquiring and transmitting the dispositions necessary for building shared understandings and agreements across a cultural and political landscape that is increasingly defined in terms of ideological and religious fault lines (see Nixon and Ranson, 1997). The capacity to read these differences against the grain of common sense understandings and received orthodoxies, and to translate these readings into ways of living together, is a practical necessity. That is the precise point at which deliberative pedagogies, or what I have elsewhere called 'pedagogies of recognition', imbued with a moral sense of what is involved in the reconstruction of a public sphere, gain political purchase (see Nixon, 2004a; Nixon *et al.*, 1997).

Learning presupposes, finally, the possibility and, indeed, as Taylor (1991) would have it, the necessity of *authenticity*. It provides the potential for living life in such a way that truthfulness and respect become what we are in our relations with one another. Authenticity is the public face of truthfulness and respect and involves the additional virtuous dispositions of *courage* and *compassion*: the intellectual courage required in seeking to be accurate and sincere, attentive and honest, and the compassion necessary to recognise and acknowledge the particular circumstantial difficulties that others face in doing so. Authenticity is central to the notion of academic excellence: the idea that, for ourselves and others, life can be lived all of a piece, truthfulness become a way of life, and respect an integral part of that life. In striving for excellence, academic practitioners are necessarily striving for authenticity. Moreover, they are doing so under conditions of work which are often deeply alienating and inauthentic. Under such conditions, courage and compassion are both the necessary conditions for, and the inevitable outcome of, the aspiration towards excellence. Excellence is a process of growth, development and flourishing; it is not just an endpoint.

Authenticity, as Sennett (2006) reiterates, is increasingly difficult to achieve within working environments that require, as a condition of excellence, a constant state of 'surrender': an acceptance of the need, in the interests of efficiency and effectiveness, to constantly let go of the past. Sennett quotes the head of a 'dynamic company' who asserted 'that no one owns their place in the organization, that past service in particular earns no employee a guaranteed place' (p. 4). As Sennett comments, it is difficult to respond to that assertion positively: 'a peculiar trait of personality is required to do so, one which discounts the experiences a human being has already had' (p. 5). Such a trait is inimical to the idea of a self defined through its storyline: a self that builds and learns, that acquires the dispensations necessary to go on learning, and that achieves a sense of purposefulness through time.

The moral unity of practice

> And the unity of a virtue in someone's life is intelligible only as a characteristic of a unitary life, a life that can be conceived and evaluated as a whole.
>
> (MacIntyre, 1985: 205)

The virtues highlighted in the previous section cannot be reduced to a set of professional skills, since, as MacIntyre (1985: 205) argues, 'someone who genuinely possesses a virtue can be expected to manifest it in very different types of situation, many of them situations where the practice of a virtue cannot be expected to be effective in the way that we expect a professional skill to be'. Nor do the virtues outlined above come ready-made. They are achieved through activities traditionally associated with universities: research, scholarship and teaching. Within and across those different activities the virtues hang together as part of a *whole* way of life: good research requires, albeit in varying degrees, accuracy and sincerity, attentiveness and honesty, courage and compassion; similarly, good scholarship and good teaching. In isolation, none of those activities is adequate to the task of ensuring that the virtuous dispositions relating to truthfulness, respect and authenticity are exercised to full capacity.

Those activities comprise a moral unity when, and only when, they mutually reinforce each other; a unity which is fractured when, for whatever reason, one or other of those activities is treated as self-sufficient. Academic practice, in other words, is a moral unity comprising activities that are a necessary but not sufficient condition for sustaining the virtues of truthfulness, respect and authenticity. The notion of teaching excellence only makes sense in the context of a broader notion of excellence that relates to both academic and institutional practice; a notion neatly summed up in the late Edward Said's (2004) categorisation of himself as a 'scholar-teacher' (see Nixon, 2006a).

The relation between research, scholarship and teaching is not, then, merely a matter of contingency. The fact that they are conducted within particular institutional settings means that they share certain ends and purposes that are structural features of those settings (see Hinchcliffe, 2006). They are dependent upon, and at the same time help sustain, a moral framework the pivotal points of which are truthfulness (accuracy/sincerity), respect (attentiveness/honesty) and authenticity (courage/compassion). Although research, scholarship and teaching are clearly very different kinds of activity, each requires a dispositional orientation towards these virtues. That moral orientation is a defining feature of the field of academic practice within which these various activities are located. As activities each is clearly very different and involves a differing range of skills and understandings. However, as moral endeavours, these activities have much in common; and what they have in common is, in part at least, a sense of moral purposefulness in respect of the virtues of truthfulness, respect and authenticity. Those involved in these different activities share what Pring (2003: 64) has called 'the deep down *feeling* concerning how they ought to act'.

In the highly stratified system that now constitutes higher education, how one acts is largely dependent on where one is located within sharp divisions of labour and across complex institutional hierarchies. Academic workers are increasingly likely to define themselves, not in terms of the integrity of academic practice, but with reference to what they see as their prime specialist activity; moreover, the goods of those specialist activities are increasingly defined, not in terms of the intrinsic goods of learning, but with reference to such extrinsic goods that are easily quantifiable and therefore amenable to measurement. It is not that these extrinsic goods are of no consequence, but that they squeeze out all other considerations. We are in danger of losing 'the deep down *feeling*' that guides right action and that constitutes the moral bases of academic practice.

It is important to insist upon the moral coherence of academic practice *as a whole*, precisely because of the increasing stratification of the higher education sector whereby deep divisions of labour are being systematically engineered and then justified on the spurious grounds of consumer choice. Within this context the notion of 'widening participation' becomes meaningless, since what students will be participating in at different points within the system will not just be different (in the naively benign sense of that term) but will differ qualitatively. The reclamation of the moral bases of academic practice, by academic practitioners, is essential if public funding is to meet public ends.

Exercising academic agency

We can set aside the passive outlook, which fantasises that blaming and accusing others contributes to justice ... active citizens improve institutions as they improve the conditions of trust.

(O'Neill, 2002: 38)

Academic excellence, I have argued, is a moral category and can only be achieved through the acquisition of the virtuous dispositions implicit in practice. This argument, it should be emphasised, is not advocating a retreat from 'care for the world' (Arendt, 1998) to the consolations of the ivory tower. On the contrary, I am arguing that academic practice is always morally orientated towards particular public goods and particular virtuous dispositions that render those goods attainable. To renege on a commitment to learning as a form of moral agency, a way of changing the world for the better, is, as Collingwood (1939) affirmed, the final betrayal of 'clear thinking' by those charged with responsibility for sustaining clarity of thought. Failure to discharge that responsibility is not simply an omission; it is a means of 'corrupting the public mind' and producing in it, as Collingwood insisted, 'a willingness to forgo that full prompt, and accurate information on matters of public importance which is the indispensable nourishment of a democratic society' (pp. 166–167).

Questions then arise as to what, as academic workers, we can *do* in order to attain the conditions necessary for achieving academic excellence. The crucial questions, as O'Neill (2002) insists, focus on institutional trust and call to account our own moral agency: how can we begin to fulfil the conditions necessary for truthfulness, respect and authenticity? How might we redefine our academic identity in the light of these virtuous dispositions? How, above all, might we support one another in this task?

First, we can acknowledge the deeply corrosive effects of current patterns of work and the unequal distribution of those effects across the workplace. Sennett (1999) shows how the steadily increasing insecurity experienced by workers is making it impossible for many of us to achieve a sense of moral agency. Moreover, he argues, it is those very elements of the post-Fordist working environment that are deemed to be worker friendly – flexibility, team work, specialisation – that are in fact creating the insecurities. They are doing so, he claims, through their re-engineering of time whereby there is an increasing reliance on, for example, worker mobility, part-time and casual contracts, and entrepreneurialism. Academic workplaces are subject to these same strains and pressures, which, it is important to emphasise, produce systemic inequalities between 'colleagues'. Not to acknowledge that 'collegial' relationships are shot through with inequality is in effect to deny the possibility of trusting relationships based on good faith; and in denying that possibility we deny the possibility of developing relationships of virtue. Honesty requires us to acknowledge these differences and sincerity demands that we be explicit regarding their impact on the quality of our working lives. Honesty and sincerity in acknowledging how deeply un-collegial our 'collegiality' actually is would be the very difficult first step in establishing new forms of professional relationship.

Second, we can be responsive to the differing circumstances of individuals – colleagues *and* students – that render the personal management of time difficult and sometimes chronically crisis-ridden. Pahl (1995) has shown how anxiety is invariably attendant upon success; but the successful very often have the option, or privilege, of living their lives in such a way that the contingent factors that engender anxiety are carefully managed through lifestyle and life choices. The less successful may make other principled choices or simply not have the options open to them: other commitments impinge on the resources of time that the more successful choose – or feel themselves driven – to allocate to work. Genuine professional relationships would, then, rely upon sensitivity to the complex and increasingly troubled interface between the personal and the professional. People do have to make choices and, of course, consequences inevitably follow from those choices, but what have to be respected in any attempt at 'virtuous friendship' are the choices that the other has made; and what has to be attended to is the impact of those choices on the other person's life chances. We can rarely in our interpersonal relationships alter the consequences that flow from another person's particular choices, but we can and should respect those choices and, where appropriate, recognise their grounding in the virtues of courage and authenticity.

Third, we can require of ourselves and others that we take responsibility for the positional power invested in us. The flatter organisational structures associated with post-Fordist work regimes render power more diffuse and therefore more difficult to locate. One's own power is thereby that much easier to deny. To deny one's own positional power, however, is to disempower those over whom one ought rightly to be exercising authority. Teachers aspire to excellence in their professional relationships with students not by denying that authority, but by exercising it in the interests of truthfulness, respect and authenticity. Recognising the equal worth of the other is dependent upon our courage in discharging that academic duty; which, if *rightly* discharged, is also a duty of care and compassion. Professional relationships, in other words, would be equal relationships precisely because they would involve a shared understanding regarding power differentials and a shared dialogue regarding how those differentials might be put to good use. Their equality would reside in their capacity for recognition. Such relationships would necessarily be difficult, but they would be honest and truthful in respect of difference. In their search for shared understanding they would be agonistic in their deliberative modes of discourse, but not antagonistic. They would reach out to the kinds of interpersonal agreement that take full cognisance of how and why we differ.

Fourth, we can acknowledge the competing priorities and pressures acting upon ourselves and other academic practitioners. We can resist the urge to possess or take over the other, to impose our views on the other, or to make unreasonable claims on the other. With the best of intentions we can sometimes create a culture of dependency, or even oppression, through our failure to recognise and respect boundaries. Without that recognition and respect academic practice cannot aspire to excellence. It remains locked in paternalistic modes of thinking and feeling. Of course, boundaries sometimes have to be negotiated and renegotiated. This is particularly true of the boundaries we impose upon our own use of time. Should I be giving more or less time to that particular group? Should I require of that individual more of his or her time in the development of a particular project? Should we, together, rethink our use of time in relation to our complex and overlapping activities? Sometimes such negotiations confront the hard realities of contractual obligations. The crucial point is to acknowledge that each of us needs to set boundaries and that the boundaries we set, although negotiable, are vital to our well-being.

Finally, we can acknowledge the diverse professional trajectories to which we are committed and to find ways of sustaining one another in pursuing those diverse trajectories. The complex nature of academic practice means that as academic workers we are constantly negotiating a professional identity for ourselves in relation to our specific responsibilities for the conduct and administration of research, teaching and scholarship. Aspiring to excellence involves combining these activities in ways that play to our own strengths and that recognise the priorities of the particular institutions within which we work. Professional identity does not come ready-made. It involves the struggle for authenticity and, as such, has to be constructed. The commitment to that struggle will, of course, take time, since we can only understand what that struggle means by listening to one another and talking with one another. The sheer crowdedness of academic life plays against this good intention. We spend our time teaching, researching, reading, writing, but rarely carve out the institutional space to discuss these activities in relation to our sense of what it means to be an academic. Yet, without this discursive space, we risk becoming isolated operatives.

Underlying these suggestions is the assumption that the achievement of academic excellence is, in part at least, dependent upon the quality of professional relationships within the academic workplace. Aristotle, in the *Nicomachean Ethics*, wrote of such relationships in terms of 'friendship' and distinguished 'perfect friendship' or 'virtuous friendship' as a relationship between equals who have their own and each others' best moral interests at heart. Such friendship is neither provisional nor instrumental, but unconditional in terms of what is good for oneself and the other: it is both inward-looking and outward-reaching. It is premised on the assumption that we become better people through the reciprocity afforded by our shared aspiration to help one another in doing so. That is why, as Pahl (2000: 79) puts it, 'friends of virtue' are also 'friends of hope' and 'ultimately friends of communication': 'our friends who stimulate hope and invite change are concerned with deep understanding and knowing'. The conditions necessary for reclaiming the quality of our professional relationships are also, therefore, the conditions necessary for achieving academic excellence (see Nixon, 2004a, 2006b).

Universities as 'moral institutions'

> Diogenes Laertius reports that Socrates once attended a play of Euripedes in which a character, speaking about practical excellence, spoke the lines: 'It is best to let these things go as they will, without management.' Hearing this, Socrates 'got up and left the theatre, saying that it was absurd to ... let excellence perish in this way'.
>
> (Nussbaum, 2001: 84)

In highlighting what academic practitioners themselves can do to reclaim excellence as a moral category, I am not minimising the need for structural change and political intervention. As Socrates well knew, excellence has to be managed if it is to flourish. One aspect of mismanagement, or plain neglect, relates to the chronic underfunding of higher education. 'In business terms', as Rees-Mogg (2002) puts it:

> British universities are over-trading and under-funded. Since the late 1970s the number of students has been dramatically increased from one in eight of the relevant age group to one in three, but the funding has not. As a result the Department for Education and Skills' own index of public funding per student has fallen by a half.

Rees-Mogg argues from this premise that there should be no further widening of access – an argument that runs entirely counter to that of this chapter. Nevertheless, his premise still holds: universities within the UK are the victims of 'the economics of idiocy'.

The policy issue is crystal clear. If we want to widen participation, we must pay for it; if we are unwilling to pay for it, then widening participation is not an option. The attempt to widen participation through inadequate funding changes the very nature of participation for the vast majority of students. For, as Rees-Mogg rightly (if somewhat priggishly) again points out, 'a good degree from a first-class university can help in getting an interview; a modest degree from the average converted polytechnic is only too likely to go into the reject pile'. The problem lies in the development of policies, by successive governments, which have manifestly failed to resist, and sometimes actively sought to maintain, the deep and historic institutional inequalities that characterise the university system as a whole.

Of course, there is a serious debate to be had as to how adequate funding levels should be achieved. It is perhaps unrealistic, given the current neo-liberal orthodoxy, to expect any government to propose raising the necessary funds by imposing higher tax thresholds on the wealthier sections of society. We cannot, in a fiercely market-driven society, perform a backward somersault into state 'welfarism' (however desirable that unthinkable option would sometimes appear). The viable options would all seem to involve some combination of public and private funding or what is increasingly referred to as 'cost-sharing' (Texeira *et al.*, 2006). Nevertheless, whatever means are employed, the goods of widening participation coupled with excellence of provision must be paid for. Without adequate funding universities are unable to flourish.

Some kind of 'basic income' scheme is one of a raft of measures that Sennett (2006) proposes as a means of countering the increasing instability and lack of solidity of institutional bureaucracies. Such a scheme 'would replace the welfare bureaucracies of northern Europe by a simpler system which gives everyone, rich and poor alike, the same basic income support to spend or misspend as the individual wants' (p. 186). According to this 'basic income' scheme (which Sennett sees as beginning to impact upon British legislation in the modified form of 'basic capital'), 'all individuals would be able to buy education, health care, and pensions on the open market; further, unemployment benefits would disappear, since everyone has the minimum annual income needed to support themselves'. Within such a scheme, as Sennett goes on to explain, 'taxes support everyone at a minimum level of life quality, but the Nanny State disappears; if you misspend your income it's your problem. Moreover, everyone gets this basic income whether they need it or not; means-testing disappears' (pp. 186–187).

Such a scheme may have advantages over funding reforms based upon income-related student loans, variants of which have been adopted in Australia, New Zealand, South Africa, Sweden, the UK and the US. Within the UK, tuition fees have been introduced for all students, but with bursaries available for the poorest and with all repayment charges tagged to future incomes (see Chapman, 2006). Notwithstanding these provisos, Callender (2006: 126) insists upon the contradictory nature of the UK government's student funding policies, whereby the desire to widen participation to higher education is being potentially undermined by the very policies government introduced to further these aims:

> The most disadvantaged students, and the very focus of widening participation policies, experience the greatest risks, hardship and financial pressures, all of which affect their chances of success and their ability to participate fully in university life. Moreover, many of the strategies they adopt to offset these risks, and their concerns and worries about debt – be it living at home or term-time employment – compound their disadvantage and increase existing inequalities among the student population. This helps explain the enduring class and ethnic differences both in the patterns of participation in higher education and in patterns of graduate employment.

The funding base is not the only consideration, however. Universities also require a strong civic base if they are to aspire to institutional excellence. They must reach out to other institutions and organisations, particularly those located within what remains of the public sector. Most universities are now acutely aware of the need to build strategic alliances with business and industry, but the role of the university in working alongside the non-profit making service sector is equally important. In developing strong working relations with institutions within that sector, universities express their commitment to addressing the social problems that 'the good society' would seek to eradicate.

Sacks (2000: 44) argues that such problems:

> are of their essence matters that lie somewhere *between* the individual and the state, between the individual who makes choices and the state which makes laws. That is why social problems are intimately related to moral institutions, because it is these which have traditionally mediated between the individual and the state.

'Moral institutions', to employ Sacks' terminology, need to share their resources of knowledge and understanding if they are to address these problems effectively. Through their research and teaching capacity, universities have tremendous resources of hope to bring to this shared endeavour.

Cross-institutional links of this kind rely crucially on the willingness of the institutions involved to develop deliberative modes of dialogue and communication. Shared understandings across institutions can only be achieved through recognition of the very real differences – of constraint, process, purpose, history, etc. – that characterise those institutions. As higher education reaches out and increasingly locates itself within the more vocationally oriented domains that have traditionally been associated with further education, those differences can only be accentuated (see, for example, Field, 2005; Parry, 2005). Mutuality of respect regarding these differences is an indispensable resource. Without the virtues of attentiveness and honesty there can be no hope of developing a common (and commonly understood) set of purposes capable of sustaining strong cross-institutional collaboration.

Partly because of the chronic underfunding referred to above, and partly perhaps because of the increasing diversification of the university sector, public perceptions of UK universities are not good. There is a general assumption among senior politicians that universities are, in the main, badly managed and a more commonly held assumption that they no longer have the capacity to compete with their North American counterparts. Rees-Mogg's flippantly disparaging reference to 'the average converted polytechnic' (quoted above) is typical of the taken-for-granted cynicism routinely displayed in the national press and broadcasting outlets by critical commentators and pundits as well as by politicians and senior figures in government.

Universities clearly have a responsibility to counter this prevailing cynicism and to argue their case. All too often, however, the case that senior university managers choose to defend is not that of the sector as a whole, but that of their own institution or institutional bloc. In a highly competitive system to argue entirely for one's own institutional interests is perforce to argue *against* the institutional interests of others. The public perception of a sector somehow disjointed or at odds with itself is thus reinforced by the spectacle of vice chancellors and principles engaged in a seemingly endless wrangle regarding their various institutional interests. Within the higher echelons of university management there are too many politicians defending their own patch and two few statespersons with a care and concern for the sector as a whole.

I am not here arguing for a bland uniformity of institutional provision. Clearly institutions need to work to their historical strengths. In so doing, they will necessarily develop specialist areas of expertise and seek to maximise their capacity within those particular areas. Through that process, they will also define the particular constituencies that they wish to prioritise. To that extent institutional diversity is a benign feature of the institutional landscape. It only becomes pernicious when (as argued in the opening section of this chapter) fierce competition between institutions becomes the major determinant of the overall pattern of institutional provision and of how, within that overall pattern, particular institutions define their educational ends and purposes. Clearly, institutions will prioritise the various activities of research, scholarship and teaching in different ways according to their particular areas of expertise and the particular external relations they are seeking to develop. In order to fulfil their educational ends and purposes, however, it is essential that these activities are seen as vital and necessarily interrelated components of both academic and institutional excellence.

Conclusion

> We are familiar with the way this language has carried all before it. We must sit on the cusp, hope to be in the centre of excellence, dislike producer-dominated industries, wish for a multiplicity of providers, grovel to our line managers, even more to the senior management team, deliver outcomes downstream, provide choice. Our students are now clients, our patients and passengers customers.
>
> (McKibbin, 2006: 6)

The erosion of public trust and confidence in the university sector puts at risk not only the institutions that comprise that sector, but the democratic ends to which they are committed. If universities are central to the good society, then all those who value the good society must seek to regain that public trust and confidence. That can only be achieved through an open and honest debate as to how best to democratise excellence for the good of the university sector as a whole. The opening up of that debate would be a vital element in a necessary and long overdue response to the systematic diminution of the public sphere. This diminution is not an inevitable result of the way things are, but is the outcome of a dominant ideology of market-managerialism.

The most powerful weapon of that ideology has been its vocabulary. That point is clearly drawn out in Clegg's contribution (Chapter 6) to this volume, with its emphasis on the 'discursive migration' of the term 'excellence' from the world of commerce and industry to that of higher education. It was also implicit in Ranson and Stewart's (1994) carefully constructed argument for 'renewing democracy' through the development of 'a public culture', was spelt out robustly by Inglis (2004) in his 'malediction upon managerialism', and has been memorably re-stated by McKibbin (2006) in his recent invective against what he sees as the 'destruction of the public sphere':

> It is a language which was first devised in business schools, then broke into government and now infests all institutions.... It purports to be neutral: thus all procedures must be 'transparent' and 'robust', everyone 'accountable'. It is hard-nosed but successful because the private sector on which it is based is hard-nosed and successful. It is efficient; it abhors waste; it provides all the answers.... The language might be laughable, but it is now the language shared by all those who command, Labour or Conservative, and is one way they wield power.

(p. 6)

One way of speaking back to that power is to decline the easy offer of its vocabulary (see Nixon, 2004a). That means, of course, mining an alternative vocabulary from the cultural and historical resources available: truthfulness, respect and authenticity are some of the linguistic resources that this chapter has drawn on to set about that task. The idea is not to deny the current ideological impasse, but to begin to build (at precise points within the sector) the wherewithal for imagining different ways of achieving excellence and for constructing a new sense of what a good society might look like.

Chapter 2

Braided practice

The place of scholarly inquiry in teaching excellence

Richard A. Gale
(The Carnegie Foundation for the Advancement of Teaching, US)

Introduction

Each year four teachers are honoured as US Professors of the Year by the Council for Advancement and Support of Higher Education (CASE) and The Carnegie Foundation for the Advancement of Teaching. Since 1981 CASE has been recognizing and rewarding individual faculty 'for their dedication to teaching, commitment to students and innovative instructional methods'. The criteria includes extraordinary dedication to undergraduate teaching demonstrated through student impact and involvement, institutional and community contributions, student and peer support, and an approach to teaching and learning characterized as scholarly (CASE, 2006). Although one might argue about the criteria and how they are demonstrated, it is the last category that is perhaps most significant: to ask teachers for a scholarly approach to teaching and learning as a prerequisite for being considered excellent might seem logical, but it is far from commonplace. Teaching awards are more often based on culminating evaluations and subjective narratives than on scholarly approaches to student learning and its systematic improvement. In championing this aspect of teaching excellence, in placing scholarship of teaching and learning as an attribute of high-quality instruction, CASE and Carnegie highlight an important feature of higher education; they make visible the understanding that teaching excellence requires more than knowledge, expertise and commitment to improving student learning; in order to be an excellent teacher one needs all three, along with a scholarly approach to the practice of teaching and learning. For when disciplinary knowledge, pedagogical expertise and scholarly inquiry are combined, not just in tandem but entwined, connecting with and reinforcing each other, they become a braided practice that is stronger, more coherent and more likely to lead to the kind of teaching that will in turn lead to significantly improved student learning. And although clearly a practical consideration, the role inquiry plays in excellent teaching is much more a conceptual issue, suggesting a new view of what constitutes evidence of student learning, what drives teaching improvement, what counts as scholarship, what it means to strive for excellence and make it commonplace in teaching practice.

This can be demonstrated by two Professors of the Year. Marilyn Repsher is an excellent teacher of mathematics. From her work with elementary and secondary school teachers preparing students for college, to her efforts at making mathematics relevant to students' lives and majors, to her teacher training at Jacksonville University, Repsher exemplifies teaching excellence in higher education. Beyond her commitments to student learning and innovative teaching, new technologies and traditional lectures, can be found an interest in and passion for inquiry, a curiosity about the practice of teaching and learning that manifests not only in questions and curriculum but also investigation and evidence. Vernon Burton has a similar interest in the process of pedagogical inquiry and the learning about student learning it yields. As professor of history at the University of Illinois Urbana-Champaign he is dedicated to helping students develop their own perspectives on the past, becoming historians in their own right using tools they know best. This attention to student work led Burton to new media as a vehicle for learning the past and communicating with a wider audience. A champion of online learning and virtual-space technologies, community collaborations and real-world connections, student intentionality and the integration of times and places, Burton has merged the often arcane discipline of history with the frequently baroque practices of hyperspace. Both teachers certainly fulfil any criteria for professional distinction, but they also exemplify a braided practice, wherein a deep commitment to and understanding of disciplinary knowledge, dedicated efforts to achieve and maintain and ideally share pedagogical expertise, and ongoing efforts to undertake scholarly inquiry to improve student learning all combine to create teaching excellence (CASE, 2006).

Scholarly teaching

Of course there is no formula for teaching excellence, and braided practice builds on what might be considered a baseline competence and commitment that all successful teachers share. To be a teacher is to be knowledgeable with regard to subject matter, the process of teaching and the assessment of student learning; in order to teach, one must be prepared in terms of content and structures. All teachers should remain current in their field, aware of the developing nature of knowledge, connected to the growth of understanding such that students have access to up-to-date information. They should demonstrate a level of awareness with regard to students and how they learn, and an excitement about both the material and practice of education. Teachers should be reflective and responsive, thoughtful about how they conduct classes, making improvements and mitigating or avoiding difficulties. Once considered information delivery vehicles helping students 'bank' knowledge for future use, today's teachers know that deep learning requires the fostering of critical engagement and active learning, even in the most passive venues.

These attributes and expectations vary according to place and purpose, but once the baseline is achieved there is another level that bears addressing, with attributes that set teachers apart as not just accomplished but as scholarly. Scholarly teachers have a different kind of commitment and a different way of approaching their profession; they are not only knowledgeable about their field but also well-informed with regard to the latest ideas about how the field is taught and how students learn the discipline. Likewise, scholarly teaching presupposes improvement; embracing the idea that teaching can and should be enhanced through systematic understanding of practice (although *engaging in* investigation shifts the focus from 'scholarly' to 'scholarship of' teaching, or scholarly inquiry, described later).

Disciplinary knowledge

Teaching excellence also requires disciplinary knowing. Whether beginning with an understanding of the periodic table or the carbon cycle, the plays of Shakespeare in Elizabethan England or the places where salt was harvested by the Anasazi of the Colorado Plateau, disciplinary knowledge is a prerequisite to any kind of thoughtful and responsible teaching; it is a given in most classrooms that teachers will have an appropriate background in their subject. Some level of expertise is necessary for all teachers, but in the quest for excellence the role of disciplinary knowledge cannot be underestimated or too narrowly defined; one must know a field to teach it, and that knowledge must be broad enough, connected enough, to anticipate and respond to collateral needs of students. Indeed, it is often in collateral uses of knowledge, at the fringes of disciplines or the points of interdisciplinarity, that learning can best be achieved. Application of disciplinary knowledge in 'real world' settings is frequently showcased as a key strategy for deep learning; when application occurs in connection with other disciplinary frameworks, other complex and illuminating knowledge sets, or other areas of expertise, it has the potential to aggregate into something more significant than the sum of its parts. Thus the ability to integrate knowledge within, across, beyond disciplines (itself a kind of disciplinary knowledge), to see links and transfer points, becomes a central feature of teaching and learning. Field knowledge also extends into the teaching practices used to communicate and collaboratively create learning in the classroom, and thus a case can be made for pedagogical experience and expertise being a logical corollary, a necessary aspect of field-based teaching excellence.

Pedagogical expertise

The adage that there is no substitute for experience is certainly true for teaching; the more time spent teaching the more one understands the necessary preparation, most successful strategies and daily challenges to be addressed. But there is a difference between experience, which includes the sum total of all classroom time and attention (as teacher and student) and expertise, suggesting a level of skill and accomplishment that bespeaks a more learned, more accomplished, more professional approach to roles and responsibilities. Expertise in disciplinary practice is at least one goal of graduate education, and it is represented in some fields by an ever narrowing focus, an ever more powerful lens through which to examine and interpret the world.

In some cases, pedagogical expertise might manifest as a teacher becoming extraordinarily well-versed and accomplished in a particular approach to teaching; some of the finest facilitators have made the seminar their life's work, and the expert lecturer is a joy to behold. Indeed, some disciplines are so committed to particular pedagogies that they trump all others – think of lab and field experiences in biology, small-group work and the seminar in the humanities, the design studio in fine arts and architecture. The technical facility necessary to effectively conduct a problem-solving session is considerable and every bit as worthwhile as that required of an expert tutor or master craftsman. To develop expertise in a field's 'signature pedagogy', a phrase used by Carnegie President Lee Shulman (2005) in discussing professional and liberal education, is rightly seen to be a significant accomplishment. But what of fields where signature pedagogies are only the beginning, or disciplines which revel in multifaceted approaches to instruction, or studies programmes linked to more than one intellectual tradition and thus free to range far and wide in approaches to teaching? Indeed, what of the teacher who dabbles in different pedagogies, seeking the most effective mode of instruction for the topic at hand, the students at table, the community at large? If pedagogical expertise can manifest itself in signature pedagogies, it can also be present in variable forms; a case could be made for expertise applied not to an exclusive classroom technique, but rather to a more pedagogically promiscuous approach.

One level of expertise begins with the premise that our diverse and ever more integrative classrooms require not singular pedagogies but varied, variable modes of instruction. The wealth of information regarding student learning styles should be enough to suggest that teaching must be more responsive to the realities of culture and context. Thus in the quest for teaching excellence, pedagogical expertise may need to be framed in terms of developmental processes that take into account the need for an expansive and ever-changing instructional toolkit involving skills and techniques, pedagogies and processes, the ability to adapt to new circumstances, improvise according to emergent needs and issues, reflect on or respond to student learning as and when it happens. Perhaps this last attribute is most pertinent, for while we think of expertise as something gained, gathered, 'banked' in a mirror image of Freire's concept of the term (1970), it may be more accurate to think of the expert as someone capable of adjustment and adaptation, resilience and realignment, critical observation and evaluation of both learning and teaching at any given moment. For what makes pedagogical expertise possible, even in the most junior of faculty, is the tendency toward observation, innovation and responsiveness that characterizes thoughtful practice and the desire to improve. And it is that desire to improve which leads to the third aspect of braided practice and teaching excellence, scholarly inquiry; for while all three aspects of braided pedagogy are important, perhaps equally so, more attention will be given here to scholarly inquiry because it is less often considered in discussions about teaching excellence.

Scholarly inquiry

Although the concept of scholarly inquiry into pedagogical practice is as old as teaching and learning, it is relatively new to the formal structures of academic life and only recently has the scholarship of teaching and learning become central and accepted at a significant number of institutions. The term scholarship of teaching and learning itself is perhaps best understood through the work of The Carnegie Academy for the Scholarship of Teaching and Learning (CASTL) Higher Education Program of The Carnegie Foundation for the Advancement of Teaching (2006). The scholarship of teaching and learning seeks to render teaching public, subject to critical evaluation, and usable by others in both the scholarly and the general community. These objectives, however, do not really get at the processes of scholarship itself, which are straightforward but far from simple.

Beginning with faculty curiosity and the natural impulse of thoughtful teachers to understand and explain the ways in which students learn (or don't learn), scholarly inquiry or the scholarship of teaching and learning often stems from a single, simple question: how do you know? This question is where disciplinary scholarship begins; it is the birthplace of dissertations and academic papers. How does a theatre historian know Scots national identity is intentionally cultivated, advanced in plays of the Scottish Enlightenment? How does a biologist know cyclic AMP and LDL trigger enhanced gap junction assembly through a stimulation of connexion trafficking? How does a sociologist know race is the key arbiter of blue-collar employment outcomes for young black *and* white men? Similar questions pertain in the quest for knowledge about student learning but take different forms, different paths. How do you know what is really happening when theatre students role-play and improvise character relationships in rehearsal? How do you know what happens if students present experimental lab results through a poster session? How do you know what works best to facilitate student openness and understanding when dealing with race and gender in online environments? These opening inquiries lead to pedagogical research, and the scholarship of teaching and learning is one way to discover answers to such persistent questions. While any systematic or scholarly investigation into teaching and learning can be viewed as pedagogical research, what sets the scholarship of teaching and learning apart from most pedagogical research is that it is undertaken by faculty who seek to examine and understand student learning *in their own classrooms* and through their own observations and analysis.

Cycle of inquiry

The process works in a four-stage cycle of inquiry, beginning with an observation that sparks curiosity about student learning that cannot be addressed without investigation. This requires a shift in viewing students and their learning, as well as the development of observational skills more akin to those of disciplinary inquiry; student work or classroom activities might be viewed as historians would previously unexamined documents or artefacts, as field biologists might a new environment or landscape. Sometimes observations are discipline-specific, but more often represent local manifestations of enduring issues (student motivation, participation dynamics, questioning strategies, knowledge transfer or persistence). Observation quite naturally leads to the need to know more, necessitating investigation of the observation and any questions observing might engender, such that evidence of student learning can be produced and a claim can be made about how learning occurs. Because most faculty are steeped in disciplinary method, investigations often follow methodologies of their field: historians might analyse student text or conduct interviews; sociologists might develop surveys or conduct focus groups. But while common methods offer immediate familiarity with process, they often prove limiting in terms of the learning about learning they can yield. As a result, many scholars of teaching and learning find that in order to answer questions they must borrow methods from other disciplines; biologists often draw on text analysis, artists might resort to experimental and control groups. As with all scholarship, method must fit inquiry, questions are often complicated and results are rarely transparent.

This raises a tangential issue regarding the nature of questions and the process of inquiry. Frequently, the questions being asked (how do students learn in small groups? or what makes active learning more effective than passive receipt of information?) are made up of other questions (what is going on in small group work? or what makes case study pertinent to learning?). As a result, the process of observation and investigation must often be broken down into component parts; sharper visions or finer details of what happens in a classroom, narrower questions yielding more specific data, each of which begins to produce an accretive idea of student learning. During the process of inquiry, three kinds of questions often arise: what is, what works and what if? What is happening when students learn? What works to improve student learning? What if something new is tried to make learning better? These questions, first articulated in *Opening Lines* (with the third labelled 'visions of the possible'), make up the most prevalent approaches to scholarship of teaching and learning investigation (Hutchings, 2000). Addressing these questions ultimately leads to data about student learning and the development of a claim.

Because all scholarship must be validated, each claim–evidence–analysis–conclusion sequence is subsequently examined by peers to determine whether it meet standards of inquiry in the field. Often this occurs via scholarly journals of particular disciplines or the journals devoted to the scholarship of teaching and learning, but work of this kind is increasingly being made public in other forums including peer review of teaching portfolios, the most complete and persistent example of which can be found at the University of Nebraska Lincoln (Peer Review of Teaching Project 2006). But whatever the venue, judgement follows the same rigorous analysis expected from any form of scholarship. This process requires all scholarship begin with *clear goals* and a researchable question, incorporate *adequate preparation* including knowledge of previous work and experience with the mode of inquiry, employ *appropriate methods* for addressing the question and providing evidence of an answer), produce *significant results* as verifiable evidence, use *effective presentation* to communicate the inquiry and the evidence as well as its impact on the field and embody *reflective critique* of the question, the methods, the results and the impact (Glassick *et al.*, 1997).

Finally, results of the investigation and findings of the reviewing peers are made public in venues likely to influence practice beyond the local and stimulate use (and investigation) of the evidence in other contexts. Thus scholarly inquiry is framed as the result of careful attention to the classroom environment, an attempt to understand student learning for the purposes of improvement and a process by which knowledge and expertise is made available for public use. Clearly this is an important way to advance knowledge of student learning within a discipline, between disciplines, across multiple fields and among colleagues in a variety of contexts local and remote; it also focuses attention on how good teaching succeeds and all teaching improves. What makes scholarly inquiry a core feature of teaching excellence, a vital aspect of braided practice, is the commitment teachers bring to understanding and improving student learning and the change commitment brings to multiple classroom environments.

Implicit in this proposition, that excellence requires inquiry, is belief that educational practice cannot remain static if it is to progress beyond the realm of rote instruction and the delivery of bankable knowledge and information. Teaching is more than a set of skills and activities that, once mastered, can be repeated ad infinitum without challenge or change; it is an intellectual practice that must be cultivated, developed over time and space, working with and responding to student differences, cultural variations and emergent needs of an unpredictable world. We often speak of students' growth and progress in much the same way, champion their development as intentional, integrative thinkers and learners. Why should we expect anything less from teachers? If we want students to become lifelong learners, ever curious, thoughtful, changing, we should likewise model that behaviour in our teaching, demonstrating a curious, thoughtful, adaptable, critical approach to instruction (beginning with our own).

Consider Daisy Hurst Floyd, professor of law at Texas Tech University, who was curious about the development of professional identity in law students: how, when, where it occurred, whether it had any impact on or was aligned with professional lives. She gathered data about students' educational experiences with identity formation before and during law school, then correlated that with experiences of practicing lawyers within a class devoted to bridging the gap between academic and practical training:

> Although they come to law school with a clear sense of purpose, many students become disengaged from the educational experience and develop reduced expectations for what their lives as lawyers will be. Many students experience law school as an isolating, competitive, and dehumanizing environment. Encouraging students to strengthen skills of reflection and self-awareness and to form connections with peers changes students' experiences. Students involved in the project report renewed hope that they can fulfill the original purpose that brought them to law school and renewed expectations that they will live balanced, healthy, and satisfied professional and personal lives.
>
> (Floyd, 2002)

The project yielded fascinating data, having a profound effect on one professor's understanding of the law and its impact on those who define its practice. Not only did Floyd change her teaching, she is now Dean of the Walter F. George School of Law at Mercer University where she is helping other faculty see and understand how different pedagogical approaches can lead to different professional identities.

David Reichard worked within the context of an upper-division free speech course at California State University Monterey Bay. He began with the observation that students did not always achieve 'deep understanding' of free speech, or at least not the depth of understanding expected:

> The study also examined the role of students' prior knowledge about law, and whether small seminars, embedded within a larger class, facilitated the development of students' deep understanding. Students prepared for and reflected on seminar discussions through public weblogs, or blogs, that chronicled their learning process through the semester, providing important scholarship of teaching and learning evidence of their learning process.
>
> (Reichard, 2004)

Through careful gathering and comparison of student data, including observations of student research partners, Reichard formed a deeper understanding of his students' deep understanding of free speech. This understanding was shared with colleagues locally and nationally, through conference presentations and ultimately publication. Furthermore, their own artefacts and evidence contributed to a larger movement in which electronic sources and structures are being used to collect more complete and coherent data on student learning in traditional and online classes.

Benefits of scholarly inquiry

The benefits of scholarly inquiry are unquestionable – beginning with deeper knowledge of student learning and greater appreciation for larger issues of the educational enterprise. Additional advantages include the collateral influence such inquiry has on how students see and understand their own academic trajectory and their own role in that experience. Time and again scholars of teaching and learning comment on changes in student awareness brought about by inquiry into classroom practice; as students see higher education as open to investigation and improvement, they begin to take a more active role in the teaching and learning process. Indeed, one inquiry into programme portfolios as a vehicle for empowerment suggests that students who view education as an evolving process of discovery, rather than a series of ossified and eternal courses, take more active and engaged roles in their own learning (Gale, 2001).

This perspective has also led to collaborative work on the role of students as co-investigators in scholarly inquiry. Scholars of teaching and learning at institutions like North Seattle Community College and Western Washington University have reported that students involved as partner-researchers in inquiry projects become more activist and intentional about their own learning and more aware of the qualities and practices of good teaching. This work on the student voice in scholarly inquiry has been accomplished in part through a collaboration organized under the CASTL Campus Program's Leadership Clusters, but it represents only one portion of the student-faculty inquiry projects underway on campuses around the world (Sustaining Student Voices CASTL Leadership Cluster 2005). Like current emphasis on undergraduate research, student participation in scholarly inquiry provides direct experience in the rationale for experimentation, the process of investigation and the influence of scholarship. But in order for scholarly inquiry into teaching and learning to be fostered and sustained it must be encouraged and celebrated, recognized and rewarded, scaffolded and supported by colleagues, department chairs and academic administrators. Fortunately, this kind of scholarly inquiry is being encouraged at institutions of higher education from Bournemouth to Budapest, Hong Kong to Halifax, Sydney to Singapore. As more colleges and universities come to realize the importance of the scholarship of teaching and learning, more administrators and faculty and students initiate inquiry projects that address important questions about student learning.

Furthermore, as college personnel begin working together on inquiry projects, they come to realize the benefits of collaboration at every stage. Student-faculty collaborations provide new windows on learning and teaching, as well as more practical views of what scholarship of this kind can and should reveal. Faculty-staff collaborations, especially institutional research or work that involves student support staff, provide complementary pedagogical and co-curricular evidence producing deeper and more complete visions of how students integrate diverse learning environments. Adding the administrative level enables institution-wide perspectives that address questions of mission and mandate, providing venues for trans-departmental collaboration. In fact, when inquiry begins to transcend individual classrooms and departments and even institutions, it has the potential for great impact, not just as collaborative but as coordinated scholarship that can be shared and compared more widely (Gale, forthcoming 2008).

The nature of braided practice

Braiding itself is understood as the interwoven combination of separate parts, each with its own coherence and often its own identity, into an overlapping and cross-connecting pattern. The virtues of braiding include greatly increased strength and carrying capacity, improved durability and resistance to external (often damaging) forces or influences. With regard to disciplinary knowledge, pedagogical expertise and scholarly inquiry, braiding suggests an interweaving cross-connection designed to influence and inform the practices of each, contributing to strength and durability while also building greater integrity into the entire endeavour. To some extent, this grows naturally out of the work championed by Ernest Boyer in *College* (1987) and *Scholarship Reconsidered* (1990). It also has roots in Shulman's three types of knowledge (subject matter content knowledge, pedagogical content knowledge and curricular knowledge), and his oeuvre on the scholarship of teaching and learning (2004). Shulman (2006) has remarked that 'everyone who professes in our institutions of higher education has an obligation, at least at the formative level, to take professional responsibility for the quality of her work, that is, to engage in the scholarship of teaching and learning'. In fact, one could draw a line of braided practice (including knowledge, theory, practical expertise and thoughtful inquiry) from Aristotle's notion of *praxis* through to William Sullivan's work on practical reason (2001). What makes braided practice so vital to teaching excellence is the way that each aspect informs and improves the others, through the establishment of important points of comparison, the confluence of ideas and innovations and, perhaps most significantly, the way in which excellence in one area strengthens and deepens the practice of others. This is especially true of inquiry, the least recognized and the most transformative of the three, and the one which has the greatest potential for changing how we know, how we teach and how students learn. The influence of the scholarship of teaching and learning on pedagogical expertise is well-documented and generally well-accepted (Hutchings, 2000; Beaudry and Bruce, 2003; Becker and Andrews, 2004; Cambridge, 2004; Huber, 2004; Hutchings and Huber, 2005). Developing a better understanding of how students learn in particular circumstances and under certain conditions, through the systematic examination of practice and the gathering of compelling data, will only serve to change and improve how faculty engaged in inquiry think about what they do in the classroom and how or why they do it. Put another way, when faculty pay closer attention to how students learn, they themselves learn how to improve their own teaching.

This was the central idea behind Mark Maier's investigation into small group work in an economics class at Glendale Community College in California. Specifically, he knew that there had been a great deal of research into cooperative learning and its impact on student achievement, but he had seen little about what actually occurs within the context of a small group, so he audiotaped students during small group work in a 'Principles of Economics' class. Initially, these conversations seemed disappointing, suggesting students were spending less time on economics than on non-class-related topics; eventually recordings revealed students working together, building cumulative learning capacity, yielding new insights and changed practice.

> The tapes allowed me to improve cooperative learning activities, for example validating the process of raising questions. In addition, I was able to document the manner in which cooperative learning structures supported efficient use of class time and relatively equal participation by all students. Finally, the transcripts showed me that students tried out new terms and concepts, often correcting mathematical errors and misinterpretation of terms that I had not anticipated. These simultaneous conversations took brief periods of time so that many more students practiced their learning and many more errors were corrected than in a standard classroom discussion.
>
> (Maier, 2002)

Although inquiry was time-consuming and labour-intensive, it resulted in changed practices that streamlined content delivery and made in-class time more efficient and productive. Thoughtful scholarship informed practice and resulted in greater pedagogical expertise. When made public within his community and beyond, Maier's insights influenced the practice of others and led to National Science Foundation funding for an inquiry project.

Likewise, the process of scholarly investigation into teaching and learning expands disciplinary knowledge through the intervention of practice, forcing a constant reexamination and reinterpretation of the most direct and the most oblique aspects of a field. All too often we approach the foundational tenets of our discipline with a cavalier or dismissive approach, reminiscent of rote learning more than critical thinking. In far too many classrooms, student are told that they must 'learn the basics on their own' before they are ready or able to grapple with the more complex and often more interesting questions at the 'cutting edge'. Yet it is at the access points of learning that the most good and the most harm can be done, for it is often in early stages that students develop a lifelong fear, familiarity or fascination with art, geology, mathematics, sociology, or any topic. Imagine what an inquiry approach to basic-knowledge courses would do for teaching and learning at the entry level of any discipline, how attention to the ways in which students gain a working knowledge of what it means to see like an artist or geologist, think like a mathematician or sociologist might inform and illuminate the field not only for students but for faculty. Scholarship of teaching and learning can also deepen disciplinary knowledge at advanced levels of instruction, including graduate and professional training; this is especially true when inquiry focuses on aspects of the field which are not readily accessible or easy to understand.

Take Whitney Schlegel, who in teaching human physiology at Indiana University was concerned about the extent to which collaborative team learning could cultivate disciplinary thinking. Students in these classes were often fiercely independent, committed to competition rather than cooperation in the quest for higher grades and standings. She created projects and processes that required collaboration in five-person teams and gathered data about their interactions through the eyes of a student designated as team historian for the project. What she found was significant for the students and for the teacher:

> Engaging students in peer collaboration with an opportunity for individual and group reflection on the process facilitates disciplinary thinking as well as the professional attitudes and behaviors necessary for collaboration in the disciplines and professions of physiology and medicine. The student voice reveals that disciplinary skills and central themes are made transparent and intrinsic in a team-learning environment when peer review and reflection are integral components of their intellectual experience. The team chronicle of their experience demonstrates that the earlier a team invests in trying to understand and develop group process the greater the academic achievement of the team.
>
> (Schlegel, 2004)

In addition to the disciplinary benefits for her students, Schlegel's inquiry provided new insights into her own understanding and communicating of principles. Through the lens of her team historians and the data they provided, she was able to develop a deeper sense of how her students made meaning of disciplinary processes that she herself had come to take for granted, and in so doing Schlegel expanded her own understanding of her field and its implications for the future of practicing physicians.

Another case for braided practice could be made with reference to the reciprocal influence of disciplinary knowledge and pedagogical expertise, self-evident and readily-acceptable features of teaching excellence. What matters here is less the impacts on knowledge, pedagogy and inquiry than the confluence and interplay of the ideas at work behind the overlapping descriptions; when dedication to excellence is framed as commitment to all three aspects of excellent teaching it has more substantial conceptual significance than can be suggested by any one attribute in isolation. When teaching is framed as a process of inquiry and a home for scholarship, it has the weight of academic impact which cannot help but influence the way we see disciplines and pedagogies. Indeed, knowledge gained through teaching and learning scholarship is often disciplinary knowledge, bearing on the way subject matter is framed, communicated and understood through the process of instruction.

Challenges and benefits

There are, however, challenges involved in this kind of an approach to excellence, especially given that not all faculty are well prepared or intrinsically motivated to conduct scholarly inquiry. Certainly the principles and practices involved are well known and available to all, given enough time, assistance and acceptance, but therein lies a central problem with defining excellence in terms of inquiry: scholarship of this sort requires investment of time, in preparation and in conducting the investigation; it requires resources in terms of data gathering and analysis; it requires community in the broadest sense of the word, supportive colleagues to critical examiners to willing audience; and it requires acceptance from the institutional powers that be.

The benefits that can be derived from including inquiry in our definition of teaching excellence are legion, and impact all concerned. Inquiry provides a pathway to adaptability, enabling teachers to see where they are successful and where they might want to make change. Furthermore, positive results can be seen in students, who benefit from the results of the inquiry, from the process of investigation which sheds light on their learning and provides serious attention to accomplishments, and from the engagement that comes with attention. Additionally, there are benefits to faculty who participate in this scholarship in the form of improved practice and knowledge, but also the pedagogical community that develops around such projects and the renewed commitment to the causes of higher education that seem to follow. Finally, there are benefits to the disciplines, in terms of how students learn the features of the field, and to institutions with such a clear emphasis on students and their success.

Learning is developmental in nature; students learn in different ways at different times in their academic lives, and the best teachers are those who can work through the needs of students with a variable and responsive pedagogy. Teaching is likewise developmental, with an often steep learning curve for the uninitiated, and the path to excellence is one of incremental improvement through trial and error, observation and imitation, instinct and instruction. But if inquiry can be added into the mix, if scholarship can be made integral to excellence, it will undoubtedly lead to thoughtful trials of innovative approaches, clearer observations about the what and how of student learning, more communal and collaborative approaches to faculty instruction. Viewing the classroom as a venue for scholarship builds a sense of responsiveness, a level of awareness that is uncommon on most campuses and unexpected by most students. Likewise, when faculty take student learning seriously, enough so that they commit time and energy to understanding what is happening in their classrooms, there is a reciprocity formed, a sense of shared responsibility for instructional outcomes, one of the many benefits of putting students at the centre of our disciplinary, pedagogical, scholarly practice. And what better component of excellence can there be than the habit of putting students at the heart of teaching and learning?

Just as the scholarship of teaching and learning requires supportive infra-structure and a culture of inquiry, braided practice has its own structural require-ments. It requires a campus culture where students are at the centre and improved learning is a goal with which all can agree; there must be a culture of excellence, a culture of inquiry and a sense of community in support of object-ives. Key to this is opportunities for collaboration wherein faculty work together, in tandem, or in concert on persistent and pervasive questions of student learning. There must be administrative support for individual faculty pursuing inquiry projects, and that support must be both in word and deed. Insti-tutions certainly benefit from practice that combines knowledge, pedagogy and inquiry, and as such should recognize and reward those who practice the schol-arship of teaching and learning. Additionally, inquiry must become a part of the collective campus vision, made vocal and visible through the actions of the insti-tution and its representatives. One of the most important conditions for success, however, also stands as the greatest hurdle: departmental awareness and accep-tance. The department, which is committed first to disciplinary knowledge and then to pedagogical expertise, is often where difficulties appear. But it is also in the department that mechanisms for encouragement and engagement, through shared inquiry and the articulation of what it means to engage in scholarship, can be put in place. There is nothing so important to student success, and the teaching that makes success possible, as departmental commitments to under-standing and improvement, especially when improvement comes in the form of inquiry into student learning. It is through commitments to understanding and improvement that current faculty will themselves achieve the goals of teaching excellence.

Looking ahead

Perhaps even more important than creating opportunities for success among current faculty is the necessity to build this approach into the professoriate of the future, junior faculty, and those entering an institution for the first time. Gradu-ate students represent the first, best opportunities for changing our view of teaching excellence, and incorporating the scholarship of teaching and learning into their disciplinary training would not only foreground the importance of student success but also set graduates on the path to teaching improvement in years to come (Gale and Golde, 2004). The same must also be done for junior faculty who have not had the opportunity to investigate student learning as graduate students, or in fact for any teachers new to an institution. If attention to scholarly inquiry into classroom practice is part of campus orientation, or if the importance of teaching investigation is immediately recognized and rewarded through mechanisms as diverse as participation in coordinated projects and teaching centre events or the institutional creation of working groups, then from the outset faculty will be predisposed to seeing their role as one of teacher/scholar. In fact, infrastructure in place to support the scholarship of teaching and learning is often an indication of how seriously an institution takes the need for teaching excellence. Finally, many institutions are committed to the preparation of future leaders, administrators and faculty and, in some cases, students who demonstrate a particular commitment to learning from student learning. Cultivation of tomorrow's leaders is just as important as preparing future faculty, but significant leadership in support of braided practice and teaching excellence begins in the same place as all scholarship, with a new way of seeing.

But any new way of seeing brings into focus other questions, such as how this idea of braided practice might fit into the current context of national policies and social expectations for teaching and learning. Katharine C. Lyall, University of Wisconsin System President Emerita, has remarked that 'higher education in the U.S. is at the center of a "perfect storm" of economic and political changes that challenge our core mission as well as the ways in which we accomplish our work'. She continued:

> Convergence of the economic and political winds ... have created a swirling vortex of new demands and changing expectations for higher education. Out of this come increasing pressures for re-examining whether the results we have traditionally produced are the ones still wanted in the twenty-first century and rising demands that we measure and value out outputs in ways that can be compared across institutions, accessed by consumers, and used by policymakers. It is here that the black forces of reductionism meet the 'while hats' of formative evaluation. And it is here, at this juncture in time and in this particular policy space, that I believe the work of the scholarship of teaching and learning can make a critical difference.
>
> (Lyall, 2006)

For Lyall, this scholarship provides answers to questions of improvement and calls for accountability, offering understanding of teaching impact and evidence of student learning. Furthermore, when scholarly inquiry is braided with scholarly teaching and disciplinary knowledge in a self-reflexive, critical helix of improving practice, it represents a coherent response to public clamours for measurable outcomes. Shulman suggested, 'we have to get more serious about our studies not only demonstrating that we take our teaching seriously – which, Lord knows, is important – but also about generating new knowledge and understanding'. He continued:

> No longer do we appear before those who set policy with only a sad story or a happy one, but we come before legislative committees, before the administrators of our institutions, before our boards with the kind of evidence that can't be ignored. As I said before, the claim of the scholarship of teaching and learning is that there are certain questions only faculty can ask. Put another way, if we fail to ask them, they won't be asked at all and won't

matter, be forgotten and ignored. Asking them and bringing the answers to the larger community is our moral obligation, and I urge you to accept it.

(Shulman, 2006)

Indeed, as the work of higher education teaching and learning becomes more public, visible and accountable to the social and political climate outside ivy-covered walls, the more it requires a coherent combination of knowledge, experience and inquiry. Through the concept of braided practice, we build a profile of teaching excellence that has greater integrity, accountability and opportunity for improvement.

There was a time when teaching excellence was defined by what others could see; student evaluations and testimonials reflected teacher's strengths and abilities within the discipline and the classroom, while faculty observations and accolades served to corroborate, augment and triangulate perceptions from another viewpoint with more experience and different standards. Now a new approach is taking hold, one that asks more of the teacher than disciplinary knowledge and pedagogical expertise. This inquiry model requires the development of a scholarly eye on student learning, one that can see beyond the obvious and help to dissect both difficulty and success in the service of improvement. This is perhaps the most challenging aspect of braided practice, demanding a commitment not only to knowledge and pedagogy but to perception, curiosity and change. Japanese film director Akira Kurosowa once commented that being an artist means never to avert one's eyes; likewise, striving for excellence in teaching means never avoiding the hard questions that constantly appear in our practice, and never repressing our need to know.

But knowing often comes at great risk, for it is far easier to settle on and repeat pedagogical approaches than to embrace inquiry as an ongoing aspect of practice. Being committed to braided practice means accepting teaching in a constant state of flux, never being satisfied with what is known, never shying away from changes that might be difficult in the short run but beneficial in the long run or for others in the field. It is indeed a conceptual shift, one that seems necessary to the idea of teaching as a profession seeking improvements in student learning, but anathema to those wishing to insure high teaching evaluations and universal praise. Yet in the quest for excellence praise is not the goal; for many teachers excellence is its own reward. That is why excellent teachers are never satisfied with recognition, never content to rest on past success and innovation. They continue to observe and question, see and change, create opportunities for inquiry and insight, evidence and occasionally failure; because in the journey that is teaching excellence, only braided practice can make the change we want to bring about for all students.

Chapter 3

Beyond performance in teaching excellence

Bruce Macfarlane
(Thames Valley University, UK)

Introduction

'Teaching excellence' is a contested concept. It is variously interpreted as teaching behaviour that is interactive rather than didactic; modelling interpersonal skills; developing a collaborative relationship with students; possessing a repertoire of teaching skills; showing enthusiasm and energy; displaying creativity; demonstrating concern for 'weaker' students; and being committed to one's own professional development (e.g. Hillier and Vielba, 2001; Skelton, 2005: 95–97). These various characteristics may, in turn, be grouped by reference to different meta-understandings of what constitutes 'excellent' teaching (Skelton, 2005: 35). However, while a number of studies have elaborated different conceptions of 'excellence', less attention has focused on which types of teaching activity are being evaluated. What, in other words, do we mean by 'teaching'? In raising this question I am joined by others in this volume who also question whether there is a secure, shared understanding of what we mean by 'teaching' (see, for example, Chapter 4).

There are taken-for-granted assumptions and dominant understandings as to what constitutes 'teaching'. These often exclude a range of practices that occur outside the formal environment of the lecture theatre or seminar room. In this chapter, I will examine how schemes to reward teaching excellence interpret the range of activities which 'count' as teaching. This is an important area for analysis as I will argue that interpretations of excellence, and evidence used to support this claim, tend to favour more performance-related interpretations of teaching practice, influenced by a creeping culture of managerial control in universities (Deem, 1998; Skelton, 2005).

Performance and performativity

The notion of teaching as a 'performance' is powerfully embedded in interpretations of what constitutes good or excellent teaching. For example, videos of 'star' lecturers were proposed by government ministers in the early development of a scheme to reward university teaching excellence in the UK (Skelton, 2005).

This understanding draws on the metaphor of teaching as theatre (Armstrong, 2003). Here, there is an emphasis on teachers replicating the skills and attributes of the accomplished actor through dress, voice projection, body language, use of props, memorising a script and convincing the audience that they are genuinely passionate and knowledgeable about their subject. In this version of excellent teaching it is essential to immerse oneself in a role and put on a bravura performance in the lecture 'theatre'. The use of actors in educational and training provision for teachers and university lecturers serves to reinforce and, to some extent, legitimise this metaphor.

'Performative' teaching implies something slightly different than teaching as a performance. The former implies that teaching can be evaluated in terms of its impact on enhancing economic performance and efficiency or satisfies measurements of good teaching endorsed by audit and quality control procedures (Skelton, 2005). An example might be vocationally relevant teaching that helps to develop students' work-related skills. While teaching as a performance is not necessarily the same as performative teaching, the dominant methods we use to judge teaching excellence are biased in favour of the dramaturgical metaphor. To demonstrate this I will focus my analysis on teaching observation schemes and student evaluation questionnaires. These instruments of evaluation are central to the evidence base used to judge teaching excellence and tend to be biased in favour of evaluating performance in the formal teaching environment. I will argue that less visible elements of teaching practice that take place 'offstage' need to play a more significant role in informing judgements about teaching excellence. Many of these behind-the-scenes activities are team-based, rather than about purely individual excellence, contributing to an 'academic citizenship' (Shils, 1997; Macfarlane, 2007) that maintains the infrastructure and broader moral foundations of university teaching.

What counts as teaching?

When I began working at a research-based UK university some years ago I quickly realised that teaching was defined in very narrow terms compared to my previous experiences at a less research-intensive institution. I asked a colleague how many hours they taught on average each week. They replied that they did no more than about six hours teaching. After initially commenting that this commitment must leave a reasonable amount of time for research activities, a different reality began to unfold. After further discussion I realised that my colleague thought of 'teaching' as *only* the number of hours they spent giving a formal lecture. His definition of teaching had omitted 'seminars' where he led a small group of students in discussion and analysis based on the week's lecture, one-to-one student advising and the supervision of postgraduates undertaking research degrees. Time spent assessing student work, giving further feedback electronically or at a distance or in preparing teaching materials was also excluded. To my colleague, and many others at the university, teaching was exclusively equated with giving a lecture.

This personal story is illustrative of taken-for-granted assumptions about the way in which teaching is often defined. While the use of active learning methods is now widely considered to be a central feature of 'good practice' (Chickering and Gamson, 1991), the lecture is still a dominant form of teaching across many subjects in universities. Ironically, despite the acknowledged limitations of the lecture in engaging learners interactively, this method has thrived in the age of mass higher education as a pragmatic means of teaching large groups of students (Apodaca and Grad, 2006). In an Australian study, it was found that 'lectures remain the most common type of teaching reported in most disciplines, even in the context of exemplary and innovative practice' (Ballantyne et al., 1999: 243). While this bias may appear contradictory to contemporary expectations that equate active techniques with excellence, lectures provide a better match to the needs and expectations of the burgeoning culture of performativity. This is because they are a publicly accessible form of teaching that is easy to observe on the basis of lecturers conforming with a narrow set of behavioural expectations.

The growth of inspection regimes for educational provision in schools, further education colleges and universities in the UK, and elsewhere, has increased the pressure to identify 'measurable' outcomes for teaching activity often defined in terms of 'standards'. These performative measures are necessary to justify inspection and regulation of educational provision (Avis, 2003). In a university context, workload planning models, a further concept imported from the business environment, identify the number of 'teaching hours' per faculty member during a week, term, semester or academic year. In a UK context, academics working at post-1992 universities have more detailed contracts in relation to teaching hours than lecturers working in 'old' (i.e. pre-1992) universities (Robson, 2006). In most post-1992 universities teaching hours do not normally exceed 18 hours per week or 550 hours in one academic year. Definitions of teaching hours include formal interactions with students such as lectures and seminars but normally omit informal interactions central to student learning such as personal tutoring responsibilities, assessment and feedback. These formal interactions with students are commonly evaluated through teaching observation and student course experience questionnaires. Hence, the performative culture quantifies and evaluates formal teaching environments, such as the lecture, but often fails to account for wider aspects of teaching practice that are harder to observe and measure. To return to the dramaturgical metaphor, teaching is defined as something that takes place 'onstage' rather than behind the scenes of such formal encounters in university life.

Teaching observation

The formal teaching and learning environment tends to be represented by the lecture and those teaching interactions that take place in seminars, workshops and laboratory situations involving a lecturer and a group of students. Interactions in such settings are the most easily observable compared with informal learning exchanges that take place through student advising (Gosling, 2002). In these less formal environments observation can prove more challenging owing to the less predictable format of the teaching and learning process and the fact that the presence of an observer can be regarded as 'more intrusive' than in a lecture (Staffordshire University, 2000). The language used in teaching observation forms is frequently based on the assumption that the focus of what will be observed will be a lecture or a teaching situation suited to an evaluation of the presentation skills of the lecturer. Phrases that guide observers to comment on 'delivery and pace', 'rapport', or 'use of audio-visual facilities' are examples of the way teaching observation tends to focus on presentation skills as something 'worth' watching (Gosling, 2002). These phrases underscore that what is being evaluated is the actors' on-stage performance.

The primary importance attached to the formal teaching environment is reinforced by reviews of the quality of higher educational provision by government agencies and professional bodies across a number of national contexts. Such reviews often seek to obtain a snapshot of teaching 'quality' through observation of the formal teaching environment, such as UK subject review, conducted during the early part of this decade (Quality Assurance Agency for Higher Education, 2000). This bias is significant as observation records are commonly invoked in schemes to evidence teaching excellence. This includes both institutional schemes linked to promotion and national excellence awards. For example, in the University of Warwick teaching profile, observation records are seen as a basis for evidence that 'performance is demonstrably excellent' (University of Warwick, 2002: 8). In the UK National Teaching Fellowship (NTFS) scheme 'feedback from peer observations' is specifically cited as constituting one of four sources of evidence that might be used to support an excellence claim (Higher Education Academy, 2006).

Records of teaching observation, or extracts from records that put the applicant in a positive light, may be used to support claims to teaching excellence across a range of promotion and award schemes. Such evidence, though, may reflect very different models of teaching observation. Some teaching observation schemes are predicated on a peer review model whereby teachers observe one another, feedback is constructive and non-judgemental and the relationship between the parties is based on mutuality as professional peers. Others adopt a development model where educational developers or other acknowledged expert teachers observe novices often in the context of a certificated university programme for new academic staff (Gosling, 2002). While educational developers are generally committed to teaching observation as a means of encouraging individual reflection, the expert-novice relationship implied by the development model can also be used as a performative tool to make a summative judgement regarding whether someone is a 'competent' teacher.

Determining competence is the unambiguous purpose of the evaluation model. In this third model of teaching observation, the observer will be a senior member of staff with either managerial responsibility or an obligation to report their judgement to others as part of an appraisal process (Gosling, 2002). It is premised on a concern about 'quality control' seen by critics as inappropriate and of limited value in a higher education context (Knight and Trowler, 2001) given that the relationship between student and teacher is more complex than a simple market analogy. The evaluation model is also linked to making teaching 'teacherproof' (Bruner, 1996) by seeking to standardise the skills and behaviour of lecturers in formal settings. 'Consistency' in processes that impact on students such as teaching or assessment is one of the principles in the implicit evaluative framework of quality assurance (Ottewill and Macfarlane, 2004). This means, for example, that some lecturers are cast in the role of replicating the lessons of others where students on large undergraduate programmes are divided into a series of parallel seminar groups. Here, the McDonaldised lecturer (Ritzer, 1998) must keep to the script if teaching is to conform to performative expectations.

These sharp differences in the principles underpinning teaching observation schemes mean that evidence is at best difficult to compare. While they rely on different sources of expertise to judge teaching excellence – peers, professional developers and line managers, respectively – they are rarely designed to recognise less visible forms of teaching. Regardless of the model of teaching observation, it needs to be understood that the credibility of the observers may be called into question. Frequently observers are assumed to possess the expertise based on their seniority or level of experience and do not receive training to carry out the function (Gosling, 2005). This means that evidence of teaching excellence derived from the comments and judgements of untrained observers may simply perpetuate ingrained practices within the teaching of the discipline (Wentzel, 1987). Even external peer reviewers working for government agencies are not necessarily sufficiently expert to pass reliable judgement. Peter Milton, commenting on the operation of the UK Quality Assurance Agency Programme Review scheme which he directed, stated that 'some of those doing the assessing probably had as much to learn about classroom presentation as those being judged' (Milton, 2002: 1).

Student evaluation questionnaires

Teaching excellence schemes hold great store by evidence of (positive) student evaluation. Much of this evidence is derived from student evaluation questionnaires (SEQs) that have long been the dominant means by which students are asked to evaluate the quality of teaching, especially in the US (Clouder, 1998; Brennan and Williams, 2004). The massification of higher education outside North America has resulted in SEQs becoming a standard feature of the evaluation of teaching across many national contexts and appears to be increasingly linked to the evaluation of teaching performance for reward and promotion purposes (Apodaca and Grad, 2006). In Canada, the 3M Teaching Fellowship programme expects applicants to submit a 'copy of the instrument used to evaluate the nominee's teaching' in addition to the data derived from SEQs over several years (Society for Teaching and Learning in Canada, 2006). In similar vein, nominees for the UK NTFS are asked to base their excellence claim on evidence from student feedback and evaluations. The Carrick Awards for Australian University Teaching, launched in 2006, has gone even further. This scheme has developed its own standardised SEQ and has stipulated that nominees must use this form to obtain and submit feedback from 30 students in making a claim for excellence (The Carrick Institute for Learning and Teaching in Higher Education, 2006).

There are numerous, well-known criticisms of SEQs. These include challenges to the reliability of some statistical techniques, the inappropriateness of assigning students a status as expert consumers together with their 'conservative' expectations in judging what constitutes good teaching, the 'halo effect' whereby teacher popularity rather than expertise is being tested and the danger that some lecturers can give students an 'easy ride' in return for better evaluations (e.g. Piercy et al., 1997; Elton, 2001; Lyon and Hendry, 2002). These and other criticisms of the SEQ fall outside the scope of this analysis. What is pertinent though is that, in parallel with teaching observation forms, SEQs often focus on the performance element of teaching. While they may appear to give students more of a voice in the evaluation of teaching, the kind of judgements called for are often narrowly framed around issues of technical competence (Rowland, 2000).

SEQs tend to be written on the assumption that students are evaluating a formal teaching context by asking questions that privilege the assessment of presentational skills over 'softer' skills associated with building relationships. Even where SEQs avoid reference to formal teaching environments the manner in which they are administered (often in-class) can privilege this context. Their extensive use is symbolic of the 'replacement of the informal with the formal' in UK higher education (Brennan and Williams, 2004: 9). They have become a ritualised facet of the teaching exchange and do not represent a genuine opportunity for students to enter into an open dialogue with their tutors (Rowland, 2000).

Part of this formality is the way SEQs seek to gain an impression of student satisfaction with respect to a range of 'levels' beyond the control of the individual lecturer. These can include the module, the year of study, the programme, the subject, the department, the faculty and the institution (Brennan and Williams, 2004). Here, students are frequently asked to comment on the quality of rooms and facilities and learning resources such as laboratories, studios, clinics and libraries. Other questions connected with the appropriateness of assessment tasks and course materials may further relate to aspects of programme design beyond the remit of the deskilled 'McDonaldized' lecturer whose role is to 'deliver' materials prepared by other more senior or experienced colleagues (Ritzer, 1998). Where SEQs seek student feedback on 'learning support' this can refer to specialised units in areas such as library and information services, student skills, dyslexia support and careers guidance.

While it is important to get students to think about teaching in a broader sense than 'onstage' performance, SEQs may more negatively infer that lecturers play little or no role beyond the formal teaching context in offering support to learners. This supports an 'unbundling' of the academic role that is beginning to erode the responsibility of lecturers for the teaching of students 'offstage'.

Unbundling

Teaching observation and SEQs are illustrative of the way that evidence used to support claims to teaching excellence conform to a diminished sense of what it means to be a teacher in modern higher education. This type of evidence privileges formal teaching contexts but, with more subtlety, narrows the focus of what 'counts' as teaching. The contemporary extension of student support services has led to a withering of the pastoral role of the academic to that of a referral agent for specialist counsellors, careers professionals, subject librarians, student debt officers, disability advisors, numeracy and literacy specialists and international student officers. Concerns about making teaching more 'efficient' has legitimised the erosion of contact time between academic staff and students. The drive for efficiency means that contemporary university environments encourage larger student groups, less contact time for individual learners and less available or approachable tutors (Christie *et al.*, 2004). New research indicates, for example, that the replacement of the lecturer's office with open plan working arrangements in some universities is making it practically more difficult to find appropriate private space for personal tutoring (Bradford, 2006). There is evidence that institutional pressures on academic staff to be more research-active encourages a culture that 'distances' the tutor from the student (Brown, 2002).

Underpinning the increasing detachment of tutors from broader elements of teaching and learning support, such as personal tutoring, is the phenomenon known as 'unbundling'. This term refers to the way that academic work is being subdivided into specialist roles such as 'teacher', 'researcher', 'instructional designer', 'specialist tutor' and 'skills advisor'. Kinser (1998) uses the term 'unbundling' in describing the way the various elements of the 'all-round' academic role had been subdivided by the University of Phoenix, the largest private, for-profit university in the world. However, this trend is also widely apparent in public universities and was recognised in the UK Dearing report on higher education as a significant future trend that would result in a smaller proportion of staff being 'core' employees (NCIHE, 1997). Unbundling is now reflected in a growing number of university appointment and promotion policies that differentiate a variety of academic roles. Edith Cowan University in Australia, for example, details five roles in addition to the 'standard academic role' of teaching and research scholar (Edith Cowan University, 2005).

Universities are now employing a growing number of language and study skills staff, a trend that mirrors the growth of less well qualified or well paid 'para' professional staff in other public professions (Robson, 2006). In the UK, healthcare assistants in nursing, community support officers in policing and teaching assistants in schools all serve as examples. Unbundling is apparent through growing use of graduate teaching assistants (GTAs), who routinely assess and grade undergraduate student work and teach seminars or tutorials (Park and Ramos, 2002). Again, this allows academics to spend more of their time on research and postgraduate tuition (Shannon *et al.*, 1998). It is another example of a practice that has spread from North America to Europe in the wake of massification and increased competition for government research funding in some contexts, especially the UK and Australia.

Unbundling is a significant phenomenon because it assigns teachers a diminished set of responsibilities and institutionalises a deskilling process whereby some lecturers are reduced to little more than curriculum delivery operatives with minimal student contact outside the formal teaching environment. During the first five years of the UK NTFS, between 2000 and 2005, the unbundling of the academic role was recognised through a separate category for nominees in 'learning support' roles. In similar vein, the Carrick Awards for Australian University Teaching has created a series of categories separate from 'teaching excellence'. These comprise citations for 'contributions to student learning' and awards for 'programs that enhance learning' with seven categories including assessment and feedback, innovation in curricula, learning and teaching, and services supporting student learning (Carrick Institute for Learning and Teaching in Higher Education, 2006). Such schemes reinforce the legitimacy of unbundling and mean that those recognised as 'excellent teachers' may play a limited, and often highly specialised, role in relation to university teaching.

Different phases of teaching

As I have sought to illustrate, much of the evidence base that underpins claims for teaching excellence is performative data. Even if we are to assume that this captures formal teaching contexts adequately, it leaves other elements of teaching practice under-represented. One way of seeking to develop a more comprehensive understanding of teaching is to detail different stages or phases connected with teaching activities. For example, 'instruction' is just one of five elements identified by Newble and Cannon (1995). Here, it is important to represent activities that are not easily subjected to performative evaluation. In pursuit of this objective, a simple distinction can be made between pre-performance, performance and post-performance teaching helping to capture a more holistic picture of professional practice (see Table 3.1).

Pre- and post-performance teaching activities take place almost exclusively out of the spotlight of the performative culture. They are activities central to teaching and student learning but are often carried out by a lecturer working on their own (e.g. planning a lesson) or on a one-to-one basis (e.g. student advising or personal tutoring). Pre- and post-performance teaching activities are not,

Table 3.1 Phases of teaching activity

Phase	Examples
Pre-performance ('offstage')	programme design; lesson planning; developing teaching materials; establishing learning opportunities in the workplace or community; reflection and review; research into teaching
Performance ('onstage')	lectures; group seminars or tutorials; workshops; experiments; practical sessions
Post-performance ('offstage')	student advising/personal tutoring; mediating on-line discussions; assessment and feedback; reflection and review; research into teaching

generally, easily observable phenomenon like watching a lecture or seminar and are similarly difficult to evaluate or gather evidence of in respect to their 'impact'. Nor would observation alone necessarily provide a reliable understanding of the complexity of these activities and relationships. This does not mean, though, that they do not contribute as significantly, if not more so, to the student experience than performance elements.

Feedback on assessment is an example of a teaching activity that is undervalued in performative terms and yet contributes significantly to a student's learning experience and their retention (Yorke, 2001). As Boud has argued while students may be able to survive poor teaching they cannot escape the impact of poor assessment practice (Boud, 1995: 35). In the UK, the standard and consistency of feedback provided to students has been the subject of particular criticism in Quality Assurance Agency reviews of the quality of teaching provision across many subject areas (Ottewill and Macfarlane, 2004). This has resulted in institutional quality units attempting to 'teacherproof' written feedback through the use of standardised tick-box style forms. However, while the adoption of such forms may have increased the consistency of teacher feedback 'justified' in relation to assessment criteria, filling a form full of tick-boxes decreases the space available for students to receive constructive and more individually oriented comments. This is an example of the impact of the performative culture on summative assessment and feedback practice. Such prescriptions treat assessment as a mere postscript to teaching and learning (Orrell, 2006) and marginalise still further the role of formative assessment. The modularisation of the curriculum in the UK has also left little scope for formative feedback on student work in the abbreviated time that tutors have before summative assessment becomes necessary (Yorke, 2001). Relationships with students, through which an understanding of their academic strengths and weaknesses may be gained, is further curtailed in a modular system with courses lasting a maximum of 15 weeks rather than a whole academic year.

Like feedback on student work, personal tutoring can make an important contribution to the student learning experience but one that is hard to evaluate or judge in purely performative terms. Personal tutoring is difficult to even define and may be interpreted in a variety of ways. At Oxford and Cambridge universities, the 'tutorial' is connected with a discussion between a lecturer and the student on the basis of the latter's written work (Robbins Report, 1963: 185). However, in broader terms, a 'tutorial system' is one in which 'the pupil comes into personal contact with his teachers, and he feels he can bring his difficulties and problems to them, and that his progress is a matter of sympathetic concern to them' (Robbins Report, 1963: 186–187). The newer English universities mimicked the Oxbridge tradition leading to a personal tutor who, apart from teaching, was expected to act as a 'guide, philosopher and friend to a given number of students' (Pashley, 1974: 179).

The principle of the 'personal tutor' may still be espoused by many contemporary institutions. However, in a mass system with large student groups one-to-one tutoring is an expensive use of teaching resource that few institutions can afford to maintain. In the context of a research-intense US university student advising 'is generally unstressed by university officers, unenforced by chairs, unrecognized by peers, and unrewarded by the institution' (Rhodes, 2001: 77). In a British context, the 'open door' policy of academic staff has been largely replaced by tutor availability for as little as one hour per week (Brown, 2002). Personal tutoring is simply not seen as a cost efficient use of a scarce resource (i.e. the lecturer's time) when alternative use of that time might be devoted to performative outcomes in relation to research. In the UK, where institutions are formalising the personal tutoring role this is largely in response to the requirements of a government policy initiative, called personal development planning, that focuses on developing the employment-related skills of students rather than their emotional or moral growth (Clegg, 2004).

Research, however, has indicated that personal tutoring does play a significant role in student retention, a matter of central concern to universities and colleges in an age of mass higher education and economic and social commitment to widening participation. While social and academic factors help explain retention (Tinto, 1993), the tutor is a key figure in the process of student integration (Gibbs, 2004). Students are more likely to drop out in their first year of study and this is where academic guidance can be crucial (Barefoot, 2004). The decline of personal tutoring, though, means that students often experience modern higher education as an impersonal, uncaring environment in which they are likely to remain largely anonymous (Barefoot, 2004).

Unbundling means that many elements of pre- and post-performance, such as the pastoral care of students, are now seen as the 'business' of those fulfilling specialist learning support roles. In the pre-performance phase instructional designers now play an increasing role in developing on-line learning materials. In the post-performance phase GTAs are acting as assessors while specialist counsellors, skills and careers advisors fulfil tutoring and pastoral responsibilities that have formerly been seen as central to the academic role. Curiously, the use of GTAs in the context of assessment of student work and managing seminar discussions is sometimes justified on the basis that what they are asked to do is not really 'teaching' in the sense that they are not delivering a lecture (Rhodes, 2001). This brings us back to the personal story I related at the beginning of this chapter as to how a colleague narrowly defined teaching in a research-based university.

As noted earlier, many teaching excellence schemes reflect the effects of unbundling by recognising separate categories for awards that often distinguish 'teaching' from support for student 'learning'. The latter category is intended often implicitly or even explicitly for those 'learning support staff' in areas such as library, careers, welfare, counselling and other specialist roles to claim excellence. While, in many respects, it is laudably inclusive to recognise these specialist support professionals, it also establishes a boundary that divides the work of 'teachers' from 'learning support staff'. It suggests that many pre- and post-performance responsibilities are largely someone else's responsibility rather than that of the lecturer.

Research into teaching may be associated with potentially pre- or post-performative teaching activities (see Table 3.1). However, such work is increasingly seen as a specialised activity. In the UK, the NTFS formerly treated research inquiry into practice as integral to a claim for teaching excellence whereby nominees would submit a project plan as part of their application. A review of the NTFS resulted in this inquiry element being decoupled from the scheme from 2006. This has reduced the cash value of a NTF award by four-fifths financing a separate stream of funds for investigative projects open for collaborative bids, including at least one National Teaching Fellow. This decoupling is significant because it formally separates scholarly inquiry from individual teaching performance (see Chapter 14 in this volume). It implies that expert teachers may not necessarily reflect on their practice or intellectualise the basis of why their practice 'works' (Blackmore and Wilson, 2005). It is yet another indicator of unbundling that is institutionalised in English higher education through the division between research and teaching funding.

Some teaching excellence schemes, such as the Carrick Awards for Australian University Teaching, enable teams of teachers to apply. Overwhelmingly, though, the dominant emphasis of both institutional and national schemes alike is to reward individuals whose teaching is deemed as excellent. This bias toward individual achievement overlooks the importance of team work in the pre- and post-performance phases of teaching. Examples of unheralded work of this nature include giving students formative feedback on their work, counselling, helping a student to prepare for a job interview, establishing a work placement opportunity or writing academic references. Activities that support the teaching of colleagues such as mentoring, second marking or sharing teaching materials are also undervalued by the performative culture and, together with supporting students outside class, are constituent elements of what it means to be a good 'academic citizen' (Shils, 1997; Macfarlane, 2007).

Conclusion

At face value, the dramaturgical metaphor is attractive: 'teaching is just like acting'. Or is it? At root, teaching, especially in higher education, is about authenticity. This is about encouraging students to speak with their own voice and to have the courage to develop their own critical perspective on propositional or professional knowledge (Barnett, 1990; Nixon, 2004b). To be authentic demands courage on the part of the teacher as well as the student; to try to teach in different ways that promote dialogue, to be honest about their own ideological or theoretical perspectives and to engage with students as co-learners (Macfarlane, 2004). This is not about acting. It is about building a relationship with students based on trust and respect.

Surveys of excellent teaching consistently point to the overriding importance of the interpersonal qualities of teachers (e.g. Ballantyne *et al.*, 1999; Hillier and Vielba, 2001). These qualities are about building authentic relationships rather than stage craft and mean that we need to assign far more significance to pre- and post-performance teaching. Such interactions need to find space to grow beyond the confines of formal teaching environments that are so often the source of attention in evaluating teaching excellence. Where pre- and post-performance teaching is recognised in excellence schemes there is a growing tendency to support performance management systems that dictate that such work is undertaken by learning support professionals rather than academics as part of their teaching role. This trend undermines understanding of the importance of teaching as about building relationships rather than simply 'delivering' formal curriculum content.

Some might argue that what should be measured is student performance as opposed to teacher performance. Attempts to judge the excellence of teachers in compulsory education are increasingly linked to the extent to which students perform well in examinations, for example. In contrast with teachers in the compulsory sector, though, many higher education lecturers both teach and set the assessment requirements for their own courses (Entwistle, 1992). This means that basing judgements about teaching excellence in higher education on student performance may place lecturers in an invidious position that threatens their objectivity as assessors. Where such performative measures exist an excellent teacher may be one with the integrity to resist temptations to inflate student grades as opposed to one who succumbs to such pressures. While such moral temptations have always existed there is a need to build a more sophisticated understanding of 'good', rather than 'excellent' teaching. This is a teaching practice that is about being committed to the virtues of what it means to be a 'good' lecturer, such as respectfulness toward students or courage to innovate in the classroom (Macfarlane, 2004). This can only be achieved if we develop a more critical understanding of what it means to be a teacher and value what goes on 'offstage' as well as 'on'.

Chapter 4

Teaching, discipline, net-work

Miriam Zukas and Janice Malcolm
(University of Leeds, UK and University of Kent, UK)

Introduction

As Alan Skelton points out in the introduction to this volume, performative and psychologised understandings of 'teaching excellence' predominate in UK higher education today. Whilst the meaning of *excellence* is a matter of public debate, some of the problems associated with 'teaching excellence' derive from the unspoken assumption that the meaning of *teaching* is clear to all – a question which Macfarlane (Chapter 3) explores in this volume. We want to begin with teaching, rather than excellence, by making a case for the use of the term pedagogy, rather than teaching. We then reflect on our ongoing conceptual work on pedagogic identities to offer a more coherent, contextualised and situated understanding which links pedagogy to issues of disciplinary and vocational practices; values, purposes and beliefs; national and institutional policy and practice; the relationships between teaching and teachers, and learning and learners, and so on. We revisit five pedagogic identities from earlier work (Malcolm and Zukas, 2001; Zukas and Malcolm, 2002a) and look at these in relation to the notion of teaching excellence, particularly in the light of Skelton's (2005) analysis. These are analysed afresh in relation to conceptualisations of academic identity which incorporate discipline, research and pedagogy, and a new identity is incorporated into the analysis – that of the educator as disciplinary actor. Drawing on actor network theory (ANT), we suggest that the force of 'teaching excellence' is inevitably undermined by the competing, entangled and powerful actor networks of discipline and research practice.

Why pedagogy?

The language used to describe the activities in which teachers engage has numerous limitations. Contemporary British discourses position teaching principally in relation to learning, so that teaching is constructed rather obliquely as what teachers do inside classrooms (or other learning sites) to bring about learning. As Skelton (Chapter 14, this volume) points out, this results in the prevailing view that teaching can only be excellent if it serves learning – the meaning of which is rarely clarified. Furthermore, it implies that teaching is a decontextualised transfer of knowledge, skills and practices to the acquisitive learner; in other words, teaching is principally about instruction and teaching methods. Yet, when we talk with teachers about their work (see for example Malcolm and Zukas, 2006), they raise issues of disciplinary and vocational practices; personal and political values and beliefs; national and institutional issues such as quality assurance; they discuss the purposes of teaching, and the relationships between teaching and teachers, and learning and learners. We have sought through the use of the term pedagogy to provide a linguistic acknowledgement of the broader cultural, institutional and historical contexts in which educational transactions and practices are situated, and to signal a challenge to the dominant and often barren discourse of teaching and learning.

Simon's (1981) question 'Why no pedagogy in England?' drew on an idea of the 'science of teaching', and is sometimes credited with having helped to reestablish *pedagogy* as an educational concept in the British discourse of school education (Davies, 1994; Murphy, 1996). Simon criticised British educational institutions for having 'no concern with theory, its relation to practice, with pedagogy' (Simon, 1981: 82), and sparked a debate about the different usages of the terms *pedagogy* and *didactics* in other European contexts, in which educators outside initial education have had relatively little involvement. Hamilton (1999), for example, provides a historical account of the ways in which specific understandings of both *pedagogy* and *didactics* have developed and dominated at different points in European history. He argues that earlier understandings of the art or science of teaching (drawing, for example, on Latin and Greek terminologies, and on the work of Comenius and Kant, among others) distinguished between the overall *purposes* of education, the scope and categorisation of *knowledge*, curricular *design* and the methods of *instruction*. Whilst *pedagogy* encompasses all of these (at least), *didactics* can be seen as a specific element or branch of *pedagogy* concerned with questions of method and technique. Whilst in many other European languages these distinctions persist and have developed through use, in English the meanings attributed to these powerful terms are fluid and indistinct, and consequently difficult to analyse. So whilst *pedagogy* has re-emerged as a common term in British educational discourse, its meaning often appears to be limited to what might more accurately be termed *didactics*.

Questions of method ('how?') have thus come to dominate British understandings of *pedagogy* in the last few years, at the expense of questions of purpose ('why?') or content ('what?'). Increasingly, the literature of both policy and practice has assumed 'individualism as explanatory mode both for learners and teachers' (Davies, 1994: 27), and implied that 'learning and teaching' – that is, an understanding of *pedagogy* as merely *didactics* – is a more fruitful concept than the broader and inevitably more complex notion of *pedagogy*. This is linked with the dominance of psychologistic explanations of learning (Hollway, 1989; Zukas and Malcolm, 2002a), and encourages a technicist view of the processes of teaching and thus of teaching excellence. It also renders teachers, power, purposes and educational contexts invisible and, in effect, beyond analysis (Malcolm and Zukas, 2001).

We have argued for some time that, in the face of the success of the simplistic 'teaching and learning' and 'teaching excellence' discourses, we need to seize the linguistic initiative by reclaiming the word pedagogy from the narrow meaning to which it has been reduced in English, as a rich and appropriately multilayered term for educational social practice. The teachers we have interviewed in the course of our research[1] often struggle to express the dislocation which they experience when they try to (or are required to) separate themselves and their communities out from their teaching, or to think of their students as decontextualised individual learners. They clearly understand pedagogy as something both broader and more fundamental than the classroom techniques, recording practices, assessment strategies, etc. which they employ, willingly or otherwise. Their experience of complying with, and resisting, the practices which shape their work, implicates both institutions and wider social and political contexts in their understanding of pedagogy. This understanding, far from focusing on only one polarised aspect of learning and teaching, instead conceives educational practice as a situated, multifaceted and complex process, involving multiple relationships and, crucially, driven by specific and often conflicting purposes, power relations and interests. We argue that *pedagogy* can be understood as encompassing all of this complexity, and thus allows us to do analytical justice to the work of both teachers and students.

A further argument in favour of *pedagogy* arises from the common positioning of *teaching* in relation to *research*, such that it is assumed that research and teaching are self-evidently and fundamentally separate and distinctive activities (Malcolm and Zukas, 2005a). The promotion of teaching excellence has been seen as one way of lessening the divide between them, not least by raising the status of teaching and encouraging pedagogic research, so that teachers are seen as knowledge producers in a more conventional sense (Skelton, 2005). But as Skelton (Chapter 14, this volume) and others have pointed out, this has backfired somewhat; separate policies for teaching and research have worked instead to maintain distinctions between them and further to promote what Trowler *et al.* (2005: 439) have termed policy bundles of 'policy paradoxes, shaping practices in contradictory ways and setting up incommensurable goals'. A fundamental problem here is the separation of research, teaching and learning (academics produce knowledge through research, which students then learn; teaching is the medium through which this transfer occurs). Elsewhere (Malcolm and Zukas, 2005a) we have argued that this is because many learning and research discourses are steeped in metaphors of acquisition (Sfard, 1998): teachers are conceptualised as providers, facilitators and mediators of some property, possession or commodity (knowledge and concepts) which they possess (know), while researchers acquire, discover or even create the knowledge which is then taught.

In contrast, what might be characterised as 'the new learning' perspectives (Sommerlad, 2003) draw on metaphors of participation, with 'knowing' understood as full participation in a community of practice (Lave and Wenger, 1991). From this perspective teachers, and potentially learners, as well as researchers, are themselves producers of knowledge. However, discussions of learning as participation often neglect the critical relationship of *discipline* to social communities of pedagogy/research in higher education. If we reject the conventional 'acquisition' argument that research is about creating disciplinary knowledge whilst teaching is about disseminating it, then the distinctions between research and pedagogy begin to blur; instead, both have to be understood as sites of disciplinary knowledge production, and pedagogy cannot then be defined or understood outside discipline. Complex inter-relationships between research and teaching *within disciplines* have to be taken into account, alongside questions of identity.

Adding the term 'excellence' to pedagogy, as we have defined it, is then something of a political act. It invites critical debate, as advocated in the introduction; it requires us to ask 'excellent for whom and for what purposes'? It challenges the disembodied tidiness of teaching, and its counterpart learning, with the mess of power relations, conflicting interests and contested disciplinary knowledge. It also invites us to consider social analyses of learning and change which take account of micro- (individual), meso- (departmental) and macro- (organisational and policy) levels and their interrelations (Trowler, 2005). It guards against the artificial separation of research, teaching and discipline which has dogged a considerable amount of higher education research. Finally, as we shall see below, to speak of pedagogic excellence is to open up issues of identity.

Why identities?

To avoid confusion, we want to be explicit here both about what we mean by the term identity and about our particular focus on academics' pedagogic identities. Chappell *et al.* argue that 'all pedagogical work is always and everywhere *identity work* of some kind' (2003: 4, italics in the original). Bernstein (1996), too, uses pedagogic identity in this way; our focus, however, is on pedagogues, rather than on learners. In raising questions of pedagogic identity, we do not intend to engage in a disciplinary war zone. Clearly, identity's sociological meaning, as the group or class to which a person belongs, is practically the opposite of its psychological meaning of 'a sense of personal *distinctness*, a sense of personal *continuity*, and a sense of personal *autonomy*' (Apter, 1989: 75; Harré, 1998). From the psychologist's perspective, a knowing, conscious subject is at the centre of individual identity; for the sociologist or the anthropologist, social relations must be the focus of attention. Our aim is to avoid the individual/social binary so frequently encountered in writing about learning; we do not intend the term 'identity' to signify something fixed, immutable, abstract and somehow disembodied.

Lave and Wenger's (1991) classic study of apprenticeship has been hugely influential in analyses of learning as participation. They use the plural term 'identities' to mean 'long-term, living relations between persons and their place and participation in communities of practice' (1991: 53), and to convey the mutability and multiplicity of these relations. However, from our point of view their conception of communities of practice is problematic, not least because it fails to challenge the representational categories of 'the social' and 'the psychological' (Nespor, 1994). Other concerns can be summarised as, first, the failure to engage with issues of power and conflict, either within communities or across communities when community members belong to multiple communities (Malcolm and Zukas, 2006); and, second, the failure to account for historical change.

Recently, we have turned to Jan Nespor's (1994) use of actor-network theory (ANT) in relation to undergraduate education, and to his definition of identities which:

> crystallize in the tensions and pressures produced as different communities of actor-networks clash. Identities are shifting, contested stakes of networking practices that seek to produce or maintain a certain configuration of social space by excluding or restricting some people and things from participation while recruiting and reconstructing others to fit into the network.
>
> (Nespor, 1994: 13)

This approach has a number of advantages over that of Lave and Wenger. First, identity is now clearly seen as contested both within and between actor-networks – individual educators draw on a wide and often contradictory range of actor-networks in their pedagogic practice. Second, it highlights the social (networking) practices in which people and things participate, so that we understand pedagogy as multifaceted and complex, involving multiple relationships with specific and often conflicting purposes, power relations and interests. Third, it has the potential to facilitate an understanding of changes over time through an examination of the genesis and development of a given actor-network.

Nespor is one of relatively few education specialists to draw on ANT (others include Hamilton, 2001; Clarke, 2002; Edwards, 2003; Edwards and Nicoll, 2004; Usher and Edwards, 2005; Mulcahy, 2006), which is not so much a theory as conventionally understood, as an emerging tradition or way of analysing particularly socio-technical entities. There are many versions of ANT or, as Latour suggests, good accounts 'where all the actors *do something* [sic] and don't just sit there' (2005: 128), but its fundamental premise, relational materiality, is generally shared. This means that 'materials do not exist in and of themselves but are endlessly generated and at least potentially reshaped' (Law, 2004: 161). Thus actors might include humans, technologies, machines, laboratory instruments, texts, policies and so on. Actor-networks are not fixed entities which are constituted by actors (one version of a community of practice, for example); instead they are 'fluid and contested definitions of identities and alliances that are simultaneously frameworks of power' (Nespor, 1994: 9).

Nespor uses ANT to explore higher education practices, looking specifically at the ways in which undergraduate education works to connect students to disciplinary practices as 'physics students' or 'management students'. He argues that the material productions of time-space (buildings, classrooms and so on) are central in enrolling students into disciplines, whilst the representational productions of space-time (textbooks, notes, lectures) are essential for the mobilisation of practice and practitioners. In this way, educational activities are connected to activities in other settings through networks that construct space-time relations. Students, therefore, are not simply being prepared to participate at a later stage in professional fields of practice – they are participating in those fields already (ibid., p. 131). This resonates with our earlier attempt, in this paper and elsewhere, to disrupt teaching and research distinctions.

For Nespor, learning is defined as being able to move oneself (and other things) through space-time networks: 'having knowledge means participating in an actor-network that organises a field of practice such as a "discipline"' (p. 132). The discipline itself exists as a stable entity 'constituted by cycles of accumulation within networks that organise flows of people through space and time' (pp. 10–11). From this perspective, teaching is no longer viewed as a straightforward cognitive transaction but, instead, as one of the many ways in which the spatialised and temporalised activities of students and teachers connect them to a *disciplinary practice*. For example, lectures and note-taking function in very different ways, depending on the discipline involved:

> Instead of simply reducing and compressing the course into a mobile product (as much management students did in their note-taking), the experience of taking notes was as (or more) important for physics students than the content of the notes. In taking notes the students were interacting with the professors' performances at the same time as they were reproducing them in immutable and mobile forms on notebook paper.
>
> (Nespor, 1994: 69)

We would argue that research can be understood in precisely the same way, as indeed the development of disciplines (for example, the changing boundaries of geography or anthropology over the last century) can be understood as appropriations of intellectual and social space. The new identity which we propose in the next section – that of disciplinary actor – is thus one which ignores, or perhaps resolves the problem of, conventional distinctions between research and teaching as forms of academic work.

Pedagogic identities revisited

In earlier work, we considered how the educator was constructed through the literature of post-compulsory education in general, and HE in particular, and thus identified a number of 'versions of the educator' (Zukas and Malcolm,

2002a). These were analysed across several 'dimensions of pedagogic identity' (ways of understanding how the versions related to each other). We now consider how each of these identities relates to ideas of teaching excellence; propose the addition of a further identity – that of disciplinary actor; and ask whether teaching excellence itself can be a successful actor network.

The educator as psycho-diagnostician and facilitator of learning

We were not the first to observe that psychology has provided the dominant framework for higher education pedagogic writing in Britain, although we can perhaps lay claim to one of the earliest critiques of the 'psychologisation' of teaching and learning in higher education (Malcolm and Zukas, 1999). Although there is a growing and vociferous body of critique (e.g. Rowland, 2001; Haggis, 2003; Nicoll and Harrison, 2003), there remains a vast and indeed growing literature which begins with a psychologised focus on learners and educational transactions, and assumes that educators need to diagnose learners' needs using learning styles, or skills, or some other individual predispositions as symptomatic indicators. Such approaches remain immensely popular despite the evidence that they are of doubtful explanatory or pedagogic value (see, for example, Coffield *et al.'s* 2004 review which identified 71 models of learning styles). Once characteristics and approaches to learning are identified, teaching becomes a matter of using techniques and tools which treat those particular symptoms; pedagogy is reduced to diagnosis and facilitation.

Skelton (2005: 21–37) has identified four meta-understandings of teaching excellence (traditional, performative, psychologised and critical) and we can see that the 'psycho-diagnostician/facilitator of learning' identity underlies a psychologised meta-understanding of teaching excellence which 'is associated with the establishment of universal procedures for teaching and learning, their successful implementation in practice and the achievement of specified outcomes' (p. 31).

The educator as assurer of organisational quality and efficiency; deliverer of service to agreed or imposed standards

When we first analysed pedagogic identities in the literature of higher education, there existed a strand of writing which focused on the contribution of teaching to the quality of an institution's activities (e.g. Elton, 1987; Ellis, 1993). Since that time, the higher education landscape has become increasingly littered with the debris of accountability instruments: targeted funding for recruiting specific groups of students, the introduction of 'transparency review' to measure the uses of academics' time and ensure that research does not subsidise teaching, the active promotion of league tables and other publicly available comparative mechanisms, and so on – similar examples can be found in many other countries as well. Indeed, it could be argued that the discourse of teaching excellence is steeped in the expectation that pedagogues are responsible for delivering the services which universities (and their paymasters) demand.

Skelton's performative meta-understanding of teaching excellence (2005: 29–31) is directly related to this identity; he suggests that this understanding has emerged as countries look to increase the productivity of their educational systems. The regulation of teaching is one strategy, alongside competition for students in a global higher education marketplace, to ensure that higher education contributes to national economic performance. Such understandings assume a meritocracy in which teachers are enforcers of standards for the purpose of systemic and economic efficiency.

The educator as reflective practitioner

The reflective practice identity has long dominated the professional discourse of higher education but, as we showed in our early work, it is frequently taken for granted as a conceptual framework for thinking about academic practice. The extent to which this is the case can be seen from Skelton's case study of the NTFS scheme, where teaching excellence is primarily about 'reflecting on one's own teaching, devising solutions to practical problems and disseminating these solutions to individual and sector colleagues' (Skelton, 2005: 58–59). At present there are clear signs of more critical perspectives on reflective practice emerging; recent contributions by Fook (2006) and others are examples of this trend in areas outside education. In higher education however, the discourse of teaching excellence seems likely to continue promoting 'reflective practice' as the panacea for most pedagogical challenges.

The educator as critical practitioner

In earlier analyses, we contrasted adult education traditions of critical writing with those of higher education. In the former, the 'why' and the 'what' of education had always been as important as the 'how'. In the latter, much critical writing had focused on the purposes of higher education and its various social, historical, epistemological and technological functions. Whilst there had been a focus on critical pedagogy within women's studies, disability and black studies, there was much less evidence of critical writing in relation to what might be called the mainstream or 'straight' pedagogy. Since then a more concerted critical discourse has continued to develop which could have a significant impact on the discourse of teaching excellence. Skelton's own view is that 'teaching excellence from the critical perspective seeks to provide learners with access to knowledge that engages prevailing social structures and interests', and teachers working within this perspective aim 'to support a process of student emancipation which seeks to give them greater knowledge and control over their lives'

(2005: 33). He is optimistic about the pursuit of such a meta-understanding of teaching excellence, and this book contributes to that project. However we would caution that a broader and more inclusive discourse of pedagogy, rather than simply of teaching, would be needed for such optimism to be justified.

The educator as situated learner within a community of practice

This model is seen most obviously in the work of Lave and Wenger (Lave and Wenger, 1991) who focus on legitimate peripheral participation (through apprenticeship) as a framework for learning the 'culture of practice'. It could of course be argued that an informal apprenticeship is in fact the traditional learning route for teachers in higher education, and as pointed out above, this idea has been freely (and often uncritically) adopted as a model or pattern for a range of practices in higher and professional education. The idea of a community of practitioners is neat and attractive, and helpfully incorporates social practice and participation into the discourse of teaching and learning. Within higher education, however, it is not difficult to identify multiple and indeed competing communities to which teachers and learners could be said to belong: disciplinary, institutional, educational-political and pedagogic communities, for example, overlap both each other and institutional boundaries in a way which renders them rather less susceptible to neat analysis than we might hope (see Malcolm and Zukas, 2005a). The structures and discourses of teaching excellence have to assume the existence of a community of practice which is generally above disciplines, schools of thought, and institutions; there may be an assumption that the possessors of teaching excellence in the form of awards (master practitioners?) are able to imbue other community members with excellence through specific forms of community participation, such as conference presentations, academic development work and so on. This may be, as Skelton's study seems to suggest, a fantasy constructed around the bureaucratic quest for performative leverage (Skelton, 2005: 171).

Pedagogic identity meets ANT: the educator as disciplinary actor

At the point when these pedagogic identities were first developed, we pinned our disciplinary colours to the mast, arguing that discipline was integral to pedagogy, and that the emergence of generic educational development had, in effect, abstracted pedagogy from existing disciplinary communities (Malcolm and Zukas, 2000; Zukas and Malcolm, 2002a). Since then, there have been signs of the resuscitation of disciplinary pedagogic knowledge and more discipline-based pedagogic research.

These disciplinary ventures may well be cause for hope, although the preliminary results often seem to reproduce the same psychologistic epistemologies which we criticised in generic approaches, uncritically 'applying' instruments and measures to disciplinary settings. This may be because notions of 'subject' rather than discipline inform these new developments. As Parker (2002: 374) comments:

> 'Subject' is reassuringly concrete – a subject can be defined, has a knowledge base which can be easily constructed into a programme of knowledge acquisition and, perhaps most importantly, of quantitative assessment ... subjects are also passive – they are taught, learned, delivered.

She speculates that the move from discipline to subject has come about because of what she calls the 'marketing practice of dissociation' where undesired associations are removed in order to enhance the product's value; so 'subject' is somehow less exclusive, more economically valuable than 'discipline'. For Parker, subjects are 'implicit packages of knowledge and skills' whilst to be engaged in a discipline is 'to shape and be shaped by, the subject, to be part of a scholarly community, to engage with fellow students – to become "disciplined"' (p. 374) – which is precisely our point.

In relation to teaching excellence, Skelton (2005) argues that, whilst Parker's work advocates reflection through which some of the unquestioned assumptions, boundary demarcations and limits to learning might be challenged, she fails to deal with issues of power, particularly in relation to its operation within disciplines. This is a critical question and we have turned to actor-network theory (ANT) to try to explore how disciplinary and other actor networks interact with and impact upon attempts to define teaching excellence as an actor network. The illumination of educational practices which ANT offers, directly or indirectly, turns on their heads many of the categories and distinctions with which we work on a daily basis. It provides an analytical framework which both accommodates complexity, and helps to clarify some of the entangled histories, interests and purposes embodied in specific policies, discourses and practices – in this case, the attempt to 'translate' teaching excellence into an accepted category of academic practice.

Teaching excellence net-work

> Strength does not come from concentration, purity and unity, but from dissemination, homogeneity and the careful plaiting of weak ties ... resistance, obduracy and sturdiness is more easily achieved through netting, lacing, weaving, twisting, of ties that are weak by themselves, and ... each tie, no matter how strong, is itself woven out of still weaker threads.
>
> (Latour, 1996)

If we use the metaphor of a net to think of higher education – perhaps something like the net found in a football goal – it is composed of lengths of rope and knots which hold those lengths together. The rope itself is made up of relatively weak fibres twisted or plaited together into a single yarn, and then fashioned into a series of knotted shapes to form a strong and flexible structure. The fibres can be thought of as the numerous elements – disciplines, policies, purposes, personal trajectories of academics and students and so on – which together constitute what we think of as the HE 'system'. Over time, areas of the net may weaken, disintegrate, fray or rot through use or disuse, and of course these can be repaired by being rewoven or replaced without dismantling the entire net. The time may come when the net contains virtually none of the original rope or knots, although its net identity remains.

The teaching and learning 'movement', of which the discourse of 'teaching excellence' is but one manifestation, can be seen as an attempt to patch up areas of perceived weakness in the net. However there is a failure to understand the complex nature of the net itself which means that the patching as currently conceived is unlikely to be successful. The patching strategy is to extract a few individual and relatively weak fibres from a strong rope, and refashion them into an entirely new patch of net which can then be reincorporated into the whole. This strategy fails to take account of the weakness of individual fibres, which lose the strength they gave to the rope by being removed from it. The new concentrated patch, made up of a small number of weak fibres and perhaps resembling a cobweb rather more than a football net, is both weak in itself and ultimately weakens the structure of the whole net.

Teaching excellence discourses and their associated practices have developed, we suggest, as an attempted solution to several perceived weakness in the net: one, the overshadowing of the importance of teaching by research; two, the need to manage academic staff to perform more effectively and efficiently; and three, to demonstrate (for global marketing purposes) that the massification of higher education has not had deleterious effects on teaching standards. It can therefore be seen that a number of complex ideas have here been brought together into a single object that can be mobilised and circulated as a taken-for-granted fact – i.e. there is a problem with teaching and learning in universities. To use our metaphor, there is a need for a new patch in the net. As Latour (1987: 131) explains:

> The problem of the builder of 'fact' is the same as that of the builder of 'objects': how to convince others, how to control their behaviour, how to gather enough resources in one place, how to have the claim or the object spread out in time and space.

In ANT terms, this is what has been called translation (Callon, 1986). Within education, Callon's ideas have been utilised in relation to the International Adult Literacy Survey (Hamilton, 2001) and an influential policy document, *Skills for Life* (Clarke, 2002), as well as by Nespor (1994).

Callon (1986) identified how the researchers in his study (of an attempt to develop a marine conservation strategy for a scallop population off the French coast) imposed their definition of the situation on other actors[2] (e.g. the scallops themselves; the fishermen) through four 'moments' of translation:

1   *problematisation*: or the way in which the researchers sought to become indispensable to other actors by defining what the problems were, and then suggesting that these would be resolved if the actors negotiated the 'obligatory passage point' of the researchers' investigation;
2   *interessement*: the series of processes by which the researchers sought to lock the other actors into the roles proposed for them by the research programme;
3 . *enrolment*: the strategies used by the researchers to define the roles they had allocated to others; and
4   *mobilisation*: the ways in which powerful actors (spokespeople) supposedly speak for others with their apparent agreement and consent.

This analysis offers an interesting framework for understanding how competing networks of discipline, teaching and research are played out, and where the nascent network of teaching excellence intersects with these established and entangled trajectories. Those who establish the notion of teaching excellence through *problematisation* (e.g. the Dearing Report [NCIHE, 1997] and subsequently the short-lived Institute for Learning and Teaching in Higher Education) get to define the problem and act as gatekeepers determining who the other actors in the network are, and what they want/need. The idea that there is a problem with teaching and learning in higher education becomes an obligatory passage point through which all actors (learners, teachers, disciplines, universities, educational developers and so on) are drawn so that it is in the interest of all those actors to pursue teaching excellence as a solution for the problems of teaching (e.g. teaching as poor relation to research; the massification of higher education and the relative decline in resources; globalised competition; economic, efficient and effective teaching). There is no room for competing arguments or issues to be raised by actors; instead the problematisation of teaching defines how those other problems are to be resolved. Ignoring the plaiting and twisting which lends strength to the net as it is, the problematisation process determines that a new patch of net must be created and somehow tied into the whole.

Interessement involves the development of strategies to stabilise the identity of the actors defined through problematisation (for example the National Teaching Fellowship Scheme, local university teaching prize schemes, programmes of educational development, HEA membership) whilst *enrolment* entails the processes by which actors are locked into the roles proposed for them (for example, through the obligations attendant upon becoming a National Teaching Fellow, the requirement to disseminate 'good practice', the accountability procedures to ensure teaching excellence, the requirement to undertake continuing professional development to remain in good professional standing, etc.).

The final step in this process – *mobilisation* – occurs when various actors are transformed into manageable entities that can be transported across space-time into – for example – selection processes and promotion criteria. This is assisted by representations (immutable mobiles, in Latour's [2005] terms) which are portable, such as application forms for teaching awards, or lists of assessment criteria. The identification and establishment of 'excellent' teachers (whether through competitions, inspection or any other regimes) relies on both the mobilisation of the actor network, and the immutable mobiles which coordinate action from within centres of power.

Power is of course a stumbling-block to the success of these moments of translation, and here lies an essential weakness of teaching excellence as an educational category and practice. The attempt to abstract teaching from other powerful and enmeshed elements of academic practice, and to define teaching excellence as the solution to the perceived problem of teaching and learning, falls at the moment of problematisation precisely because it fails to enrol powerful agents in the cause of the network. If, for example, high-status universities or esteemed academics are uncommitted to the idea that teaching can be or should be separated out from discipline or research in order to be 'fixed', then the meanings being attributed to the 'problem' cannot be stabilised in the first place.

Pedagogy as net-work

We have shown that teaching excellence is doomed as a strategy for patching the net of higher education, because the problematisation of teaching of which it is part ignores the existing plaiting, twisting and knots which give the net its strength. However pedagogy, rather than teaching, offers a broad understanding of educational practice as situated, multifaceted and complex. Pedagogy cannot be disentangled from knowledge production or understood outside discipline. In other words, pedagogy is twisted together with disciplines, purposes, policies and so on to make the yarn which makes the knotted shapes which, in turn, form the structure of the net of higher education. It is clear, therefore, why the obligatory passage point of the 'teaching and learning problem', and the accompanying mobilisation of the actor network of teaching excellence will not succeed. This is not to deny the continuing problems of globalised competition, the relative decline in resources, or the ongoing polarisation of teaching and research. But instead of looking to teaching excellence for a solution to such problems, we have, instead, to return to our metaphor of net-work. Rather than the extraction of weak fibres to form a cobweb, as in the case of teaching excellence, the whole rope might be strengthened through more intricate plaiting and twisting of discipline, purposes, policies, academics and students with pedagogy. Such a net would still have areas of relative weakness and would constantly need patching, but, in Latour's terms, strength (for the net of higher education) comes from 'netting, lacing, weaving, twisting, of ties that are weak by themselves' (Latour, 1996), rather than from the creation of new nets.

Notes

1 Our research on academic identity in post-compulsory education includes a series of fifteen extended and semi-structured interviews with teachers in the UK and Australia. and builds on an earlier bibliographic study of the construction of teachers' pedagogic identities in the literature of higher education (see Malcolm and Zukas 1999; Zukas and Malcolm 2002a).
2 Callon uses the term 'actant'; for reasons of simplicity, we refer to actors throughout.

Chapter 5

Integrating research and teaching

Understanding excellence

Angela Brew
(University of Sydney, Australia)

Introduction

The relationship between research and teaching is central to questions about the nature of higher education and to what constitutes excellence within it. In the context of the contemporary Western university, external accountability and funding measures appear to be driving research and teaching apart. Efforts to integrate research and teaching within universities have been increasing in recent years and these defy this trend.

There are a number of reasons why teaching and research should be progressively integrated. Three key ones are important in this chapter. First, as Ron Barnett (1997) argues, higher education needs to be inquiry-based so that students develop the skills needed to be able to cope with the complexity of a world which we cannot at any time fully understand. It is a world in which: 'There is a high degree of uncertainty; there is no clear-cut direction but many competing ideas, theories and methods, and no one is in overall charge' (Nowotny *et al.*, 2001: 115). The nature of this world is central to questions about what kind of higher education should be provided for students. In an uncertain, ambiguous and what Barnett (2000a) calls 'super-complex' world, professionals need to be able to evaluate evidence, to take decisions on the basis of the evidence available, to work collaboratively and to present arguments logically and cogently. These are the skills of research and inquiry. This suggests that students, the professionals of the future, need to be involved in learning how to generate, evaluate and communicate knowledge alongside researchers.

Yet studies of students' conceptions of and ideas about research have consistently shown that they tend to be unaware of the research being carried out in their institution even when they are studying in a 'research-intensive' university (Jenkins *et al.*, 1998; Zamorski, 2002). These studies have also shown that students do not like learning about research methodology and fail to see the reasons why they should do so (Murtonen, 2005). Making research and inquiry central to their studies brings students closer to the research activities of the university and helps them to see the importance of research and inquiry skills for their future working lives.

The second reason for integrating research and teaching rests on the nature of academic work, and in particular the way academics manage to fulfil research and teaching goals simultaneously. This questions the advisability of viewing research and teaching separately (see, for example, the work of Colbeck, 1998 and 2002).

Third, academics have been asked to take on a range of new teaching agendas in recent years. In Australia this includes engaging in curriculum reforms, integrating generic and specific graduate attributes, combining or rationalizing degrees and subject areas, evaluating programmes to meet institutional demands, responding to various strategic initiatives, not to mention coping with more students, accommodating more international students and teaching courses more flexibly. The list of demands is endless. However such challenges are not going to cease so a critical issue is how academics grow their capacity to cope with continual change. In my own institution, the scholarship of teaching and learning, through which the academic frames and investigates questions about their teaching and their students' learning, is providing the means by which teaching is able to be improved through a process of inquiry and continual renewal (Hutchings and Shulman, 1999).

Mass higher education, accountability requirements, new professional demands, internationalization, together with epistemological uncertainty all create a problematic environment for today's academics. Conflicts in values and practices are an everyday occurrence. Academics are finding that the ways they would like to teach and to research are compromised through lack of time or resources or through competing demands that are placed upon them. The result is frequently demoralization, frustration and a culture of complaint. In this context, institutions committed to the integration of research and teaching will be encouraging an evidence-based approach to the challenges of academic practice. This means that people are enabled to come together to solve problems that they face as higher education professionals. The challenges of academic practice are viewed as questions for investigation. An example of this is the University of Sydney Faculty of Veterinary Science which has worked to improve teaching and student learning through a 'shared leadership' programme. Individuals and groups systematically investigate problems and seek solutions based on a knowledge of the literature of teaching and learning in higher education.

So there are good reasons for bringing research and teaching together and indeed in Australia, as elsewhere, there is now considerable evidence that not only are research-intensive universities renewing efforts to integrate research and teaching, but so too are institutions that are not particularly strong in research (Brew, 2006a). It would be encouraging to think that the distinctions between teaching, learning and research could break down and that the academy could become a place where both academics and students in their different ways develop the strategies, techniques, tools, knowledge and experience needed to address complex, important and difficult problems of the world today.

Strengthening the relationships between research and teaching has implications for what is thought of as a university and what the purposes of higher education are. The values and assumptions on which current higher education practice is founded are called into question. The integration of research and teaching transforms the responsibilities of people who work in universities changing or questioning their roles. It poses questions about the nature of knowledge and who should be involved in developing it. It questions the ways in which spaces in universities are arranged and challenges those responsible for campus planning to think differently. It fundamentally questions the relationships between students and those who teach them.

These issues provide some important challenges to contemporary discussions of excellence in higher education. Measures of excellence need to be able to capture the dynamism of a continually changing scenario. As understanding of the differing ways in which research and teaching can be integrated is enhanced, the possibilities for its development grow. In this chapter I explore the implications associated with the integration of research and teaching and then examine the consequences for different views of excellence.

Inclusive and scholarly knowledge-building communities

The way the relationship between research and teaching has traditionally been viewed has been to see research and teaching as occupying quite separate and competing domains of the university: academics generating knowledge, and then transmitting knowledge to students typically through lectures. I have suggested why students need research and why academics need to engage in inquiries within their academic and professional workplaces. If students are progressively engaging in research and inquiry, the university community becomes more like a partnership of academics, academic leaders and managers, students and general staff. A more inclusive, inquiry-focused higher education then results. I have argued elsewhere that we need to create inclusive knowledge-building communities where academics and students work in partnership to generate knowledge (Brew, 2006a). In this way research, teaching, learning, scholarship and professional practice become integrated. I want to briefly mention six interlinked aspects of inclusive and scholarly knowledge-building communities:

• There is, as I have indicated, a shift towards inquiry or research-based modes of teaching and learning where students have to construct their knowledge to produce new world views. Student-focused conceptual change approaches to teaching and learning have become the norm (Prosser and Trigwell, 1999). At the University of Sydney, for example, problem-based learning is being implemented in many professional areas. Initially it was introduced into the Graduate Medical Program and has now been extended to dentistry, pharmacy and veterinary science courses. Inquiry based learning is now commonplace, for example in engineering and agriculture, as well as in numerous units of study across the university which are focused on investigation.

- Such communities see knowledge as being diffuse – constructed through communication and negotiated in particular social contexts (i.e. Gibbons and colleagues' 'Mode 2 knowledge': Gibbons *et al.*, 1994). The emphasis in this kind of higher education is on the construction rather than the imparting of knowledge; encouraging approaches to learning that involve students in artistic and scientific production, emphasizing uncertainty; in other words, engaging students in inquiry.

- Learning is viewed as a social practice involving mutual engagement in a joint enterprise with a shared repertoire. It is carried out by academics and by students. Learning grows through participation in inquiry groups. This can involve students engaging with academics in summer undergraduate research scholars' programmes (e.g. in The Australian National University), or working with academics within special independent units of study (as at Murdoch University in Western Australia). It can also be implemented with large student cohorts. For example, the first-year biology course at the University of Sydney has 1,000 students who participated in a survey of airborne fungal spores in the Sydney Basin. Such an extensive survey had been impossible as part of an existing research project (Taylor and Green, 2006) because of the expense and time constraints in surveying such a large area. The teachers comment:

> The initiative transformed a classic laboratory exercise, teaching students about sterile techniques in microbiology, microscopy and use of keys for fungal identification, into part of an existing research project determining presence of potentially allergenic fungal spores in the air. Each student collected samples from their home suburbs in Sydney and surrounding areas and identified the colonies growing on their plates. The resulting data set (1,000 samples) was then analysed using GIS to map distributions of fungal genera across the Sydney Basin, and students wrote a short report on the findings.
>
> (Taylor and Green, 2006)

- The development of inclusive academic communities where both students and academics engage cannot take place without the relationships between students and their teachers changing. For if research and teaching are integrated then the separation between academics and students begins to break down. Participation in learning is as an equal. This does not mean that everyone is equal in the sense of having equal skills and knowledge. Equality here is about treating individuals as fully participating human beings with things to contribute as well as things to learn. So this involves continually being aware of the power issues that serve to undermine the contributions of others. It also means exercising humility with respect to one's own views (Brookfield and Preskill, 1999) and it involves democracy in the sense in which Dewey used the term, where education is about nurturing human growth and development. This is a particular challenge when large cohorts of students are involved as in many courses in Australia. In this respect, for example, the University of Sydney has set up specific strategic initiatives to encourage inclusive practices.

- This kind of higher education demands that research and scholarship are defined broadly. Conceptions of research are oriented towards understanding and the development of meaning. The researcher is in the focus of awareness (see Brew, 2001b), for research in this model includes the growth not just of socially useful knowledge but also of personal meaning. Teaching and learning and academic practice become processes of research and scholarship. Academics learn to critique the underlying ways of thinking and acting through a reflexive approach to their work.
- Finally, scholarship becomes central to academics and students. Scholarship here is not simply a set of different kinds of activities but, rather, scholarship is viewed as the quality of the way academic work is professionally done for both students and academics. This view of scholarship as a quality emphasizes academic professionalism: the attention to detail, meticulousness and rigour and an emphasis on having the skills, knowledge and techniques for effective academic practice as a professional within a specific disciplinary domain (Brew, 1999).

Teaching excellence and knowledge-building communities

If the serious and systematic pursuit of the integration of research and teaching leads to the development of inclusive scholarly knowledge-building communities with these characteristics, how are we to understand excellence in this context and what are the challenges in developing it? Skelton (2005: 22–34) suggests there are four contemporary understandings of teaching excellence:

- *Traditional*: in which excellence is perceived as disciplinary mastery, the development of criticism, logic and accumulation of approved knowledge.
- *Performative*: where excellence is viewed in terms of contributions to economic performance, ability to compete in the 'global higher education marketplace' and where there is state regulation to maximize individual performance.
- *Psychologized*: where teaching excellence is viewed as a relationship between teacher and student; the aim being to develop students' deep approaches to learning.
- *Critical*: the aim of teaching excellence here is to empower students through

a process of emancipation achieved by participation in critical questioning of the nature of knowledge and what it means to be educated.

Skelton suggests that in the contemporary university, teaching and learning practice is dominated by performative and psychologized perspectives of excellence. Traditional perspectives are in decline and critical perspectives are marginalized. In this chapter I illustrate how the move towards a new kind of higher education in which research and teaching are truly integrated, shifts the balance between these perspectives, elevating the status of critical perspectives and suggesting new ways to understand traditional, performative and psychologized perspectives on excellence.

Critical perspectives question the veracity of traditional, performative and psychological perspectives. Inclusive scholarly knowledge-building communities involve a different set of values and assumptions about the nature of higher education, research, scholarship and knowledge than currently exist, so I want to explore these different assumptions in order to understand how higher education needs to change if excellence in the integration of research and teaching is to be achieved. The values and assumptions in a higher education system with little connection between research and teaching need to change when research and teaching are integrated. Inclusive scholarly knowledge-building communities are based on a different set of values. So strengthening the relationship between research and teaching leads to conflicts in values and challenges to entrenched hierarchies. These tensions have implications for the balance between different perspectives on excellence.

Judging excellence

Excellence through performativity

When excellence is viewed in terms of performativity, measures of productivity in research and teaching take precedence. Research is judged in terms of the amount of research grant money obtained, the number and/or quality of publications of 'research-active' staff, or as in the proposed Research Quality Framework in Australia, 'research impact', and so on. Teaching is typically judged in terms of student evaluation, knowledge of subject matter, quality of planning and preparation, clarity of course objectives, rapport with students, as well as scholarly teaching outputs, etc.

In Australia, as in the UK, governments have separated funding for teaching and research. There are very good economic reasons for this. However, it does not match the way academic work is carried out and it works against the integration of research and teaching. Colbeck (1998, 2002) argues that in the normal course of an academic's daily work, they manage to pursue both teaching and research goals simultaneously for about one-fifth of the working week. The shortage of, and highly competitive nature of, research funding results in teaching subsidizing research in many areas. Further, equipment purchased for research is routinely used for teaching and vice versa.

The process of knowledge generation by academics and the learning done by students has, by and large, traditionally been viewed as separate. Even where there has been an attempt to involve students in research it more often than not has involved undergraduate students as an audience for research (Zamorski, 2002) and has not engaged them in research activity. While US national funding bodies encourage undergraduate research, in Australia as in the UK, funding councils do not and it is not until the later years of a doctorate that students are considered able to carry out independent research. In contrast, if the relationship between research and teaching is viewed not as oppositional, but rather as the development of inclusive scholarly knowledge-building communities (Brew, 2006a), all who work in the university are engaged in inquiries to build knowledge; each person contributing different kinds and levels of understanding and skills. This involves a redefinition of what is understood by research, scholarship and teaching and new ideas about who should be involved in each of these.

The scholarship of teaching and learning has been influential in the development of a body of research about teaching and student learning which is neither teaching nor research, but occupies a liminal space between both activities. Debates about whether pedagogical research aspects of the scholarship of teaching and learning should be considered as research by disciplinary research council funding panels highlight this. Further, the involvement of undergraduate students in research practices involving conference presentations, publication of original research through journal articles and books (see for example Chang, 2006) as well as engagement in various forms of interdisciplinary teamwork focused on inquiry all challenge conventional ideas of research and publication and question who are the researchers in the university. Undergraduate research schemes, where students engage in real research with an academic or a group of academics during a summer or winter vacation, have been a feature of US higher education for some time, and are now growing in the UK (Blackmore and Cousin, 2003), but they are limited in Australia. When they engage in such schemes between the first and second year, undergraduate students become research associates and get to know the staff and the department from a different perspective during the period in question. Once a student is treated as a colleague, the distinction between staff and student has begun to blur.

If staff and students are more firmly integrated, research output should take account of not just the output of staff but also of the work of students and their contributions to scholarly knowledge. The integration of research and teaching within a framework of the scholarly knowledge-building community questions individualistic notions of research performance. Nowotny *et al.* (2001) suggest that we are moving towards a situation where the development of knowledge takes place within what they call a 'Mode 2 society'. They suggest that not only are there so many more 'actors' or forces (political, social, economic) having a say in how research should be organized and conducted, but the integration of research in society is now affecting ideas about what knowledge is and how it is assessed. The increasing number of contexts in which research is carried out, the proliferation of demands for scientific knowledge in specific contexts and the mix of practices, methods and beliefs which now constitute it has, they argue, changed our understanding of the very nature of research. This is exemplified in the Australian government's measures of 'research impact' which include social, economic, environmental and cultural benefits (DEST, 2006).

This opens up new debates about the impact of research which can no longer be viewed narrowly in terms of impacts on the research community. Society has an interest. Contributions to the global marketplace become more diffuse when the contributions of students and the ways in which they have been integrated into the knowledge-building process are taken into account. It is not that performative notions of excellence are no longer useful, but the integration of research and teaching within scholarly knowledge-building communities highlights the limited range of performative dimensions in current higher education practice.

Traditional excellence

Traditional notions of excellence as the acquisition of disciplinary knowledge are also called into question. Again, it is not that the acquisition of disciplinary knowledge is unimportant; rather, the ways of acquiring that knowledge are transformed. When students are engaged in inquiry-based learning, questions about who the learners are and who has what knowledge are raised. Since research is a process of learning (Brew and Boud, 1995), both students and teachers are learners. Further, the integration of research and teaching means that although we can assume that the teachers have a broader range of disciplinary knowledge than their students, it is possible that students may develop knowledge of specific topics which is new to the teacher. It is common practice for doctoral students to end up knowing more about a particular subject than their supervisors do. Inquiry-based learning at undergraduate level may also do this, albeit on a more limited scale. Indeed, excellence in terms of the acquisition of disciplinary knowledge may well need to be defined in terms of the extent to which students' knowledge transcends that of their teachers.

The building of knowledge is a community concern. Bereiter (2002) suggests that knowledge-building starts from the questions of participants and that these may be students or expert researchers or professionals. Yet in the contemporary university, the relationship between teaching and research is an asymmetrical one where power and prestige are concerned. In spite of numerous efforts to redefine the nature of academic work to create a more even balance (e.g. Boyer, 1990), and in spite of initiatives to reward teaching through award schemes, research output remains more highly prized than teaching and researchers continue to have more kudos than teachers. Academics also have more prestige than students. These relationships of power and prestige are reinforced by the economics and politics of funding regimes, for example the funding of research and teaching separately, also the practice of evaluating teaching and research separately. Research is a valued commodity; a kind of reward for hard work at the junior levels. Research with its high status is preserved for those who have, as it were, successfully 'played the game'. Research-based learning questions all of this. It encourages a reflexive critical questioning of academic work, a view of teaching as a form of research, expanded ideas about who is capable of doing research, expanded ideas about the nature of research and, if students are to be involved in the scholarly community, changes in the discourse of higher education. This suggests that traditional notions of excellence as the mastery of disciplinary knowledge do not go far enough. They do not take into account changes in the nature of knowledge nor the social factors that dictate who is considered worthy to develop it.

Nowotny *et al.* (2001) argue that in a Mode 2 society, knowledge is generated as much outside universities as within. Professionals, academics and others in society negotiate the appropriate areas of investigation and discuss and generate knowledge within what they call 'transaction spaces' (p. 103). In a higher education where research and teaching are integrated, students participate in such knowledge generation. The distinctions between theory and practice, between research and consultancy, between research and professional practice, break down in an evidence-based process of coming to understand phenomena in a complex society where everyone has an interest in knowledge generated through research. What disciplinary knowledge is and the process of acquiring it is now much more complex than traditional notions of disciplinary excellence suggest. New, expanded definitions are required.

Psychological perspectives on excellence

Higher education has traditionally embodied notions of what constitutes excellence in teaching and learning and that, as Skelton (2005) has pointed out, has moved away from the acquisition of received disciplinary knowledge to encompass 'student-centred' approaches which focus on the development of 'deep' approaches to learning. At the University of Sydney we have found that such approaches can be helpful in shifting new university teachers away from didactic lecturing and towards supporting students in acquiring disciplinary knowledge through a meaningful and participative process.

In the context of inclusive scholarly knowledge-building communities, such perspectives which Skelton refers to as psychologized perspectives (following Malcolm and Zukas, 2001) on excellence are, however, limited. This is because they do not encompass the complexity of types of learning and engagement involved in the integration of teaching and research in inclusive scholarly communities. What a deep approach does not require is any critical engagement with the subject under study. Yet this is a hallmark of inquiry-based approaches to teaching and learning where students develop academic judgement in relation to disciplinary knowledge; in other words, they do not simply understand it.

They become capable of critiquing it and this critique may extend to the very questioning of the nature of disciplinary knowledge itself.

Critical engagement

So we need to go beyond definitions of excellence in teaching and learning which focus on the student's experience of a deep approach to require critical engagement with the subject of study. Excellence as critical engagement with the subject is essential to the integration of teaching and research. The development of scholarly knowledge-building communities demands it. A deep approach to learning is not enough; it is merely a starting point.

Serious integration of research and teaching suggests that the relationships between staff and students need to be redefined. There is an ambiguity in contemporary higher education with regard to the ways in which students are treated. Scholars, who value collaborating and sharing ideas within a constructively critical framework and who hold to the importance of ethical practices in the equitable treatment of individuals, none the less tend to treat students as a separate class of human beings. The requirements of mass higher education have led to practices which set academics apart from students, particularly undergraduates, in a kind of academic apartheid situation. Yet many academics would espouse values of participatory democracy and equity. Such a values conflict is demonstrated most poignantly in the strict ways in which hierarchies are maintained. Not only are students entering the university taught separately from students entering in other years, but even when students are encouraged to engage in research- and inquiry-based learning, this is more often than not carried out away from the research activities of their teachers. Undergraduates, in particular, are kept 'at arm's length' from the research of the department (Brew, 2006a: 70). There is a sense in which research is preserved for those who are judged worthy. Postgraduates are permitted to do research because they have participated in the kind of 'submissive waiting' that Bourdieu (1988: 88) talks about in relation to academic careers:

> The exercise of academic power presupposes the aptitude and propensity, themselves socially acquired, to exploit the opportunities offered by the field: the capacity to 'have pupils, to place them, to keep them in a relation of dependency' and thus to ensure the basis of a durable power, the fact of 'having well-placed pupils' ... implies perhaps above all the art of manipulating other people's time, or, more precisely, their career rhythm, their curriculum vitae, to accelerate or defer achievements as different as success in competitive or other examinations, obtaining the doctorate, publishing articles or books, appointment to university posts, etc. And, as a corollary, this art, which is also one of the dimensions of power, is often only exercised with the more or less conscious complicity of the postulant, thus maintained, sometimes to quite an advanced age, in the docile and submissive,

even somewhat infantile attitude which characterises the good pupil of all eras.

To suggest, as I have done, that the serious integration of research and teaching questions the ways in which academics and students relate to each other, indicates that more inclusive discourses need to be used when referring to and addressing students. The language of higher education where, for example in Australia, students are frequently referred to and treated as 'kids', is inappropriate in a more inclusive higher education where academics and students work together on generating knowledge in a scholarly community.

Engaging in a process of reflecting on teaching and learning in a scholarly way leads to a critical engagement with teaching and learning. As Rowland (2000) points out, sooner or later when one begins to inquire into an aspect of one's teaching, particularly in the context of a collaborating supportive group, one begins to question one's values; the values that underlie the teaching that one does. Exploring one's values leads to a questioning of the relationship between the teacher and student and a recognition of the ways in which one's unintentional actions affect the students' behaviour and outcomes. This happens, for example in the Graduate Certificate in Higher Education which my colleagues and I teach at the University of Sydney. We encourage academics to question the values of teaching; a process that frequently leads to a consideration of the ethical dimensions of teaching and when this happens, ethical tensions manifest themselves. Personal ethical imperatives are seen to be set aside in conforming to institutional imperatives and constraints. Tensions between personal and institutional goals come to light. Excellence in a critical perspective does not consist in the resolution of these tensions. Rather it is in the recognition and critical engagement with them including engaging students in their consideration that excellence in teaching becomes possible.

Excellence as a process

Differing perspectives on excellence create a range of different and sometimes conflicting demands on higher education institutions. While the integration of research and teaching lends itself, as I have argued, to critical perspectives on excellence, institutions, departments and course teams nonetheless are required to perform to measures derived from contrasting views of the nature of excellence. In an earlier publication (Brew, 2006a: 157–168), I suggested that the extent to which research and teaching are integrated can be measured on a number of different dimensions, namely: the extent and nature of research activity; the use of evidence-based academic practice; the extent to which there is a research-based curriculum; whether a culture of inquiry is being encouraged; whether communities of scholars are being developed; whether research organization is aligned with teaching organization; and whether teaching enhances research. These dimensions now provide a framework for summarizing key questions about excellence in the integration of teaching and research and examining the tensions which come about through the marriage of different, sometimes competing, measures of excellence.

The extent and nature of research activity

Performative requirements within higher education such as research assessment exercises tend to assume narrow definitions and distort the nature of research. They tend to work against a university's capacity to integrate research and teaching influencing recruitment and driving senior academics to seek ways to escape from teaching. The integration of research and teaching demands wider definitions of research, opening up who does research within universities and encouraging all to be involved in some form of inquiry, research and/or scholarship no matter what their position or role. Critical perspectives on excellence in the integration of research and teaching suggest that participation in research should be extended with opportunities and funding for undergraduates to collaborate with academics in real research projects even at the lower levels of undergraduate education. Creative opportunities to rethink relationships within institutions of higher education are needed so that student researchers, general staff researchers and scholars work with academic researchers collaboratively. This means that excellence in the integration of research and teaching moves away from questions about whether staff are research-active to questions about whether all are engaged in some form of inquiry through which they learn. It focuses on the questions that are being asked about the nature and extent of research activity within the institution.

Excellence in the integration of research and teaching also demands an opening up of who decides what counts as research within universities and within society including governments and research councils. Broad definitions of research are needed including, for example, scholarly work leading to the production of textbooks, undergraduate student research conferences and journals, and creative and artistic works, etc. The integration of research and teaching also means that pedagogical research by academics and by students is valued for its capacity to continually update teaching and contribute to knowledge through publication and discussion. The integration of research and teaching relies on there being a balance of high quality researchers in the subject discipline, and in subject-specific and generic pedagogical research and scholarship. Some academics are active in both.

Evidence-based academic practice

Excellence in the integration of research and teaching necessitates that teaching and learning are evidence-based. It follows from the pursuit of pedagogical research that curriculum decisions are based on informed knowledge of the literature on teaching and learning in higher education together with well-founded evidence of students' responses, learning experiences and outcomes. Inquiring into teaching, as we have seen, leads academics to develop a critique of their practice, and the values and assumptions that underlie it. Their epistemological and onto-logical beliefs and assumptions are challenged. So institutions integrating research and teaching will have schemes to develop disciplinary academics' pedagogical research skills. They will undoubtedly have high quality courses in pedagogy for academics to take and they may well have research grant schemes for research on teaching, and rewards for scholarly outputs in teaching and learning.

Inquiry is central to a university, but is all too often confined to the disciplinary domain. In institutions that are serious about the integration of research and teaching, inquiries into problematic aspects of academic practice become part of the everyday life of the professional. An evidence-based approach to academic practice is also true of the way in which the institution is managed. In such institutions new knowledge that will help the institution to confront and solve the problems that it faces and develop the policies and strategies that are needed, is built within a spirit of inquiry and investigation.

A research-based curriculum

Excellence in the integration of research and teaching leads to the curriculum mirroring research processes and activities. A research-based curriculum means that research is more visible and that spaces are opened up through integrated campus planning so that there are places where students and academics can meet for discussions on research. This means that assumptions about students not being ready or able to engage in research are seriously and systematically challenged and more integrated relationships between students and teachers developed. Students at all levels participate in research and inquiry within their courses.

A culture of inquiry

Traditional and performative views of excellence reinforce academic hierarchies. The integration of research and teaching leads to a critical questioning of hierarchies and redefinitions of who are the researchers and learners in higher education. A key element of a research-enhanced context is thus a self-reflexive culture; one which takes an inquiry based approach to understanding itself; to examining how it makes decisions, how students are integrated and how disciplinary understanding can contribute to knowledge of its practices. So where research and teaching are being integrated there will routinely be critical questioning of the way research in the area is informing both the process of research and teaching and learning. Important questions to ask would include: what can disciplinary knowledge and theories contribute to understanding of teaching and learning issues? How can disciplinary research inform teachers' understanding of their teaching and their students' learning? What is the nature of knowledge?

How are we learning together? Researching teaching, or pedagogical research, is only a first step. I have already suggested that the ultimate goal of the scholarship of teaching is a scholarship of academic practice. The skills of research and inquiry are applied to the academic workplace and embedded in the ways in which academic work is done (Brew, 2006b). Within a research-based higher education, students are involved in such inquiries as a routine matter.

Communities of scholars

The scholars in a university where research and teaching are integrated are 'students', 'staff' and 'faculty' or 'academics' as I have suggested. They also include 'general' or 'support' staff many of whom have research and inquiry roles. Excellence in a community of professional scholars in a university where research and teaching are integrated, then, means broadening out the community of scholars. I have suggested that such communities need to be inclusive. This means acknowledging that different participants have different things to contribute as well as to learn. Excellence involves creating universities as places where communities of scholars work together on common interests, the contributions of each person being valued no matter what their level of prior knowledge and understanding. This again draws attention to the importance of setting up structures, systems and strategies that will minimize negative effects of power and prestige that define hierarchical positions within universities. Excellence does not necessarily mean that hierarchical positions do not exist, but it does mean that there is an attempt to understand and counter their negative effects.

Research-aligned teaching

In evaluating whether a higher education institution is seriously integrating research and teaching, questions need to be asked about the extent to which the learning needs of both academics and students are being met by how the university, or indeed particular faculties and departments, are organized. Opportunities for cross-disciplinary, and trans-disciplinary exchanges, and for multi-disciplinary research may suggest new forms of organization. What is key is whether the curriculum is aligned with the research strengths of the department (including pedagogical research), so that the learning needs of the students are aligned with the learning needs of academics.

Excellence in the integration of teaching and research demands that these activities are jointly supportive of each other both in policies and in structures and strategies for implementation within any given institution. So that maximum benefit can be made of such cross fertilization, institutional structures and systems are needed that go beyond separate treatment of teaching and research, for example through separate teaching and research committees. Such integration is not facilitated when policy at a national level goes against it, for example, through the separate funding or evaluation of teaching and research, or when the spread of research to undergraduate scholars is discouraged through research councils as in the UK and Australia, for example. Leadership at national as well as institutional levels is important to the development of excellence in the integration of research and teaching.

Teaching-enhanced research

There is evidence that teaching stimulates disciplinary research through questioning by students, and through the results of the research and inquiry projects that students engage in (see for example Neumann, 1992; Smeby, 1998; Kirov, 2003). Teaching also stimulates pedagogical research. So the relationship between teaching and research is mutually beneficial.

Conclusion

This chapter has considered the process of integrating research and teaching as a dynamic critical challenge to assumptions which underlie contemporary perspectives on excellence. So the question remains whether universities, their departments, course teams as well as individual academics can achieve a level of excellence in integrating research and teaching. This chapter has set out a number of aspects of integration which provide critical insights on contemporary attempts to measure or establish excellence. I have suggested that excellence in integrating research and teaching lies in the critical pursuit of strategies and approaches that reconceptualize research activity, implement evidence-based academic practice and research-based curricula; that develop a culture of inquiry and inclusive communities of scholars; that align teaching and research organization; and that enhance research through teaching.

Part II

Policy and discourse

Chapter 6

The demotic turn – excellence by fiat

Sue Clegg

(Leeds Metropolitan University, UK)

Introduction

Excellence has become ubiquitous as a popular slogan, indeed the oxymoron 'excellence comes as standard' has thrown off its ironic resonance and is now routinely used to promote an astonishing variety of goods. A Google search of the precise phrase (23 May 2006) came up with 513 matches – including an employment agency, mailing machines, caravan parks, Yarra Honda (cars), hookloaders and, perplexingly, 'naked opera' (which fortunately applies to attempts to demystify, rather than states of undress). The dictionary definition promises: 'The state or fact of excelling; the possession chiefly of good qualities in an eminent or unusual degree; surpassing merit, skill, virtue, worth. etc.; dignity, eminence', and excel is defined as: 'to rise above others' with biblical and religious connotations. While some of the examples in this book might fit into this elevated usage, in terms of prizes and in the exceptional characteristics of some scholars, the demotic of excellence sits uneasily alongside these meanings since anything less than excellence could be understood as failure. This is the tone Neave (2005) identifies, commenting from a European perspective on the peculiarities of policy 'à l'anglaise', on the recent UK government's policy statement on The Future of Higher Education (DfES, 2003). In his view the White Paper is linguistically and eschatologically 'decidedly demotic' (Neave, 2005: 17). Analysing the language he argues that:

> Here is a document closely akin to the sales brochure, drawn up in a curiously foreshorten even staccato language …. As – words – and sentences – become shorter so the vision conveyed is one of dynamism enforced, vigour, vim and fierce resolve injected directly into the hearts of all associated with the higher educational enterprise – which is to say virtually everyone from vice-chancellor to first year student.
>
> (Neave, 2005: 17)

Neave (2005) is using the idea of demotic language, which is the popular form of a language addressed to the (Greek) 'demos' or people, to draw our attention to the ways in which policy documents use a language that politicians (in this instance) suppose to be popular. I am suggesting that the language of excellence, which is ubiquitous as an advertising slogan, shares this characteristic. It seeks to present itself as popular, after all who could want anything less?

Moreover, excellence is being used not merely as a descriptor but as part of the 'evaluative state' (Neave, 1998, 2005) which now explicitly codifies excellence in relation to public purpose. Stratification has become an instrument of public policy rather than a mere descriptor of esteem; league tables and other metrics produce and codify difference. This is clearest in research where strenuous efforts have been made to identify and concentrate rewards on the best. Throughout the White Paper there is a double usage of excellence as involving selectivity, drawing on the more literal meaning of surpassing and unusual, particularly in relationship to research, alongside the claim that the sector as a whole should deliver excellence in teaching. The sections on teaching in the White Paper move across these meanings – 'delivering excellence' implies a general aspiration, the proposals for Centres **for** Excellence in Teaching and Learning (CETLs), which have been lavishly funded as a result of a competitive bidding process, combines reward for excellence with the aspiration to achieve excellence across the sector, while direct reward for excellent teaching implies special achievement. However, the White Paper's overall tone balances praising the achievements of higher education, aligned with the needs of the economy and the personal benefits to individuals, with an elaboration of the threats to the competitive position of universities especially in relation to research. Meanwhile learning and teaching have become an object of strategy in the UK, and in other parts of the anglophone world (Patterson, 2001; McWilliam, 2004; Clegg and Smith, 2006). This is part of the process whereby higher educational institutions are simultaneously deemed to be more independent of the state financially and in terms of governance, and yet are becoming more regulated through centrally set performance indicators and targets and called upon to deliver key functions in terms of supplying flexible, adept workers for the 'knowledge' economy.

In this chapter, therefore, I want to inquire more closely into these discourses of excellence and into whether the proclamation of excellence does in fact guarantee its execution. In particular I want to trace the discursive migrations of the terms from its origins in commerce and industry and track some of its evolution from its roots in quality. This starting point grounds my discussion of teaching in the understanding of the tensions between craft and mass production. Moreover, it locates the subject of excellence as being the organisation and its relationship to the external environment. Teaching excellence becomes one of the ways in which the organisation orientates itself to the client/customer/student, and as these terms are far from synonymous they will themselves come in for scrutiny as the sector in England braces itself for the introduction of a limited quasi-market and prepares itself for, what some vice chancellors desire and most anticipate, a fuller market and proportionally decreased public funding. This background will be used to locate the different meanings of excellence at play in discussions of teaching and learning, and explore the contradictory sites of practice produced in part by these policy and pedagogic texts. The conclusions offer some reflections on whether and how teachers might write themselves back into these texts, and whether there are discourses more appropriate to higher education in which a dialogue can take place. Unless some dialogue occurs many (good as well as bad) teachers will be left articulating the language and practice of professional craft while governments, funding councils and some vice chancellors articulate a language of organisational improvement. Without this engagement the discourse of excellence is likely to be damaging to our attempts to understand ourselves, producing excellence as a rhetoric set adrift from roots in practice.

Migrations

Even a cursory examination of higher education in recent years reveals the number of migrations of concepts and terminology from business. Quality (Morley, 2003), audit (Power, 1997), risk (McWilliam, 2004; Clegg, 2006), and the pressures of commercialisation and marketisation (Naidoo and Jamieson, 2005) have created a climate of performativity in which academics are required to display their competency and expertise (Morley, 2003). McWilliam (2004), in her analysis of changing the academic subject, points to the ways in which academic knowledge is being made over as 'professional expertise' (McWilliam, 2004: 156). Drawing on the earlier work of Mary Douglas she points to the ways in which risk has come to feature in the academy and:

> the ways that rationalities of risk can work as a logic for naming a particular set of practices as 'risky' and also for determining what sorts of mechanisms ought to be put in place to minimise the now apparent danger.
>
> (McWilliam, 2004: 153)

It is not that the idea of managing risk is inherently bad, but that its discursive location within the structures of audit begin to transform an academic's relationship to his or her own work; what counts is 'the degree of intimacy that academics have with the record' (McWilliam, 2004: 159) not with the student, or with the research. I want to argue that excellence fits within this network of related terms and belongs to an organisation change approach to higher educational institutions which has its origins elsewhere in discourses of organisational change and management. Such discourses do not simply translate as Deem and Brehony (2005) have shown, nor are they seamless. Nonetheless, the cumulative effects of re-description are real and it is worth enquiring, therefore, where 'excellence' appears in this pantheon?

One simple answer to this question is that 'excellence' is the latest in a series of transformations in the ways management gurus and organisational experts have sought to re-describe and refine efforts at improvement. I want to argue that at the heart of this transformation is the move from craft,[1] and that this is why these transformations create such particular tensions within the discourse of teaching. Ideal typical craft can be understood as activity where the craftperson monitors their own activities based on the accumulation of skill. Long apprenticeship is of course fundamental to craft, but crucially the craft worker makes interiorised judgements of quality, about what is good, based on standards common to that profession. Craft pieces were often produced at the end of an apprenticeship precisely to demonstrate that skill. These pieces, not infrequently beautiful objects in themselves, were imbued with considerable personal pride. While such systems were highly regulated the judgements about the quality of the thing were based on handed down precepts and by the master craftsman (most commonly male) himself. Mass production, accompanied by an increasingly rigid division of labour, destroyed this connection between the end-product, judged to be worthy or not, from the process of its manufacture and this in turn initiated a wave of management innovations designed to control the quality of such outputs. There has been a movement from the early twentieth century with the advent of statistical process control, through to quality processes and techniques from the late 1940s under the influence of innovations in Japanese manufacturing, to work on teams and leadership and continuous improvement. The general move has been from inspection to the development of various standards and Total Quality Management in the 1970s and early 1980s, to the development of Balanced Score Card and the Excellence Models from the late 1980s and into the 1990s (Barrett, 2006). Each move claimed improvement on the last but in practice incorporated elements of earlier thinking and purpose.

The details of this journey are of course of considerable interest to students of organisations but need not detain us; the point of relevance is that all these models take the interests of the organisation in its (competitive) environment as their central concern. The Higher Education Funding Council with its concern with risk management (HEFCE, 2006), and funded projects looking at particular models of excellence (Consortium of Excellence in Higher Education, 2003), necessarily takes this sort of approach when thinking about the success and viability of the organisations it funds, but that should not distract us from the extraordinary migration of concepts from the commercial sphere into higher education. The first and most obvious point is that the direction is all one way, moreover, whatever the precise terminology the general thrust of organisational excellence is away from forms of governance that have generally been recognised in the educational literature as characterising universities until the last decades of the twentieth century. Excellence, therefore, comes to us as a term with a particular genealogy and discursive location. It cannot be understood as a neutral descriptor, rather higher education has become colonised by a language not designed to debate the purposes and functions of higher education, and in which the notion of any form of organisational exceptionalism on the part of higher education is rejected outright. The organisational literatures that are being drawn on to justify the adoption of these models are explicit on this point

(Barrett 2006);[2] organisations have the same generic characteristics and, there-fore, lessons from other sectors are applicable to higher education.

Identifying the broad story above has the advantage of dramatising one of the tensions around teaching excellence, namely teaching's long held status as craft and professional expertise with interiorised standards held dear by its practition-ers, as against the newer discourses of improvement and excellence which depend on the judgements of others. I am using craft here as co-terminus with a Schönian sense of professional practice as I have argued elsewhere that the case for the uniqueness of strictly professional ways of knowing is misleading in terms of the characterisation of an epistemology of practice (Clegg, 1999). The important point to note, however, is that once there is a shift to a mass system the cosy closed world of the craft professional is no longer seen as a guarantor of quality, and governments and others insist on external judgement being exer-cised. Stephen Ball (2003) describes these processes at work in the compulsory education sector, and in his impassioned defence of teaching as a craft points to the detrimental effects of performativity on teacher professionalism. In higher education much of this judgement is peer-based, but this should not beguile us into thinking that it is self-regulatory in a craft sense. The major shake up of higher education systems across the globe have involved an alignment of educa-tion systems to the needs of the economy (Brown and Lauder, 1997, 2001), and a rejection of the premise that educational professionals can self-regulate and control the quality of what is produced. Jackson (2000), for example, in his defence of the introduction of learning outcomes across the sector argues that the alternative was not a return to the acceptance of professional judgement characteristic of elite systems, but rather direct control in the form of an imposed common curriculum. He, therefore, defends the practices and guidance offered by the Quality Assurance Agency, which is the national regulatory agency for higher education in the UK, as incorporating the need for professional judge-ment. However, it is clear that this repositions professional judgement in radical ways as part of audit not as self-regulation in the older sense.

There are, of course, good reasons why one might be in favour of such a move. Guilds and professional organisations have long protected inherited privilege and this was undoubtedly a feature of higher education (Scott, 1995; Collini 2003). A system that educated a mainly male elite to fulfil elite or semi-elite roles was rightly and properly criticised by those from the radical left and by feminists, as well as being open to challenge from the political right which began a generalised assault on the idea of professional autonomy from the 1980s onwards. Moreover, the quality of the 'products' from higher education is ideo-logically contestable. Whereas, to follow my craft metaphor, the skill involved in a cut glass vase might be apparently flawless, whatever the aesthetics of the matter, it is not at all clear that the learning of the products of universities were anything like as flawless. The women's health movement exposed the lack of learning of many medical professionals and over the recent decades few disci-plines have survived without radical critique of the forms of knowledge and values they fostered. Mary Evans (2004), in revisiting the novel *Lucky Jim*, reminds us of the class snobberies of higher education, and the quality of the learning that went on in universities was openly contested by new groups of students who moved into the system in the 1960s and 1970s, many of whom went onto populate newer higher educational institutions as lecturers. So, as Nixon *et al.* (2001) and others have argued, there can be no simple defence of the past. My story is not simply one of craft good/management bad. It is possible that some higher education teachers were awful craftspeople (although the evidence for this assertion is often little more than anecdotal), and the move towards opportunities for professional development grounded in appropriate theory can only be welcomed. An epistemology of practice is neither uninformed nor a-theoretical, teaching is a concrete science which involves retroduction from practice as well as drawing on abstract scientific concepts (Collier, 1997; Clegg, 2005). Therefore, any defence of proper professional autonomy should go hand-in-hand with forms of inquiry into practice and a rigour in its self-evaluation, as well as debates about the underlying purposes of higher education (Nixon *et al.*, 2001), and the proper exercise of professional judgement (Macfarlane, 2004).

However, moves away from craft and increasing regulation, as many contributors to this volume demonstrate, involve hidden complexities. Being able to judge the quality of a widget depends on being able to specify it within known parameters. The parallel shift concerns how to specify the learning, not necessarily the attributes of the teacher, but the outcome (Clegg and Ashworth, 2004). Here, we are in all together more troubled waters, and if we think in terms of excellence these questions become even more troublesome, especially as other metaphors and migrations enter the fray in the form of students as consumers in semi-marketplaces, and remembering that the subject of 'excellence' outlined above as deployed in policy discourse is the organisation, or even the system as whole. While teaching excellence may not be an oxymoron, therefore, it does appear to be a rather more complex coupling than might be supposed.

Excellent teaching and learning

The idea of excellence in teaching and learning implies that there are standards against which these things could be judged. As Skelton has shown, however, both in this volume and in his book (Skelton, 2005), there are very different framings of what this could mean depending on the paradigm from within which the question is posed. Unlike goodness 'excellence' does carry within in it some notion that it is by definition unusual. This is precisely the meaning that has been used in judging the products of higher education in the research field. Indeed so rare is this commodity that in the next research selectivity exercise panels are to be called upon to make judgement about three different categories of international excellence. Whatever the 'charming absurdities' (to borrow a term from McWilliam, 2002) of this position, it does not in principle distort normal language usage beyond recognition. However, the situation with teaching is rather different where delivering excellence is rather something that is aspired to across the board. This comes much closer to the discursive position of the term within the organisational excellence movement, which focuses on continuous improvement. Even the CETLs initiative, which was competitive and selective, had at its core the spreading of excellence. In this section, therefore, I want to spend some time considering the possible contradictions excellence poses for teachers and for the central dilemma of teaching as essentially being based in the refinement of professional craft.

One of the implications of recent shifts in teaching as many commentators have noted is the reversal of teaching and learning and its transposition into learning and teaching. One reason for this is of course that once the goodness of the practice becomes transposed from the interiorised judgement of the craft professional to a potentially measurable outcome then it is the student's learning that becomes a measure of success. At one level this has always been true, the success of the pupil in examinations and gaining qualifications and skills reflects, sometimes vaingloriously, back on the tutor. However, mere examination success in terms of passing while serviceable in an elite system has come to be distrusted in the context of mass education where concerns about standards have come to play a major part (McWilliam, 2004). There is a curious paradox in that the more students are successful the more this provokes anxiety about standards. This relates to the more literal sense of excellence being rare and unusual, if more and more people are achieving a degree then it cannot have the same worth as it once did – it no longer signifies excellence. Moreover, it is widely recognised that funding per capita has fallen while numbers have expanded, institutions are thus claiming 'excellence' in a context where in purely market terms the value of the product might be expected to have fallen (as indeed in purely economic terms the value of a degree has). There is no doubt some of the scares over standards are fuelled by straightforward class prejudice and scepticism that many people of working class origin can benefit from education. Furedi (2004), for example, claims that the discourse of widening participation is responsible for the 'dumbing down' of universities. Additionally, fears over standards feed other sorts of anxieties as the middle class seeks to secure traditional markers of distinction and preserve intergenerational cultural capital (Ball *et al.*, 2002). Nonetheless, the standards debate does point to some instability within the discourse of excellence. The response to the standards issue in most government-funded mass education systems has been to more towards quality assurance and enhancement. Excellence represents one more approach to this same organisational problem, how to demonstrate continuous improvement in an increasingly competitive market, albeit one that is simultaneously regulated in ways that restrict its full operation.

How then to calculate excellence, or even goodness and the maintenance of standards, in learning and teaching? One answer has involved the development of various instruments for measuring the student experience (e.g. HEFCE

National Student Survey). Internationally these take various forms, but all are vulnerable to the criticism that they are not measuring learning as such, but rather 'customer' satisfaction with the conditions of learning. In organisational excellence models one of the key terms is 'customer' and while there may be some conceptually less problematic customers for the 'services' of higher education, for example catering and accommodation, students as customers is an unstable idea. Even the notion of 'choice' of university is misleading as Ball *et al.* (2002) have shown. While there may be legitimate aspects of university life where students do feel and behave as customers, the central core pedagogic relationship, in most of its elements, cannot be understood as such. Customer implies paying for a service, but although students pay fees the essence of the contact is a two way one in which they have to contribute much in terms of work and intellectual engagement if they are to succeed. The active contribution of students in their learning is a topic that has attracted considerable interest in the pedagogical literature, and good teaching encourages and promotes this involvement, but this, it might be legitimately argued, should be an element of all good teaching, not simply of the excellent. The crux of the dilemma, however, is that even good teaching cannot guarantee good learning; students can and do fail, sometimes for reasons which are neither under the control of the teacher or the student (Yorke and Thomas, 2003; Yorke, 2004). Moreover, even failure is complex since failure to complete a course is not necessarily personal failure in the lifeworld of the student who may have achieved considerable learning. Arguably success is equally subjective, although not necessarily when viewed externally in terms of the crude metrics of government calculation of the economic benefits of higher education in both personal (earnings) and national (increased competitiveness) terms. However, what is clear is that judging the goodness or excellence of learning and teaching is by no means simple.

In practice many of the attempts to demonstrate and produce excellence in teaching revolve around notions of organisation improvement in delivery, and in making the outcomes of learning more legible. The fundamental shift, therefore, is one that thinks excellence in terms of outcomes not inputs – metaphorically judging the quality of the widgets produced. The example I have already cited is the specification of learning outcomes, which involves attempts to get agreement about what the learning is, both for assessment purposes for the student, but also as a way of judging the coherence and pedagogical rationality of courses and programmes. However, specification and explicit texts, while they might offer an appearance of 'transparency', and a benchmark against which good teaching and learning (or even) excellence could be judged, in practice turns out to be much more slippery. As we showed in our research (Clegg and Ashworth, 2004) the language of learning outcomes is at best a shorthand that teachers use. At worst, according to Hussey and Smith (2002), it represents a fundamental category mistake and acts to stifle creativity. In complying, teachers translate their reasoning into the approved form, but these translations involve moving from the 'knowledge how' of enacted practices into 'knowledge that' type statements which are at best approximate. These translations, as with the migrations described in the first section, come with a price. Avis (2000) argues the need to analyse '*enacted practices*' (p. 46) and points to the dangers of technicised processes, and the way in which the textual practices of learning outcomes produce 'readerly' texts which limit the scope for agency on the part of students and staff. These readerly texts are part of a prescribed language of audit, review and evaluation based on common templates. In contrast 'writerly' texts invite the reader to write themselves in, but despite the rhetoric of student control of their own learning, the texts available to students in the form of learning outcomes rarely allow them to write themselves in. Many who championed learning outcomes, and indeed other new teaching and learning technologies such as Personal Development Planning, did so for what they believed to be good pedagogical reasons aimed at making it easier for students without the requisite cultural capital to second guess the obliquer mysteries of academic practice. However, these good reasons in and of themselves cannot suppress the contradictions. The enactment of practices always takes place in concrete historical circumstances and these circumstances, as we have seen, involve successive migrations of discourses and techniques from commerce and industry, all of which are based on the replacement, not the celebration of, craft. The experience of many teachers is thus of reduced autonomy at a time when they are increasingly extorted to facilitate their students becoming more independent and self-actualising as autonomous learners. Moreover, stripped of any foundation in critical and feminist pedagogies, many of these innovations cease to have any radical content (Clegg and David, 2006).

In practice, when it comes to the messy business of judging and rewarding teaching excellence on the ground, the professional craft-like nature of practice, what might be deemed practical wisdom, becomes evident and the not inconsiderable difficulties of what might count as 'evidence' of excellent teaching re-emerges. As both Frame *et al.* (2006) and Skelton (2005) note, judgements in earlier rounds of the National Teaching Fellowships (NTF) relied heavily on notions of reflection. However, they interpret the possibilities for critical potential of reflection, as operationalised in the scheme, rather differently. My own view is that reflection should involve critique and reflexivity and a turning outward of the gaze towards the conditions of practice, as well as an analysis of minutia of practice (Clegg, 1999), but that in practice much of what passes for reflection in contemporary higher education fails to do this. The significance of properly theoretically informed reflection, however, is that it locates teaching in an epistemology of practice, and as a concrete not abstract science. The recent debate about the need for 'evidence-based' teaching and learning does not, as I have argued elsewhere (Clegg, 2005), necessarily involve a more sophisticated theoretical understanding. Rather 'evidence-based' often acts as a signifier for a return to inappropriate positivist inflected forms of measurement. In the case of individual awards (and in judging the CETLs) there has been a move away from reflection in favour of 'evidence'. However, many of the forms of 'evidence' deployed, e.g. external examiners' reports, scores from subject review, etc., rely on tacit peer judgements rooted in craft. Despite efforts at standardisation, external examiner and audit reports and the like depend on deep insider professional knowing, and similarly while students can and often do generously praise their teachers this hardly constitutes 'evidence' of teaching excellence. I am by no means arguing that such judgements are simply subjective or worthless, rather that in proclaiming them as 'evidence' we misread them. Rather than seeing them as thoughtful acts of interpretation appropriate to the practice itself, they are transposed into a positivistically conceived rhetoric of evidence.

One of the paradoxes Skelton (2005) points to, and Rosie *et al.* (2006) also highlight, is the divergence between teaching excellence understood from the perspective of 'ordinary' teachers and those conferring awards. Achieving an award involves the careful presentation of self in terms of the rules articulated. This is not to decry the merit of winners of either CETLs or NTFs, merely to point out that competition itself involves measuring oneself against a socially sanctioned, and essentially inter-subjectively co-constructed, set of norms. How these norms come into being is itself worth of scrutiny since what is regarded as excellence tells one much about the prevailing mores of those who have leadership in the teaching and learning field. Clearly practices which fit within the established pedagogical literature are likely to be recognised, but this is a circular argument. As Haggis (2003) and others have pointed out, the range of conceptions in the teaching and learning literature have until recently represented a narrow set of the possible approaches which could be taken to researching the field. Moreover, in institutional contexts, almost by definition, reward is likely to go to those who express the values and culture of the organisation. Rewarding teaching thus easily slides into the sorts of organisation excellence discourses described above. However, in practice universities have had difficulties in dealing with individuals who achieve external recognition, and the experience of award winners is both divergent and gendered in terms of the extent to which awards confer career and other sorts of advantage (Frame *et al.*, 2006). Moreover, different sorts of capital are valorised across the sector as divisions widen between research intensive universities and those institutions where teaching is more central to their self-definition and the available sources of funding.

Reflections

Teaching excellence, therefore, seems to occupy an odd place in terms of thinking about teaching. Excellence is by definition selective, yet even many of those involved in devising rewards for excellence recognise its community base. Despite the transmogrification of many aspects of teaching into 'outcomes' through the application of a limited number of hegemonic theoretical perspectives, teaching retains an essentially reflexive craft like quality. This can be adduced, as I have suggested above, on purely theoretical grounds. Attempts to codify teaching knowledge by treating it as a technique grounded in the abstract sciences like psychology provide an ideological gloss, rather than guaranteeing real substance. Metaphors derived from the improvement, organisational change and other managerial discourses are misleading when they migrate into pedagogy. Some indicators for organisations (including higher education) may be amenable to continuous improvement, although whether the claims for profound cultural change are well grounded is more questionable. Excellence in some spheres might be an appropriate signifier. However, if these metaphors and translations are taken too literally there is a danger that any scepticism towards the seductive rhetoric of excellence becomes interpreted as being simply an argument for an ossified status quo – who could sanely be against excellence? However, the opposite of excellence is not stasis, but might involve co-construction with students about what good learning in any particular context might look like. This might involve conflict as well as approval; learning can be a disturbing and painful, as well as pleasurable, experience (Meyer and Land, 2005). It also involves reflection on the real conditions of practice both for students and teachers, in which resources, most often experienced as time, are lacking. The critical pedagogy literature has wrestled with the issue of how education might have emancipatory implications for its participants for many years. Central to these concerns is the recognition that pedagogic love or pleasure, variously theorised (McWilliam, 1996; Darder, 2002, 2005; Rowland, 2005), is at the heart of teaching and the idea that higher education can create new horizons for its participants. This is not based on complaisance, but on the contrary takes as its challenge the conditions of learning, and ongoing, critical, collective inquiry into the project in hand. I would take this to be what 'good' teaching attempts.

I have argued that in relation to research excellence there are, albeit distorted, metrics for rewarding the winners. This might make some sort of sense, at least in the most expensive bits of science. However, it makes no sense applied to students and teaching and learning. Excellence as a tactic for rewarding teachers might seem to bring benefits and enhance the prestige of teaching, but we should recognise that that is precisely what it is; a tactic to compensate those who dedicate themselves overwhelmingly to the pursuit of knowledge through teaching rather than in research or management. This mirroring move has led Barnett (2003), among others, to analyse 'learning and teaching' as a sort of counter ideology to research, and Nixon (2004b) to insist on the significance of the unity of academic practice. While more competition in the form of fees will undoubtedly mean that the differences in conditions under which students learn and teachers teach will increase, this should not be glossed with 'excellence'. We know that those places where mostly middle class students study will offer elite provision, but that does not mean that their teachers are more 'excellent' although their degrees, as now, will be worth more in the marketplace.

Organisational excellence is based above all in embedding excellence so that everyone produces to the highest quality and strives to do better, a sort of über-Fordism, except that instead of being micromanaged through the division of labour, staff are expected to internalise the values of the organisation. The interesting question is whether and how these values align with the interiorised values of professional craft skills based in knowledge of the practice of teaching and learning. The only way that can be checked out is through real dialogue, but if excellence acts as a cover for avoiding that debate then the organisational implications look bleak. These are not matters unique to education. Wherever craft knowledge and professional know-how comes into conflict with organisational imperatives, and examples in the UK include health and creative artists in large organisations, then tensions arise. The irony is that most actors recognise the contradictions of their situation all too well. The question is how to deal with them. In the classroom teachers and students can still enact writerly practices; however, many teachers feel that critical engagement, pedagogic love and pleasure are becoming more difficult to nurture. Higher education's official self-descriptions are increasingly decoupled from practice, and the demotic language of policy seeks to suppress the very real contradictions of practice by fiat. My own preference would be to pose the question of what might be good values and good teaching for higher education and to leave the currency of 'excellence as standard' to those who want to market hookloaders, which we are assured: 'are manufactured to the highest standards for waste construction and municipal applications throughout the world'.

Notes

1 I am particularly grateful to Mike Papius and Peter Ashworth who, in their different ways, have contributed to this insight, although of course any distortions are entirely my own and should not be attributed to them.
2 There are of course other more critical literatures as in any disciplinary domain.

Chapter 7

Policy discourses about teaching excellence in a transforming South Africa

Ruth Searle and Sioux McKenna
(University of KwaZulu-Natal, South Africa)

Introduction: the South African policy context

The past 12 years have seen a number of sweeping changes in South African higher education, both in response to global trends, and also as part of the restructuring processes needed to remedy the multiple problems created by apartheid. In 1994, when South Africa had its first democratic election, the higher education system was highly fragmented, segregated and differentiated. The new government inherited a three-tier system of universities, technikons and colleges, with different institutions within each tier catering separately for different racial groupings: Indian and coloured, African and white. These institutions had been funded differentially. The geographical locations of African institutions further isolated them and created particular difficulties. In addition, students entering the system came from a much more varied educational background than previously, many from schools which were part of the under-resourced Bantu education system and who were thus underprepared for higher education in many ways. At this time of transition there came a flurry of higher education policy and discussion documents. This chapter looks at some of these texts and asks questions about the ways in which teaching excellence is positioned through the documents.

In this changing landscape of South African higher education a number of interesting tensions now exist which are reflected in both policy and practice. Kraak (2001: 88), for example, examines the tensions and contradictions in key policy documents such as the 'Size and Shape' document (CHE, 2000) and the *Higher Education White Paper of 1997* (DoE, 1997) which are the result of different ideological positions. He identifies the pull as being between the driving forces for economic development and the imperative for social justice. Moore and Lewis (2002: 1) describe these possibly conflicting demands which seek to restructure higher education (and influence the ways in which teaching takes place) as: 'a response to developments in the global economy and the changing role of higher education internationally, and a local concern for economic development, social reconstruction and equity'. Managerial and accounting discourses, now prevalent in higher education policy, focus on efficiency, effectiveness, audits, viability and throughput rates, indicating a strong drive for South Africa to enter the world arena on a competitive and equal footing. These discourses tend to overshadow and work in contradistinction to the discourses, particularly important in the South African context, of redress, social justice, equity and non-racism.

The introduction of a suite of mechanisms such as the National Qualifications Framework (NQF), the South African Qualifications Authority (SAQA) and the Higher Education Qualifications Committee (HEQC) have allowed for the development of a single unified higher education system, registration of degrees and accreditation of degrees and a level of equivalency between qualifications which is very different from the fragmented and unequal system that existed previously. This unified system works towards providing widening access, and better opportunities for all, although it will take much to address the under-resourcing and other problems embedded in the previous system. In particular special attention has had to be paid over the past 12 years to the quality of teaching and learning at both the undergraduate and postgraduate levels. However, the NQF, SAQA and other such mechanisms also greatly increase government control and introduce a level of bureaucracy that may become stifling (Bundy, 2004). It is clear that the mechanisms and policies intended to shape and guide higher education may be used in a variety of ways, and there is certainly a tension between development and compliance, between autonomy and control and how these develop over time.

These tensions seem to be resolving and there is a subtle pendulum swing in the role of South African universities away from socio-economic transformation towards becoming a producer of resources for national competitiveness and economic growth (Kraak, 2001; Fataar, 2003). Thus, in South Africa, as elsewhere, 'the national Higher Education agenda has been made subservient to the global reform agenda' (Maassen and Cloete, 2002: 22).

When the economic and social sanctions against South Africa were lifted as apartheid ended, international trends such as massification, mergers and increased student diversity hit our higher education sector all at once, and at a point in time when the challenges of rectifying a severely skewed system were paramount. Increased student diversity was immediate and quantitatively greater in South Africa than elsewhere (for details see: Hall *et al.*, 2002; Bundy, 2004; Cooper and Subotzky, 2001). The simultaneous imperatives of social justice and economic development, and the need to enter the global market on a competitive basis, has created a complex higher education environment within a multifaceted society. The implication for teaching of the global reform agenda is that it is increasingly being seen as an activity primarily aimed at producing human resources for economic development. The pressure to produce such resources in an efficient manner results in a severe challenge to individual academic professionalism, academic freedom and transformative, responsive and reflective teaching.

Framework of analysis

Our analysis underpinning this chapter attempts to deconstruct the ways in which teaching is framed within various national policies and documents in the South African higher education arena. The documents we have considered are the *Higher Education White Paper* (DoE, 1997), *Towards a New Higher Education Institutional Landscape* (known as the 'Size and Shape' document, CHE, 2000), *The National Plan for Higher Education* (NPHE) (DoE, 2001), the new *Funding Formula for Higher Education* (DoE, 2004), the *Higher Education Quality Committee* (HEQC) *Audit Criteria and Framework* (CHE, 2004a, 2004b), and the *HEQC Improving Teaching and Learning Guides* (CHE, 2004c).

In looking at these texts we wanted to consider not only the ways in which teaching is positioned in the South African context but also the implications of such positioning for the classroom. Foucault (1980: 100) uses the term 'discourse' to describe how institutions name, define and regulate their practices such that a discourse is the place where 'power and knowledge are joined together'. Discourses are thus very powerful in structuring both knowledge and social practices. The discourses of teaching that we refer to in this chapter are not only direct references to teaching but also the ways in which teaching practices are framed and constructed within the documents. For example, *The National Plan for Higher Education* (DoE, 2001), describes in detail the multiple aims of higher education but makes scant reference to the role educators should play in realizing these aims.

The transformation of higher education, within an emergent democracy, positions all discourses as being 'in transition'. Because the norms and values of our society are in a general state of flux, so too are the discourses constructing education. Kraak (2001), in describing four overlapping policy phases between 1989 and the present, illustrates the transitional nature of the policy discourses. During the first phase (1989–1994), it had become evident that a negotiated settlement was possible. The anti-apartheid agenda shifted to that of preparing policy frameworks for the new democracy. Tensions between 'popular democratic' and 'economic rationalist' discourses 'were muted by the consensus-building dictates of the day' (ibid., p. 87). The second phase, which Kraak (2001) calls the legislative era (1994–1997), culminated in the Higher Education Act of 1997 (DoE, 1997), which represented a 'compromise set of policy propositions that balanced the demands of the competing discourses'. A 'policy implementation' phase began in 1994 and became more evident between 1997 and the present. During this period 'the limits of state power begin to surface and ... policy idealism in education is inevitably mediated by the structural constraints and political limits facing the new state' (Kraak, 2001: 87). The current period, which Kraak (2001: 87) terms 'a vacillating state', is one in which there is 'significant policy doubt, retraction and reversal'. These shifts in policy discourses have great impact on the ways in which teaching excellence is constructed nationally, institutionally and by individual educators.

We have used four 'ideal-type' understandings of teaching excellence – traditional, performative, psychologized and critical (see Skelton, 2005: 21–37) – as a framework for analysing the documents. In using Skelton's understandings as a mode of analysis, we ran the risk of forcing data into discourse categories that we already had in mind rather than letting them emerge from the data. But we used various methods (such as peer review) to critique our analysis and sought validity in Carspecken's sense of the soundness of argument rather than the truth of statements (1996: 56). As this chapter shows, there is some evidence of all four of these understandings in the documents but, in the light of the implementation of national quality mechanisms, the National Qualifications Framework and an outcomes based approach to education, we raise particular concerns about the implications of a performative discourse.

Traditional understandings of teaching excellence in the South African context

Teaching excellence, as a phrase, has largely been avoided in the new South African policy context. This is understandable in a country undertaking massive social reconstruction; terms like excellence carry connotations of privilege. Like so much else in the transformational context of South African higher education, the notion of 'excellence' is contested. The idea of teaching excellence is often dismissed for its traditional associations with social elitism and the aim of cultural reproduction. As Skelton points out, teaching excellence in a traditional understanding is 'associated with mastery of a discipline' through the 'careful digestion of approved knowledge' (2005: 27). Within this limited traditional understanding, teaching excellence in South Africa can be seen as the domain of the more elite institutions, whose student body comes from the top socio-economic sector of society; student groups which racially remain predominantly white. Verkleij (1999: 2) maintains that 'institutions which are regarded to be the best, based on their reputation, act as role models. This makes "excellence" something practically unreachable (and frustrating) for all other institutions having different histories, cultures and funding opportunities'.

Whilst the importance of 'bright students' for success in higher education continues to dominate mainstream thinking, it is tempered by a growing critical awareness that 'brightness' relates to the degree to which students' cultural capital (Bourdieu and Passeron, 1973) is acknowledged within the value system of the South African higher education environment. The debate about student preparedness and access has engendered an ongoing curriculum debate about, for example, whether it needs to be more Africanized and whether there needs to be more acknowledgement and exploration of indigenous knowledges. The call for higher participation rates in higher education (for example, DoE, 1997, 2001) is often collapsed into a call for more locally situated teaching and learning. This politicized debate is taking place at the same time as there is a recognition that higher education must contribute to national performance in the global economy. The tension between these two competing discourses – between economic imperatives and social justice concerns and between local and global concerns – is thus often played out in discussions about curriculum and pedagogy (Nkoane, 2005). A Council for Higher Education colloquium report indicates that:

> The political imperative is manifest in calls for developing indigenous knowledge and acknowledging the African context in professional education: We don't want a situation where simply because Oxford University focuses on this type of curriculum that in South Africa we simply do that.
>
> (CHE, 2002a: 88)

One of the consequences of the politicization of higher education discourses is that educators, institutional managers and national policymakers focus on the drive for equity, and distance themselves from terminology which could be linked to old regimes and troubled ideals. In a society where access to education was systematically controlled according to race group, any notions, such as 'teaching excellence', that could be interpreted as harking back to the apartheid regime must be rejected for more politically neutral terminology, such as 'teaching quality' and 'best practice'.

The term 'excellence' is thus rarely used in reference to teaching in any of the documents we considered in this study. Where it is used, there is a subtle specification that the term is not to be understood in an elite, traditional way but is meant in an inclusive and contextualized manner. For example, the HEQC Founding Document which sets up the National Quality Council, states that their hope is that a minimum standards context will 'provide the foundations for the development and support of *excellence at all levels* of higher education and training' (CHE, 2001a: 8, our emphasis). The HEQC Audit Criteria document outlining the criteria for auditing institutions asks institutions to consider a general open-ended question about excellence: 'What are the *unique and distinctive ways* in which the institution enriches and adds excellence to the higher education sector and society – nationally, regionally and internationally?' (CHE 2004a: 10, our emphasis).

Psychologized understandings of teaching excellence in the South African context

The existence of a psychologized understanding of teaching excellence within the documents is very limited. Skelton (2005: 31) characterizes this understanding as:

> associated with the establishment of universal procedures for teaching and learning, their successful implementation in practice and the achievement of specified outcomes.... Psychologized understandings of teaching excellence focus primarily on the transaction between individual teacher and student.

Teaching is rarely presented in South African higher education policy in terms of the individual relationships between learner and educator. However, some evidence of a psychologized understanding of teaching excellence can be found in national documents related to the implementation of an outcomes-based approach to education (OBE).

OBE has been strongly critiqued in South Africa (see, for example, Jansen, 1999), given its basic behaviourist underpinnings. Luckett and Webbstock (1999: 3) raise the concern that:

> outcomes or competency-based education is premised on an out-dated behaviourist psychology which assumes a certain uniformity and pre-dictability in human behaviour. The outcomes based method of curriculum design epitomizes linear, instrumental reasoning in which micro-level action and behaviour in the classroom is meant to be determined by pre-specified learning outcomes and assessment criteria.

Essentially, students are expected to demonstrate outcomes determined by teachers, ensuring that far from being student-centred, control remains with the teacher. The reductionist tendency of the outcomes approach may engender a system which ignores the learning that emerges from educational encounters which have not been pre-determined, but which may be every bit as important. With the specification of intended outcomes, many of the unintended outcomes become undervalued. There may be a tendency to teach to the outcomes, especially with the pressures for throughput in limited time periods.

The outcomes-based framework of education in South Africa has generally been interpreted in fairly technicist ways within higher education institutions, with great emphasis on performative systems. For this reason, we return to OBE later in the next section.

Performative understandings of teaching excellence in the South African context

Efficiency discourses in policy

The policy tensions between discourses premised on social transformation and equity, and those premised on accountability and efficiency in the higher education context discussed in the introduction to this chapter have implications in terms of performative understandings of teaching excellence. Skelton states (Introduction, this volume) that 'A performative teaching excellence is attractive to policy makers and institutional managers given its emphasis on the three 'E's of economy, efficiency and effectiveness'. The White Paper on Higher Education of 1997 captured the 'equity/efficiency' tension clearly:

The South African economy is confronted with the formidable challenge of integrating itself into the competitive arena of international production and finance.... Simultaneously, the nation is confronted with the challenge of reconstructing domestic social and economic relations to eradicate and redress the inequitable patterns of ownership, wealth and social and economic practices that were shaped by segregation and apartheid.

(DoE, 1997: 5)

The RDP (Reconstruction and Development Programme) was published in 1994 as the macro-economic policy framework during the period of transition and attempted to develop the economy while simultaneously reallocating social goods. 'However, by the mid-1990s it had become clear that the RDP was unrealizable. The limitations of South Africa's very narrow tax base and pressures to open up the economy to the global market led to a shift to a neo-liberal, monetarist, macro-economic policy Growth, Employment and Redistribution (GEAR)' (Luckett and Webbstock, 1999). One of the consequences of this shift is that higher education has now been constructed as a vehicle for economic growth 'under the influence of the steering media of money and administrative power' (Kemmis, 1998: 22).

But while higher education has a clear responsibility to meet the current demand from industry and government for skilled labour (see, for example, DoE, 1997; Skills Development Act No 97 of 1998), this demand should not result in the development of a skilled labour force that is unable to meet the need for the advancement of knowledge. 'Invoking notions of efficiency to make Higher Education less wasteful and self-indulgent may well produce important pedagogical and social benefits', writes Singh (2001: 9). But she goes on to express apprehension about the trend of narrowing the higher education context 'and the disturbing implications of such trends for achieving this and for the broader values and purposes often associated with Higher Education'. In particular Singh expresses concern that the bid to make higher education more efficient should not detract from the goal of developing a critical citizenry.

The shift in *The National Plan for Higher Education* (DoE, 2001) to a discourse more overtly economically driven was, according to Fataar (2003), indicative of attempts to align higher education policy to the macro-economic policies of GEAR. By the time *The National Plan* was released in 2001, 'an economic rationalist discourse had come to settle on the Higher Education discursive terrain' (Kraak, 2001: 86). Kraak tells us that 'Contestation has occurred over the extent to which globalisation and the forces of economic modernisation should be ceded a major role in the reconstitution of post-apartheid HET' (Kraak, 2001: 85). This contestation may have done some good in that transformation issues remain in the National Higher Education Funding Formula, but by and large the efficiency discourse seems to have won over the equity discourse and is expressed through an increasing concern with accountability.

After highlighting the economic and social challenges facing higher education, the *White Paper* (DoE, 1997) tells us that:

> Against this backdrop, higher education must provide education and training to develop the skills and innovations necessary for national development and successful participation in the global economy. In addition, higher education has to be internally restructured to face the challenge of globalisation, in particular, the breaking down of national and institutional boundaries which removes the spatial and geographic barriers to access.

It would seem, therefore, that excellent teaching in higher education in South Africa is increasingly seen in terms of economic development rather than social transformation. This is further exemplified by the frequent calls for curricula to be responsive to the needs of industry.

A performative approach to teaching excellence is a particular danger given the macro-political tensions discussed. The pull towards an economic rationalist discourse brings with it strong pressures to teach that which industry or government demands. Sometimes this is understood as being an immediate set of skills necessary for a specific job. Researchers (see, for example, McKenna and Sutherland, 2006) have raised concerns about whether the technical training of students ignores their capacity for critical engagement, problem solving and other flexible practices that industry ultimately requires in today's knowledge-based world.

A 'high-skills' or 'economic rationalist' discourse not only leaves little space for discourses of equity and transformation, but can also easily be misinterpreted as requiring teaching that simply transfers a specific set of workplace skills to a set of learners. Economic rationalist discourses sometimes translate into production-line teaching and learning, more progressive discourse is appropriated and used as a mask in a way which ensures that critical engagement can be shut down as anti-transformation. Thus it is difficult to resist notions of efficiency or effectiveness, which often run counter to any argument for more developmental teaching processes, smaller classes or more time without seeming to be unproductive or dilatory.

The economic needs of post-apartheid South Africa, coupled with the increasing demand for globalized knowledge and skills, make it difficult to argue against the primacy of performative training practices. 'The role of Higher Education in facilitating social benefits is viewed mainly through the prism of responsiveness to the "market"' (Singh, 2001: 11). Participation in a global economy cannot occur under terms that take no cognizance of our country's history or social development needs.

Outcomes-based education

In performative understandings of teaching excellence, systems are reified and the actual learning process becomes invisible. The collection of evidence and the production of policies – these become quality in and of themselves, distanced and neutralized from the ideological terrain of the classroom. 'Tensions arise when the functioning of the system and sub-systems start to over-ride the logic of what makes sense to individuals in their local contexts and the demands and constraints of the system begin to colonise people's lifeworlds' (Luckett and Webbstock, 1999: 11).

A possible example of such an 'overriding' system was the introduction of OBE in South Africa. OBE was part of an attempt to align education to national and labour needs through a single integrated curriculum structure. But within the national move to OBE has come a subtle framing of teaching as an input within an industrial model premised on inputs, outputs and throughputs. Programme outcomes are registered nationally as part of the accreditation process. Outcomes, therefore, are predetermined and inherently problematic. Teaching excellence then becomes very rooted in the economic production process and systems are highlighted over contexts. This is reinforced in the funding policy for higher education in South Africa where the formula is based on terminology such as on 'teaching inputs' and 'teaching outputs' (DoE, 2004).

Quality assurance through institutional audits

The quality movement in South Africa, like that in the UK, also grapples with an inherent tension, that of being both evaluator and developer. This tension manifests itself through the terminology as it shifts between 'quality assurance', 'quality promotion', 'quality management' and 'quality enhancement'. On the one hand, mechanisms for tracking, monitoring and evaluating, that is, all the judgmental aspects, are a central focus within the national quality documents. On the other, there is constant reiteration in these documents that enabling and supporting development is key, and that bodies such as the HEQC see this as part of their mission. Webbstock (1999) outlines the need for institutions to balance these aspects:

> Universities will need somehow to strike a balance in whatever quality assurance systems they implement, between satisfying external authorities that they are being accountable, and in putting effort into bringing about improvements in quality where they think it is necessary. These are directions which are potentially antithetical; too much time spent on satisfying external bodies can lead to a 'culture of compliance', in which many quality assurance activities are undertaken to comply with demands, and which use up much time which could otherwise have been spent on improving the core functions of the university.
>
> (Webbstock, 1999: 16)

Although the institutional audit framework document, developed through the HEQC, stresses the developmental aspects of audit processes, there is a very real tension inherent in HEQC documents (in particular between the audit framework document and the audit criteria and programme accreditation documents) between quality enhancement for development and the need to use quality assurance processes to address serious issues of mismanagement, incompetence and corruption evident in several institutions. The two key areas of institutional audit focus are governance and teaching and learning. In the compliance model that seems to be developing within some institutions, the letter of the criteria are being fulfilled (down to the smallest example provided) rather than the spirit of quality development which is so emphasized in many of the national quality documents (such as the audit framework document).

A key concept underpinning the introduction of the HEQC and the idea of institutional audits has been stakeholder inputs. The criteria were drawn up by academics from across various institutions, and all other institutions and stakeholders were called upon to comment on the process at various stages. The audits were piloted, resulting in amended criteria and audit procedures. The entire process is based on the notion that audits are undertaken by a 'panel of peers'. This inclusive process was intended to ensure ownership by the sector and reduce a performative approach to quality. The view was taken that an active involvement and iterative process would lead to a more critical engagement with the audit criteria and prevent institutions interpreting the criteria in reductionist ways.

However, Bundy (2004: 15) is cautious in his discussion of the introduction of institutional audits in South Africa and wonders whether 'South African Higher Education [will] become subject to the negative aspects associated with "the audit culture" elsewhere?'. Bundy proposes a need to be alert to the unintended outcomes associated with national audit procedures where the response to the policy becomes one of providing documentary evidence bearing little relation to classroom practice, or of educators who comply with 'correct' procedures but with little thought or enthusiasm, choosing rather to expend time on other aspects such as research. An example of this may be in completing templates for the registration of programmes or modules, or writing learner guides for students in courses because such documents are mandated, rather than because they are necessary for the learning process. Completion of such document templates, after a while, may be done quite automatically, copying from previous examples rather than as a reflective activity.

It is our view that if institutions enforce a performative approach to institutional audits, they run the real risk of suppressing teaching excellence. Teaching decisions become systems-driven rather than based on sound educational reasons, and in contexts such as these, there is no space left for contextualization and reflective teaching.

Quality monitoring through programme accreditation

Despite the attempts to ensure a participative and consultative process, as described above, the HEQC has the very real power of closing down programmes. The effect this has had on institutions has been to increase the tension between developmental discourses and a more authoritarian approach to monitoring teaching practices. In 2003, the HEQC reviewed MBA degrees and the resultant de-accreditation of a number of programmes sent shockwaves through the higher education community, and clearly signalled that government would play a much greater role in the whole educational quality process. In the latest round of programme reviews (2005), a similar process has been followed with the Masters in Education degree. The authoritarian aspects of such national processes can be used by institutional management as a threat to ensure compliance among educators. The documents for programme accreditation in particular emphasize the role of quality processes for monitoring and assurance purposes, and claim that stipulating 'minimum standards is intended to protect students from poor quality programmes, safeguard the credibility of qualifications and facilitate articulation between programmes and providers' (CHE, 2002a: 7).

From an analysis of the programme accreditation documentation, it is clear that the criteria for programme accreditation are about minimum standards rather than about excellence. The criteria state the minimum standards evidence which must be produced for accreditation. Our concern is that these lists of evidence can be interpreted by institutions as the standards themselves.

The CHE explain their view that there should be a gap between the 'facts' of minimum standards and the 'norms' of best practice to allow for the 'diversity and uneven levels of development in the system' (CHE, 2001a: 4). The HEQC sees minimum standards as a necessary measure: 'To instil public confidence in the quality of Higher Education provision, facilitate articulation between Higher Education institutions and programmes, and provide the foundations for the development and support of excellence at all levels of Higher Education and training' (CHE, 2001a: 9).

Our concern is that institutions may content themselves with complying with the minimum standard 'facts' rather than striving for excellence. Even worse, in a performative mode, institutions interpret these minimum standard 'facts' as a set of rules and regulations to be rigidly adhered to as if they were the definitive requirements of best practice rather than as a set of practices to be contextualized and critiqued.

Encouragingly, however, there is an awareness by the national quality body, the HEQC, that while the use of minimum standards may be necessary to address the variable levels of quality in the current environment, it brings with it the danger of compliance-driven quality. After a national review of all MBA programmes, for example, the CHE published a report entitled *From Minimum Standards to Excellence: Next Steps in the MBA Review*, the purpose of which was to 'shift the quality focus from compliance with minimum standards to a discussion about improvement and excellence, based on an identification of the trends, weaknesses, strengths and innovations in management education in South Africa' (CHE, 2004a: 2).

The minimum standards nature of some of the national quality discourse is, nevertheless, particularly problematic for institutions working with a performative understanding of teaching excellence. Teaching excellence, or 'best practice', can, in performative mode institutions, come to mean teaching practice which provides measurables mentioned (as examples) in the national quality documents. For example, the only acceptable evidence of programme reviews could be those that are in a format that can be tabulated and archived, rather than including methods that are less quantifiable but impact meaningfully on the ways in which teaching occurs. For example, where teaching is understood to be the 'lecture', student evaluation of lecturers and courses elicit feedback on the *performance* of the lecture (Chapter 3, this volume) and fail to elicit feedback about the teaching that occurs through informal discussions, close interpersonal relationships and in settings outside of the classroom. These aspects of teaching generally lack documentation and are difficult to quantify so do not count as valid evidence. Excellent teaching is less likely to be valued in institutions working in a performative mode of quality assurance because they can only value that which can easily be measured.

Critical understandings of teaching excellence in the South African context

In a critical understanding of teaching excellence, education is not only about interactions between teacher and learner (as in the psychologized understanding) but also about the potential of education to change society. Higher education's role in society in a critical understanding is not just about developing manpower (*sic*); it aims to develop a critically engaged citizenry. This is particularly vital given South Africa's history. There is evidence within national documentation of endeavours to create critical spaces. For example, in an attempt to retain the developmental aspect of audits, institutions are required to prepare self-evaluation reports in which they demonstrate their own audit process against the 19 criteria and four open-ended questions. The role of the audit panel then is to verify and comment upon the findings of the institution. While we have discussed the national and institutional contexts that may prevent this from happening, the process is designed to encourage both individual and social transformation by requiring a critical reflection on practice and ownership of the evaluation by the institution themselves.

Dr Prem Naidoo, from the HEQC, asked at a conference presentation in 2005 why the open-ended questions of the audit process were so underemphasized by institutions in drawing up their portfolios. He suggested that this was indicative of the lack of ontological debate about the purpose of the university and the nature of best practice (Naidoo, 2005). The audits run the very real risk of becoming performative check lists despite the best efforts of those involved in overseeing the audit process. As higher education gets caught up in national economic rationalist discourses, so the power of institutional management increases to dictate not only how resources are allocated but also what is valued in terms of teaching. In some cases the new managerial style has co-opted the audit process and used it as a threatening lever over academics. Any documentation that arises from the HEQC is interpreted as commands rather than as an opportunity for critical dialogue.

The HEQC discourses in themselves, however, seem to encourage a degree of criticality and are facilitative of change. For example, the Improving Teaching and Learning Guides produced by the HEQC state that 'self-evaluation can produce useful knowledge for reflection and improvement and contribute to curriculum innovation and creativity. The need for reflection and deliberation by those who teach should be recognised and encouraged by institutional managers' (CHE, 2004c: 27). But institutions can subvert these national documents and use them as rules and regulations. There is a panic around the audit and accreditation process that has little or no link to debates about teaching excellence.

The HEQC seem aware of the need for discussion around what constitutes teaching excellence and have not fallen into the trap of defining teaching excellence in the form of a performative checklist of criteria or 'tips for teachers'. In their Improving Teaching and Learning resources (CHE, 2004b: 9) they state that '"good practice" is contingent, context-dependent and defies generic description'. But sadly, in our experience, HEQC documents such as this one, and even the Audit Framework document, are read with far less scrutiny than the list of institutional audit criteria and programme accreditation criteria. The lists of criteria, with their examples of evidence, are not only poured over but read as being for literal implementation.

We therefore cannot assume a shared critical understanding of the term 'teaching excellence' in this politically volatile environment. If an institution, department or educator calls for 'excellence', we believe they need to overtly contextualize it as being within a framework that sees excellence as a hallmark of diversity and equity.

Conclusion

Within policy there is a precarious balance between encouraging developmental and formative approaches and more technicist approaches to teaching excellence. The forces at play in the transforming South African higher education landscape are pulling in a variety of directions. Within national policy and institutional processes, there remains the potential for critical engagement with notions of teaching excellence, but educators need to assert their professional authority to realize this potential. While traditional understandings of teaching excellence are not particularly visible at present due to the political incorrectness of elitism in our society, there is nevertheless the possibility that these will gain ground in an environment that encourages comparison on a global level and competes for scarce resources. A psychologized understanding of teaching excellence remains embedded within specific staff development programmes, where educators may be encouraged to implement generic procedures to ensure that learners demonstrate set outcomes. With the introduction of national quality mechanisms in the particular macro-context of South Africa, the most prevalent understanding of teaching excellence appears to be a performative one. Educators may find themselves being pushed into compliance mode in a way which works against teaching excellence. Teaching becomes focused on providing specified evidence rather than being creative, responsive and reflective. While there are evident tensions within the flurry of higher education policy shifts in South Africa, space has been made within quality documents for critical engagement. Academics at all levels now need to claim these spaces, to consider the implications of policy implementation and to resist any construction of teaching excellence that is conceived in reductionist ways.

Chapter 8

Critiquing excellence

Undergraduate research for all students

Alan Jenkins and Mick Healey
(Oxford Brookes University, UK and
University of Gloucestershire, UK)

(Is) teaching excellence an exclusive or inclusive concept?

(Skelton, 2005: 22)

Attending a top 20 public research university has its advantages. You are able to utilize the facilities that hundreds of millions of dollars in annual research funding provides. At The Honors College you will benefit from all these resources while experiencing the nurturing climate and elite peer group typical of a small liberal arts college.

University of Arizona (n.d.)

I propose that all colleges and universities provide an opportunity for all undergraduates to conduct research – to create knowledge .... Research promotes critical and creative thinking, the habits of mind that nurture innovation; creates a sense of intellectual excitement and adventure; and provides the satisfaction of real accomplishment.

(Ellis, 2006)

We aim to take Royal Holloway forward by building on research strengths to provide quality teaching .... Top class researchers make excellent teachers and students benefit from the enhanced quality of the education they receive.

(Hill, 2003)

The relative contributions that teaching and research make to higher education has recently been brought into sharp focus. Massification raises fundamental questions about what constitutes an appropriate curriculum for a diverse student population. At the same time government and research funding bodies have begun to support the concentration of research within particular institutions.

Here we consider these trends through the lens of 'excellence' and the various meanings of that term both to deepen our understanding of the roles of teaching and research in universities and to explore conceptions of excellence. We espouse a critical perspective on teaching excellence (Skelton, 2005) and concentrate not on the properties of individual teachers but on system-wide values, policies and practices. We in part focus on what Skelton (ibid., p. 33), in his analysis of teaching excellence, terms 'issues of epistemological authority and control'. For example:

1   What counts as knowledge?
2   How is what counts as knowledge organized?
3   How is what counts as knowledge transmitted?
4   How is access to what counts as knowledge determined?
5   What are the processes of control?
6   What ideological appeals justify the system?

We proceed by pointing to the system-wide pressures that are fracturing what some have described as the 'teaching–research nexus'. We go on to consider the particular claims that some research-intensive universities make for the distinctive qualities of their teaching and consider these in the light of the research evidence on teaching-research relationships. We then return to a consideration of values and examine what distinguishes higher education from high school and vocational education arguing, following Barnett (2000a), that an understanding of 'supercomplexity' is what should distinguish higher education for all students. While recognizing that high-level research will be concentrated, we draw out the policy implications for two broad ideal types of universities, the 'research-led' and the 'research-informed'. Our focus then moves to the national level and explores how national policies and funding can ensure that all students in all higher education institutions benefit from research. In the conclusion we consider whether and how this discussion contributes to our understanding of teaching excellence. Our discussion draws upon evidence largely from the UK, Australasia and North America.

Fracturing the teaching-research nexus

In post-Second World War Anglo-America the importance of what has been termed the 'teaching–research nexus' (Neumann, 1994), i.e. the academic linking the roles of teacher and researcher to benefit student learning, has been a central feature of the espoused values of university education. This was powerfully expressed in the UK government's *Robbins Report* on the then future of higher education (Committee on Higher Education, 1963). This argued (para 555) that university staff should both teach and carry out research on the grounds that:

> The element of partnership between teacher and taught in a common pursuit of knowledge and understanding present to some extent in all education should become the dominant element as the pupil matures.... It is of the utmost importance that the ablest who are capable of going forward to original work should be infected at their first entry to higher education with a sense of the potential of their studies.

Such views have been strongly expressed in other national systems. Thus in New Zealand, the Education Act (1990) states that 'research and teaching are closely interdependent and most of their teaching is done by people who are active in advancing knowledge' (New Zealand government, 1990, s162 cited in Woodhouse, 1998: 41). Relatedly the New Zealand's Academic Audit Unit 'is required to audit not only the research policies and procedures of the university, but also how it links research and teaching, and the effect of this link' (Woodhouse 1998: 39).

However, the importance of linking teaching and research at the level of the individual academic and within the university as a whole is now under question from two main forces. First, the growing body of research on the teaching–research nexus; and second, paradoxically, from the increased importance governments give to research that restricts its immediate benefits to the few institutions, staff and students who are deemed 'excellent'.

Historically the value of the teaching–research relationship was an article of faith, or perhaps more kindly an expression of fundamental beliefs about the nature and purpose of higher education. Yet several research studies, particularly at the level of the individual academic, have questioned this close connection (Jenkins, 2004). In a large meta-analysis of the research considering the relationships between research productivity and student evaluations of individual teachers, Hattie and Marsh (1996: 529) concluded that 'the common belief that teaching and research were inextricably intertwined is an enduring myth. At best teaching and research are very loosely coupled'. Relatedly other studies at the level of the institution and the department have shown that, while many institutional mission statements proclaim the value of linking teaching and research, the policy framework often does not support such links (Jenkins et al., 2003). Indeed, the pressures for research productivity and the valuing of high-level research at the expense of teaching may in fact weaken the linkage between teaching and research. These studies demonstrate that we cannot simply assume a productive relationship between research and teaching. And even if such a relationship was to exist and benefited student learning we cannot assume that it works 'naturally'. Institutions, departments and individuals need to give serious thought about how to support or reinvent the teaching–research nexus (Jenkins, 2004; Jenkins and Healey, 2005).

There is increasing evidence that institutional policies for research may be fracturing the potential links between teaching and research in the lives of academics and in the experience of students, particularly at undergraduate level. The reasons lie in the policies of governments and of some university leaders which promote the view that 'high-level', 'cutting-edge' research needs to be concentrated in particular universities and departments. Research is now increasingly seen as central to national prosperity and in need of concentration within those research-elite universities, departments and individuals where it will be most productive. In this context the meaning and the value of 'research' has been narrowed and made into a commodity. Its wider roles, for example, in contributing to our wider social understanding and in developing student learning have been removed from many academic and policy discussions of research (Brew, 2001a, 2006a).

The post-Second World War period has also seen the growth of a mass higher education system with high student participation rates and the creation of many more higher education institutions. Research funding is now increasingly competitive between and within universities. Though the form of such national funding varies, the effects are broadly the same. This fracturing of the teaching–research nexus arguably has a particularly detrimental effect on the quality of the learning experience of students. High-level researchers tend to concentrate on a limited view of research focusing on those activities that have high currency in national research ratings and national league tables and give limited attention to those investigations and publications, such as textbooks and integrative research and scholarship, which can directly support student learning and wider societal understanding. Furthermore, much teaching at undergraduate level is often done by poorly paid and poorly supported sessional and part-time staff (McNay, 1999; Pocklington and Tupper, 2002; Hersch and Merrow, 2005). So as Nixon argues in this volume (Chapter 1) 'if the appeal to excellence means anything at all, that meaning has to be sought in conditions that are shot through with alienation and inequality'.

Conceptions of excellence in universities and a selective misreading of the research evidence

Governments and national systems are then faced by these twin pressures of funding a mass higher education system and developing high-level research. In state systems, where governments are directly and centrally responsible for higher education policy, these pressures are dramatically revealed in, for example, recent responses of the UK, New Zealand and Australian governments.

In 2003, 40 years after the *Robbins Report* had argued for the importance of the teaching–research nexus, the UK government projected and planned the future of UK higher education. The White Paper, *The Future of Higher Education*, comments in some detail on excellence in both research and teaching. It argues that to achieve research excellence, research needs to be concentrated in 'our *leading* universities' and these institutions are also called 'the *best* universities' (DfES, 2003: 31, emphasis added).

> Looking at Nobel prizes, or at citation rates for scientists, indicates that although our position is still strong it is declining.... International comparisons show that other countries, like Germany, the Netherlands and the USA ... concentrate their research in relatively few institutions.... This suggests we need to look again at how our research is organised, and make sure we capture the benefits of concentration, and that we have a number of institutions able to compete with the best in the world.
>
> (DfES, 2003: 13–14)

In these discussions of how policy might support research excellence the needs of students and wider societal understanding are conspicuous by their absence. Chapter 3 considers how to establish excellent links between higher education and business. Chapter 4 is titled 'Teaching and learning – delivering excellence' and states (pp. 46–47):

> All students are entitled to high quality teaching, ... We will also celebrate and reward teaching excellence.... Centres of Excellence in Teaching will be established to reward good teaching at departmental level and to promote best practice, ... The National Teaching Fellowship Scheme will be increased in size.

The White Paper then having argued that these policies will deliver 'teaching excellence', which is never explicitly defined or indeed its possible meaning(s) discussed, draws on the Hattie and Marsh evidence of student evaluations and research productivity discussed above to argue that (p. 54):

> At present, the 'University' title is reserved for institutions that have the power to award both taught degrees, and research degrees. The right to award research degrees requires that the institution demonstrate its strength in research. This situation is at odds with our belief that institutions should play to diverse strengths, and that excellent teaching is in itself a core mission for a university.... *It is clear that good scholarship, in the sense of remaining aware of the latest research and thinking within a subject, is essential for good teaching, but not that it is necessary to be active in cutting-edge research to be an excellent teacher.*
>
> (emphasis added)

This is at best a misreading of that research and its policy implications. For what that and related research indicates is not that research productivity and knowledge is unimportant to effective or indeed 'excellent' teaching, but that the two are not necessarily automatically linked. Indeed the authors of the research cited by the White Paper draw a very different conclusion from their research (Hattie and Marsh, 1996: 533):

> The strongest policy claim that derives from this meta-analysis is that universities need to set as a mission goal the improvement of the nexus between research and teaching. The goal should not be publish or perish, or teach or impeach, but we beseech you to publish *and* teach effectively. *The aim is to increase the circumstances in which teaching and research have occasion to meet, and to provide rewards not only for better teaching or for better research but for demonstrations of the integration between teaching and research.*
>
> (emphasis added)

In a later paper Hattie and Marsh (2004: 1) state that:

> Overall, we have consistently found that there is a zero relationship between teaching and research at the individual academic and at the Department level. *The greatest misinterpretation and misrepresentation of this overall finding is that it leads to the conclusion that research and teaching should be separated for funding purposes* (emphasis added). This conclusion could meaningfully be made *if* the correlation was negative, but it is not. Zero means that there can be as many excellent teachers *and* researchers as there are excellent teachers, excellent researchers, and not-so-excellent teachers or researchers. Zero does not mean that there are *NO* excellent teachers *and* researchers. It could be claimed that Universities have survived with a zero relationship, but that does NOT mean that all academics within those institutions are EITHER researchers OR teachers. *The fundamental issue is what we* **wish** *the relation to be, and then we need to devise policies to enact this wish.*
>
> (emphasis added)

So any discussion about what is 'excellent teaching' or 'excellent research' and what if any should their relation be in a university, comes back to the fundamental questions of 'what is a university?', 'what is higher education?', 'what is research?', and also to the questions posed in the introduction, such as 'what counts as knowledge?' and 'how is access to what counts as knowledge determined?'.

This issue is not confined to the UK. Interpretations of the research evidence and the role of research vis-à-vis university status is an international issue. Thus in New Zealand the Tertiary Education Minister recently suggested lifting the requirement that undergraduate degrees must be taught by people involved in research (Cullen, 2006). A year earlier, in Australia, Brendan Nelson, the then Minister for Education, Science and Training, asked 'Why can't we have Universities that make a conscious decision to specialise in outstanding teaching and scholarship but do very little research?' (Nelson, 2005).

The distinctiveness of university education and the implications for teaching-research relations

There is an extensive literature about the nature of the university and its restructuring under the influences of massification and the pressures for research and economic competitiveness. In the final analysis such discussions come down to what one values in education and indeed in the wider society. We concur with Skelton and his use of Barnett's work as giving us a way forward:

> First of all, we need to identify what we mean by 'higher education' so that any expression of teaching excellence is directed towards this end. As Barnett (1992: 15) notes, it is impossible to discuss concepts like quality

and excellence 'unless we have a reasonably clear conception of what might be included under the umbrella concept of "higher education"'. Any consideration of teaching excellence must therefore address the broader concept of higher education to which it contributes.... Different conceptualizations of higher education will have a significant bearing on what we understand by teaching excellence. For example, an excellence devoted to the production of a skilled workforce will have a different quality to that which seeks to develop student autonomy.

(Skelton, 2005: 21–22)

And to which we would add, in the context of the concerns of this chapter, the need to specify what, if any, is the role of students as researchers during their higher education experience. For while one can still generally assume that at postgraduate level the curriculum is one which is largely research-based and most of the teachers are involved in research, that is often no longer the case at undergraduate level. We are persuaded by Barnett's (2000a) argument that the central role of the university should be to help *all* students cope with 'supercomplexity'. He distinguishes between complexity and supercomplexity in the following way:

A *complex* world is one in which we are assailed by more facts, data, evidence, tasks and arguments than we can easily handle *within* the frameworks in which we have our being. By contrast, a *supercomplex* world is one in which the very frameworks by which we orient ourselves to the world are themselves contested.

(Barnett, 2000b: 257, emphasis in original)

He later argues that:

Under such conditions, a double educational task arises: first, bringing students to a sense that all descriptions of the world are contestable and, then, second to a position of being able to prosper in such a world in which our categories even for understanding the situation in which we are placed, including understanding ourselves, are themselves contested.

(Barnett, 2004: 252–253)

In such a world knowing produces further uncertainty as research continually reshapes our understanding. Barnett (2000a: 163) argues that teaching and research are:

activities (that) are separate and distinct and are not to be confused. However, research is a strong condition for teaching: being engaged in research of a frame-developing kind and projecting those frames to wide publics is a strong – although not exactly necessary and certainly not sufficient – condition of teaching that is aimed at bringing about supercomplexity in the minds of students.... Institutions but also their students have the right to expect that their lecturers are engaged in research.... *The issue, then, is whether ... the lecturers ... adopt teaching approaches that are likely to foster student experiences that mirror the lecturers' experiences as researchers.*

(emphasis added)

Barnett's view as to the importance of students' understanding of supercomplexity is reinforced by the arguments of the social theorist Anthony Giddens. In a range of influential publications, Giddens has argued that, in order to understand and operate in the complex globalised worlds they live, individuals need to understand this complexity and to use that knowledge to both shape their 'private' lives and to be active citizens. This process he called 'democratising democracy' (Giddens, 2002).

From this we argue that *all students in all higher education* institutions whether termed university or college, should learn in an environment which goes back to and reaffirms the values advocated by Humboldt who, in founding the University of Berlin in 1810, argued that 'universities should treat learning always as consisting of not yet wholly solved problems and hence always in a research mode' (quoted by Elton, 2005: 110). Without such a focus any discussion of what they are experiencing as being 'excellent teaching' lacks meaning. It may have a value for example in aiding employability – indeed the student and the institution may achieve 'excellence' at achieving such a value – but to us that is not what characterizes *higher* education. Furthermore to state, as did the 2003 UK White Paper, that those universities with a strong research focus are the 'leading universities', are the 'best universities', tells us much about the underlying values that shape the system. Such perspectives and implicit conceptions of excellence bring us back to the key issues of 'how is what counts as knowledge organized?', 'how is access to what counts as knowledge determined?' and 'what ideological appeals justify the system?'.

The White Paper in effect reaffirms that in the UK there is not only a differentiated higher education system, but also a stratified system with those institutions producing high-level, world class, cutting-edge, research at the apex of that system. As Sir Howard Newby, then Chief Executive for the English Higher Education Funding Council stated, 'the English ... do have a genius for turning diversity into hierarchy' (Newby, 2003: question 455). For all the rhetoric of supporting research excellence, the White Paper represents a restricted conception of the social role of research and in effect what is seen as research. Conceptions of research excellence that support undergraduate students' involvement in research are excluded from the policy discussions of research policies and funding. Conceptions of research excellence that would support society's understanding and involvement in knowledge complexity are not part of the discussions and decisions on research policy. Relatedly conceptions of 'teaching excellence' that try to ensure student involvement in research are also not central to the policy deliberations.

Although the detailed discussion above is from the UK higher education system, the issues are worldwide. Thus in the US, the highly influential Carnegie Classification originally designed as a research methodology to analyse institutions was used by others to rank institutions by measures such as research productivity. Thus the 1994 classification identified seven categories, for example, Research Universities 1 were defined as having 50 or more doctorates per year and 40 million dollars or more per year of research income from outside grants. Furthermore, while its original intended purposes included preserving 'and even increasing the diversity of institutions of higher education by type and by program; resisting homogenization' (cited in McCormick, 2000), the effect has been to push institutions to move up the 'Carnegie ladder' through increasing 'measures' such as numbers of staff with doctorates. As Lee Shulman (2001: viii), President of the Carnegie Foundation, observed: 'One pernicious effect of the Carnegie classification … is the tendency for many institutions to emulate the model of a large research university'. There are similar critiques of how UK league tables similarly reflect and accentuate system-wide pressures to see a narrow view of research excellence as central to national institutional classification and identity (Brown, 2006).

Proceeding towards policy

To proceed to policy formulations we have to recognize the complexities revealed by the increasing research evidence on teaching-research relations (Jenkins, 2004; Healey, 2005). Pragmatically we also have to recognize that national systems and individual institutions have to deliver effective and excellent teaching in contexts where research resources and, in particular, staff with high research expertise, will be unequally distributed between and within universities. However, we believe that higher education institutions should be striving towards certain core features without which excellence should not be asserted. These include:

- There should be a significant amount of exploratory and investigative learning and assessment (i.e. teaching in research mode).
- All curricula should in part focus on helping student understanding of (disciplinary) knowledge supercomplexity.
- Students should be encouraged to feel part of the university's research and scholarly culture.
- University policies, particularly those with respect to teaching and research, should be based on research evidence.

We think the central way to bring teaching and research together in *all* types of higher education institutions lies in the curriculum, for this lies at the core of the student's experience. This moves the focus away from the research skills of individual staff to whether the student learns actively as a researcher, is assessed in research mode, and whether the curriculum is clearly based around current issues in the discipline(s) studied. Stating that the undergraduate is entering and participating in the world of research does not necessarily mean that the student is actively constructing new original knowledge (though that may happen). But to say that the student learns as a researcher, is to state that the university, particularly through its curricula, supports students in gaining new insights and opportunities to learn about research and the way knowledge is constructed.

Clearly there is logic in Howard Newby's comment that 'We cannot possibly sustain world class research in the 90 universities in England.... It is simply again not practical to think in those terms' (Newby, 2003: question 445). For clearly certain types of research, particularly in the sciences, do need concentrated high-level funding for equipment; and there are grounds for most research funding going to those staff who will be most effective in ensuring high-level research outputs. And pragmatically we have to recognize that governments and institutions will tend to think and act that way. But recognizing such system-wide pressures for research concentration also reinforces the need for counter-vailing policies. National research policies also need in part explicitly to focus on the needs of students in higher education to understand knowledge complexity. This requires them to be both the recipients of research through up-to-date curricula, and actively involved in developing their understanding of the provisional and contested nature of knowledge through involvement in research and inquiry.

There will be significant differences between the ways individual universities both help students understand knowledge complexity and also link it to other desired goals of the particular university, such as student employability or service learning. In particular there will be significant differences in the way that students learn as researchers between those institutions that have high numbers of staff with strong research skills and research facilities, here referred to as *research-intensive*; and those institutions where most staff are focused on teaching, particularly of undergraduates, which we here label as *research-informed*.

We now proceed to draw out the implications for policy and practice in these two ideal types and then in national systems. Here we sketch out broad directions for policy and practice. Specific examples of possible national and institutional strategies are outlined in Jenkins and Healey (2005) and Jenkins *et al.* (2003). Suggestions for curricula are discussed in Healey and Jenkins (2006).

Teaching-research relations in research-intensive institutions

Here our focus is on those institutions with high-levels of research funding and where most academic staff are directly involved in cutting-edge, high-level research. These institutions can offer society, staff and students particularly valuable and indeed excellent ways of handling the relationships between teaching and research. To achieve this though they have to go beyond statements that proclaim that the existence of high-level research and researchers somehow make the teaching at such institutions better or in some automatic way excellent. For paradoxically the view that the best researchers are the best teachers, both ignores the research evidence (Jenkins, 2004) and leaves unstated or at best implicit what is high-quality or excellent teaching. It also ignores the central problems that research-intensive universities face in delivering effective teaching. The institutional and individual staff's focus and requirements for research may easily lead to a devaluing of teaching; and the potential benefits of staff research and university research resources may remain hidden or distant from the student. As the Boyer Commission (1998: 5–6) report on US research universities dramatically, and perhaps confrontationally, stated: 'Nevertheless, the research universities have too often failed, and continue to fail, their undergraduate populations ... thousands of students graduate without ever seeing the world-famous professors or tasting genuine research'.

We think the ways forward for such institutions, while also producing high-level research and striving to meet the core higher education features stated above, is to develop:

- University policies for appointment, staff development and, in particular, promotion, which explicitly value those staff whose central function is supporting student learning.
- Curricula which integrate staff discipline-based research with teaching, including: recognizing the particular needs of year one and two undergraduate students and bringing them into the research world of the university; and ensuring that all undergraduate students receive opportunities to learn through research (Kinkead, 2003).
- Policies and structures that enable undergraduate students to benefit directly from the research resources of the university.
- Those graduate students who are likely to go on to teach in universities, to be supported in their graduate studies to become effective teachers as well as researchers; and recognize that many of them will go on to teach outside research-intensive institutions.
- Research policies which ensure that the knowledge generated by staff and students is communicated and shared with wider society.

Teaching-research relations in research-informed institutions

Most undergraduate teaching is done outside the institutions of the research elite. To ensure effective teaching-research links, the research-informed institutions too need to develop policies that value this linkage. Paradoxically they need to be aware of assuming or claiming the effectiveness or even excellence of their teaching simply because of their focus on this activity. Such claims need to be evidence-based. They should also conceptualize and develop research in a way that is consistent with their institutional identity. This may mean challenging dominant views of what counts as 'research'.

Furthermore, while such a strategic research focus may well be part of their institutional identity, such institutions need to guard against that research focus resulting in a devaluing of teaching especially of undergraduates and even further removing the undergraduate student and many staff from the worlds of research and scholarship. It is likely that research policies and funding need to at least in part focus on supporting the undergraduate and postgraduate curricula and on supporting all academic staff, including part-time staff, to be involved in some form of 'advanced scholarly activity', which Brown (2003) defines as:

> the creation of new knowledge, or the critical reinterpretation and transfer of existing knowledge … (which meet three criteria)
>
> iii results in a visible output in the public domain,
> iii carries peer esteem; and
> iii contains an aspect of innovation/originality.

This includes not only research activities, but also, for example, involvement with professional bodies, engagement with knowledge transfer, leadership in the community, acting as an external speaker and refereeing. Particular attention needs to be directed at communicating the importance of research to undergraduates, many of whom will not necessarily be strongly or immediately disposed to seeing its value to their own education or life beyond the university. And most of all an understanding of supercomplexity and development of abilities to undertake, appreciate and engage critically with research need to be at the centre of their curriculum, as for us these are features which distinguish *higher* education. Thus, in addition to the core higher education features noted above, such institutions should demonstrate that:

- All academic staff are supported in being involved in some form of advanced scholarship.
- University policies for promotion explicitly value those staff whose central function is supporting student learning.
- University research policies are in part targeted to support students' understanding and abilities as researchers and the currency of staff's knowledge in their discipline or professional area.
- If university policies support high-level research (and or consultancy), institutional and department leaders ensure as a minimum that such research does not have an extra value that undermines the institutional focus on student learning; and the institution seeks ways to ensure the wider dissemination and involvement of staff and students in that research.

- University research and promotion policies explicitly value those staff whose research focuses on broad integrative scholarship, research that is directly engaged with the needs of society, and, in particular, scholarship that focuses on support for student learning.

Teaching-research relations in national systems

All national systems, from those where policy is centrally directed by government as in the UK to the more diverse systems such as the US, need to consider explicitly how to support effective teaching-research links throughout the sector while also recognizing that much high-level research will be selectively funded between and within institutions. Our question here is 'how can this be achieved and how does it relate to this book's focus on teaching excellence?'.

What the UK government has done is to proclaim and profess conceptions of teaching excellence which are not linked explicitly to broader academically-based social and political goals. They have developed policies to reward 'excellent teachers' and 'excellent teaching departments' that mask a system that is hierarchical and where the 'leading' universities, departments and individual staff are those focused on 'cutting-edge' research. This leaves many students and staff on the fringes of the worlds of research with research funding concentrated in selected institutions which are seen as our 'leading/best universities'. Justified by the mantra of teaching excellence, enhancement policies for teaching give extra funding to staff and students in departments rated as 'excellent', but these departments do not have to show any evidence of enabling students to understand supercomplexity. And students and staff in departments and institutions that are not considered excellent receive less funding; which may well further distance them from the possibility of research-based curricula. Furthermore, research funding and policy is in effect a closed system with little thought as to how it could positively impact on student learning. Indeed the government directed Higher Education Funding Council for England has stated: 'Despite the evidence of a synergistic relationship between teaching and research, we make no recommendation about this: it would be wrong to allow teaching issues to influence the allocation of funds for research' (HEFCE, 2000: 29). This takes place in a context where the financial unit of resource that supports students and teachers is for most being reduced: whether these funds come directly from an embattled 'public purse' and/or from private funds or sources.

This chapter was written at a time when there was considerable discussion about the future organization and funding of UK research, in particular whether the RAE (Research Assessment Exercise) should be replaced (DfES, 2006). But in these discussions the needs of students and wider societal understanding have rarely surfaced. Similarly in discussions in Australia and New Zealand regarding changes in research funding, this issue is also largely absent. The main focus of such discussions is on high-level, cutting-edge research for the few.

However, two recent developments in the US present potentially more valuable conceptions of teaching and research excellence. Earlier we showed how the use of the Carnegie Classification had resulted in narrow conceptions of research excellence dominating the system. In 2006 a new classification was announced that 'focused more on what colleges teach – and to whom – than on the highest level of degrees awarded and research capacity' (Jaschik, 2006). Furthermore, McCormick said that 'other voluntary categories would be created, with the first probably being institutions that show strength in taking steps to improve undergraduate education', and measures are to be created that support teaching scholarship and research that includes community engagement (reported by Jaschik, 2006). Here we may be seeing the emergence of a more critical and integrated conception of teaching and research excellence.

Second, and perhaps more significant than the change in the Carnegie Classification, there is the changing thinking, values and policies of the US National Science Foundation (NSF). One of their three core strategies is the effective integration of research and education which:

> at all levels infuses learning with the excitement of discovery. Joining together research and education also ensures that the findings and methods of research are quickly and effectively communicated in a broader context and to a larger audience.
>
> (NSF, 2000)

With these perspectives and values the NSF radically redesigned its programmes and grants. This led to a whole range of policies and funding streams to bring teaching and research together (Kaufman and Stock, 2004). Some of these funding streams are specifically targeted to support undergraduate students (and staff) as researchers in institutions outside the research elite. In 2006 NSF announced a major new programme, Undergraduate Research Collaboratives (URCs), to 'enable large numbers of students, including first- and second-year students, from across the full spectrum of postsecondary institutions to participate in research' (NSF, 2006).

In discussing this programme Ellis (2006) notes that:

> New types of institutional partnerships are a particularly promising aspect of the URC awards.... Especially noteworthy has been the participation of two-year institutions that traditionally have been outside the research mainstream. A project led by the University of South Dakota, for example, embraces community and tribal colleges. Nearly half of all undergraduate students attend community colleges, and those students represent a huge, diverse, largely untapped talent pool.

We see these changes as being particularly significant for the NSF is a major source of competitive funding for institutions and thus is likely to directly impact on US institutional policies; while the national and international reputation of the NSF has the potential to impact on the thinking and policies of other national systems.

In a more limited way there has been some changing of thinking and policies in the UK. For example, the response to the government's proposals to create teaching-only universities together with fears as to the impact of the RAE on teaching–research relations, led to the government establishing the Research Forum to examine teaching–research links in the context of growing research selectivity. That group argued that:

> research and teaching are essential and intertwined characteristics of a university ... (and that).... *It is becoming clearer that those students who are not learning in an HE environment that is informed by research, and in which it is not possible to access research-related resources, are at a disadvantage compared to those who are.*
>
> (Research Forum, 2004, emphasis in original)

This led to the creation of a special fund in England to support 'research-informed teaching' outside the research elite, with funding being in reverse proportion to funding through the RAE (HEFCE, 2006). These funds are relatively small in comparison with the sums some institutions earn though the RAE. However, what is most significant is the shift in government thinking with the recognition that students need to learn in a research-informed environment. It remains to be seen whether other countries, such as New Zealand and Australia which are embarking on their versions of the RAE, will also recognize the need to retain and enhance research-informed teaching environments. In New Zealand in the same speech that the Tertiary Education Minister talked about the willingness to 'look more closely at our concept of what constitutes a degree' and in effect remove the explicit link to research at undergraduate level, he also argued that New Zealand higher education institutions should form distinctive roles and not all try to include the research focus characteristic of the university sector. This argument was justified by appeals to excellence. 'What the government is seeking is excellence within types of provision; excellent ITPs, excellent PTEs, excellent universities, excellent wananga'[1] (Cullen, 2006).

Conclusions: towards a teaching excellence in research mode

In conclusion we focus on what we have learned about teaching excellence through the prism of the relationships between teaching and research in the contemporary university.

In part our conclusion is that the word 'excellence' has little or no meaning unless it is set in a wider political, social and educational agenda. If we use that word we need to take the noun 'excellence' and ask of it excellence of what, for whom, and to what ends? Or relatedly we need to put alongside our conceptions of teaching excellence words, such as 'equity' and 'parity'. We need, as does Bowen (2004: 2) in his discussion of excellence in US higher education, to give teaching excellence a definition or an objective: *'thought of broadly as educating large numbers of people to a high standard and advancing and disseminating knowledge'* (emphasis in original).

At times in writing this chapter, as we have thought about and investigated the literature on teaching excellence, we have considered that the word 'excellence' should be removed from the language and values of education. For at present the phrases 'teaching excellence' and 'research excellence' are being used to strip away from many students, staff and the wider society the intellectual and social benefits of understanding how research can contribute to the richness with which the world can be experienced and understood.

Alternatively if teaching excellence is seen as a more inclusive concept – as something to which we should all aspire in pursuing educationally and socially valuable goals for all students and staff in higher education – then it offers a way of reshaping the relationship between teaching and research that is consistent with the democratic goals of a mass higher education system. In our view this reshaping needs to involve students being able to appreciate and investigate the supercomplexity of knowledge and this should represent the central goal of all higher education institutions. The *excellence* of national systems and all higher education institutions need then to be investigated and pursued through this lens. Pragmatically and recognizing the need of society for high-level cutting-edge research – and that universities should be central sites where such knowledge is created – then this goal has to value institutional diversity and recognize, as does in part the revised Carnegie Classification, a more varied conception of what is seen as excellent practice and policy in higher education.

We have argued that all higher education institutions should be striving towards certain core features, including that there should be a significant amount of exploratory and investigative learning and assessment; all curricula should in part focus on helping student understanding of knowledge complexity; students should be made to feel part of the university's research and scholarly culture; and university policies should be based on research evidence.

To ensure excellent teaching, national policies need to be designed explicitly to support all higher education institutions strive to achieve such excellence. In that context there may be a case for selective national awards to individuals or departments in so far as they are for their contribution to such system-wide goals. But 'excellent' national policies are those that are directed to reaching for system-wide success in ensuring that national and institutional research and teaching policies are at least in part directed to supporting all students obtain an understanding of supercomplexity.

Note

1 ITPs: Institutes of Technology and Polytechnics; PTEs: Private Training Establishments; Wananga: Maori Tertiary Education Institutions.

Chapter 9

Tertiary teaching matters
Political economy of a New Zealand centre for tertiary teaching excellence

Joce Jesson and Richard Smith
(University of Auckland, New Zealand and
Auckland University of Technology, New Zealand)

Overview and introduction

This chapter provides both a critical and personal view of the work and processes of a government-appointed body called the Aotearoa/New Zealand Teaching Matters Forum. The chapter uses documentary analysis to critically unpack the 'official' documentation and consultation responses of the tertiary sector to consultation about tertiary excellence. We acknowledge that the government-appointed body did achieve some success in reaching consensus and producing a report for the New Zealand Cabinet on Teaching Excellence. However, we raise questions about the supposed 'apolitical' and 'democratic' process of this initiative.

The primary objective of the forum, as set out in its initial Terms of Reference, was to provide advice to Cabinet on the establishment of a National Centre on Tertiary Teaching Excellence. However, at the same time there was a requirement to engage with the wider education sector on options for supporting effective teaching and learning. The forum was established at the end of 2004 as a group of individuals (rather than stakeholder representatives) who had an interest in 'teaching excellence'. The forum included people with a range of expertise from across the tertiary sector. The forum, while 'nominally' independent of government, was supported by a project team from the Ministry of Education (MoE), the Tertiary Education Commission (TEC), and had some involvement from the New Zealand Qualifications Authority (NZQA).

An initial discussion document *Teaching for Learning: Proposals for a National Centre for Tertiary Teaching Excellence* (Teaching Matters Forum, hereafter TMF, 2005a), was developed and then the forum held a series of consultation meetings in an attempt to engage democratically with the whole New Zealand tertiary sector including universities, institutes of technology and polytechnics (ITPs), wānanga (indigenous Māori tertiary universities),[1] private training establishments (PTEs), industry training organisations (ITOs) and institutions of adult and community education (ACE). The diversity of the perspectives around the concept of tertiary excellence – held by executives, managers, teachers, academics and learners of these different organisations – meant that each part of the sector was promoting their own interests and perspectives on the contested notion of 'quality'. Despite the laudable aim of creating a centre, many people in tertiary education felt it was promoted primarily to support the needs and interests of the universities rather than other types of tertiary providers.

Unpacking the concept of teaching excellence underlying the initial and subsequent report was like unravelling cooked spaghetti. There were no definitions and somehow it was thought to be self-evident. The academic unions were convinced that this was simply another plan to get academics/teachers tied down to performative teaching standards and even more audits. In the battle over purpose, location, and name for the centre, what was lost in the final report was any real conceptualisation of tertiary teaching excellence. The politics of the establishment of the centre is bound up in various ongoing attempts of different and various governments since 1987 to establish a unified sector that collaborates together, and provides the whole population with greater access to tertiary education.

A brief background/historical section is provided on the reforms to the tertiary education sector to contextualise the discussion on the establishment of the tertiary teaching centre.

Background

Until 1990, tertiary education in New Zealand was strongly bifurcated. On one side was a centralised, bureaucratic system under the Department of Education responsible for funding and administering polytechnics, colleges of education and vocational training. On the other hand were seven universities guarding their considerable legalised autonomy under the claim of academic freedom within triennial grants from government, and a restrictive entry through school examinations (see Sullivan, 1997; Olssen, 2002). Participation in tertiary education was comparatively low overall compared to other countries, especially those from the OECD. At the same time there was considerable pressure from a strongly emerging Māori voice for self-determination to create improved access and participation for Māori learners.

In spite of enormous opposition from the universities, legislation was pushed through. The Education Amendment Act of 1990 sought to establish an integrated tertiary system covering all forms of provision within an outcomes-based, corporatised model monitored through a series of new agencies. So from 1990 all tertiary institutions became self-managing, able to compete for student places through EFTS (Equivalent Full-Time Students) funding. The most important of the new agencies were the Tertiary Advisory and Monitoring Unit (TAMU) and the New Zealand Qualifications Authority (NZQA). The role of the NZQA was to accredit and monitor all qualifications in both the upper school sector and the tertiary sector area. Moving all tertiary institutions into this same funding regime was quickly accompanied by caps on central funding, forcing institutions to generate alternative funding sources, increasing competitive pressure on the emerging institutions, and pressure on degrees (Peters, 1990, 1997; Butterworth and Tarling, 1994; Butterworth and Butterworth, 1998).

The public justification for the huge changes in higher education was to create a better match between the needs of the 'customers' (students) and the providers (the various tertiary institutes (TEIs), universities, polytechnics, colleges of education and wānanga). It would, as the minister of the time put it, 'make tertiary education more efficient by making them more aware of the real costs of courses' (Goff, 1990). In each organisation, marketing strategies were reviewed and swish sales pitches launched, to lure potential students. In order to attract students, one area that was focused on by the polytechnics and PTEs was the quality of teaching and learning they offered (e.g. UNITEC, 1993).

Quality is a very easy idea to claim but it is much harder to define. Quality is a mixture of perception, emotion and behaviour mixed in together with some physical facts. It is thus a highly context dependent concept (see Skelton, 2005: 21–24). For example, in the manufacturing industry the quality of some output can be specified as meeting a particular pre-specified plan. When a machine is broken or it is making flawed products there is a problem which can be identified and replaced. However, in totally human systems, the specification of quality becomes much more difficult. The first thing many tertiary teachers experienced in relation to the reforms, in 1991–1995, was the development of simplistic and expensive quality assurance systems requiring hours of their own mainly unpaid time to document. Obviously the whole country wanted quality tertiary education and the new standards monitor was the NZQA. In order to gain accreditation for the newly established degrees – and the funding – complex quality assurance systems were required in all NZQA-accredited institutions. These showed on paper just how the institution claimed to assure the quality of its programmes, their curriculum and their delivery.

Every aspect of the higher education process thus became subject to detailed specification and measurement with every nook and cranny of the system becoming rendered capable of being documented (and audited). It was as if education were a giant engineering system. Scientific measurement and objective reasoning invaded all aspects of the organisation. Courses specified predetermined learning outcomes, assessment is projected to measure these outcomes and the resources of time, space and people needed to meet these outcomes are then quantified and costed. The organisation is thus illuminated by the cold light of science (usually the science of economics), in an engineering model of production. Within this model, student course evaluation became a key indicator of course quality. Performativity became the mode of operation with staff 'performing' to the feedback of students perceived as 'customers'.

The quality assurance system established by NZQA sought to assist the 'customer/student' in making decisions about which course/programme/degree/institution to choose. Within this system, statistical relationships are used as if they are real numbers and measures of performance are all seriously reported annually as part of the high cost glossy annual reports to parliament. The presentation of the institution has become much like the public company reporting to its shareholders, and seeking new customers. Image was now everything for customer recruitment, and the use of the glossy prospectus and 'advertorials' in newspapers, popular magazines and television advertisements has become more widespread.

The introduction of student tuition fees in 1990 and a student loan scheme were important planks in the government's new market model of tertiary education creating student demands for better and more effective teaching. Furthermore, the government promoted rhetoric of 'educational services' created the situation whereby the students as 'customers' were able to insist on practices they associated with value for their money, further reinforcing the climate of measurement. Class size nevertheless grew from a norm of 15 in 1990 to around 30 in 2000 (Tertiary Education Advisory Commission [TEAC], 2001).

At the same time the increased competition between various institutions rapidly reduced traditional tertiary sector cooperation and collaboration. Thus by 2000, ten years later, while there was considerable individual institutional autonomy of institutions, there were also enormous pressures on funding accompanied by strong accountability pressures of measurement and student demand (Peters, 1997; Peters and Roberts, 1998; Codd, 2002; Ashcroft and Nairn, 2004).

However, the new competitive environment did not end the original bifurcation. The universities managed to continue very much as they had previously under their claim of academic freedom, and continued to be very concerned that their share of the funding system had become eaten up by the polytechnic or PTE 'invaders'. Under the auspices of the New Zealand Vice-Chancellors Committee (NZVCC), universities quickly set up their own parallel systems for course audit and monitoring – the Committee on University Academic Programmes (CUAP). This was separate to but aligned with the NZQA. The universities, perceived as the 'leading providers' in the sector, did not want to be 'controlled' by an outside body – thus maintaining their traditional academic independence.

What transpired however, under the terms of the new complex funding arrangements, was that universities were forced to agree to have increased research funding separated out of the student-based funding formula (based on EFTS – or as it is colloquially referred to in New Zealand, 'bums on seats'). Research performance of individuals created a mechanism for a new funding regime of research auditing and funding called the Performance-Based Research Fund (PBRF), which was implemented in 2002 (see Hall *et al.*, 2004; Ashcroft, 2005; Smith and Jesson, 2005b; Roberts, 2006). Nevertheless the pressure on tertiary institutions to be able to identify the elements of quality teaching and to improve access and participation by disadvantaged groups continued.

As a response to the opportunities available through new funding incentives, Māori groups established wānanga (Māori universities) – premised on Māori pedagogies and these began to form a separate system from many traditional institutions. A large number of Māori students (often traditionally marginalised within the Pākeha-dominated education system) enrolled in these new institutions, seeking both second-chance education and Māori-oriented knowledge, and creating a huge largely unforeseen growth in tertiary education (Bishop and Glynn, 1999; L. Smith, 2006).

In the emerging model, quality assurance systems including those of teaching had in effect become an arm of a marketing system. If a student chose one institution on what that organisation said about its own quality – what did that infer about the others? There was thus very little critical distance between assessment, learning outcomes and marketing. So student perceptions of lecturers became *the* de facto measure of the quality of teaching, the course and the programme. While the validity of student perception evaluation scales used across different courses, different lecturers, ranges of levels or classes of students was recognised as dubious, it was given recognition through university promotion systems and in the external auditing systems (see Sullivan, 1997).

What became more insidious, however, is the way that 'performativity' of teaching through student evaluation undermined any intellectual version of teaching quality, pressurising teachers to see student perception as the only way to understand good teaching. What was also emerging was the unintended consequences of a funding environment in which only university research – not teaching – was being monetarily valued (Smith and Jesson, 2005a, 2005b). When research quality became measurable by output in the PBRF, quality tertiary teaching came to be regarded as somewhat of a mystery; measurable only through inputs like teaching hours, or the indirect notion of learners' perceptions. In spite of government talk about quality of teaching being a factor in funding, tertiary education providers continued annually to report only the required teaching quality of ratios of students/academic staff member as EFTS:FTE (equivalent full-time students:full-time teaching equivalents).

The next section of this chapter looks at the specific initiative put in place to reward quality tertiary teaching. Whilst we both applaud the initiative as countering the primary academic focus on research, we contend that compared to the monetary rewards and esteem given to research, the incentives offered to teaching by the initiative are small and likely to be devalued. Changing academic identities in the light of 'performativity' has been considered in depth in recent literature. Ball (2003) argues that performativity can be seen as a mode of state regulation in which professional and institutional 'output' becomes more important than beliefs or values underpinning professional work (see also Harris, 2005).

Universities in Britain, North America and Australasia have entered the global marketplace as entrepreneurial institutions (Codd, 2005). Universities have been reconstructed to become providers of services to individual clients or customers (Delanty, 2001). They have been reconstructed as businesses run by managers who are expected simultaneously to be both accountable and enterprising (Codd, 2005); and academics/teachers who work within them are seen primarily as performers.

Blackmore and Sachs (2000: 2) have suggested: 'For academics, there are now a range of performativities required – teaching, research, consultancy, development and community service, measured largely in dollar terms – in terms of internal measures of academic performance'.

It is this sort of comment that underlies concerns about the auditing of teaching (see also Middleton, 2005a, 2005b; Morris Matthews and Hall, 2006; Roberts, 2006) and the 'performative' cultures of higher education in the UK and elsewhere (see Avis, 2003; Barnett, 2005a).

Instituting teaching awards

Initially in 2001 the government did try to counter criticism of the hollowing out of practice through performativity by establishing a series of annual awards for excellence in tertiary teaching through the NZQA. The stated aim of these awards was to recognise and encourage excellence in tertiary teaching and provide an opportunity for teachers to further their careers and share good practice with others (NZQA, 2001). Furthermore, the awards are based on the following premises about what constitutes excellence in teaching:

> Those excellent teachers have commitment to their subject, knowledge, enthusiasm and the ability to stimulate learners' thought and interest. Their portfolios will show that they are organised and well prepared, with aims, outcomes and assessment criteria. Above all, it must be evident that the nominee(s) are student focused and committed to advancing understanding of the subject they teach, and to lifelong learning.
>
> (NZQA, 2001)

In spite of universities regarding the NZQA as their *bête noire*, they are a small, yet powerful ensemble compared with other parts of the tertiary sector. The universities have fewer tertiary teachers overall than their counterparts in polytechnics and other providers. However, despite this, the elaborate system set up by NZQA to assess the submitted portfolios of teaching was based largely on the traditional university model of preparation of a portfolio for promotion, and the implied lecture-based model of delivery. The culture of portfolio preparation in universities is based on a model of individualistic proclamation in research, teaching and service that was an anathema to many working in polytechnics or PTEs.

The collection of and documentation of practices relating to the assessment of teaching assessment privileged university teachers over their colleagues employed in polytechnics (ITPs) or in PTEs. The time, experience and support required to assemble and submit the portfolio was more readily available in universities compared to the more managerial environment of the new polytechnic or PTE sector. Moreover, most of the university centres of professional development ran extra programmes and workshops specifically to assist this portfolio preparation. Whilst we do not have any empirically based evidence to support this point, it is something we both know from personal experience of working in this domain.

The stated purposes of the teaching awards were to:

1 Recognise and encourage excellence in tertiary teaching
2 Encourage and promote good practice
3 Enhance career development for teachers by valuing and rewarding excellent teaching practice.

(NZQA, 2001)

However the resulting awards have not encouraged a more unified sector nor have they met the unstated (or at least implied) goal of providing models of good practice. They have, however, been successful in colonising institutes of technology and polytechnics (ITPs) with university-based models for documenting good teaching. In fact, of the ten awards worth $210,000 annually allocated, the university sector has received 80 per cent of the awards.[2] This outcome, in our opinion, reflects the resource-rich status of universities who are able to actively encourage and support staff participation, than any statement about the quality of teaching within these institutions.

One of the earliest casualties of the 1990 reforms and the competitive market environment was the regional tutor training or academic development unit originally established to serve a regional group of polytechnics. These units had been very effective at spreading new ideas quickly across the sector, building a sense of the role of the academic as pedagogue, and supporting reflective practice as a legitimate model for teaching improvement. They had also served to validate good adult education practices in their organisations, as they helped the identity shift of the new academics from that of disciplinary expert to pedagogue. In the increased fiscal pressure after 1990, only those units in bigger or merged organisations survived, mainly through seeking to interest staff in the ITPs and PTEs in the creation of higher qualifications, or in providing services for failing students. However, many of those working in such units still persisted in their calls for more recognition of good teaching, and more innovative practices.

The final section outlines the creation and development to date of the National Centre for Tertiary Teaching Excellence.

Creating a National Centre for Tertiary Teaching Excellence

In its *Statement of Tertiary Education Priorities* (STEP) for 2005–2007 (through the TEC), the government clearly signalled their continuing commitment to improve the quality of teaching as well as the quality of research:

This STEP reinforces the key message of the Tertiary Education Strategy – it is essential for New Zealand's economic and social development goals that the quality of teaching and research improves and is better connected to business and communities. To secure best value from the public investment in New Zealand's tertiary education, we are emphasising the quality and relevance of tertiary education provision. This STEP is about making participation count by improving learner achievement and progression to higher levels of study. We will [be] increasingly focusing on raising the performance of the tertiary system.

This requires increased commitment by tertiary education organisations to:

Take responsibility for, and actively work to improve, the quality of their teaching to ensure that all students and learners gain the best value possible from their participation in tertiary education; ensure that students and learners access excellent education and training that is relevant to their needs, to those of employers and community groups and to New Zealand's broad national goals, and that students and learners increasingly progress to higher levels of learning and qualifications; and enable their knowledge, teaching, and research activities to better support innovation in all aspects of New Zealand life and the social, economic and intellectual development of New Zealand.

(Tertiary Education Commission, 2005)

This clearly pointed up government requirements about good teaching yet raised concerns about more audits. Following on from this, literature reviews were commissioned by the Ministry of Education (MoE) on what constitutes 'good tertiary teaching', how to improve tertiary teaching practices across the higher education sector and evidence of best practice.

One review undertaken by Prebble *et al.* (2004) identified the following attributes of good tertiary teaching:

Effective teachers are those who:

- are knowledgeable about their subject;
- adopt an organised and systematic approach to their teaching;
- are enthusiastic and interesting;
- respect their students;
- have high expectations of their students' performance.

The authors further concluded that:

- good teaching has positive effects on student outcomes;
- through a variety of academic development interventions, teachers can be assisted to improve the quality of their teaching.

None of these findings were very surprising, but they created more pressure within the sector for identifying good teaching practices. It came as no surprise, therefore, that towards the end of 2004, the government appointed a body to consult with the broader tertiary sector on the development of a National Centre for Tertiary Teaching Excellence.

The initial flurry of scepticism towards the idea of a centre came when an initial document about it was released in April 2004. For example fears about the requirements of even more auditing were expressed from institutional managers, academic developers and staff through their unions and professional associations. There were concerns that even more and tighter controls would be put on teaching quality. Staff within the sector were apprehensive that this would lead to increased compliance, and a movement of funds from supporting teaching to administrative and compliance audit of teaching. However, those making important decisions (e.g. the government and an increasingly large educational bureaucracy) had no real recognition of the complexity of the task of teaching, nor the constraints of funding.

The response from the Teaching Matters Forum was that the model suggested for the creation of Centre for Tertiary Teaching Excellence required wide consultation in order to create the necessary sector support and buy in (Forum, 2005a, 2005b, 2005c):

> The Teaching Matters Forum, in undertaking its task, identified that sector consultation on the issues was needed in order to develop recommendations which were robust, well considered and in line with the views and opinions from the sector participants, including diverse learners across a wide range of learning settings.
>
> (Forum, 2005a: 3)

In order to reassure the range and the number of stakeholders the forum sought extensive written and verbal feedback on the proposal, and also ran a series of very well attended workshops seeking input from across the whole sector and the statement was repeatedly made that:

> As with all good education, the learner will remain the focus, and the vision for the centre will be to achieve the best possible educational outcomes for learners in the tertiary sector. The centre will support all tertiary education organisations (TEOs) and groups who work with teachers and learners, including existing networks and professional bodies, while remaining relevant and accessible to individual teachers. Its roles will include building and maintaining networks to spread individuals' and organisations' best practice right through the sector.
>
> (Forum, 2005a)

Specific sessions were also held for staff involved with Māori learners, as well as other learner representatives, staff developers and foundation learners. Discussions were also held with those involved with Pasifika learner interests.

Overall in the final report there was broad support for a national organisation which would support teaching and learning, and promote the importance of effective teaching and learner-focused cultures. There was also general support for the idea that the centre would help provide more research evidence about tertiary teaching and learning that was New Zealand-based or at least applicable to New Zealand. There was also general support for raising the status of teaching, improving teacher 'training', and developing flexible learning styles which cater for the diversity of learner needs and situations across all TEOs.

There was, unsurprisingly, less support for the idea that the centre would be funded by the institutions themselves, as the final report noted. What was surprising, however, was that no other alternatives were put forward either by the forum nor other sector representatives. In other words what appeared to be what was wanted by all was a financially well-supported centre that was funded centrally, but responsible to the needs of the whole sector.

A very strong and vigorous push was mounted for the centre to be Māori-focused in order to meet the needs of Māori learners. This came through an organisation called AMPTEE (Aotearoa Māori Providers of Training, Education and Employment) and a large group of Māori academics. Their submission stressed the need for a self-determined solution for Māori by Māori. Similarly, there was a strong call from those in the Adult and Community (ACE) sector to recognise their particular pedagogical approaches, and the needs of those students with limited literacy or numeracy.

A somewhat different message came through from the consultation focus groups held with Pasifika people. While there was general support for the idea of the centre, what they sought was a say in its governance. As one person was reported to have said:

> unless Pasifika are represented at the highest level of the national centre then we will as a sector have more of the same. There is not a lack of good will to see Pasifika achieve. There is a lack of capacity.
>
> (Forum, 2005a: 20)

The name of the centre was something about which there was some deliberation – which was reconciled finally by renaming it *Ako Aotearoa* (a Māori term recognising simultaneously teaching and learning).[3] Overall the big issues were over the funding of the centre, its location and management. These were not solved in the final report but left to be worked out later. The meaning of teaching 'excellence' did not appear to be an issue which was hotly contested. The notion did not surface in the material given out for consultation. It would seem that, given the difficulty of coming to an agreed definition of what is meant by this somewhat nebulous term, little discussion about it took place and so this meant it was confined to the 'too hard' basket.

While the sector consultation suggested a stand-alone centre, the final model agreed with government was for a centre that was institutionally-based yet responsible for meeting the needs of improving teaching across the whole sector.

The questions around the funding and governance of the centre the forum raised were responded to by Cabinet and the sector group was recalled for a while (Teaching Matters Working Group, 2005). Following this, the government in 2005 announced that it would be making available four million dollars per year for a National Centre for Tertiary Teaching Excellence to promote and support effective teaching and learning. There was no way that this centre could risk being captured by one group at the expense of any other. Somehow it had to appeal to everyone. The message of the formal invitation to submit a proposal to develop and provide a centre was clear:

> It is intended that the Centre shall operate as a collaborative, cross-sector entity. Therefore this invitation applies to groups of TEOs, or consortia of TEOs and sector peak bodies working together. While an individual TEO may apply, it would need to clearly demonstrate the ability to build and have TEO involvement from across the tertiary sector.
>
> (Forum, 2005c; Tertiary Education Commission, 2006)

Although the consideration of the proposals to develop a centre was to have occurred by May 2006, somehow the complexity of the task seemed enormous and at the time of writing (June 2006) there had still been no official response.[4] There were initially two competing bids from some 'unlikely' alliances in the sector, both led by universities with a loose amalgam of wānanga and polytech-nics/institutes of technology.

We have recently been informed that neither of these bids made a successful case for the fledgling centre. One bid was rejected early on, while the other con-sortia was asked to extensively revise and resubmit their proposal, focusing particularly on literacy. Both bids, we have been told, were initially rejected for focusing too much on research and not enough on the 'pedagogy of tertiary teaching'. The meaning of this was unclear, although it may refer to a lack of focus on promoting particular methods or models of teaching.

Thus, at this point, we still wait for the final outcome, still somewhat scepti-cal of whether there will be a genuinely 'innovative' centre, whether it will be a recreation of what was cut back in 1989 (with the demise of the regional tutor-training and academic development units), or a struggling, underfunded centre attempting to please everyone with little chance of doing this successfully.

Conclusion

In all of the hot air around the structure and the funding of the centre, the con-cepts of effective or 'excellent' tertiary teaching and its context specific nature seems to have been lost. We consider this to be both unfortunate and disappoint-ing. As committed tertiary educators we want all students to be taught by quality tertiary staff in all institutions. However, we are unsure of whether the proposed National Centre will be able to promote, let alone deliver upon, such lofty ideals.

We are left with several unresolved issues and questions for consideration and debate:

1 We predict that despite the claims in the documentation that the proposed centre will represent the interests of the whole sector, the universities will take a lead position and perhaps 'colonise' it with their vested interests and particular practices. This will mean that the centre will help to maintain their entrenched and somewhat privileged position.[5] There is evidence that this previously happened when universities took advantage of their greater resources and standing to support staff applying for the tertiary teaching awards (in which they have been very successful). There is also considerable evidence that the university sector has benefited most under the PBRF research funding redistribution (see Ashcroft, 2005; Middleton, 2005a; Smith and Jesson, 2005a, 2005b; Roberts, 2006).

2 Furthermore, and aligned to the issue above, it has been noted (Hall *et al.*, 2004; Middleton, 2005a, 2005b; Morris Matthews and Hall, 2006) that a critical concern of many academics is that the PBRF will impact negatively on the quality of teaching provided by tertiary institutions. For example, staff time will be directed to research at the expense of maintaining or enhancing the quality of teaching. Moreover, in relation to the investing of resources into research rather than teaching, Smith (2005: 52) maintains that in reality the majority of funding (approximately 70 per cent) into higher education institutions in New Zealand will remain sourced from teaching and not research. An institution would be clearly unwise to jeopardise the quality of its teaching programme which provides the largest proportion of its revenue, to pursue more research which provides a smaller proportion of revenue.

3 Despite the specific vagaries of funding allocations to teaching and research in higher education in Aotrearoa/New Zealand, an equity concern remains. This is the parity of esteem of teaching and research (see Middleton, 2005a). The government through its educational agencies (principally the TEC) has allocated merely four million dollars to the establishment of a National Centre for Tertiary Teaching Excellence. This is a very small budget in relation to the investment into the PBRF research auditing regime which allocated 18.2 million dollars in its first year (2004). For us the message is clear: for universities (but perhaps not the whole diverse tertiary sector) 'quality' (assured) research is clearly more valued than 'quality' teaching.

4 We believe that the roles/activities below are ones that should *not* be undertaken by the National Centre (and these are in line with what the Forum, 2005a, 2005c, warned against):

   • regulation (such as teacher registration) or quasi-regulatory activities;

- significant focus on fee for service activity;
- major funding allocator;
- competing for research funds with other sector researchers.

If the National Centre develops a role as a standard setter or sector monitoring agency, then this would conflict with its focus on collaboration and support. It is clear that the National Centre is not intended to be a regulatory agency. But we argue that the centre should not take on quasi-regulatory roles such as the application and monitoring of standards and or qualifications. Such roles would conflict with the centre's operating style as a catalyst and a leader.

However, this does not preclude the centre having a role in exploring the need for the development of standards/competencies for tertiary teachers. Inevitably, as the forum itself noted, there is a fine line for the National Centre to tread between developing knowledge and information, and being seen to set standards (Forum, 2005a: 24–25).

We are concerned that the National Centre would be encouraged in the future to take up a regulatory function and become a standards setting body – much in the same way the PBRF monitors and evaluates research (see Jesson, 2005). We ask is it a forerunner to a policy change which might 'audit' the teaching dimension of our professional lives as tertiary educators?

5   We predict that the new tertiary teaching regime will be setting up grounds for further differentiation in the sector and a return to the earlier bifurcation as occurred through the imposition of the PBRF (Smith, 2005; Smith and Jesson, 2005b).

6   Our final unease is that this development will pave the way for 'compulsory' qualifications in tertiary teaching for those engaged in higher education teaching (as are being proposed or occurring in other geographical domains, e.g. the UK and Sweden, see Trowler and Bamber, 2005). We are not against the notion of staff voluntarily engaging in professional development to improve their own tertiary teaching and undertaking postgraduate qualifications. However, we do vehemently oppose further qualifications being a 'mandatory' requirement of employment which we see as adding to the already spiralling credential-inflation of our higher education institutions, and adding to the already high workloads of professional staff. Whilst it may be the aim in a competitive environment of CEOs and staff in professional development units to increase enrolments in further tertiary teaching qualifications – there is a need for creditable evidence that this is both necessary and justifiable on more than just financial grounds.

What becomes of this brave initiative to create *Ako Aotearoa* remains a mystery at the time of writing this chapter, as it is still in the process of being conceptualised before it can be actualised. However, as both supporters and critical commentators of the proposal to date, we believe there are still some interesting political and pedagogical skirmishes ahead and that its development will make an interesting project to research for some time to come.

Notes

1 This is a controversial and highly contested term. Whilst Māori academic and the wānanga themselves claim a literal translation of Māori University, the Pākeha (New Zealand people of European origin, mostly from the UK originally), who work in the Pākeha-dominated universities, prefer the term Māori higher education institutions.
2 These awards first began in 2002 and until 2006 there had not been an overall winner gaining the $30,000 Prime Minister's Supreme Award for Tertiary Teaching from outside the university sector. In fact of the 49 awards presented between 2002–2006 there have been only ten recipients in other tertiary institutions outside the university sector: two by college of education staff, two from wānanga, and six from polytechnics or institutes of technology.
3 In the Māori language the term 'ako' means both teaching and learning – and it encompasses the reciprocal relationship of these two processes.
4 The TEC announced its decision on the successful tender for the contract in August 2006. This was a consortium of institutions headed by Massey University. The consortium includes AUT University, the University of Canterbury, Christchurch College of Education, UCOL and Manukau Institute of Technology. The Centre will comprise a national centre in Wellington and regional hubs in Christchurch, Palmerston North and Auckland. Bryan Gould (former UK Labour politician and former Vice Chancellor of Waikato University) was announced as their Chair of the Board.
5 Additional contextual note: there are currently eight universities in Aotearoa/New Zealand. The latest institution to gain university status was AUT University (Auckland University of Technology), which had formerly been a polytechnic. It was granted university status in January 2000. By the end of 2007 there will no longer be any standalone Colleges of Education – they are merging with their local universities or have already done so in the past decade.

Chapter 10

Centres for Excellence in Teaching and Learning in England

Recognising, celebrating and promoting excellence?

David Gosling and Andrew Hannan
(University of Plymouth, UK)

Introduction

The Centres for Excellence in Teaching and Learning (CETLs) initiative is a central feature of the strategy of the Higher Education Funding Council for England (HEFCE) to raise the status of teaching in higher education. This initiative is designed to 'recognise, celebrate and promote excellence by rewarding teachers who have made a demonstrable impact on student learning and who can enthuse, motivate and influence others to do the same' (HEFCE, 2005: 9). A principal policy objective is to rebalance the perceived emphasis within the sector on research achievement. At a briefing for CETL staff in May 2006, a senior HEFCE officer claimed that an intended outcome for the CETL initiative is to 'achieve esteem for teaching excellence that is at least comparable with that accorded to research'.

The importance of the CETL initiative is signalled by the funding it has received – £335 million. This represents the HEFCE's largest single funding allocation to enhance learning and teaching. The funding for this single initiative is equal to the total funding allocated to all of HEFCE's other teaching quality enhancement initiatives over a ten year period from 1999 when the Teaching Quality Enhancement Fund (HEFCE, 1999) was initiated. In early 2005, 74 CETLs were allocated funding of up to £2 million for capital expenditure and £500,000 per annum for five years. An extra £20.86 million was shared amongst the established CETLs in 2006 on a pro rata basis. This significant volume of funding is being directed towards an untested strategy, which has generated considerable scepticism among both educational development professionals and senior managers (Gosling and Hannan, 2007). The only UK precedents, in higher education, for a strategy based on rewarding excellence as a means of promoting teaching quality are the early phases of the Fund for the Development of Teaching and Learning (FDTL) where the requirement to have achieved high Quality Assurance scores was quickly modified and the National Teaching Fellows Scheme, which, as Skelton (2005 and Chapter 14, this volume) has argued, has been only a limited success.

In this chapter we explore the ways in which the rhetoric of the CETL initiative was transformed from the ideologically-laden conception of the original proposal into a more eclectic and pragmatic 'developmental' discourse. Not surprisingly, the interpretation of the policy initiative has been further modified through the process of its implementation. We argue that, although CETLs are doing interesting work in teaching, learning and curriculum development, there are serious doubts about whether they can meet the expectations of the policymakers. One of these doubts centres on whether staff engaged in teaching and supporting learning will be seen to be rewarded in the ways that were intended. We also examine the implications of the democratic conception of excellence that was operating in the selection processes for the CETLs' capacity to influence teaching and learning across the HE sector. We deconstruct the underlying ambitions of the policymakers and question whether the category of 'excellence' remains meaningful in this context.

This chapter is based on research undertaken by the authors and supported by the University of Plymouth. We have investigated how members of staff from different types of institution came to understand the initiative, how they responded to its requirements and how the bidding process itself shaped the proposals. We have also investigated the effects of both failure and success on individuals and institutions in the bidding rounds and the way in which proposals have begun to be put into effect. During the bidding phase we interviewed 24 members of staff, six of them twice, who were bid-writers or bid coordinators (and sometimes both) for a total of 26 CETL proposals from 15 institutions (Gosling and Hannan, 2007). We have subsequently undertaken a further 12 interviews with representatives from CETLs, approximately one year after their formation, to investigate the underlying ideas informing their development. A detailed analysis of the second stage bid documents of 20 CETLs and of HEFCE's publications relating to the CETL initiative has also been undertaken (Gosling and Hannan, 2006).

Evolution of the initiative

CETLs were first announced in the government White Paper in January 2003. The original idea was couched in terms of the government's desire to 'celebrate excellent practice in teaching departments'. It was said that 'The very best will be designated Centres of Excellence, and given funding of £500,000 a year for five years to reward academics and to fund extra staff to help promote and spread their good pedagogical practice' (DfES, 2003: paragraph 4.28). Departments coming close to, but not quite meeting, the standard required to become a Centre of Excellence were to be given 'commended' status. Centres of Excellence, it was announced, would also be able to bid for capital funding, to ensure that the 'learning environment and equipment gives a better experience to students, keeps pace with the skills of lecturers, and plays its part in raising the status of learning at an institutional level' (DfES, 2003: paragraph 4.30).

The original proposal was based on the idea that the way to raise teaching quality was to reward excellent teachers through a competitive and selective process that would identify where teaching excellence lay and invest further in it so that it would have an impact across the whole higher education sector. As such it was essentially a political initiative that was consistent with the then dominant neo-liberal ideology which had been embraced by both Conservative and New Labour governments. Neo-liberalism assumes the superiority of competitive market mechanisms to achieve quality and efficiency (rather than the consensual processes of traditional professions), celebrates achievement as a characteristic of individuals' efforts (rather than of collectivities) and places increased emphasis on choice for the consumer as an incentive to improve performance in public institutions (rather than on internally agreed criteria for improvement) (Olssen et al., 2004). Although there are many variants within the broad concept of neo-liberalism, a common feature is the assumption that by encouraging enterprise, private endeavour and entrepreneurialism, public sector institutions will rise to greater achievements. The pursuit of self-interest is assumed to be the dominant human motivation. Success therefore needs to be rewarded even if this increases inequalities, because, it is argued, the whole of society ultimately benefits from allowing the highest achievers maximum freedom to pursue their ideas. Therefore an 'enterprise' culture, within an environment of self-regulation (rather than state regulation), which allows the most successful to receive their well-earned rewards, is to be actively pursued as a policy objective. Not surprisingly this ideology has been promoted by those who stand to gain most from it, the capitalist corporations, but successive governments, which have become increasingly dependent on these corporations, have been willing allies in its pursuit, though with subtle differences in approach and emphasis (Hall, 2003).

The proposals for CETLs may be seen as ideologically motivated within this neo-liberal tradition. Rather than spread the available funds on an egalitarian basis, policymakers preferred a competitive process which awarded relatively significant financial sums to a limited number of institutions (54 out of a total of 132 universities and colleges). The CETLs were treated like venture capitalists – encouraged to take risks, allowed considerable freedoms in the use of their funding, and subject to only 'light-touch' regulation. The CETL strategy was the antithesis of supporting the weakest and bringing them up to a satisfactory standard through collective endeavours. Instead 'the very best' were to be given a free-hand to develop interesting and bold ideas on the assumption that others would wish to emulate them because of their demonstrably excellent practice. It was also assumed that the best departments would be able to attract more and better students by virtue of their designation as 'Centres of Excellence' and because of the enhanced funding at their disposal.

Although this philosophy continues to inform the strategy of the CETLs, the original idea was modified in some significant ways. First, although the intention to identify 'beacons' of excellent practice has been maintained, the designation of the centres was changed from Centres *of* Excellence to Centres *for* Excellence in Teaching and Learning (HEFCE, 2003). This apparently minor change of preposition from 'of' to 'for' marked a significant shift in approach, because it signalled that the centres were not only being recognised for the excellence already achieved, but they would also be required to show how they would develop their excellence in the future and extend it beyond their own practice. In other words, a developmental role was imposed on them. We will argue that this had important consequences for the manner in which the CETLs were chosen as well as for how they were expected to operate.

The second shift was a departure from the proposal that it was 'the very best' departments that would be recognised and asked to 'spread their good pedagogical practice'. Rather, the statement is made 'We do not believe that the focus of a CETL need be a single department' (HEFCE, 2003: paragraph 19). Bidders were encouraged to define 'distinctive practices' that 'could be based in a department at subject level, or equally could cut across subject department, faculty, or institutional boundaries'. Examples of cross-cutting themes were provided based on 'forms of teaching', 'ways of conceptualising, organising or supporting student learning', 'ways of designing the curriculum', 'a goal of higher education' or 'an identified issue or problem area in teaching in HE' (paragraph 20). We will examine the significance of this widening of the terrain within which excellence could be demonstrated later in this chapter.

A further important feature of the CETL initiative was the decision to give the responsibility to bidders to define excellence in their own way, provide a rationale for their conception of excellence and to provide 'a track record' not only of activities relating to the proposed CETL, but also 'the fit with the institution's strategic objectives and Learning and Teaching strategy, and how excellence is currently recognised' (HEFCE, 2003: paragraph 37). It appears that there was an intention to reward institutions for having made significant progress towards developing a strategy for learning and teaching and for having means of recognising (in unspecified ways) teaching. These points were reinforced in Annex C which provided example models of CETLs that were said to 'prompt institutions into thinking broadly and creatively about the opportunities that this proposal creates to define excellence that is truly mission-driven' (p. 15). This shift towards consideration of how bids were nested within institutional strategies clearly favoured universities and colleges which had given some priority to teaching. It meant that the 'excellence' being rewarded was no longer simply a characteristic of teachers, but was in part regarded as a feature of whole institutions.

When the invitation to bid was published in January 2004 (HEFCE, 2004), the idea of the 'commended' designation had been dropped because of anxieties about 'unintended consequences for those who fail to secure a CETL' (paragraph 14). The intention of the Funding Council for the CETL initiative was now said to be:

to strengthen the strategic focus on teaching and learning by directing funds to centres that reward high teaching standards, promote a scholarly-based and forward-looking approach to teaching and learning, and where significant investment will lead to further benefits for students, teachers and beyond.

(HEFCE, 2004: paragraph 11)

The focus had shifted away from looking back to excellence already achieved to looking forward to what the CETL would be able to achieve in the future and extending this to others:

We envisage that CETLs will sustain and stimulate further excellent practice through teaching that is informed by scholarly reflection, developed through innovative and adventurous thinking, extended through tested knowledge to learning in new contexts, and multiplied by active engagement in dissemination of good practice.

(HEFCE, 2004: paragraph 16)

We have shown how the rhetoric of the CETL initiative shifted from the original announcement in January 2003 to a year later when the invitation to bid was announced. We have suggested that these changes were significant in signalling a shift in the CETL policy but, as we shall now argue in the remainder of this chapter, the resulting ambivalence has had unintended consequences which threaten to undermine the success of the whole enterprise.

Rewarding excellence

Despite the modifications discussed above, the central idea remains that 'the CETL initiative is aimed at recognising and rewarding existing excellence' (HEFCE, 2004: paragraph 24). The implicit model is as follows

1   an institution, or some sub-section of it, is awarded a CETL on the basis of having been judged to have 'excellent practice';
2   the CETL will further develop that excellent practice by reflective, scholarly and research activities;
3   this excellence will be further multiplied through the process of dissemination of good practice.

Thus from the outset the CETL initiative has sought to be a way of providing rewards at the institutional level in the form of substantially enhanced funding, improved status and standing, and an opportunity to further establish reputation through the activities associated with the CETL. In other words a direct appeal was being made to the interests of senior managers whose institutions stood to gain considerable market advantage by being awarded a CETL. For this reason, many felt they had 'no choice' but to bid for CETL funding, even if they did not approve of the policy, as this respondent indicated:

> It is not going to do anything about teaching and learning in the wider sense of the institution.... We are doing lots of other things about teaching and learning. If I look at what we are doing now, I can see a real difference from what we were doing 5 or 10 years ago – I can't quantify it, it's all intuitive stuff. I don't think this bid is going to have that impact ... people are largely after it for much more lumps of money.
>
> (N.B.S.16)[1]

The strategy of the Funding Council depended on the CETL initiative having sufficient financial and symbolic capital for it to be worth the effort to bid for a CETL and, as we have reported elsewhere, the effort required was extreme (Gosling and Hannan, 2007). Because the symbolic capital was somewhat contentious, or at least an unknown quantity (as we will discuss below), the £2 million capital funding played a significant role in the Funding Council's strategy. The provision of new or refurbished buildings and/or extensive new equipment, could provide a material and public symbol of the enhanced status of the institution. Some institutions with CETLs are clearly exploiting this opportunity in their marketing strategies by drawing attention to their Centre for Excellence, not just as a notional title, but as a physical space with obvious benefits to existing and future students.

It is also important to note that the 'vision' for the CETLs included the idea that the reward element should extend to the individual members of the teaching staff who had been judged to be excellent – 'the purpose of CETLs is to reward teachers for excellence within a defined learning or programme context' (HEFCE, 2004: paragraph 28). The Funding Council envisaged that a proportion of the funding would be used to:

> reward excellent practitioners through financial or promotional schemes or in other ways, including by giving more time and opportunity to teach and reflect on teaching, provision for staff visits, better facilities for teaching, and increased opportunities for improved staff-student interaction.
>
> (HEFCE, 2004: paragraph 41)

However, this aspect of the policy proved to be more difficult than the policy makers envisaged. In the first place, the way of identifying who were to be treated as the 'excellent staff' proved to be contentious:

> We needed to select a group of staff who were nominated as the core people, who were the named excellent people to be at the centre of each of the CETLs. Because there was no clear system for doing that, no criteria, no appointments, panels and so on, so that was partly done on the sort of buddy

process, partly done on who do you think will look credible on paper when their mini CVs are presented, who happens to have published in learning and teaching, who happens to have worked with the LTSN[2] centres as they were – so that the whole issue of identifying the named excellent people, who would be the first to be rewarded, was a little bit problematic and I would find it hard to say that that was done in an objective or scientific way.

(N.C.S.1)

Second, the notion that those preparing the bids would be the same individuals who would receive the rewards for being successful was found to be unrealistic in a number of CETLs. On the contrary, in some cases, the people writing the bids stood to gain very little from all the work invested in preparing the case to be awarded a CETL:

For the people who have been working for me planning it, it has been nothing but a punishment and a lot of work, and they aren't going to be the people who benefit, it is going to be other people who benefit I suspect. The people who will benefit will be individuals whose time will be bought out so they can do the things which are involved in it.

(O.BC.SF.5)

Indeed, it was clear that many academic staff involved in CETL bids rejected the reward element of the initiative: 'The teachers themselves said we don't want one of us to start getting £1,000 for being excellent, we think that is really awful and divisive' (O.B.S.8).

Because the idea of rewarding specified staff was seen to be problematic, some CETLs were designed in a way which would keep open the question of which staff would ultimately benefit from the funding. Some successful bidders went so far as to indicate that in the implementation of the CETL they felt the need to downplay the reward element, because of the resentment that it was feared would follow internally: 'I think the biggest challenge is going to be making sure that the CETL is not seen as something that is rewarding just some parts of the University, that it's you know, X department again' (N.B.S.18).

Far from accepting the premise that those who have been successful should receive additional funding, considerable effort was invested to ensure that all departments in the institution stood to gain from the award of the CETL.

The policy as envisaged could only be successfully implemented in institutions that already had a way of rewarding staff, although even here there was an unwillingness to use the reward element in a way which gave financial benefits to individual academics:

We had already, as part of the HR (Human Resources) strategy and HR funding, put forward proposals for rewarding staff in relation to teaching and learning so really it was a further development of that rather than something that was entirely new ... (so we) said this is a scheme that we are putting in place and we would expect that staff who were involved in a centre to be able to benefit from this scheme.

[interviewer] In terms of promotion and such like?

Well, potentially or more in terms of perhaps relief of teaching, opportunities for staff development or for purchase of equipment and so on.

(N.C.SF.12)

In these ways we have found that institutions were unwilling to change existing practice in order to meet the requirements of the CETL initiative. This has meant that, in institutions that have a strong commitment to egalitarian ideologies, a central tenet of CETL policy is being negated or minimised because individuals who are charged with implementing the CETL(s) within their institution reject the neo-liberal competitive ideology which was the political foundation of the initiative.

The meaning of excellence in the CETL initiative

Harvey has argued that the notion of 'quality' in a higher education context can be understood in several ways. He suggests five types of quality:

Quality as exceptional performance
Quality as perfection or consistency
Quality as fitness for purpose
Quality as value for money
Quality as transformation

(Harvey, 2002: 253)

While all of these types of quality may be present in a CETL's area of work, the designation of 'excellence' seems to imply that there is evidence of 'exceptional performance'. Furthermore, when something is judged to be 'exceptional' this entails making a comparative judgement that a performance is significantly above the norm. Nevertheless, 'exceptional performance' does not necessarily imply that what is excellent is the highest performing example of its kind.

It is true that all CETL bids were required to demonstrate that the department(s), or the institution(s), had achieved a certain standard above the norm in respect of the theme or subject that was to be the focus of the CETL. However, the nature of the selection process means that it is not possible to conclude from the award of a CETL that the individuals involved, singly or collectively, are the highest perform-ing teachers, or that the bidders are 'the most excellent'. In this respect the award of a CETL is significantly different from the award of the highest rankings in the RAE, the Research Assessment Exercise,[3] which does make judgements about which are the highest achieving research departments within their field and directs significantly greater resources to those who achieve this top ranking.

One rather obvious reason for this difference is that, whereas it is in the interests of all the top research departments to put themselves forward to be considered and ranked in the RAE, since they all aspire to receive funding by virtue of their research quality, CETLs could only be chosen from the bids that were received. Institutions were restricted, according to their size, as to whether they could submit one, two or three bids (plus a collaborative bid), and in fact some institutions did not submit as many bids as they were entitled to. Furthermore, since the selection process was designed to either accept or reject the bids received, it follows that no overall ranking of teaching quality could be made.

The reluctance to rank departments for teaching excellence represented a retreat from the original political goal which was to reward 'best' departments. The retreat appears to have occurred for both pragmatic and principled reasons. It was clear that any process involved in making a judgement about the 'best' teachers would be far too costly. Any suggestion that panels might visit competing institutions and observe teaching 'practice' was ruled out as too expensive, too time-consuming and an unreliable basis for judging excellence. It was not possible to make use of existing information about comparative measures of teaching performance since this did not demonstrate which department or institution was in any sense 'the very best'. There was no confidence that the immensely expensive Teaching Quality Assessment (or Subject Review as it was later called) had yielded anything like reliable evidence of teaching excellence (Newton, 2001; Morley, 2003; Ottewill and Macfarlane, 2004). Internal processes, including comments of external examiners, or student feedback, are also inherently unreliable as proxy measures of comparative teaching quality.

There is also a theoretical consideration that makes any comparative judgement about teaching problematic. The notion of excellence in teaching is highly contested because any claim to excellence must be relative to the goals being pursued (Skelton, 2005: 21-37). Excellent teaching relating to enhancing student employability, for example, might be very different from excellent teaching to create critical researchers. If no single set of criteria can be found that would meet universal agreement, then no judgement of overall excellence is available. In the US, the National Student Engagement Survey (NSSE, 2006), as well as earlier work by Astin (1993a), for example, has enabled comparative judgements to be made, based on some agreed criteria of what constitutes 'effective educational practices' (Kuh and Pascarella, 2004). However, in the UK there is no equivalent long term research data available, although the recently introduced National Student Survey and the other data gathered at the Teaching Quality Information website (www.tqi.ac.uk) may in time provide what is necessary.

The consequence of these considerations was that each bidder was required to specify what they considered to be excellent about their practice, what criteria were being used to make that judgement and what evidence was available to show that these criteria had been met. Some in the bidding process grappled with the concept of 'excellence' through a process of critical debate, while for others it was treated uncritically as if it was self-evident: 'At the top of the organisation it was sort of taken for granted that we had pockets of teaching excellence lying about the place' (O.B.S.8).

Some claimed that the notion of excellence presented no problem because reputation and testimonials from a variety of sources concurred in the judgement of excellence:

> We didn't have any difficulty defining excellence but that was mainly because, once we had found the material, others tended to do that for us, in that the external examiners, visitors, people who were interested in what we were doing all provided their own testimonies, but I don't think excellence was a problem.
>
> (O.B.F.11)

Several were suspicious that there would be a hidden, unspecified set of criteria operating in the selection process, and did their best to second guess what would most impress the Funding Council (Gosling and Hannan, 2007): 'I think there was a feeling that there would be support for institutions that were trying to achieve a particular mission and therefore were demonstrating excellence in that context' (N.C.F.14).

Others tried to pick up clues about what the selection criteria would be from meetings they attended with the Funding Council: 'There became a lot more emphasis on dissemination internally but also dissemination externally and through the HE Academy – that you should have links with other bids – how you are going to reach employers' (N.B.S.16).

But the lack of clarity about what constituted excellence and what evidence would count for demonstrating excellence created real anxiety for bidders trying to determine if they had guessed correctly:

> Some people have felt that because the notion of excellence was very much left open for you to define that they were writing almost in a vacuum. You never know if you have got it right ... when you write the bid you have to say, am I going to hit the right buttons to get the tick from the assessor's checklist?
>
> (CHE.B.F.20)

In the absence of any clear guidance about what evidence of excellence was required, some bidders drew on a broad range of sources:

> We tried to draw fairly broadly upon sources of information because it was not entirely clear what evidence would be most convincing so we used a range of things; obviously Quality Assurance Agency subject review reports, external examiners' comments, comments from students that had been collected through our old internal process of quality monitoring.

Where there were professional bodies involved, if they had made written reports and had comments which we could draw upon we would use those as well. So we used a fairly broad base of evidence and as I say partly because it was not clear what the funding council would find most convincing really.

(N.C.SF.12)

The decision to allow multiple definitions of excellence and the lack of any judgement of rank ordering of teaching quality have continuing consequences for the CETL initiative. Across the sector it is well understood that bidding is a rhetorical act that requires specific skills. The explanation for some institutions being awarded multiple CETLs may not be that those institutions had more excellent teaching, but rather that they had managed the bid-writing process exceptionally successfully. It is also clear from our research into the bidding process that some individuals and groups devoted much more effort to bid-writing for a CETL, and were more successful in gaining institutional support for their efforts, than in other institutions. As a result, those who have been awarded the title of 'excellence' are not necessarily regarded by others as the undisputed leaders in their pedagogic field:

It was to build on existing excellence. Well, if you look at the existing evidence that was quoted, things like the Fund for the Development of Teaching and Learning awards and the teaching quality assessment scores, very little of either of those was judged on classroom teaching and outcomes for students.

(N.C.F.14)

Although this comment may look like a case of 'sour grapes' by those who were unsuccessful, the conclusion drawn is actually intrinsic to the selection process itself. The important consequence is that the idea that the 'excellent' will 'disseminate' their practice to others on the basis of their being found to be the 'best' may be undermined in the eyes of some by the perceived lack of legitimacy of the designation of 'excellence'.

In recognition of this reality, some CETL directors chose to emphasise their responsibility to develop excellence rather than their having been rewarded for being excellent. That is to say they emphasised that the Centre's role was to research and promote excellent practice, without presupposing that excellence has, or indeed will be, achieved. This more dynamic understanding of excellence reflects the fact that, somewhat paradoxically, CETL bidders were required to strike a delicate balance between arguing that some level of excellence had been achieved, but also that further development of that practice could also occur. This clearly implies that being excellent was not to be regarded as an absolute state as endorsed in the Invitation to Bid which states that 'We do not attempt to define excellence in absolute or "gold standard" terms' (HEFCE, 2004: paragraph 50).

A further issue is created by the multiplicity of definitions of excellence that were encouraged by the CETL initiative. Because each bid defined excellence in its own way, there was no consistency in what is to be regarded as 'excellent'. Indeed CETLs even within the same broad subject area may be premised on contradictory values and incompatible practice. For example within the design field, one CETL is advocating 'a distinctive form of experiential learning that is student-centred, research-led and resource-rich, it blends learning-through-making and learning-through-interpretation in creative design where object scholarship is central' (HEFCE, 2005: 13) while another, also involving design students, talks in terms of students being 'carefully prepared for learning that is designed, supported and assessed with strong employer and professional body input and thus highly relevant to professional development' (HEFCE, 2005: 40). Ideologically, and in practice, these two CETLs are operating with conceptions of excellence that are very far apart.

Does this matter? It has been argued that the language of excellence has become 'increasingly hollow and meaningless' (Walker, 2006: 138) and the appeal to excellence 'marks the fact that there is no longer any idea of the university, or rather that the idea has now lost all content' (Readings, 1996: 39). In our view it is right that excellence in teaching should remain a contested area for debate and that striving for excellence should be regarded as an always incomplete process. The significance of taking this view is its implication for the 'dissemination' of outcomes from CETLs, since it follows that if excellence is indeed contested then no simple causal theory of transferability of 'best practice' across the sector is defensible. What is needed is a more critical debate about the meaning of excellence and the different kinds of teaching excellence that may be pursued. Such a debate cannot take place without consideration of what the role of the university is in a modern society. There is little evidence that this debate occurred during the process of awarding CETLs in 2004–2005.

Democratisation

Another consideration which seems to have been influential in the decision to allow multiple, and self-defined, conceptions of excellence relates to the strategic goal of the CETL initiative. Informal conversations with key personnel suggest that the unspoken goal of the initiative was to reward and invest in institutions where teaching was being taken seriously as a strategic objective as demonstrated through an active teaching and learning strategy (there is a hint of this in HEFCE, 2004: paragraph 52). Although there was no explicit intention to exclude institutions which had a strong research orientation, it was intended that institutions which were primarily teaching orientated should be able to access this generous funding as a reward for their commitment to teaching and student learning. The widening of the criteria and the abandonment of any 'gold standard' of excellence, discussed earlier in this chapter, and the decision to allow thematic areas of excellence (HEFCE, 2004: paragraph 29), are evidence of the desire to democratise the conception of excellence. In order to achieve this objective, it was necessary to design a selection process that would not simply reflect existing reputational hierarchies.

As Astin pointed out, and his comments about the US apply equally to the UK, 'excellence' in higher education tends to be viewed in two ways:

> The *reputational* view equates excellence with an institution's position in the hierarchical pecking order that is so much part of our folklore in American higher education, a folklore we quantify by doing reputational surveys. The *resources* view equates excellence with such things as the test scores of entering students, the endowment, the student-faculty ratio and the size of the library.
>
> (Astin, 2000: 182)

He goes on to say that since the two views are mutually reinforcing they produce the same rankings. He also argues that reputational and resources approaches to excellence are flawed because they fail to address the key issue of the education of the student. So he suggests 'Why not define the "excellence" of institutions in terms of their ability to develop the talents of the students?'. He calls this a 'talent development view of excellence':

> Its premise is that excellence lies in the institution's ability to affect its students favorably, to enhance their intellectual and scholarly development, and to make a positive difference in their lives. The 'most excellent' institutions are, in this view, those that have the greatest impact – 'add value' as economists would say, to students' knowledge and personal development.
>
> (Astin, 2000: 182)

This argument has been taken up more recently by Kuh and Pascarella (2004) when they challenge the received view about what makes a college excellent. They suggest that 'In the minds of most people, the best colleges are those that are the most selective' (p. 53). By looking at the findings from the National Survey of Student Engagement, they conclude that 'our results clearly show that institutional selectivity is a weak indicator of student exposure to good practices in undergraduate education' (p. 56) and that 'attendance at a selective college or university in no way guarantees that students will be more likely to engage in effective educational practices than their counterparts at less selective schools' (p. 57).

In line with this thinking, the Invitation to Bid stated that the CETL initiative will use 'measures or evidence of the value added by teachers' engagement with students' as a 'characteristic of excellence' (HEFCE, 2004: paragraph 50), though as Brown (2006: 13) has pointed out 'no-one has yet come up with a robust way of measuring such "value added"'. So clearly did this send a signal to elite institutions that they could not assume that their excellence would be regarded as self-evident that, when one self-regarding elite institution succeeded in reaching the second round when most of its self-defined peers did not, it began to doubt whether it should even be playing this particular game:

> In fact when we got through the first round and I went back to talk to some colleagues in [my university] who are in research management they were horrified when I told them that X university and Y university hadn't got through the first round. They said well, we shouldn't have got through the first round either, it is obviously a bad thing to have got through the first round! There was a lot of feeling that this was an initiative aimed specifically at teaching-based institutions.
>
> (O.B.S.8)

Actually the distribution of CETLs between so-called 'old' (that is pre-1992) and 'new' (post-1992) institutions was approximately equal, with 32 for the former and 31 for the latter. If we consider the number of institutions with CETLs, 24 are new universities and 22 are old universities,[4] and a further eight are university colleges. Of the 18 Russell Group universities (the most prestigious research-intensive universities in the UK) 11 were awarded CETLs. However:

> despite dominating the national 'league tables' for teaching quality, only one of the top six ranked institutions in England won a single 'Centre for Excellence in Teaching' while several teaching-focussed institutions with much weaker quality records acquired up to four each.
>
> (Gibbs, 2005: 7)

On balance, the lack of any direct correlation with the normal 'reputational' rankings suggests that the CETL process may be judged to have succeeded in 'democratising' teaching excellence. Although it is too early to judge whether the symbolic capital of being awarded a CETL will be sufficiently strong to overturn the normal perceptions of the stratification of higher education in the UK, it seems unlikely that this will be the case. Equally, although the funding for the CETLs is generous, it is not sufficient to make much of a dent on the enormous differentials between the capital wealth of institutions, nor does it come near to being a counterbalance to the resources available through the RAE:[5]

> I thought there was a big problem in resourcing teaching in the light of political drivers around the RAE but having a CETL wasn't going to significantly change that especially if you are not promising them past the first five years.
>
> (O.B.S.8)

Far from the policy altering the perception of staff who have been devoted to developing teaching within research institutions, the allocation of CETL funding is not regarded highly by some: 'It seems to me that I and the rest of us have put a huge amount of effort into these things and I'm not sure that it's not just a sop to shut us up' (O.B.S.13).

To this extent CETLs are unlikely to alter significantly an institution's self-perception about the status of its teaching or the perceptions of others of its status – though in the case of the two institutions that were awarded four CETLs this general conclusion may not apply. Nevertheless, there is some evidence of a new elite being formed based on the achievement of National Teaching Fellows, FDTL projects and now CETLs because these are all mutually reinforcing. For those institutions that have none of these awards, other means of making the claim for, and communicating, teaching quality will need to be found. Little is known at present whether awards such as these will have an impact in the competitive market for students.

Potential for development

As we have seen, it was intended that there should be a strong element of reward in the CETL initiative, but there was a price to be paid for this 'reward'. This was the requirement to present a 'business plan' which would 'support the case for further investment' (HEFCE, 2004: paragraph 61). Furthermore the case had to demonstrate that the CETL 'can achieve value for money' (HEFCE, 2004: paragraph 35). The bidding process therefore required institutions to show, not only that they had achieved a threshold of excellence, but that the proposed Centre had the potential to give a return on the money invested. The return looked for was both in terms of 'internal' development within the institution and also 'external' impact across the sector.

The inclusion of judgements about the potential for development in awarding CETLs marks a further point of difference from the RAE. In the RAE, departments do not have to put forward a business case for how they will spend the funds awarded for their research activity. They, therefore, do not have to demonstrate 'value for money' of the investment – rather they compete for receipt of the funding on the basis of their past performance. In the case of the CETLs, the panel's judgement about the feasibility of the development plan was critical.

The grounds for making this claim, in the absence of direct access to the adjudication criteria,[6] rest on two characteristics of the CETLs. The first relates to the distribution of subjects. HEFCE have published an analysis of what they refer to as 'the subject spread of funded CETLs' (HEFCE, 2005: 10), based on the number of times a particular subject term was used to describe the scope of bids that were subsequently approved for funding. However, the picture emerging from this analysis is misleading, since some subjects which appear to be represented by a CETL do not in fact have one relating principally to their interests. For example under 'linguistics, classics and related subjects' there appear to be seven CETLs, but in practice there is no CETL that is involved in developing classics teaching. Similarly by classifying 'historical and philosophical studies' together, the absence of a philosophy CETL is hidden. We cannot read into this that there is no excellent teaching in classics or in philosophy, nor that proposals that would have benefited those subject communities were not available. On the contrary, these subjects were judged to have high quality teaching in the Quality Assurance Agency's subject review process and there is good reason to think that there is a significant need, and therefore room for potential to be realised, for pedagogical research and development within them (Macdonald-Ross, 2005). It is simply that the adjudication of the bids has had the result of excluding those subjects from the CETLs. Furthermore, the selection of relatively few humanities CETLs exacerbates the failure of these subjects in another recent competitive bidding process, the Fund for the Development of Teaching and Learning.

The second ground for arguing that it was the development of 'projects', rather than the excellence of the teaching, that was critical in the selection process is the nature of the pedagogic focus of the CETLs. If we consider the published summaries of the CETLs (HEFCE, 2005), which might reasonably be viewed as a way of identifying what was considered to be their most important features, we find that 32 of the 74 CETLs explicitly mention virtual learning, web-based resources, e-learning or similar terms. Also, there is a notable emphasis on student preparation for employment running through most of the CETLs. In 52 of the summaries terms such as work-based learning, placements, career management skills, professional development and employer partnerships are mentioned.

We suggest that the bias towards funding CETLs with an emphasis on computer-based learning and employability-related themes cannot be interpreted to mean that these are areas of teaching where there is noticeably more excellent practice. On the contrary, both these areas might be argued to be relatively new and developing fields where excellence remains to be further defined. It seems more likely that the emphasis in these directions reflects the dominance of the vocational/instrumental view of higher education and the desire of the Funding Council to further promote the use of e-learning.

What seems to have happened in the CETL selection process is that the term 'exceptional' has been interpreted not in the sense of 'exceptional quality' but rather in the sense of being distinctive or innovative. If this is right then the CETLs do not necessarily reflect the 'brightest and best' in teaching in higher education in England, rather they reflect the particular choices made by the selection panel to favour certain sorts of bids. There are CETLs which managed to buck the general trend, but that does not undermine the claim that innovative teaching processes have generally been favoured over traditional teaching methods. This illustrates one way in which the neo-liberal project of rewarding 'the very best' was abandoned in favour of more developmental approach. By funding development projects, rather than rewarding excellence in the sense of 'the best', the selection process has undermined its own rhetoric.

A further issue here is that the emphasis on the use of new equipment creates a difficulty for the ultimate transferability of the CETL outcomes. If the capital spend is integral to the success of the pedagogy then the work of the CETL will not be easily transferable to other institutions that are not also in receipt of the munificent CETL funding. Consequently, where the approach being adopted by a CETL is predicated on new capital spending, there are serious questions about the replicability of its findings to other less generously funded parts of the sector.

Policy aspirations for the CETL initiative

HEFCE has been clear about the aspirations it has for the CETLs: 'Collectively, they will mark a significant change in the standing and aspirations of teachers in higher education and in the depth and confidence of sector-wide understanding of what constitutes effectiveness in teaching and learning' (HEFCE, 2004: paragraph 20).

This aspiration refers to a significant change across the whole sector, so, from a policy analysis perspective, the key issue is why did the policymakers prefer to offer large sums to a minority of 'winners' rather than spread the resources over all HEIs? Clearly with the funds that they have at their disposal it is very likely that the CETLs will bring significant benefits to the institutions, or the parts inhabited by the CETLs, that have been 'rewarded'. But, as one recipient of a CETL award confided to us, after visiting another technology-led CETL, the impact on institutions which have not been awarded a CETL is questionable:

> They're building wonderful new shiny offices, wonderful shiny new kit. It's great for those students, fantastic for those students. I went to one where the students have got a wonderful new media centre, so for those students at XX University – what that is contributing to the sector is absolutely negligible, but for those particular students, for that particular university that's great.
>
> (O.B.S.24)

The question that remains is by what mechanisms, or by what processes of organisational change, will the CETLs bring about the aspirations of the policymakers to transform the status of teaching in higher education across the whole sector?

We can only speculate that the thinking was based on the psychology of both financial and status incentives. As we have argued in this chapter, the idea seems to have been to offer rewards which would be sufficiently attractive to provide a reason for research-intensive universities to give greater priority to teaching and to reward those institutions which were already treating teaching seriously. But, as the following parable illustrates, offering prizes does not always alter behaviour in the ways intended:

> One day there were children at a lovely party. The party was being spoiled because some children were being well-behaved but others were being naughty. Unfortunately the naughty children were getting all the attention and even the well-behaved children secretly wished they could be naughty too.
>
> The grown-ups decided the answer was to give out some sweeties (lots of them), but only to the nicely behaved children. They reckoned that the naughty ones would want the sweeties so much that they would stop being naughty and behave just like the good children.
>
> When the sweeties were first offered, all the children tried to show how well-behaved they were, but when it became clear that only the children who the grown-ups decided were good would get the sweeties, the naughty ones just carried on being naughty.
>
> Some of the naughty children thought 'I didn't want those sweeties anyway, because I've already got lots of sweeties and I can always get more when I want to'.
>
> Others thought 'It's really so much more fun being naughty (and everyone looks up to me because I am so naughty), so I can do without the sweeties'.
>
> Some thought, 'If only horrible goody-goody children like that get the sweeties, I'm glad that I didn't get any. I wouldn't want anyone to think that I was a good-goody. I prefer to be in the naughty group'.
>
> But then the naughty ones noticed that some of the children who were getting the sweeties weren't really good children at all, but were only pretending to be good so that they could get the sweeties. They thought 'That's not fair. While they were pretending to be good, so that could get some sweeties, they were being just as naughty as they were before. But they are just getting better at making the grown-ups think they are good'.
>
> The grown-ups noticed that the good children, who had been awarded the sweeties because they were well-behaved, carried on being well-behaved and felt very happy. However, there were lots of well-behaved children who didn't get the sweeties and they were very unhappy. Some naughty children were very pleased they got the sweeties without having to stop being naughty and the naughty children who didn't get the sweeties just carried on being naughty and began to think of ways they could steal the sweeties from the good children while they weren't looking.

Conclusion

The policy of focusing on and rewarding 'excellence' has proved to be contentious in a variety of ways that we have explored in this chapter. Since many bid-writers were uneasy with the ideological assumptions of a selective and competitive process, many have done their best to subvert or ameliorate the potentially more severe effects of divisiveness both within their institutions and across the sector. Writing this in late 2006, there is as yet little evidence that the CETL initiative has led to significant changes of behaviour in either teaching or research-orientated institutions that will substantially enhance the status of teaching, or redress the balance in perceived status between teaching and research. However, it is still too early to make judgements about this, although the continuing doubts about whether there will be another round of CETL awards has undermined the incentive for those institutions that did not succeed last time to learn from their mistakes.

What implications does the CETL initiative have for our conception of teaching excellence? As we have argued in this chapter, the neo-liberal project of rewarding 'the very best' was moderated by a more democratised concept of excellence. As a consequence reputational hierarchies and taken-for-granted notions of the 'very best departments' have been challenged. Relatively low status institutions committed to widening participation in higher education have been awarded CETLs and this may contribute to a wider debate about what we understand by excellent teaching. However, the resilience of traditional hierarchies should never be underestimated. There are ambiguities about how excellence was understood during the selection process and there may be subsequent doubts about whether the CETLs can succeed in demonstrating their excellence in ways which others recognise. There are evidently concerns about whether the CETL initiative can indeed 'celebrate, recognise and promote excellence' as effectively as was intended, notwithstanding the amount of money invested.

We end, nevertheless, on an optimistic note. It is clear already that, within the institutions that have been awarded a CETL and those working in partnership with them, we are beginning to see a process of intensive development of the higher education curriculum. New ways of interacting with other institutions and with employers have been introduced and tested. There has been considerable technical innovation. Pedagogical research is being conducted into the impact of these changes. The higher education landscape in England has undoubtedly been changed by the introduction of CETLs. We shall observe with interest how widespread those changes become and how far teaching and learning achieve the enhanced status hoped for by the authors of this initiative.

Notes

1 Individual interviewees are coded in terms of their institution (N for post-1992 university, O for pre-1992 university, CHE for then college of higher education, FE for collaborating further education college), their own role (B for bidder, C for a coordinator or manager, BC if both) and the end result of the application or applications with which they were involved (S for success, F for failure and SF where the person was involved with more than one bid with different outcomes).

2 Learning and Teaching Support Network. This was comprised of 24 Subject Centres

and the Generic Centre. From 2004 the Subject Centres were incorporated into the Higher Education Academy.

3 The RAE is a national exercise conducted every six years to assess the quality of UK research and to inform the selective distribution of public funds for research by the four UK higher education funding bodies.

4 This includes two constituent colleges of the University of London.

5 According to the official government website (at www.hero.ac.uk/rae/AboutUs/) around £5 billion of research funds were expected to be distributed in response to the results of the 2001 RAE.

6 The researchers were refused permission to interview members of the CETL selection panel.

Part III

Developmental initiatives

Chapter 11

National strategies for promoting excellence in teaching

A critical review

Vaneeta-marie D'Andrea
(Central Saint Martins College of Art and Design, UK)

> At the best of times, faculty perceptions of rewarding 'teaching excellence' are outdated or non-existent, and are inevitably slow to react to the paradigm shifts in pedagogical methodologies that may be taking place. Appropriate reward or promotion systems thus do not develop at the same pace as curriculum reform, despite the increasing need to recognise the role of educators in student learning and innovative curriculum.
>
> (McLean, 2001: 9)

Introduction

In Skelton's (2005) earlier book he raises a number of important questions about how the notion of teaching excellence in higher education is understood and promoted, mainly in the UK, and with some examples from around the world. In this chapter I build on his work, and some of my earlier publications, by critically examining[1] similar questions in the context of international comparisons. I also apply Skelton's ideal type schema of teaching excellence and other scholars' work to examples of national schemes working to promote excellence in teaching. Although I am now convinced that rewarding teaching excellence needs to be context specific, my experience tells me that international comparisons provide many lessons for the local level and vice versa. Least of which, they prevent time wasted on reinventing the wheel in either context.

The debates surrounding what does or doesn't constitute teaching excellence (see Goldsmid *et al.*, 1977;[2] de Winter Hebron, 2001; Hillier and Vielba, 2001) and the criteria to assess it (see Elton, 1984, 1987) are not specifically considered in this chapter mainly because both areas are the focus of other chapters in this book. However, key understandings from work by scholars in both areas were applied to the process of creating the list of questions that I pose in the section to follow. In the interest of space, definitions of excellence, per se, are also not considered separately; instead they are highlighted in the discussion that follows when appropriate.

One noteworthy consideration from among the early debates on teaching excellence, is the corollary question posed about what constitutes 'excellent learning' (de Winter Hebron, 2001). Although Barr and Tagg's (1995) work on shifting the emphasis from teaching to learning had been around for half a decade, singling out *learning* in the context of defining teaching excellence was well ahead of the current discussions. In view of the fact that public concerns for the quality of the student learning experience have prompted the recent emphasis on teaching excellence, it is curious to me that *learning*, which is the goal of teaching, has been neglected in other work on the subject of teaching excellence to date.

National teaching recognition schemes:[3] key questions

The starting point for this chapter centres on a list of questions I have raised previously about higher education teaching recognition systems (D'Andrea, 2003). They are used here to help frame the discussion. Most of the questions considered have been deliberated at other times by a number of scholars in the field of teaching excellence. However, in this instance, in line with the focus of this chapter, I am limiting the discussion to the context of national schemes only. These questions help to identify the key issues that are most useful to local institutional or national policymakers when developing schemes to recognise teaching excellence.

It seems to me that the key question that needs to be asked of any scheme to recognise teaching is: what is the purpose of the recognition scheme? In other words, are the outcomes of a recognition scheme 'fit for purpose'? Some purposes have included defining the recognition as: an honour, a reward, a research grant or funding for scholarly activity on teaching/learning and/or any combination of these. Directly related to the purpose is the question of how does the scheme's design help to achieve it?

If the purpose of a teaching recognition scheme is to raise the status of teaching per se, making it an honour, reward or a grant could achieve this goal. Most awards in academe have been for outstanding contributions to research, the list is long and well-known to most academics. Thus, the first awards for teaching were designed to create similar recognition for teaching and influence the value placed on this element of the academic role. If the purpose of the scheme is also to change attitudes towards teaching as a professional activity, again, any of these approaches to recognition of teaching will suffice because any of them could inspire other academics to take teaching more seriously.

However, if the scheme is being designed to bring about change in approaches to teaching an honour and/or reward alone will not be sufficient. This is because the main outcome of these awards/rewards will be to recognise the person or team's contribution to the student experience but this does not in and of itself necessarily influence the work of other teachers to become excellent in their approach to teaching and learning. A grant to carry out research or scholarship on approaches to teaching and learning would only be sufficient if it included an element of 'going public' (see Shulman, 1993) with the outcomes so that they could be shared and debated among colleagues.

If the scheme is attempting to act as a change agent to improve the quality of the learning experience for students, none of the three (honour, reward, grant) will be able to achieve this without a linked infrastructure to create the critical mass needed to influence this change (see D'Andrea and Gosling, 2001). The development of a critical mass of pedagogic scholars ties in closely with another question: whether award/reward recipients have any obligation to give back anything to the sector, their disciplinary group, their institution, their faculty/school/department, and/or their students? If the answer is yes they do have an obligation, this would require the design of the recognition schemes to have built-in expectations and opportunities for sharing and exchange to take place within the usual academic fora: for example, professional seminars, conferences, journals and books.

Some other related questions come to mind, for example, do awardees have an obligation to provide some service to the academic community in order to influence the majority of academics to engage with teaching as a professional activity? Similarly do they have a professional obligation to be a role model for new colleagues and provide a form of mentoring on teaching and learning as often occurs during postgraduate study when research-related skills are being developed? Correspondingly do awardees have an obligation to report their work to the larger academic community as is done with their subject-based research? The answers to each of these questions would, again, influence the design of the recognition scheme.

There are other related questions that concern responsibilities the scheme itself needs to fulfil in order to achieve other types of outcomes. For example, if the purpose is to not only acknowledge excellence but to promote its continued development, is there an obligation for the scheme to provide awardees with professional development support such as, think-tank style residential seminars to enhance their teaching even more? Some of these questions are less theoretical than others since some have been addressed by national teaching recognition systems currently in place.

Cross-national comparisons of national schemes to recognise excellence in teaching

Information is available on several national recognition schemes, albeit to differing degrees of comprehensiveness. Table 11.1 summarises this data for Australia, Canada, New Zealand, Sweden, the UK and the US. This section of the chapter considers the overall patterns evident from the summary data in this table and attempts to answer the questions posed in the previous section in order to get a clearer picture of the structure and function of these schemes.

Work at institutional level to recognise and reward excellent teachers has in most cases preceded the development of national recognition schemes.

Meta-level studies of institutional schemes provide some important lessons for those developing national level schemes. For example, the work of Gibbs and Habeshaw (2002), carried out in the UK, identified a number of outstanding issues and useful outcomes related to institutional schemes. They found that often there was confusion between definitions of competence and excellence (and leadership), which meant that it was unclear what schemes were seeking to recognise, i.e. what their purpose was. Also they noted that the emphasis was more likely to be on past performance and not future enhancement of teaching and learning. Furthermore they indicated that the impact on teaching developments was greater when smaller awards were given to larger numbers of staff compared to the impact achieved from big awards to a select few. They found that team awards can be just as important as individual awards in achieving the goals of a recognition scheme. Finally, they pointed out that the short-term glitz of prizes create fewer permanent long-term gains for teaching careers and core roles of academics than recognition programmes that are embedded in the academic life of the recipient via, for example, promotion schemes. The national schemes discussed below demonstrate both similar confusions and similar positive outcomes.

In addition to this work, Skelton (2003) has added three key issues which national schemes would ignore at their peril. First, he indicates that not only, as Gibbs and Habeshaw found, is excellence confused with other dimensions of professional behaviour its meaning is 'highly contested and situationally and historically contingent'. He went on to note that: 'There ... needs to be an awareness of how criteria for "teaching excellence" and /or lists of attributes of excellent teaching relate to meta-level concepts' (2003: 188) and the broader purposes of higher education. Second, if educational change is a goal of the scheme then it must seek to recognise how 'ordinary' teachers understand change as well as those singled out for recognition. He maintains that 'ordinary' teachers only accept and adopt new practices if these are underpinned by values they share. Thus for change to occur through a recognition scheme this would have to be built into a dissemination process. Third, and contrary to my previous views, he sees rewarding the Scholarship of Teaching and Learning (SoTL) as a means of bridging the relationship between teaching and research.

Purposes of the teaching recognition schemes: stated and/or implied

The main purpose of all national recognition schemes, reviewed for this chapter, is raising the profile of teaching and learning through some kind of award that is meant to attach lifetime acclaim to the recipient (see Table 11.1). Whether knowingly or not, each system embodies the work of the UK higher education researcher Lewis Elton, who noted a decade and a half ago that 'if teaching is to take its rightful place by the side of research, there must be appropriate rewards for teaching excellence' (1991: 112). At about the same time that Elton made these comments, the Higher Education Research and Development Society of Australasia (HERDSA) produced a *Checklist for Valuing Teaching*. Item no. 35 of this list asked the following questions in the context of the Australasian region: 'Are there awards, prizes, incentives or forms of recognition (other than promotion) ... for excellence in teaching? Is such recognition available for both individuals and groups?' (Boud, 1990: 163). Preceding both Elton's comment and HERDSA's questions North Americans, halfway around the world again, had begun to take the initiative to reward teaching through both awards and fellowships. For example, in the US the Council for Advancement and Support of Education (CASE) awards had been in place since 1981 and in Canada the prestigious 3M Fellowships had been functioning since 1986.

The third oldest scheme to be developed was designed specifically as an honour. The Society of Living Pedagogues which was in existence in Sweden from 1990–2004 (hgur.hsv.se/activities/lps/index_lps.htm, accessed 18 April 2006) was essentially a closed society not unlike the royal societies of learned scholars and researchers in the UK and the so-called 'privileged' societies (Edgerton, 1994) in the US. Membership was through nominations from members or from the Union of Students at higher education institutions. Interestingly the status of members was further acknowledged by their work as disciplinary higher education experts to the Council for the Renewal of Higher Education. Another unique dimension of the scheme was an expectation that 'members [would] also take an active part in the training of new faculty, sharing their experience of problems in undergraduate education with new colleagues' (hgur.hsv.se/activities/lps/index_lps.htm, accessed 18 April 2006). Funding restrictions brought an end to governmental financial support in the mid-1990s (personal communication with A. Lundh, 2006) and it appears the organisation ended its activities in 2004. Its website is scheduled to be discontinued at the end of 2006.

The rewards offered by the various national schemes vary from membership of a prestigious and privileged exclusive society to think-tank residential retreats to personal prizes in excess of the equivalent of £20,000. The Council for Advancement and Support of Education (CASE) in the US awards four prizes annually while there are 250 prizes given annually by the Carrick Awards for Australian University Teachers. The latter reflects the point made by Gibbs and Habeshaw earlier that the more awards the more likely there could be greater impact.

In Scotland the PROMOTE project has studied institutional and departmental approaches to rewarding and recognising teaching. The interviews with awardees indicate that 'the importance of financial reward lies not in motivation for recipients, but, as interviewees regularly repeated, in formal acknowledgement by the institution of the value of what is being rewarded – achievement and excellence in teaching' (Earl and Mcarthur, 2003: 17). Similar feelings were expressed by others in the study from different universities across Scotland. This, it would seem, is an important understanding for national schemes to apply as well.

Table 11.1 Focus of national recognition schemes for teaching excellence (stated or implied)

Focus of awards	Australia	Canada	New Zealand	Sweden	UK	US
Raise profile/status of teaching	✓	✓	✓	✓	✓	✓
Recognise and celebrate individual impact on student learning		✓	✓		✓	
Provide national focus for institutional T&L schemes					✓	
Recognise and encourage excellence	✓	✓	✓		✓	
Promote good practice		✓	✓		✓	
Encourage 'going public' with teaching ideas			✓	✓		✓
Enhance career development		✓				
Highlight innovative and practical approaches to student learning	✓					✓
Encourage changes in approaches to teaching					✓	✓
Encourage research or SoTL				✓	✓	✓
Promote mentoring, on teaching, of new academics						✓

Other rewards include trophies and exclusive membership identity pins; both the Living Pedagogues and the Carnegie Scholars have lapel pins. The latter are given out ceremoniously at the end of the first residential programme. In some cases rewards are combined with grants to engage in scholarship or research that have specific outcomes required. There are two that clearly require this type of activity of the recipients: the Carnegie Scholars (CS) programme in the US and the National Teaching Fellowship (NTFS) Scheme in the UK (see Skelton 2005, Chapter 10, for a comparison of the NTFS, CS programme and the Canadian 3M awards).

For Elton (1991) excellence and change are inextricably intertwined. He suggests that without change there is or can be little excellence. In his view:

excellence in teaching should be measured at least in part by the following:

a   the willingness and ability to change
b   resource provision to engender change
c   the institutional climate in which change is to take place.

(Elton, 1991: 109)

Several national schemes appear to encourage some kind of change in approaches to teaching and learning and, in effect, are designed for the kind of change agency at national level that Elton describes at local institutional level. Thus these schemes would be, in Elton's view, promoting excellence as well as acknowledging it. The schemes that include a requirement for scholarship or research also include an expectation for dissemination of the work; again this includes the NTFS and CS programmes. The CS programme holds an annual conference for CS Fellows, and now other interested parties, where scholars 'go public'. The UK NTFS Fellows are encouraged to present their work at the national conference of the Higher Education Academy (HEA) which in fact also provides administrative support for the NTFS competition.

Again few programmes provide direct support to the recipients. The Swedish system provided support for regional chapter meetings of members 'where current undergraduate issues are being discussed' (hgur.hsv.se/activities/lps/index_lps.htm, accessed 18 April 2006). The 3M programme in Canada brings all winners together at a three-day retreat to build a recognised teaching and learning 'community'. The NTFS has recently done something similar for its winners. The CS programme requires recipients to attend three separate 'think-tank' style residential seminars, lasting over a month in total. These are undertaken during the first year of the honour in order to develop and complete a SoTL project and build a community of teaching scholars.

Other issues linked to teaching recognition schemes

A number of other issues arise when considering comparisons of national schemes to recognise excellence in teaching. A few of these are considered below.

Student experience

One of the interesting findings of this review of national recognition schemes is how few directly require student views or involvement. In fact, the CASE award is the only one that requires letters of support from the candidates' students. And like the NTFS scheme in the UK, it has a student on the selection panel as well. In Sweden students could nominate candidates for the award of Living Pedagogue. Despite all the talk in higher education about increasing the student voice, it appears that it is somehow lost in the discussions of excellence at national level.

It seems to me that the student voice would be more represented if the following actions were taken:

1   students, via their representative organisations, nominated the candidates for the awards as was done in Sweden;
2   the selection criteria were explicit about the importance of undergraduate education as evident in the CASE award in the US which states:

The primary characteristic the judges consider is an *extraordinary dedication to undergraduate teaching*, which should be demonstrated by excellence in the following areas:

- Impact on and involvement with undergraduate students;
- Scholarly approach to teaching and learning;
- Contributions to under-graduate education in the institution, community, and profession; and
- Support for colleagues and current and former undergraduate students.

(case.org accessed 10 April 2006)

3   students were directly involved as novice researchers in any grants or scholarly activities supported by the rewards.

Research and teaching

The academic debates on what constitutes excellence in teaching have often been made through a comparison of the outputs of research and teaching. Elton (1991) and Edgerton (1994) have both presented eloquent cases for how this is both needed and how it can be done. The AAHE project *From Idea to Prototype: The Peer Review of Teaching* (Hutchings, 1995) was the first attempt at national (US) level to establish how teaching excellence could be assessed in ways similar to that of research. Both Edgerton's and Hutchings' work on the teaching portfolio paved the way for further developments to assess teaching in ways equal to research. More recently discussions on the scholarship of teaching and learning (SoTL) have added to this (Huber, 2000; Skelton, 2003, 2005; D'Andrea and Gosling, 2005). Skelton's (2003) argument that:

excellence and SoTL need to be connected is quite thought provoking for me. My view has been that when they are combined they confound each other and can limit the possible development of a pedagogic scholarly community. I was uncertain that the connection would be possible since, when some scholars are singled out as excellent and others not, individual recognition can be a limiting factor to building a scholarly community. However Skelton's argument that it is important to link the two is so carefully constructed that I find it quite convincing. It has, in fact, caused me to reconsider my own views.

(D'Andrea, 2006)

In Skelton's view linking the two challenges a performance focus to teaching excellence and shifts it to excellence 'grounded in experience and accumulated wisdom' and the opportunity to disseminate teaching scholarship with greater authority (Skelton, 2005: 151).

Quality enhancement and assurance

Where national higher education systems include a separate quality assurance (QA) review function, using excellence awards as a quality indicator could help to refocus the quality review to enhancement (QE). Elton's (1992) distinction may help to understand how this is possible. His view is that *quality As* are assurance, accountability, audit and assessment and *quality Es* are enhancement, enthusiasm, expertise and excellence (cited in Kulski and Groombridge, 2004: 46). Teaching excellence awards at Curtin University in Australia provide a direct link between QA (accountability and assessment) and QE (excellence and enhancement) through 'a portfolio-based approach to documenting teaching and learning' (Kulski and Groombridge, 2004: 55). For example:

Participation in the Teaching Excellence Award in 2000 was, for the School of Architecture, Construction and Planning a watershed experience. Documentation of the School's achievements in teaching and learning, and feedback from the 2000 judging panel, was affirming and motivating. The School's participation in 2000 stimulated greatly increased interest in teaching and learning, which is reflected in many ways in this (the 2002) submission. The overall impact on the School's performance has been substantial and there has been a clearly observable change in the teaching culture.

(quoted in Kulski and Groombridge, 2004: 54)

At a national level a portfolio approach similar to the one used in the 3M programme in Canada could be used to shift the quality review processes from assurance to enhancement in those countries, such as the UK, where quality assurance systems prevail. A portfolio review would allow for a more holistic approach to the quality process by focusing on a range of qualitative teaching and learning activities and outcomes.

Professional disciplinary links

In a UK study (Warren and Plumb, 1999: 250), 'none of the institutions visited offered Faculty – or discipline-based awards'. If teaching awards have any value for improving the educational experience of students within specific subject disciplines and if, as others have indicated (Henkel, 2000; Becher and Trowler, 2001), disciplinary affiliation is an academic's primary allegiance, then it would seem that disciplinary associations have a responsibility to promote the teaching in the field by rewarding and recognising its own; in effect creating the next generation of disciplinary teaching scholars. A number of professional disciplinary organisations in the US have been doing so for several decades including the American Sociological Association, among others. However, even when there is the will to do this it can take significant time and energy to make this happen. As for example in medical education in the UK: 'Across almost a century, calls for reform were strikingly similar and included suggestions for rewarding and improving teaching. This call has been repeated persistently to the present day' (Aron *et al.*, 2000: 6).

Interestingly only one national scheme, the Carnegie Scholars programme, was based on disciplinary categories in the first instance and only since 2005 has it not been defined by disciplinary identities.

Final comments

Finally, in the end, no matter how well intended, erratic procedures (Knapper, 1997; Skelton, 2005), vagueness and lack of transparency (Menges, 1996), whether merit is considered part of the process (Edgerton, 1993) and tokenism (Weimer, 1991) are all seen as undermining the effectiveness of teaching awards as a mechanism for rewarding excellence. Each national system would benefit from reflecting on how these difficulties might be overcome.

Summary analysis, comment and forward actions

This section applies a number of analytical tools to data gathered for this chapter on national teaching recognition schemes. In the first instance Menges' (1996) 'simple' tests of effectiveness of reward schemes (if somewhat crudely applied) provides a set of factors which could be interrogated further. Second, Skelton's (2005) four-fold typology of meta-understandings of teaching excellence adds a theoretical dimension to the analysis. Edgerton's (1993) report of the American Association of Higher Education's study of faculty (staff) priorities provides an interesting penultimate point about how little change has occurred in over a decade of thinking about rewarding and recognising teaching and how little the current national schemes have taken account of previous understandings and scholarship on recognising teaching. Finally, because this chapter is focused on national schemes, the potential of these for influencing national policies on teaching and learning is considered.

Menges has three tests to determine the effectiveness of teaching awards, albeit at institutional level:

1   the selection validity test;
2   the faculty motivation test; and
3   the test of public perceptions (see Figure 11.1).

As can be seen in Figure 11.1, each test has several aspects and a series of questions that could be applied to the national schemes under review in this chapter. Under the selection validity category accuracy and representativeness are both seen as essential tests of effective teaching awards. If the questions listed under accuracy are asked of the national schemes reviewed here, it is unclear from their own descriptions what core values underlie them other than to promote and value teaching and learning. However in the case of 'awareness of the criteria and procedures' these are now, because of the web, available to anyone who is interested. What is less well known is the exact process used in selecting winners. Huber cited in Bartlett (2003) outlined the process for the CASE awards in the US and Skelton (2005) discussed this in regard to the NTFS in England. Bartlett notes how difficult most judges find the process of selection and Skelton (2003) recommends changes to the NTFS process to make it, as he notes, 'less adversarial'. Future plans of the recipients are as far as can be determined only implied in those national schemes that include project work. Whether recipients are superior to the criteria would only be applicable to those schemes that are seeking to locate excellent teachers per se, such as the CASE and Carrick awards. Similarly only the Carnegie scheme appears to have attempted to achieve representiveness, and only by disciplinary identity. Reports in England have suggested that the NTFS failed to represent the work of ethnic minorities (THES, 2000). In effect most schemes would fail the validity test.

Tests of motivation include numbers of awards available, range of awards to choose from and value commensurate with efforts to apply. Overall, as noted earlier, the full range of awards across the national schemes varies greatly with the Carrick awards coming closest to meeting these parts of the motivation tests. The NTFS scheme claims to provide significant feedback to unsuccessful applicants and seems to be the only scheme that would pass this element of the motivation tests. As for evidence of increased motivation against data such as increased numbers of applications, positive outcomes from the awards, increased discussions on teaching (including both formal and informal contexts), more innovations in teaching and concrete measurable outcomes in teaching evaluations, little is known at this time but it would be interesting to explore through further research whether there is any evidence of such outcomes in local and national excellence schemes.

Regarding tests of public perceptions, it would appear that in both the UK and the US there is some evidence that the NTFS and Carnegie schemes have provided increased support for funding innovations while the glitzy media coverage in the UK and Australia suggest the coverage of teaching excellence is broader but possibly not necessarily more positive. As for answering potential students' questions about the quality of teaching or funders' questions about aspects of teaching and learning, the overall limited number of awards could not ensure the answers to the former and the data available about awardees is too limited to ensure answers to the latter. Only a few schemes could claim to pass the tests of public perceptions.

1 Selection validity test
 • Accuracy
 o Reflect core values of institution
 o Faculty awareness of criteria and procedures
 o Triangulated data sources
 o Consider future plans of applicant as well as past successes
 o Recipients are superior to award criteria
 • Representativeness
 o Fair representation of fields
 o Fair representation of types of institutions (original had institutional situations)
 o Free of gender and ethnic bias [or any other demographic bias]

2 Test of motivation
 • Ensuring incentive value
 o Are there a sufficient number to warrant the effort to apply?
 o Is there a menu of awards to choose from?
 o Is the value of award as great as effort to apply?
 o Is feedback given to unsuccessful applicants?
 • Giving evidence of increased motivation
 o Are there increasing application rates?
 o Do recipients report positive outcomes after receiving the award?
 o Has informal discussion about teaching increased?
 o Do agendas of departments and committees contain more teaching related items?
 o Are teaching innovations more common?
 o Have course evaluations become more positive?

3 Test of public perceptions
 • Is media coverage more extensive and more positive?
 • Are questions about quality of teaching from prospective students more easily answered?
 • Are funders questions about aspects of teaching and learning better informed?
 • Has external funding for support of innovations increased?

Figure 11.1 Menges' three tests of effectiveness of teaching awards (based on Menges, 1996: 7–8).

Skelton (2005: 21–37) has provided a very useful four-fold typology to analyse understandings of teaching excellence in higher education. These include: traditional, performative, psychologised and critical. When national schemes are located within these four meta-understandings of teaching excellence, more and more are moving to fewer individual awards and becoming less psychologised in the process while possibly more performative in their focus. None could claim to be aimed at social critique, participatory dialogue or emancipation. And although most schemes promote innovations in teaching they tend toward more traditional social elite cultural reproduction models. In sum, the national schemes are not easily mapped against these four definitional types of teaching excellence which would seem to indicate there remains a great deal of confusion regarding their intent and purpose.

If the survey of faculty priorities carried out by the American Association of Higher Education, and reported by Edgerton (1993), is added to this analysis of national teaching recognition schemes, three of the 14 points under a heading entitled *Rethinking Recognition and Rewards* are especially relevant to the findings reported in this chapter. Although the points refer to faculty/staff reflections on their institutional situations, the three points are worth re-stating in light of national level activity in this area during the past decade:

Rethinking recognition and reward
12. While teaching awards to individual faculty are increasingly seen as a token gesture, some institutions are contemplating interesting steps that could strengthen the role and impact that teaching awards can have.
13. In the commendable focus on re-examining their formal reward system, campuses may be neglecting opportunities to foster the intrinsic interest faculty have in teaching and professional service.
14. There is new talk of shifting the focus of evaluation and accountability from individual faculty to groups of faculty, especially academic departments. But most campuses are sneaking up on this agenda rather than tackling it head on.

(1993: 22–23)

Reflecting on the earlier discussions in this paper, it would appear that there is still work to be done at national level in all three of these areas. As is noted below, only two countries (US and UK) have contemplated strengthening the role and impact of teaching awards through creating cohorts of recognised teacher-scholars who are encouraged to engage in national debates on teaching and learning in higher education, let alone lead them. In most instances the awards are made and then little is heard from the awardees again. The shift from individual to group recognition is now possible in several schemes, for example the revised NTFS scheme now includes a new option for project teams to apply for awards however the teams still must include at least one individual national winner.

Finally, if as Hillier and Vielba have noted: 'Public definitions of excellence are rooted in particular ideologies and models of education and are located within particular political agendas' (2001: 7), policies at both local institutional and national levels could benefit from the development of cohort groups of award winners who could systematically influence higher education policy at these levels. This has only occurred in the UK through the NTFS interest group within the Higher Education Academy and in Sweden via the work of Living Pedagogues who served as experts to the Council for the Renewal of Higher Education representing their own substantive disciplines. It would seem that, if the main goal of national higher education teaching recognition programmes is to increase the status of teaching in society at large, then not to support the development of groups of award winners to engage in national debates on higher education teaching and learning is certainly a lost opportunity.

In summary, although well-intentioned, the policymakers in charge of the national teaching awards schemes reviewed in this chapter could benefit the current schemes by:

- reflecting on the decades of research available on teaching excellence in higher education;
- using Menges' tests to understand more about the effectiveness of the scheme;
- applying Skelton's meta-understandings to more fully articulate the purposes and underlying values of the scheme;
- creating a link between the awards/awardees and outcomes which are beneficial to higher education as a whole.

Notes

1 Here, I am guided by Skelton's (2005: 11) explanation of a critical approach to include:

1 'understanding teaching excellence as a contested concept';
2 seeking 'to identify the values and assumptions that underpin any understandings';
3 and bringing 'conflicting perspectives to bear on thought, action and self-reflection'.

2 It is interesting to note that Goldsmid *et al.* cite Moore and Tumin's work.
3 The questions raised here were originally prepared for discussions held by a UK Joint Task Group on Rewarding Excellence in Teaching. I was a member of this consultation group during 2003 in my role as Co-Director of the Higher Education Funding Council for England, National Coordination Team. I write here in a personal capacity.

Chapter 12

Teaching excellence in higher education in Japan

An evolving agenda

Hugo Dobson and Yukako Mori
(University of Sheffield, UK and Nagoya University, Japan)

Introduction

This chapter explores the motivations behind and impact of debates and initiatives surrounding teaching excellence in Japanese higher education institutes (HEIs). Following necessarily brief introductions to the idea of teaching excellence, the state of Japanese HEIs and the position of teaching and learning therein, the chapter explores recent initiatives and the main actors in the promotion of a teaching excellence agenda in Japanese higher education, including university teachers, students, government representatives and employers.

These developments have taken place within the contexts of a shift in Japan from an elite to a mass educational system over time, the concept of 'students as consumers' in an increasingly competitive and free-market environment, the responsiveness of higher education to the state of the Japanese economy and institutional diversification within Japanese HEIs. These issues are of concern in most developed societies but have particular significance in Japan as a result of its declining birth rate. Ultimately, discussion of teaching excellence in the Japanese context has tended towards a 'performative' understanding (see Skelton, 2005: 29–31).

What is teaching excellence?

Teaching excellence is a slippery term. For anybody who works in a HEI, it is commonly heard and generally regarded as something that should be worked towards. However, many academics and students would agree that it tends to be inchoate and subjective. Nobody is likely to dispute the desirability of excellence in the teaching and learning that takes places in HEIs. However, what teaching excellence means concretely, beyond simply having a flair for teaching, often goes unexplained. In its place is presented a monolithic teaching excellence that is regarded as a worldwide movement, promoting a single unified understanding motivated by a neo-liberal retreat of the state. This culture of excellence ensures that everybody strives for excellence believing that this excellence is attainable. No zero-sum game is operating. Everyone can be excellent. So runs the mantra.

Like many recent initiatives and concepts, teaching excellence finds its origins in the US. Some decades ago HEIs in the US introduced a number of strategies in response to the diversification of the student body and the perceived decline in the status of teaching relative to that of research. In particular, the work of Ernest Boyer and the Carnegie Foundation for the Advancement of Teaching promoted discussion of excellence in a number of US research-intensive universities (Frost and Teodorescu, 2001). Since then, a number of studies have been published that put forward their own understandings of, and route maps towards achieving, teaching excellence (Astin, 1993b; Frost and Teodorescu, 2001; Allen and Allen, 2003; Ruben, 2004). Debates in the UK on teaching excellence have centred upon common concerns and similar solutions (Elton and Partington, 1993).

To cite a non-Western context, the discussion of teaching excellence in Malaysian HEIs has been very closely framed around and motivated by the norm of developmentalism and enhancing Malaysia's economic indicators. The policy push provided by the administration of Prime Minister Mahathir aimed at projecting the Malaysian economy through the industrial stage of development and firmly into the post-industrial stage, embracing along the way the role that information and communications technology (ICT) has to play in a globalizing economy (Mazelan *et al.*, 1999).

However, the above discussions of teaching excellence have tended to be handbook-type approaches to becoming an excellent teacher. In contrast, Skelton (2005) has sought to engage with the debates critically and to this end provides an alternative and more critical framework for analysis. Skelton's critique understands teaching excellence as a contingent term whose meaning is dependent upon the underlying socio-economic and political contexts (Skelton, 2004: 452). In addition to the importance of context, Skelton's critical approach is built upon four understandings of teaching excellence: traditional, performative, psychologized and critical (Skelton, 2005: 21–37).

The first of these understandings is the traditional and emphasizes the original mission of Western European universities to encourage students to master their chosen subject. It is also built upon the elitism of higher education. In other words, teaching excellence results from the best institutions with the best facilities that attract the best students. A performative understanding of teaching excellence rests upon the performance of a HEI within the global economy. In marketing itself to the outside world and running the university as a business, measuring and quantifying activities such as teaching are seen to be crucial. Thus, teaching is a practice, and whether it is excellent or not, can be measured empirically and rewarded appropriately, alongside a whole host of statistical data on the university experience that is transparent and accessible by the user or potential customer.

Psychologized understandings of teaching excellence place the onus upon the relationship that exists between teacher and student and how this can obstruct or facilitate the student's learning experience. It is this relationship – not the respective individuals – that can result in excellence in teaching. It follows that the teacher is responsive and flexible in meeting the student's learning needs, otherwise a relationship cannot begin to flourish and excellence cannot be achieved. A critical understanding of teaching excellence is concerned with identifying and challenging existing power structures and systems of control, in addition to giving a voice to those who have been previously denied. Critical theorists stand in contrast to traditional and performative approaches by regarding the teacher's duty as one of assisting students in this quest (Skelton, 2005: 31–37).

It is often the case that the performative approach dominates the discussions of government, university managers, students who see themselves as customers and their fee-paying parents. Its primary enemy has been the traditional understanding of teaching excellence. Psychologized approaches are what are often found in induction courses for junior academics in HEIs. Critical approaches have yet to exert much influence on policy and practice (Skelton, 2005: 36–37).

The Japanese higher education system

In terms of hard figures, the importance of the Japanese higher education sector is clear. It is the second largest in the world after the US, with 508 junior colleges (234,000 students), 63 colleges of technology (59,000 students), 3,444 specialized training colleges (792,000 students) and 709 universities (2,809,000 students) as of 2004 (MEXT, 2005: 2–4). Within this system Japanese higher education is divided into public and private universities. Public universities tend to have a higher reputation than private universities and are organized in a hierarchical structure with the University of Tokyo at the very top; and within the University of Tokyo, the Faculty of Law playing a key role as the source of the majority of Japan's post-war politicians, bureaucrats and businessmen – the 'iron triangle' that has ruled post-war Japan. Next comes Kyoto University and the pre-war imperial universities. On the private side of the ledger, there are a number of universities close in reputation to that of the University of Tokyo, such as Waseda and Keio Universities.

Figures clearly demonstrate the massification of Japan's higher education system. In 1947 2.9 per cent of 18-year-olds attended a HEI, by 1980 this figure had risen to 38 per cent and by 1999 the figure of students in higher education had risen to 60 per cent (Goodman et al., 2007: 5–6). Private universities have chiefly contributed to this massification (Tsuruta, 2003: 126). In 1949, 92 private universities and 68 national universities existed; by 2000 there were 479 private and 99 national universities (Yoshida, 2002: 45).

The Japanese academic year begins in April and as regards admission to universities, entrance examinations are the key determinant. In fact, they have generated a mini-industry in crammer schools and a mindset that focuses family resources upon ensuring success for their children in entering the best university (for a detailed discussion see Takeuchi, 1997; Mori, 2002). As the Japanese higher education system is based upon the reputation of the university, it places 'more importance on the student's ability at the time of entrance, rather than on what has been achieved through the university experience' (Yonezawa, 2002: 128). This is an aspect of the system that has infuriated employers.

Once accepted, Japanese students experience an undemanding four years of rest and relaxation before they enter the world of work. They usually graduate with the minimum of effort and it has been argued that 'the role of universities in generating and imparting knowledge is less important than their capacity to define social status' (Hayes, 1998: 197).

The position of teaching in Japanese HEIs

The outsider's perception of the Japanese education system tends to be positive. For example, in January 1991, a UK government team of inspectors visited Japan to conduct a survey of its education system. The resulting report, entitled *Aspects of Upper Secondary and Higher Education in Japan*, found that:

> [The Japanese education system has] made a substantial contribution to the development of a powerful, competitive economy, a civilisation in which there is little petty crime and an economy in which the basic technological infrastructure is sound.
>
> (cited in Phillips, 2003: 174)

This positive perception of Japanese universities is backed up by a number of international rankings that have placed Japanese universities high up their tables (Asiaweek, 2000; ARWU, 2005; THES, 2005).

However, the extant literature on Japanese higher education argues against this apparent position of excellence (and even competence), especially when it comes to the quality of teaching. McVeigh regards higher education in Japan as a 'myth' and has argued that:

> There is a dark spirit plaguing the Japanese university classroom. It is the ghost of opinions suppressed, voices lost, self-expressions discouraged, and individuality restrained. This ghost is malevolent, and in its vengeance demands silence, self-censorship, and indifference from the students it haunts.
>
> (McVeigh, 2002: 3)

Refusing to fall back on cultural stereotypes based on Confucian learning such as 'shyness, modesty and humility', McVeigh blames the socialization of the system by university administration, the government and big business and is highly negative as to the possible success of any reform movement as a result of entrenched interests (McVeigh, 2002: 237–260).

Goodman has explained the problems that had emerged in learning and teaching in Japanese HEIs by the end of the twentieth century:

previously under the guise of academic freedom and a belief in the specialist nature of academic work, the teaching of academics had been left almost completely up to individuals. They designed their own syllabi, taught their own courses, set exams for their own students and marked their students' papers, all without external evaluation or reference to colleagues. The result was that, while some teaching was excellent, much of it was described as routine and unimaginative and, just as seriously, there was no coordination between courses within and across departments. A vicious circle developed as students became disillusioned and stopped attending classes; meanwhile, professors decried the lack of student commitment, yet still continued to graduate them on the basis that this was the university's duty after it had accepted them.

(Goodman, 2005: 14–15)

Lee-Cunin (2005) is one of the few to have focused upon Japanese student perceptions of the whole university experience and one of the many aspects she highlights is the feeling that teaching is often too specialized and distant. Typical student reactions were:

I have been doing my best to listen to the lecturer seriously and also to read the textbook but it does not make sense to make such an effort in his class. I want the lecturer not only to talk but also to consider how to teach, keeping in his mind what the students can understand.

(quoted in Lee-Cunin, 2005: 149)

Since students are spending a lot of money as well as time, I think that teachers should try to improve their skills in teaching. I think there are many teachers who do not make an effort to improve the way they teach although they are spending time on their own research.

(quoted in Lee-Cunin, 2005: 154)

A survey of graduates of well-established preparatory school demonstrated that 40 per cent of science students have problems understanding their lectures, whilst 30 per cent understand practically nothing (Mori, 2002: 38–39).

The 'big bang' and teaching excellence

The context in which recent Japanese discussions of teaching excellence have taken place mirrors that of the UK in several ways. First, the link between the education provided at university and the 'real world' of work and business has been of great concern over the decades and reforms have sought to enhance the economic utility of higher education, especially at a time of recession in the 1990s. Second, and closely related to the previous point, Japanese students have over recent years become much more savvy customers. It was decline of student interest in science and technology courses as a result of the poor quality of provision at national universities that led to serious attention being focused upon the problem by the government (Asonuma, 2002: 118). Third, globalization is impacting upon higher education systems across the world and has led to either cooperation or conflict as governments and people either embrace the opportunities that globalization provides or resist the pressure to converge. Japan is no exception and the internationalization of Japanese higher education has commanded a great deal of attention both in terms of internal internationalization, as seen in the goal of Prime Minister Nakasone Yasuhiro's administration (1982–1987) to invite 100,000 foreign students to Japan by 2000, and external internationalization, as seen in the relatively small but nevertheless economically significant number of Japanese students who choose to study overseas.

However, the major difference is that whereas the UK has experienced a 'massification' of higher education over recent years, the Japanese system reached this stage some time ago and is now having to combat a declining birth rate and pool of student customers. Japan's population is predicted to continue to decline to a level where the number of places available at Japanese HEIs will equal the number of graduating high school students (for a detailed discussion of demographic change and Japanese higher education see Kinmonth, 2005). Once demand meets supply in Japan's higher education system by the end of the current decade, as is predicted, all students, regardless of ability, will be able to enter university and the changing nature of the student body will create the demand for remedial skills. To an extent this is already happening and universities have taken appropriate measures in their teaching practices (Yamada, 2001: 286).

In response, on 1 April 2004, Japanese universities underwent a process of reform known as the 'Third Fundamental Reform of the Japanese University System', or the 'big bang' that seeks to make Japanese HEIs more accountable. The reforms of Prime Minister Margaret Thatcher's administration (1979–1990) in the UK provided a model to a certain extent (Goodman et al., 2007: 7). However, the reforms find their ideological roots not only in the UK but also as part of the overall orientation of Prime Minister Koizumi Junichiro's administration (2001–2006) that advocated 'structural reform with no sacred cows' (The Japan Times, 2 May 2003).

The 'big bang' reforms were touted at the time as representing one of the most radical phases of reform in Japanese higher education and can be regarded as the culmination of previous reform movements that date back to the end of the Second World War and the US Occupation of Japan. The reforms can be summarized as follows. First, 89 national universities became Independent Administrative Institutions (IAIs). Second, the Ministry of Education, Culture, Sports, Science and Technology (MEXT) relinquished much of its power in decision-making to the presidents of national universities in areas such as staff recruitment, budgetary matters and curriculum development. Third, market principles were introduced into the Japanese higher education sector as exemplified by the establishment of for-profit universities. Fourth, competition for research and teaching funds was introduced as evidenced respectively in the establishment of the Centre of Excellence (COE) and Centre of Learning (COL) programmes. In its first year of adoption, 664 HEIs applied to become a COL and 80 were successful; in 2004 554 HEIs applied and 58 were successful; in 2005 410 HEIs applied and 47 were successful. However, the funds available for this initiative were much smaller than those released for the complementary COE programme in research. In addition, approximately only 10 per cent of Japan's four-year institutions were recognized and the winners tended to be those institutions mentioned above that conducted teaching in English (Eades, 2005: 306). Fifth, the creation of more rigorous internal and external evaluation systems that are linked to funding. And finally, the introduction of accountability into higher education so that students as customers can make informed choices based on published information when selecting their HEI (Eades, 2005; Goodman, 2005: 1–4; Hatakenaka, 2005).

With these motivational factors and contexts in mind, a number of recent initiatives have sought to identify, assure or promote teaching competence and teaching excellence respectively in Japanese HEIs. The extant literature tends to make little or no distinction between the two, possibly as a result of the previous underdevelopment of the quality issue, as is discussed in more detail below.

Faculty development

It may surprise the outsider but many Japanese professors possess neither doctorates nor teaching qualifications. Partly as a result of a lack of financial or professional incentives for Japanese academics to enhance their teaching, Japanese professors fail to see teaching as a core part of their professional identity (Hayes, 1998: 201). In short:

> many professors are research-oriented and indifferent to their students and to the their [sic] teaching. They do not care how students perceive their courses because students are expected to keep up with their course work even if it seems boring or irrelevant.
>
> (Altbach and Ogawa, 2002: 3)

However, over recent years and as a result of the massification of higher education, staff development (or faculty development (FD) as it is more widely known in Japan and will be used here) has become a buzzword on Japanese campuses. It now occupies a great deal of university time and there is considerable discussion on how academics can gauge how their teaching has been received by students and improve it accordingly.

Some attempts at FD had been attempted previously, especially in response to the student unrest of the late 1960s and predominantly in the discipline of medicine (Seki, 1995: 132–133). Recent attempts have been more sustained and multifaceted. In the case of Kyoto University, FD takes place at three levels:

1 university-wide activities such as the hosting of a number of continuing symposia on the subject of FD that have been well attended by a good proportion of staff;

2 department-level activities that vary across the university but include the holding of training sessions particular to the job description and level, questionnaires, role plays and the dissemination of outcomes across other departments;

3 through the Centre for the Promotion of Excellence in Higher Education (for more details, visit http://www.highedu.kyoto-u.ac.jp), which has also organized both top-down and bottom-up activities such as symposia as above, projects on peer observation to promote a variety of teaching styles beyond those familiar to graduates of Kyoto University, and also cooperation with individual departments at Kyoto University in addition to other universities and research institutes (Tanaka, 2003: 16–20).

Three types of FD have been highlighted in Japanese HEIs:

1 the top-down type of FD led by the organizational level;

2 the grassroots level whereby enthusiastic individuals or groups of individuals take an interest in improving their teaching;

3 a synthesis of the above two groups into a systematic, organizational and substantial type of FD (Inoshita, 2003: 30–31).

Along the lines of the final type, a number of universities such as Keio University and Okayama University have used student feedback to improve teaching and have invited students to sit on newly created student-faculty committees.

As a result of recent reforms, the professional identity of Japanese academics may be changing from one based purely on research. As Ogawa suggests:

> a new campus-wide culture is indispensable in order to integrate all university constituents. In fact, at a faculty development seminar recently conducted by a national university, one professor stated, 'the most important outcome of the seminar should be to change the consciousness of those professors who are responsible for reform as a member of the university'.
>
> (cited in Ogawa, 2002: 105)

In addition, the decline in the power and autonomy of faculties and the increase in influence of university presidents are expected to expedite this process.

Teaching methods and assessment

Ogasawara has argued that Japanese universities were slow to react to the shift in the utility of an undergraduate education:

[Teachers] used to stick to the archaic view that students were more or less mature learners with basic skills and were able to find their own academic interests without the explicit guidance of teachers. Because of this attitude, professors in major research universities were not necessarily keen to improve their teaching strategy and teaching skills for a long time. Besides this, too much specialization, especially in the fields of humanities, natural sciences, and technologies, made it difficult for students to understand the relevance of undergraduate education to their own interests and future jobs.

(Ogasawara, 2002: 56)

The Japanese word for 'study', *benkyo*, originates from the Japanese word for industry; in other words, 'academic achievement is mainly obtained by one's effort, not by natural talent' (Takeuchi, 1997: 191). In contrast, the concept of *ikiruchikara* (a zest for life) has been repeated in recent discussions of higher educational reform. By stressing that learning can be fun and promoting a 'liberal, flexible and comfortable school life', this approach addresses widespread social concerns that too much pressure is being placed on Japanese youth through constant examinations (Tsuruta, 2003: 125).

In line with this thinking, a number of institutions have sought to address the criticisms of general education by introducing a range of teaching methods such as smaller seminar groups or interdisciplinary approaches. By 1998, the vast majority of universities were making efforts to alter their teaching methods (Yoshida, 2002: 51–52). This also led to the creation of a number of new interdisciplinary schools that were widely diversified in what they were offering. These have been termed 'faculties with new labels' and the buzzwords that are often repeated include international, culture, information, comparative and environment (Poole and Amano, 2003: 162). Hagi International University's Faculty of International Information demonstrates this trend (Akabayashi, 2006). The diversification in the nature of Japanese HEIs has been focused upon by one of Japan's most well-known educational researchers, Amano Ikuo. In particular, he has conducted case studies of little known, regional institutions such as Miyazaki International College, Hokkaido Information University and Aomori Public College which: 'engage in unique approaches to higher education not commonly found in Japan such as American-style liberal arts courses in English, education focused upon strictly graduate-level education, greater accountability in teaching, innovatively designed campuses, and faculty-student collaborative research' (Poole and Amano, 2003: 152). What is more, these institutions have 'continued with curriculum reform, syllabus-based teaching, innovation in teaching methods and class evaluation by students' (Poole and Amano, 2003: 162). The trend has been captured by Arimoto (1997: 206) as follows:

This shift [the massification of higher education] necessitates a teaching revolution from a traditional standardized style acceptable for the former classes of homogenous students to new styles appropriate to classes of the heterogeneous students. Innovation relating to teaching can be realized by a variety of methods: by having classes with smaller numbers of students; with general education by means of seminars for freshmen; using Socratic substitutes for lectures; having tutorial systems; and providing office hours. The first thing that every institution should do is not imitate other institutions, but establish its own aims of education and innovations in teaching.

Recently, to this end, a number of initiatives have been noted including: the publication of syllabi; the increased use of small-group teaching; faculty development with a view to spreading best teaching practice; the increased use of ICT; student evaluations of classes; and classes conducted in non-Japanese languages (Doyon, 2001: 457–458). Thus, the emphasis is placed on distinctiveness and individualization, but only insofar as it can be used to distinguish an institution and market it to an increasingly savvy student customer.

Goodman *et al.* have argued convincingly that the more radical initiatives in Japanese higher education are being promoted in institutions traditionally regarded as lower down the hierarchy: the *senmon gakko*, or vocationally-oriented HEIs (Goodman *et al.*, 2007: 15–16). In the 1970s and 1980s, these schools were described as:

> able to quickly accommodate changing demands for skills, they had thrived in many fields of training – providing special skills in cosmetology, cooking, typing, accounting, etc., or preparing for such paraprofessional jobs as kindergarten teacher or nurse – and attracted many high school graduates.
>
> (Amano, 1997: 133)

The schools have unregulated curricula, are responsive to the needs of employers and stress vocational, not academic, qualifications. For example, the teaching of English in universities tends to be focused on traditional reading of literary classics, whereas in *senmon gakko* the focus is on practical communication skills (Goodman *et al.*, 2007: 18; for a detailed discussion of how English is taught in Japanese universities see Poole, 2005).

It appears that the competition amongst institutions for a dwindling number of students is what has galvanized these institutions into action. The gap in the market was created when two-year junior colleges made the decision to repackage themselves as four-year institutions; a strategic decision that failed insofar as they were forced into competition with more highly regarded institutions. *Senmon gakko* filled the gap that was created above them (Goodman *et al.*, 2007: 12). The proportion of 18 year olds going to these vocational schools has doubled over the last 15 years from 10 per cent to 20 per cent (Goodman *et al.*, 2007: 15; see also Kinmonth, 2005: 125). The attractiveness of these schools was increased when the law was relaxed in 1999 so that completion of a course at a *senmon gakko* could lead to transfer to a university. This also contributed to the surprising phenomenon of Japanese students dropping out of traditional universities with good reputations in order to join vocational schools, or attending both.

Postgraduate education has been identified as a crucial link with the business world and society in general (Hada, 2005). However, it has also been criticized as deficient in the past in terms of quality and quantity. Traditionally, postgraduate programmes in Japan were purely for the training of future academics and companies provided their own on-the-job training and did not reward postgraduate degree holders with higher salaries. Postgraduate programmes were seen to be largely irrelevant to the practical world of work and often were simply developed to enhance the reputation of the institution rather than generate revenue or train high-quality graduates. Engineering and law graduate programmes were taught by academics with little experience of the 'real world' and tended to be either irrelevant or undersubscribed (Nakayama and Low, 1997: 250–252; Ushiogi, 1997).

Changes in postgraduate education include the introduction of law schools promoting a more practical education delivered outside of traditional teaching hours (Ushiogi, 1997: 243). On 1 April 2004, a number of universities opened the doors of their new law schools in order to increase the number of lawyers in Japan and reform their training by making it more practical and less theoretical. This is not the only ideological motivation for the establishment of these schools. The discipline of law is responding to the introduction of market principles by hunting out and securing new markets. There has also been an expansion in the numbers during the 1990s from 61,884 MA students in 1990 to 119,406 in 1997; similarly doctoral student numbers have increased from 28,354 to 52,141 over the same period (Ogawa, 2002: 93). The number of adults studying within these programmes has risen from 963 in 1987 to 5,317 in 1997 (Yamada, 2001: 288).

Evaluation

Traditionally, 'the quality issue has been regarded in Japan as comprising simple numerical matters – the number of students per faculty, staff, building area or facility, etc.' (Yonezawa, 2002: 130). Only in recent reforms did evaluation begin to be taken seriously. With the objective of gauging whether students, parents, society and government are getting value for money for their investment in higher education, student evaluations have been introduced in Japanese HEIs (Arimoto, 1997: 205–206). Since 1992, universities have been required to conduct internal assessments and a number have conducted external assessments (Ogawa, 1999). According to Yonezawa, by 1998 83.7 per cent of universities had introduced self-evaluation processes, whereas only 15.1 per cent had introduced external evaluation processes (Yonezawa, 1998).

Only in 1996 did the University Accreditation Association conduct the first evaluation of 20 HEIs (Arimoto, 1997: 206). A number of faculties at Japanese universities have conducted external evaluations and this new development has been described as:

> an epoch-making phase in the history of higher education in Japan. It provides striking testimony to absorption of the market principle by the academy, demanding increased teaching quality to the extent that faculty themselves presume to examine the academic profession itself.
>
> (Arimoto, 1997: 206)

As regards attitudes towards teaching specifically, the shift has been noticeable and a matter of life or death for Japanese HEIs:

> evaluation of teaching quality has been underdeveloped in this country and even consumers have paid little attention to it. Recently, however, consumer attitudes to teaching have been rapidly changing to the extent that teaching innovation is said to be indispensable. The supply of information to consumers regarding the quality of education is becoming more and more important for the university's survival.
>
> (Arimoto, 1997: 204)

Japanese universities have also been forced to compete in the university rankings that have been published over recent years by a number of media outlets and private companies. Probably the most high profile of these has been the *Asiaweek* ranking, partly because the President of Tokyo University Hasumi Shigehiko refused to allow his institution to be included in the 2000 rankings, even though it was likely to be on top (Yonezawa, 2002: 135).

Internationalization

Student mobility has been on the rise for many years and Japan is no exception to this engine of globalization. This impulse was evident in Prime Minister Nakasone's attempt to promote the internationalization of Japanese HEIs in the 1980s, although his goal of hosting 100,000 foreign students in Japan by 2000 never materialized until 2003. As of the turn of the millennium, the number of foreign students in Japan (78,812 in 2001) was similar to the number of Japanese students studying abroad (76,000 in 2000) (Tsuruta, 2003: 124).

The need to attract international students provided motivation for the improvement in the level and reputation of Japanese higher education. In the language of the Japanese government, 'to raise the quality of education and the efficiency of administrative systems at each institution of higher education so that universities can appropriately serve all students from various cultures' (Horie, 2002: 69). The establishment of centres for international students at major universities has been one organizational and visible sign of the importance of this strategy. More importantly, however, has been the educational emphasis that has been placed upon studying overseas for Japanese students and bringing international students to Japan and allowing them to interact with their Japanese peers. Exposure to international students is regarded as an enriching activity for Japanese students (Horie, 2002).

One area in which Japanese universities have been active is the establishment of links with HEIs in North America, Europe and Australia/New Zealand. It is often the case that non-Japanese institutions are regarded more highly for the quality of their teaching and securing a qualification in English is highly valued. External internationalization of this sort essentially provides universities with a competitive edge in marketing their individuality.

Finally, there has been an increase in recent years in the number of programs with an international perspective and the number of faculties and universities with 'international' in their title. A number of institutions have sought to improve teaching by providing instruction in English. Christian universities such as International Christian University and Sophia University have led the way (Umakoshi, 1997: 263–264). Finally, a number of non-Japanese institutions have established branches in Japan and promise students a non-Japanese university education; Temple University of the US stands out as the most high-profile example (Umakoshi, 1997: 269). However, in recent years many of these institutions have experienced numerous problems and have been forced to downscale or close down (see Mock, 2005).

Conclusions

Globalization, the massification of Japanese higher education, the rise of the student customer, the introduction of market principles and the perceived need to satisfy external stakeholders have led Japanese HEIs to move away from a traditional approach to teaching excellence based on reputation and elitism. However, the shift has been to an essentially performative understanding of teaching excellence in Japan. Psychologized or critical approaches have made little impact so far although FD and student evaluations might serve to promote these approaches in the future.

How have teaching excellence and recent reforms been perceived in Japan? Some resistance at the individual level is being articulated. Hasumi Shigehiko, former president of Tokyo University and head of the Japan Association of National Universities attacked the performative understanding of reform when he stated that: 'University reform was proposed only as part of administrative reform that was aimed at reducing the number of civil servants. However, unlike tax collection or immigration control, it is clearly not possible to make university education and research more efficient merely by meeting numerical goals' (*The Japan Times*, 16 March 2001). However, although the rhetoric of teaching excellence as promoted by MEXT and Japanese universities may not be universally accepted, it is now firmly on the agenda of Japanese HEIs. In fact, and in contrast to Hasumi's statement, it has been argued that universities have been passive in their reaction to recent reforms. According to Yamamoto Shinichi, Japanese professor and former MEXT bureaucrat:

> perhaps surprisingly for anyone who knows about universities in Japan, there has been no particular campaign of opposition to the reforms from either the universities or staff associations. It is rather as if they are expecting the reforms to improve their own teaching and research environments.
>
> (Yamamoto, 2005: 95)

The diversification of the student body in Japan as universities chase a diminishing number of students and try to create new markets might lead to the introduction of new approaches to teaching. Some research also points to the likelihood that these changes and recent reforms will lead Japanese academics to change their professional identity to embrace more closely the role of teacher as well as researcher, or quit when faced with the necessity of doing so (Poole, 2005: 263–264). In any case, this possible diversification is presented in terms of a performative audit culture and is a matter for the future.

Although it is the second largest higher education system in the world and possesses a distinctive history and development, the example of Japan is not one that threatens to upset the monolithic worldwide teaching excellence movement. So far, in line with the cultural practice of borrowing instrumentalized at the time of the opening of Japan to the West in the nineteenth century and during the US occupation after the Second World War, the Japanese government and HEIs have taken on board the recent experiences of the US and UK and applied them to their own particular features in promoting the reform of higher education in general and teaching excellence specifically. Despite radical changes and some isolated examples of resistance based on traditional and elitist views of higher education, the Japanese experience highlights the globalizing power of the worldwide teaching excellence movement and its emphasis on performativity.

Chapter 13

Teaching excellence in context

Drawing from a socio-cultural approach

Joëlle Fanghanel
(City University, UK)

Introduction

In this chapter the notion of excellence is explored with reference to the policy context from which it emerged, and conceptually problematized through a socio-cultural theoretical lens. Alongside other contributions to this book, this chapter interrogates current understandings of excellence and questions its usefulness in moving practices forward. It poses basic questions about excellence which are intimately linked with conceptions of teaching and learning – 'whose excellence?', 'excellence in what?' and 'excellence for what?' It proposes that examining excellence with reference to the context of practice highlights it as a relative value, and as an inadequate tool for enhancing teaching and learning practices in higher education (HE). First though, this chapter explores the ways in which excellence is conceptualized in higher education today, scrutinizes the outcomes of enhancement policies through a recent formal evaluation (CHEMS, 2005), and examines what can be learnt from looking at excellence through a socio-cultural framework.

The capture of excellence in higher education in the UK

Excellence as it is operationalized at present in HE practices in the UK – mainly through individual awards – tends to be understood 'performatively' and evidenced through examining processes and behaviours that are perceived to be amenable to analysis and judgment. This approach provides 'measures' of excellence which can then be 'made available for public scrutiny' (Skelton, 2005: 30) and is intended to go some way to guarantee that the state gets a good return on its investment in teaching and learning. It is also underpinned by what might be called a dispersion theory of change (whereby excellence will spread through example, emulation and dissemination). Initial criteria for the UK National Teaching Fellowship Scheme (NTFS), for instance (see Skelton, 2005: Chapter 3 for a full discussion), epitomize the notion that identifying components of excellence will enable its replication. This perception of excellence locates it within an essentialist, functionalist, technical rational frame, where teaching and learning is perceived abstractly (theoretically), as a component of a system whose direction can be inflected through circumscription and emulation of specific behaviours. It is however a view of excellence that is seriously challenged by a growing body of literature over the past decade or so, which has emphasized the need to rethink understandings of teaching and learning by bringing to the fore its 'situated' nature in practice (Lave and Wenger, 1991; Seely Brown and Duguid, 1996; Cheetham and Chivers, 2001). Some studies have also stressed the need to take account of power relations (Contu and Willmott, 2003) and ideological positionings (Trowler, 1998) when reflecting on teaching and learning. Empirical studies on academic development further question the validity of technical rational models to capture agentic and structural complexities inherent in the contexts of practice which are in fact crucial in determining individual behaviours (Fanghanel, 2004, 2007 forthcoming). It is therefore important to try and capture excellence in context.

How to capture excellence in context?

Analysis of context can be formalized through a socio-cultural theoretical framework, and this is the stance taken in this chapter. Such an approach focuses on activity (Engeström, 1999) rather than on individual actions, and takes into account the historicity of the activity (how and why practices became what they are), with reference to the tools mediating practice, and to the macro-sociological framework underpinning it (communities, rules and conventions of these communities, and the way labour is organized and distributed within them). To illustrate this capture of context, it might be useful to go back to Leontev's definition of 'activity' through the metaphor of the primeval hunt in which one beater's action can only be understood in the perspective of the whole hunt (Leontev, 1981). Transferred to teaching, this metaphor emphasizes the impact of many factors on teaching which include local conditions and specificities. So for example, in a socio-cultural perspective, examination of teaching/teaching excellence would not specifically focus on how a lecturer operates in the seminar room, but on the relation between what this lecturer is doing in the course of all his/her interactions with students and the broader context. It is not however just about seeing the 'bigger picture', but also about understanding the societal and historicist foundations of the activity. It would thus be fair to say that there are different types of hunts, with different conventions, specific types of historicity attached to them, where different tools are used and with different types of involvement for the hunters involved.

A 'critical' socio-cultural approach will also examine context with reference to the agency of individuals within it – a dimension that is not much explored in Engeström's work on activity systems (Engeström, 1987), and rarely problematized in the more people-focused socio-cultural perspective of Communities of Practice (CoP) theory (Lave and Wenger, 1991). The way in which Lave and

Wenger account for acquisition of expertise is through an apprenticeship model of practice, in which newcomers are gradually introduced to the arcane practices of the trade through a process of 'legitimate peripheral participation' in communities of practice, mainly through a diet of increasingly complex activities and observation of 'old-timers' practices. It is useful to interrogate this consensual and 'naturally-occurring' notion of legitimate participation by looking at power issues and possibilities for individual agency in communities of practice. In the systemic approach considered here, agency is taken into account through Giddens' stance on agency and structure (Giddens, 1984).

A critical socio-cultural apprehension of practice inflects the way we might conceive of excellence. It provides arguments for thinking of excellence in the following ways:

- excellence as a systemic concept (excellent environments, rather than excellent people);
- excellence in context (what is excellent in one context may not be in another);
- excellence as agency (choices made by individuals in response to a context);
- excellence as a collective agenda for change (a transformative function).

This approach shapes a view of excellence as systemic, environmentally sensitive and agentic, and therefore less coherent and easy to label than ranking and distinctions might imply.

Drivers for the excellence framework in the UK

Measuring, seeing and rewarding competence

Quality, competence and excellence are relatively new concepts in HE. They emerged from a context which has brought the teaching function to the fore and outlined new and diverse roles for academics. Over the past two decades – with the widening access agenda and an increasingly diverse student body – the role of the lecturer has become more complex, embracing remits outside of teaching and research, and including the need to ensure successful learning through support that necessitates some knowledge of basic learning principles (e.g. diagnosing students learning skills, helping students develop meta-cognitive or professional skills, fostering reflective learning). This has been shored up by academic development programmes for HE lecturers that rest on the assumption that improvement to teaching will come from a better understanding of teaching and learning, which in turn should generate improved learning. A pathway for competence is encapsulated in this notion, and the necessity of competence for HE lecturers – recently embodied in the publication by the Higher Education Academy (HEA) of professional standards for teaching in higher education –

has gradually emerged from this. To a large extent, competence (and the derived notion of 'excellence') is based on the performative understanding of practice highlighted earlier, emphasizing outcomes and the measurement, categorizing, and ranking of performance. The increased visibility of teaching performance – in the shape of 'league tables', distinctions, quality comments posted on an institution's website – has significant market implications. The emphasis on teaching performance has also triggered a movement towards rewarding teaching and reappraising academic careers so as to address in particular the imbalance in prestige between teaching and research. Discreet career paths for progression to professorship on the basis of a lecturer's teaching record have appeared (Skelton, 2005: 42). This of course needs to be considered under the moderating light of increasing job insecurity and casualization of labour in HE (Kinman *et al.*, 2006) which are as real as are attempts to reward excellence of the few.

Teaching excellence competing with research excellence

A crucial issue in defining academic roles concerns the relationship between teaching and research and a re-conceptualization of this nexus has recently taken place (Jenkins *et al.*, 2003). The notion of teaching excellence appeared in academic discourse with the Dearing Report (NCIHE, 1997), which outlined the government's vision for the future of higher education in the twenty-first century and initiated a number of changes for the teaching agenda in HE, overtly setting out to 'redress the imbalance between teaching and research' in higher education (8.9) and establishing the Institute for Learning and Teaching in Higher Education (ILTHE) to take this agenda forward (8.61). Dearing clearly called on institutions to consider rewards and promotions paths that took account of the new emphasis on teaching to remedy 'inadequate recognition of teaching excellence' (14.6), thereby seeking to inflect long-standing academic norms. A new emphasis on teaching excellence, rivalling research excellence, was born, and with it, the related discourse instantiated in policy texts and institutional missions. It is interesting to note that a parallel wave of developments on teaching in the US gave rise to the Scholarship of Teaching and Learning (SoTL) movement, which in the wake of Boyer's seminal work on the meaning of scholarship in higher education in the late twentieth century (Boyer, 1990), focused on scholarship rather than excellence to bring about teaching and learning enhancements. SoTL is a complex and ill-defined movement which contains at the same time the notion of enhancement for the benefit of collective and individual practice, and the concerns for better rewards for 'individual teaching efforts' (Kreber, 2003: 95). Regardless of its emphasis, SoTL – in its many shapes and interpretations – is a major tool in rebalancing the teaching and research nexus (D'Andrea and Gosling, 2005: 160).

The impact of technology

Public reflection on teaching over the past decade or so, and the new deliberate emphasis on quality and excellence, were therefore to a large extent informed by the increasing visibility of an activity which had hitherto remained hidden behind closed doors. This became particularly central to the debate with the advances of Information and Communication Technologies (ICTs) from the mid-1990s onwards. At the same time as globalization was transforming HE into a global market, so did the nature of the activities within it change to become an object under scrutiny. While the internet has enabled 'extensive horizontal communications that cannot be controlled or effectively censored by national societies' (Urry, 2002), new forms of distributed learning have concurrently triggered the reassessment of the student-teacher relationship in higher education (Lea and Nicoll, 2002), new forms of knowledge (Gibbons *et al.*, 1994) have emerged, as well as new pluralist parameters for learning (Billett, 2004) and, some claim, a degree of democratization (Giroux, 1997).

Emphasis on quality, professionalization and the derived notion of excellence, however, has not shifted other strong competing agendas for the teaching function – competition with research and the increasing challenges of 'flexibility'. Academic roles and contexts have become more complex and diverse, and excellence appears a reductive notion to address the complexity of the challenges for teaching and learning in HE in the twenty-first century. Looking at how the concept emerged in the UK within a programme of enhancement policies, I suggest that these policies have had a relatively limited impact in promoting effective change, and offer explanations as to why this might have been the case.

The emergence of excellence: UK policies for enhancement and excellence

UK excellence policies emerged to a large extent from the Dearing Report (NCIHE, 1997). The government's 'prescription of national excellence in teaching and the management of learning' (NCIHE, 1997: para 8.11) for UK institutions was at the heart of the excellence vision. The ILTHE, later to be merged into the Higher Education Academy, was assigned the role of recognizing individual excellence through the NTFS 'for those attaining the highest levels of excellence in teaching' (NCIHE, 1997: para 5.61). This initiative was part of a battery of initiatives aimed at enhancing the teaching and learning function in UK HE institutions. I focus on two defective aspects in the policy approach underpinning these initiatives – a functionalist understanding of change, and an inadequate attention to the meso level where academic/disciplinary groups operate in practice.

Functionalist linkages for enhancement initiatives?

Although enhancement initiatives pre-date the Dearing Report, post-Dearing approaches, in particular the Teaching Quality and Enhancement Fund (TQEF) established in 1998, sought to be more focused (by making reference to specific themes) and institutionally embedded (through institutional teaching and learning strategies) than had previous approaches such as the initial Fund for Development of Teaching and Learning (FDTL) or the Teaching and Learning Technology Programme (TLTP) (HEFCE, 1998). This embedded approach emphasizes the functionalist understanding of organizational cultures underpinning this initiative. In this perspective, change is perceived as being achievable through elaborating a vision which identifies common goals and related actions for different functions of an organization, and for individuals within them. TQEF initiatives were articulated at different operational levels – the micro level of practice (development programmes for individual lecturers, singling out excellent teachers, etc.), the meso level or subject level (through the continuation of the FDTL projects, and with the setting-up of Learning and Teaching Subject Networks – a collection of resources for teaching and learning in the disciplines subsequently known as 'Subject Centres'), and the institutional level of universities' teaching and learning strategies. Subsumed in this policy approach is the idea that institutional cultures can be shifted by focusing activities through staff development initiatives, rewards and clear corporate goals and implementation strategies.

In the formal evaluation carried out by HE Consultancy Group and CHEMS Consulting of these enhancement initiatives over the period 1999–2005, the evaluators explain that despite the integrated strategy, and the aim to impact at different levels of practice, 'TQEF was not explicitly managed to produce synergistic effects, although it was assumed that they would develop' (CHEMS, 2005: para 1.29). This approach of the policymakers reflects the limitations of the functionalist approach – things do not necessarily fall into place, and more sophisticated theories of change are needed to promote effective cultural change (Trowler *et al.*, 2005). It appears from this evaluation that the linkages between the different initiatives did not systematically occur. The results of their findings can be summarized as in Figure 13.1.

It is clear from the visual summary below that connectivity between the different levels was inadequate. Initiatives are shown to operate in a vacuum, with defective connection to organizational structures and policies, limited impact on disciplinary communities and, in some cases, little chance of impacting outside of the initiative itself. Problems of transferability and dissemination to other institutions, and other disciplines from the work of NTFs and FDTL groups are presented as two of the main barriers to change in these initiatives (see CHEMS, 2005: Chapter 8).

This highlights the limitations of policies based on functionalist understandings of organizational cultures in which group norms, beliefs and values are not

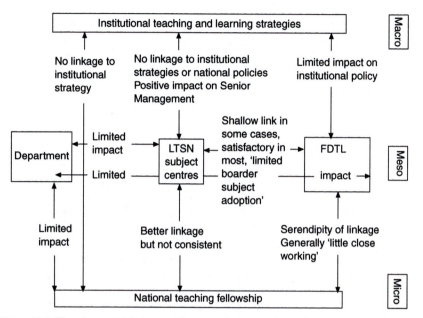

Figure 13.1 The degree of linkage and impact between the different strands of TQEF with reference to levels of practice, using report to HEFCE (CHEMS, 2005) as a source.

perceived as important ingredients. Universities are in fact 'loose-coupled' institutions (Weick, 1976), and the 'gaps' identified at the different levels of practice are inherent in the complexity of the system. I focus now on the limited impact identified at the meso level of practice.

A crucial lack of impact at the meso level of practice

Trowler *et al.* suggest that while seeking to operate at both the structural and the individual levels of practice, enhancement initiatives in the UK, to a large extent, have left aside the meso level of practice (Trowler *et al.*, 2005: 435), where disciplinary culture is in fact enacted. One significant excellence initiative at this level was the FDTL (Phases 3 and 4) which rewarded excellence by limiting access to funding to those departments which had obtained excellent teaching quality scores through the official assessment by the Quality Assurance Agency (national regulatory body for UK institutions). Since then of course a remarkable (for its exceptionality and the significance of its investment) initiative has been launched – the Centres for Excellence in Teaching and Learning (CETLs) – which is also aimed at the meso level, bringing together clusters of expertise focused on the disciplinary dimension of practice or around a specific pedagogic theme. Preliminary findings as to the impact of CETLs are considered in Chapter 10 in this book. Anecdotal accounts indicate that providing relatively small teams with extensive levels of resources has created tensions within some universities, although Gosling and Hannan's research also indicates that some CETL teams were keen to share the benefits of having secured a CETL with other departments in their institution. The danger still exists that unless serious attention is paid to dissemination and transferability of their work (CHEMS, 2005: para 8.14), such teams run the risk of having limited impact.

An initiative apparently directed at the meso level of practice such as FDTL behaves like an individual initiative, connecting to an extent with the LTSNs but having little impact on the institution and more crucially on the discipline, outside of the institution where the project is funded. Further, the success of its connectivity with other levels is dependent on the status (CHEMS, 2005: para 1.23) or influence (5.24) of the FDTL leader. These findings help us refine our apprehension of the meso level of practice. Though socio-cultural theory and empirical research (Trowler and Cooper, 2002; Fanghanel, 2004) indicate that this level is crucial to effect change, the CHEMS report is a reminder that a group needs legitimacy to qualify as a meso level player; if this is not the case, it remains a collection of individuals with little room for impact and manoeuvre. CoP theorists have earmarked the meso level of practice (the local disciplinary/pedagogic community in higher education), as a crucial unit for developing behaviours and understandings of practice, and reifying of practice through artefacts. What CoP theory does not tell us explicitly is that by virtue of its very agentic nature, this level is also the most likely to engender collective or individual resistance; this could also account for the limited impact of FDTL.

A socio-cultural framework for excellence

Having established that functionalist approaches to organizational cultures have their limitations in effecting coherent and joined-up change, and having emphasized again the need to focus on the meso level of practice – where teams work together, implement a curriculum, socialize students into a discipline, solve problems and realize policies – I now consider what theories of teaching underpin the notion of excellence, and how socio-cultural theory might provide insights to reframe this understanding.

What excellence?

Excellence as exemplified in initiatives like the NTFS and other forms of institutional awards is based on an understanding of teaching practice which focuses on individual performance, and a 'psychologized' understanding of teaching and learning (Malcolm and Zukas, 2001), anchored in a psychology-related conceptual framework, and focusing on cognitive processes and one-to-one or one-to-several interactions. A substantial body of literature on teaching in HE focuses indeed on such processes with specific reference to beliefs about teaching (e.g.

Entwistle *et al.*, 2000; Hativa *et al.*, 2001) or conceptions of teaching (e.g. Ramsden, 1992; Prosser and Trigwell, 1999). This is an influential body of literature which has become a dominant model in accounting for teaching and learning in UK educational development programmes (Malcolm and Zukas, 2001). This approach to teaching and learning is reified in the use of instruments such as the Approaches to Teaching Inventory (ATI) (Prosser and Trigwell, 1999), the Study Process Questionnaire (SPQ) (Biggs, 1987), the Approaches to Studying Inventory (ASI) (Entwistle and Ramsden, 1983), and concepts such as 'student-focused' approaches (Prosser and Trigwell, 1999), learning styles (Honey and Mumford, 1982) or 'deep and surface learning' (Marton and Säljö, 1976). These studies have obviously served an important function in highlighting the complexity of the teaching-learning nexus and in having shifted the emphasis from a delivery-focused understanding of teaching to a focus on learning, and on the experience of teaching and learning in situ. However, the nature of context as captured through these approaches tends to be highly situated. Prosser and Trigwell, for example, define a teaching context as 'the teaching and learning situation the teachers find themselves in' (Prosser and Trigwell, 1999: 159). These studies as a result yield a view of teaching as abstracted from the social and political realities of practice (Ashwin and McLean, 2005).

Studies that have focused on 'sophisticated' conceptions of teaching or award-winning conceptions and approaches – thus seeking to capture the essence of excellent teaching – emphasize 'expanded awareness of teaching and learning' linked to 'strategic alertness to classroom events' (Entwistle *et al.*, 2000; Entwistle and Walker, 2002), reflection as a form of knowledge-building, (McAlpine and Weston, 2000: 371) and conceptual orientations that include multi-dimensional apprehensions of teaching, complex and differentiating conceptualizations of criteria for teaching evaluation, and a commitment to obtaining information from others (Dunkin and Precians, 1992: 501). These conceptions of excellent teaching pay very little attention to the impact of the context of practice, although the social dimension of learning is acknowledged. Where attention has been given to the context of teaching practice in this literature, it has often been within a very narrow definition of context illustrated above.

The limitations of such approaches to teaching and learning (regardless of the degree of expertise of the practitioners involved) are clear. They tend to ignore local departmental differences, disciplinary specificities (although some studies have focused on specific disciplines) and the degree of fragmentation in the institutional landscape, particularly acute in the UK. Even recent studies (Henkel, 2000 for example) which clearly take account of the 'divide' between pre- and post-1992 institutions in the UK – disregard the tremendous diversity within both groups and the proteiform nature of culture (Alvesson, 2002: 170), making totalizing assumptions about the way academics function within systems. They do not look at practice as a set of recurrent behaviours embedded in routine (Giddens, 1984) and therefore governed by organizational cultures and professional/academic imperatives.

Excellence put to the socio-cultural test

Throwing a socio-cultural light on excellence uncovers its contextual components and shows the limitations of this concept to effect change. Empirical work carried out elsewhere using a socio-cultural methodological framework (Fanghanel, forthcoming) has examined the impact of context by interrogating the make-up of communities, the role of individuals within them, and the responses of individuals and groups to structures which may be constraining practice. Factors that appear silenced in the literature cited above emerged as a result of adopting this perspective. They concern disciplinary and pedagogical beliefs, the roles of the departmental community and of the institution in inflecting approaches to teaching and learning, and the impact of external factors (such as professional bodies and industry, national agendas and regulatory frameworks). The realities of academic labour, working conditions and career patterns were also shown to impact significantly on the way lecturers approach teaching. Finally, the specific status of the research-teaching nexus in the work context played a crucial role in orienting teaching practices. In the following section I examine the practice components that need to be taken into account when thinking about excellence. I show first, through an illustrative vignette, how socio-cultural context might be experienced in practice.

Experiencing teaching and learning in the broader socio-cultural context

Dr Liz Brown has been employed as a post-doc researcher in the department of bio-chemistry at a long-established 'traditional' university for the past 11 years. During this time, she has been on 27 research contracts. Although her interests have always been directed towards research, when Professor King decided to retire, she applied for the position of lecturer that became vacant as she felt she could no longer cope with the uncertainties of short contracts. As a junior member of the departmental team, she was asked, at very short notice, to take over all of Professor King's lectures, and to teach on a number of seminars within the BSc programme – Professor King had been considerate enough to leave her his lecture notes. She was also asked to supervise students on the BSc and to keep her previous lab engagements – a team of six postgraduate students involved in her research project – which would run for the next ten months.

Towards the end of her first semester the Head of Department approached her to design and coordinate a new module for the following year. This was to engage students in the ethics of bio-chemistry studies. Within a few weeks she wrote her module description. Liz believed in developing students' intellectual skills across the spectrum, rather than confine them to a straight and narrow curriculum. She thought generic intellectual development was more important than introducing students to a set syllabus. She introduced very innovative content that included topical issues on fertility research and innovative teaching methods such as self-assessment and group presentations moderated by the students. She thought this would shift the balance of power in favour of the students, but realized she had to prepare herself for a tug of war with the Head of Department who would certainly not find this quite in line with the way Professor King approached his teaching. She was less prepared for the reaction of her colleagues who openly belittled her approach during a departmental meeting, claiming that it totally contradicted the way bio-chemistry was generally being taught, not just at this university, but else-where too.

As the term went by, Liz realized she was increasingly neglecting her research. This really worried her for, although she enjoyed the teaching, her main purpose in ever starting on an academic career was to achieve an international research profile. She felt that in order to do her job properly, she needed to engage with the students as much as possible, and she had decided that her office was open to all students when they needed to see her. She was extremely popular with her students and was really proud of having established such a relationship with them in so little time. She was however concerned that she was gradually confined to teaching while some of her senior colleagues seemed to be able to take time out to work on their research and publish. Where would she find time to do any research in the next couple of years as a module convenor and with a heavy teaching load? Would she remain confined to the status of lecturer for years to come? Should she start to think of a teaching approach that would not take up so much of her time?

In a socio-cultural perspective, as illustrated above, actions (and cognition) are examined from within the social and cultural contexts in which they occur, rather than simply with reference to intellectual or psychological processes, or performance; this enables the capture of excellence as context-related and cul-turally constructed. The context for defining excellence would thus include the department or teaching team and the students involved; the way teaching prac-tice is organized including its interface with management priorities, other acade-mic roles, disciplinary or departmental location, and conventions related to the discipline, the curriculum, views of learning, teaching and excellence held at individual or collective levels. This brings to the fore the structures, conventions and beliefs within which excellence might be conceptualized. The dynamics within the communities themselves can be examined by critically interrogating the notions of 'mutual engagement' and 'shared meanings' (Wenger, 1998), central to CoP theory. A focus on *competing* rather than *consensual* inter-subjectivities provides an insight into the complexities of these communities, and emphasizes issues of agency, power and legitimacy inherent in real situations. Focusing thus on structures and communities emphasizes contextual pressure points which are relevant (capable of acting as enablers or as disablers) to the discussion of excellence in higher education environments:

The institution

A number of institutional regulations can come in the way of teaching and learning and thus thwart any enterprise to change practices; they include regulations that may be perceived as hindering learning (e.g. regulations on group work, e-learning, preference for certain methods). However academics can and do adapt their practices where they find regulations at odds with their beliefs (Trowler, 1998). The way an institution perceives of the relative value of teaching and research will also impact on how much emphasis is put on teaching. Signals sent by institutions that emphasize the value of research over teaching are likely to deter a focus on teaching excellence.

Departments

Departments come in many shapes and forms; a number of universities still hold on to 'traditional', relatively well-defined and circumscribed departments, while a number of institutions have opted for large 'post-modern' structures, where 'fields' are brought together for pragmatic rather than epistemic reasons. These create very different dynamics – a sense of collegiality (sometimes 'contrived', see Hargreaves, 1994) in the former, and much looser connections in the latter – which can induce a sense of freedom (associations are made with 'kindred spirits') or a sense of chaos and anomie (without referents to anchor practice). Such contrary structures will breed very different individuals and teams, and within them different understandings of excellence in teaching. Developing practice at this level is however crucial in terms of the impact it might have on student learning. Harnessing these dynamics will therefore be critical to promote enhancement of practice.

Pedagogical beliefs

Pedagogical knowledge may of course be perceived as an indispensable component of excellence. In theory, a sound knowledge of teaching and learning is likely to lead to sound practice. However, partial knowledge or unquestioned beliefs – sometimes deeply-seated in institutional/discipline-based principles – can come in the way of excellence when taken-for-granted assumptions are not subjected to critical examination. It is not uncommon to come across academics whose beliefs about student motivation and ability lead them to adopt approaches and methods aimed at mitigating what they perceive as a fundamental flaw, and strategies which could be labelled as 'remedial' (for example, broken-up lectures, short assignments). Such strategies involve shifting the burden of responsibility for learning onto students and making assessment more complex. Discussions of excellence would need to take account of pedagogical beliefs and problematize taken-for-granted assumptions.

Disciplinary identities

While a significant body of literature focuses on the epistemological specificities of the disciplines (e.g. Donald, 2002), a socio-cultural approach emphasizes the role of communities and ideologies in constructing an individual's ideas of a discipline. Disciplinary identities are less coherent than is generally accepted, and as a result perceptions of excellence within a discipline are likely to be diverse. Further, structural elements such as the status of a discipline in a department (its centrality or periphery to the main departmental emphasis), or the locus of the discipline in a curriculum (for example the teaching of soft psychology skills in the medical curriculum) also impact on how an individual relates to his/her discipline and how the discipline is perceived in the community of practice. Outside of its structural context, excellence within a discipline, might be misconstrued.

Academic labour

The nature of academic labour and the frameworks for staffing in universities inevitably impact on the notion of excellence; this point was raised in the CHEMS evaluation, as a barrier to change (CHEMS, 2005: para 7.43). In a recent report published on stress and work-life balance in UK academics, it was established that 59 per cent of the respondents employed on a full-time basis worked more than 45 hours in a typical week, and 21 per cent worked generally more than 55 hours (Kinman and Jones, 2004: 19). These data are to be put in the context of increasingly complex and demanding roles referred to at the beginning of this chapter. In addition, 42 per cent of academics in higher education are employed on a fixed-term basis (Kinman and Jones, 2004: 19). This raises a number of questions about who can have access to excellence, and offers a sober reply to Skelton's question regarding the extent to which teaching excellence is an inclusive concept (Skelton, 2005: 22–23).

The teaching–research nexus

Dearing emphasized the prescription of excellence for UK research: 'the main, though not exclusive, focus should be on excellence and on areas of national need, however identified' (NCIHE, 1997: para 5.61). He offered a similar prescription for teaching excellence, as outlined at the beginning of this chapter, without problematizing what this excellence might be, who might have access to the status of excellence, and what such excellence might be meant to generate for the public good. As a result of such vagueness, searching questions are only beginning to be posed (Jenkins *et al.*, 2003; Skelton, 2005). The teaching–research nexus is epistemically problematic, the articulation between the two activities not clearly explicated by evidence (Hattie and Marsh, 1996). The link between research and teaching in terms of generating excellence needs to be problematized (Chapter 8, this volume), and nurtured through adequate policy and curricular strategies (Jenkins and Healey, 2005). Teaching remains a lower status function in higher education (Hannan and Silver, 2000), the activity itself largely undervalued and 'atheoretical' (Rowland, 2003). This nexus is experienced as a turbulent zone by academics who outside of elite institutions bear the brunt of conflicting policy 'bundles' (Trowler *et al.*, 2005).

Excellence and ideology

Perhaps the most crucial question to ask about excellence is in relation to what academics believe is the purpose of a university education. Skelton's work (Skelton, 2005) has clearly outlined competing conceptions of excellence. 'Traditional' understandings reflect elitist views of education and the purpose of HE as 'cultural reproduction'. 'Performative' understandings see access based on merit, and focus on the functionalist dimension of HE in its relation to the economy. 'Psychologized' understandings focus on the student in the immediate context, and on learning understood in a 'relational' way, stressing interpersonal skills, personality and communication styles (Skelton, 2005: 31). 'Critical' understandings 'share an interest in and a commitment to emancipation' (Skelton, 2005: 32). A few remarks can be made in relation to this categorization:

- it reflects different ideologies of higher education, and of the purpose of a university education which are not often taken into account when examining teaching in higher education. This categorization can be related to Trowler's work on educational ideologies (Trowler, 1998: 69–80) where he identifies 'traditionalism' as reflecting an elitist belief in a limited pool of talents and emphasizing the discipline dimension, and specifically the 'purity' of that dimension which on the whole should remain untouched by mercantile preoccupations attached to the economic agenda. The 'enterprise' ideology on the other hand, emphasizes preparation for work and a focus on generic and vocational skills development. 'Progressivism' focuses on personal development and student-centred pedagogies while 'social constructionism' is a transformative ideology meant to empower students to redress inequalities and change society. Notions of teaching excellence within these different ideological perspectives will be diverse and probably contradictory too.

- Educational ideologies are reflected in academics' understandings of pedagogical roles and of appropriate teaching methods (Skelton, 2005: 35). Trowler also found that there were direct ideological connections to the way the curriculum is delivered and that, for example, academics with a 'progressivist' ideology tended to favour active pedagogies. They also focus on different elements of teaching practice (discipline, regulations, teacher-student relationship and material conditions, see Skelton, 2005: 35). In other words, different values will support different teaching and learning approaches.

Skelton identified that currently the performative and psychologized versions were the most common ideologies of excellence, reflecting dominant paradigms for understanding teaching and learning practices. Other positions are however legitimate, which again implies plural and competing perceptions of excellence.

Conclusion

The complexity of practice as uncovered through a critical socio-cultural framework provides an unlikely cradle for the notion of excellence. This chapter has shown that it becomes a problematic concept when considered in the context of actual academic structures and communities. It has highlighted the relativistic, context-sensitive nature of excellence, and the necessity to envisage systems in any apprehension of practice. It has also indicated that agentic and ideological responses within these systems render the notion still more problematic as a basis for enhancing practices. Does its relative value imply that one should therefore adopt an 'anything goes' conception of excellence, celebrating diversity and idiosyncrasies? In doing this, is there a risk that the academic community might lose its 'criticality'? (Barnett, 1997). Should one dismiss it as a meaningless concept (Readings, 1996) and focus on something altogether different?

This chapter has argued that excellence was a problematic and inadequate notion to promote enhancement of teaching and learning practices, and it suggests that focusing on the collective dimension of practice with a change agenda in mind would be more useful for the public good, and the advancement of teaching and learning. While excellence of the few is unlikely to impact significantly on practices, and excellence of many conjures up relativity and contingency, a focus on change and development anchored in the realities of practice, and on the way academic groups operate in their interaction with learners, would benefit the HE community. The emphasis on excellence tends to deflect emphasis away from the meso level where most of the dynamics of practice are enacted.

Acknowledgement

I would like to thank Paul Trowler for his very useful comments on an early draft of this chapter.

Chapter 14

The National Teaching Fellowship Scheme 2000–2006

Rest In Peace?

Alan Skelton
(University of Sheffield, UK)

Introduction

The focus of this chapter is the National Teaching Fellowship Scheme (NTFS) which was launched by the Higher Education Funding Council for England (HEFCE) in April 2000. The NTFS is a national level award scheme which seeks to recognise and reward excellent higher education teachers in England and Northern Ireland. In this chapter I look back over the scheme during the period 2000–2006 and undertake a 'critical' review (see Skelton, 2005: 10–14) which considers some of the changes in its structure and organisation. I draw upon research and evaluation studies undertaken during this period to examine the impact of the scheme on the higher education (HE) sector and the way we think about teaching excellence. I argue that recent changes to the NTFS (2006) will have far-reaching implications. In particular, the 'decoupling' of the individual award from the project strand may have fundamental consequences, since it suggests that teaching excellence is primarily about recognised performance (e.g. in the lecture theatre or seminar room) rather than ongoing inquiry into one's own practice. I consider two different interpretations of decoupling to stimulate thinking about its potential impact. I consider the broader context within which NTFS changes need to be understood, paying particular attention to the Higher Education Academy's new framework for scholarship into the student learning experience. I conclude that the new arrangements for the NTFS only serve to undermine its radical potential. The view of what constituted an excellent teacher that was implicit in the original NTFS – someone who teaches consistently to high standards, who undertakes systematic enquiry into their own practice and collective activities as part of a fellowship – has been replaced by a vision which is much more conservative. I argue that a dualistic framework of thinking which separates teaching from (pedagogical) research has prevented the NTFS from realising its full potential. We are left with a scheme which is easier to administer and manage, but one which lacks real potency.

The significance of awards for teaching excellence

Awards for teaching excellence are now commonplace in higher education operating at departmental, disciplinary, institutional and national levels. Some are
relatively small-scale affairs whilst others are accompanied by significant monetary reward, high profile ceremonies and enthusiastic media coverage. The first
award was given in 1957 at the University of California in the US (McNaught
and Anwyl, 1993), the country which offers the most awards (approximately
29,000 per year). In recent years awards for teaching have proliferated in many
countries around the world, particularly in the UK, South Africa, Canada, the
US and Australia. Awards for teaching are therefore part of a much larger and
growing 'world-wide excellence movement' (McDonald, 1990; Fritzberg, 2000)
and 'awards industry' (Arena, 2001).

Given their increasing prominence in higher education, it is important that
we consider what significance award schemes have for our understanding of
teaching excellence. Whilst awards appear to be simply a way of recognising
the positive contributions of our best teachers, it is crucial that we engage with
them critically, to identify their implicit assumptions and values. Sometimes it
is difficult to see beyond the detailed application procedures, criteria and
selection processes of awards to understand what they fundamentally stand for
in terms of teaching excellence. In order to clarify how teaching excellence is
being constructed in higher education, therefore, we need to examine award
schemes and the specific forms they take. The purpose of this chapter is to
offer a critical review of the NTFS between 2000–2006, exploring what
implications the scheme has for the way we think about teaching excellence.
The NTFS is a significant contributor to what might be termed a growing and
emerging 'official discourse' on teaching excellence in higher education.
Linked to HEFCE teaching and learning policy and offering significant financial rewards (initially £50,000), the NTFS carries considerable authority and
symbolic appeal. Many institutions have developed their own awards based on
the NTFS model (HEFCE, 2002). The implicit messages about teaching excellence that are conveyed through the NTFS are therefore permeating higher
education institutions.

The introduction of the NTFS: from 'star videos' to individual awards

The impetus for the NTFS came from the Dearing Report (NICHE, 1997) with
its emphasis on improving the quality of teaching and learning in higher education. In the aftermath of Dearing, government ministers were committed initially
to the idea of producing videos of 'star performers' to identify and disseminate
teaching excellence, but this soon lost favour and attention shifted towards a
national level award scheme. This shift was partly due to rank and file opposition to the star videos concept and partly due to the fact that national award

schemes appeared to have been introduced successfully in a number of other countries.

Linked to subject and institutional level developments through the Teaching Quality Enhancement Fund (TQEF), the NTFS formed part of an integrated strategy to raise the profile of teaching and learning in higher education. Initially the Institute for Learning and Teaching in Higher Education (ILTHE) was invited to manage the scheme taking on a range of responsibilities including: the establishment of a national advisory panel (NAP); the preparation of background information to enable the panel to identify criteria for excellence; and the development of a process to select winners. The scheme was open to all staff involved in supporting the student learning experience and eligible institutions were invited to identify a candidate to proceed to the national level competition. The first group of 20 award winners were identified in July 2000.

The socio-political context of the scheme – for example, the need for it to emulate the most prestigious awards in other countries, to attract significant publicity and to be treated seriously within the research-intensive culture of UK higher education – helps to explain why such a large sum of money (£50,000) was given to each of the award-winners. A comparison of national award schemes undertaken in 2000 by the author (see Table 14.1) shows a number of similarities and differences. It also indicates that the financial rewards offered by the NTFS surmounted those of leading 'competitor' countries.

The radical potential of the NTFS

Award schemes for teaching excellence come in a range of different shapes and sizes. Warren and Plumb (1999: 246–249) provide a useful framework for understanding different types of award, their purposes and key characteristics. In

Table 14.1 A cross-national comparison of award schemes for teaching excellence

Name of scheme	Nature of awards	Locus	Emphasis
Australian Awards for University Teaching	$40–100k; 16 awards in four categories (individual; themed; institutional; overall)	Subject-based individual awards	Reward and development
Canadian 3M Teaching Fellowships	Expense-paid three-day retreat	Generic: no subject-based categories	Mainly reward
NTFS (England and NI)	£50k; 20 individual awards	Generic: no subject-based categories/ quotas	Reward and development
US Professors of the Year Program	$5k; four awards, one in each of four categories	Generic: no subject-based categories/quotas	Mainly reward

a study based on 11 UK and seven overseas institutions they identified four main types of award, namely:

- *Traditional award schemes*: these give prizes in recognition of past performance.
- *Teaching fellowship schemes*: these confer the title 'teaching fellow' for a period of time and encourage award winners to meet together to share ideas and undertake collective developmental activities.
- *Educational development grant schemes*: these support specific projects and innovations in teaching and learning.
- *Promotion/bonus schemes*: these involve the creation of promoted posts which emphasize teaching (e.g. Readerships in Teaching) and/or salary increments or bonuses for teaching-related innovation and/or achievement.

Most teaching excellence award schemes adopt one of the models referred to above and the most common is the traditional prize (Warren and Plumb, 1999: 247). From the outset the NTFS was a very ambitious scheme which was evident in its design. It had considerable radical potential for the reasons listed below.

- *Its scope and potential value* – the NTFS sought to combine the benefits of a traditional prize, a development grant and a fellowship within one scheme, recognising past achievement but also supporting future development. Nominations needed to provide evidence of excellent practice together with detailed plans of a systematic project that would be undertaken. The creation of a fellowship meant that award-winners were to take part in collective activities to promote teaching excellence – for example, meeting together to discuss ideas and common development threads and disseminating their joint work at conferences and through written publications. Through these collective activities, the scheme was intended to offer 'added value' – to promote teaching and learning more widely in the sector and to influence colleagues' ideas and practices.
- *Systematic inquiry: teachers as 'knowledge producers'* – the requirement that award-winners would undertake research and development projects was also a radical feature of the NTFS. This conveyed the message that teaching excellence was not just about past performance – it required systematic reflection on practice and a commitment to ongoing inquiry. The project element and the belief that award-winners' development work should be widely disseminated also suggested that practitioners could be involved in generating legitimate knowledge about teaching and learning in higher education. This support for practitioner research implied that the development of pedagogical understanding and practice was not the sole preserve of 'ivory tower' educational theorists – excellent teachers located in a variety of higher education disciplines had both the right and capability to contribute.

- *The development of hybrid methodologies for pedagogical research in higher education* – the expectation that disciplinary practitioners would contribute in this way and carry out pedagogical projects was also radical in its potential implications. It suggested that practitioners might legitimately draw upon methodologies with which they were familiar within their own disciplinary communities to begin their enquiries. This opened up the possibility that higher education pedagogy might benefit from new and emergent 'hybrid methodologies' – radical fusions of disciplinary and established educational research methodologies to suit the specifics and dynamics of higher education teaching and learning contexts (see Stierer and Antoniou, 2004).

- *The creation of a new distinctive 'voice' on/for teaching excellence in higher education* – once the first 20 NTFS award-winners had been announced it was clear that they represented a potentially powerful voice on teaching and learning matters in higher education. They were a high profile interdisciplinary group who, given the status of their awards, had the authority to speak out on pedagogical issues. What might this new and powerful group have to say about teaching excellence in higher education? And were these views consistent with those of politicians and leading policymakers? Clearly the NTFS offered a new potential platform for the expression of 'grassroots' opinion on teaching in higher education.

The NTFS 2000–2006

During its formative years, the NTFS underwent a small number of changes following internal review by the ILTHE. These changes were relatively minor and given the socio-political pressures on the scheme its initial structure remained intact during the first three years of HEFCE funding (2000–2003). In 2001 a decision was taken by the ILTHE to only require project proposals to be submitted alongside the general application once a candidate had been short-listed for an award. At the time this appeared to be essentially a technical matter, but with hindsight it indicated a growing tension between the two main parts of the scheme – between recognising past achievement and supporting future development. Informal feedback even at this stage may have suggested that applicants were finding the design of project proposals time consuming and/or problematic. Indeed in my own study of the NTFS I found that there was considerable uncertainty amongst potential applicants as to the meaning and purpose of the 'projects'. Some thought that in order to submit a project proposal significant previous experience of designing and conducting educational research was required which discouraged them from applying (see Skelton, 2005: 72).

A formative evaluation of the TQEF carried out in 2001 included a review of the NTFS and its impact on the sector (CHEMS Consulting/Critical Change Consultants, 2001). This evaluation stated that the NTFS had received a mixed reception from the higher education community – award-winners themselves felt affirmed by the recognition and played an important part within their own institutions in raising the profile of teaching and learning. Impact beyond this, however, was somewhat 'patchy'. The evaluation report suggested that capacity for future change may rest more on the collective work of the fellows than their individual contributions. It recommended that a more coordinated approach to publicising the outcomes of the projects be adopted and noted that some teaching fellows were relatively unfamiliar with networks that supported the scholarship of teaching and learning. The report concluded that 'opinion on the scheme remains divided and unclear' (ibid.: 23). However, the potential of the teaching fellows – in creating 'synergies' between the separate strands of the TQEF – was noted.

Between 2000–2001, I undertook a study of the NTFS which focused on its first year of operation (see Skelton, 2002). I was interested in the implicit assumptions behind the scheme and how it conceptualised the slippery concept of 'teaching excellence'. Supported by a research grant from the Economic and Social Research Council, I explored three interrelated question areas which went beyond operational issues

1 how 'teaching excellence' was being understood within the NTFS;
2 the key characteristics of the NTFS as a development mechanism and strategy;
3 the impact the NTFS was having on the professional lives and identities of the award-winners.

In relation to the first of these questions, I found that teaching excellence within the NTFS was underpinned by a model of 'reflective practice'. This model of reflection draws principally on psychological theories of learning and teaching. In the light of this finding, I recommended that a critical review of the NTFS be undertaken to consider the conceptual legitimacy of the reflective practitioner model. I suggested that such a review might address whether a 'psychologised' form of reflective practice recognises sufficiently the diverse disciplinary backgrounds of potential NTFS applicants and allows them to place their enquiries within a broader social and political context.

In terms of the second question, the research found that the NTFS would benefit from a more explicit strategy for change. I recommended that this should clarify the status of the knowledge being generated by the award-winners and how the fellowship was meant to be impacting more broadly on the sector. I suggested that the award-winners may benefit from both administrative and academic support for their projects. The latter could be provided by experienced educational researchers acting as mentors who could help award-winners develop their research plans and possibly hybrid methodologies. I found little evidence that award-winners were working effectively as a fellowship to raise the status of teaching and learning within the sector. Experiencing a sense of camaraderie but also exhibiting typical characteristics of any interdisciplinary group split by subject, age, experience and interest, the NTFS holders did not feel part of a team with a sense of purpose and shared values. I concluded that for this happen, the TQEF National Co-ordination Team (NCT) would need to provide further support and guidance.

With respect to the third and final question, many of the award-winners reported that their 'teaching identities' had been validated through the NTFS. Becoming a national teaching fellow meant that their contributions to teaching were treated seriously even in the most 'research-intensive' institutions. This encouraged some people to contemplate a career as an educational developer within the disciplines. Others commented that the intensification of their teaching identity in the light of the NTFS created dilemmas for them: they were not sure whether to pursue a career in educational development work or remain as a subject specialist. One award-winner suggested that being recognised for teaching in an old 'research-led' university could be disadvantageous to a research profile and promotion. In the light of my study I concluded that a critical review of the NTFS should consider how the scheme might support a more productive relationship between teaching and research in higher education: the place of the project, the scope for disciplinary-based pedagogical research and achieving equivalence in value between teaching and research awards were all identified as significant issues that needed to be addressed.

Despite the reservations noted in the formative evaluation of the TQEF and in my own study referred to above, the 2003 White Paper entitled 'The future of higher education' reported that the NTFS had been 'highly successful' and announced that the scheme would be expanded to increase the number of fellowships from 20 to 50 (DfES, 2003: 53). This change was introduced formally in 2004, so that 50 teachers received the reward of £50,000. This expansion may have been prompted by growing criticisms that institutional nominees who were unsuccessful in the NTFS received no reward for their efforts. Increasing the number of fellowships was one way of addressing this problem. It ensured that the scheme managed to reach into a greater number of institutions where the influence of award-winners was likely to be felt more strongly.

Three award-winners from 2001 undertook a study of the NTFS focusing on the period 2000–2003 (Frame et al., 2003). This study was based on questionnaire returns from NTFs who had won awards during the first three years of the scheme, and focused on the following four areas: the selection process within institutions; the personal significance of winning an award; how the award was perceived within institutions; and what difference the award made to the person's work at national and international levels.

The study made a conceptual distinction between awards and rewards. The latter was taken to be not simply a financial commodity – rather it was primarily seen as a complex concern that could bestow other benefits such as feelings of pride and confidence. This insider perspective on the NTFS therefore emphasised the subjective experiences of teaching fellows and their responses to the scheme. An NTFS reward was viewed as being primarily about what a teaching fellow made of it, and what they could make of it depended on the different regimes of truth that were operating within different departmental and institutional contexts.

The study found that the majority of NTFs had been selected through a written nomination as part of an institutional selection process. Thereafter, becoming a NTFS winner increased pride and confidence amongst the majority of respondents, although there were marked gender differences. Women on the whole noted these aspects as rewards more than men. In some contexts, becoming a NTF could be a millstone – being labelled as a teacher could be damaging in a research-intensive institution and sometimes little interest in the scheme was expressed by colleagues and institutional managers. Only 50 per cent of NTFs reported that they had been involved in staff development activity. Scheme impact on departmental and institutional practice was therefore limited, although some NTFs were developing international links to support their work. The authors concluded that there was some underusage of the scheme to support development beyond the individual level. However, they also noted that some NTFs commented that it would be a shame if the personal reward element of the NTFS was abandoned. A further comment from one NTF indicated that the NCT may have got the 'wrong end of the stick' in focusing on the project as a basis for pedagogical research. These comments clearly indicate tensions in the scheme between reward and development with the NTFs – perhaps unsurprisingly – tending to emphasise the personal reward element. The study also indicated tensions between whether the award was primarily for individuals or for the higher education sector as a whole.

Recent changes to the NTFS: decoupling excellence from scholarship?

In 2006 the NTFS was substantially restructured following a summative evaluation of the TQEF (CHEMS Consulting/Higher Education Consultancy Group, 2005). Whilst this evaluation reported that the NTFS had made a significant impact in terms of raising the status of award-winning individuals, it found little evidence of impact beyond this at departmental, institutional and system levels. The report therefore questioned whether there had been any 'added value' from the NTFS in terms of its broader contribution to teaching and learning in higher education, stating that:

> It is difficult to escape the conclusion from the responses of all groups that revisions to the scheme aimed at maximising its future value for money should consider decoupling the individual award (as a prize for past performance) from the project grant.

> (ibid.: 45)

The revised scheme consists of two strands: individual awards and projects. 50 awards of £10,000 are to be given to recognise and reward individual excellence, and this money may be used for personal development in learning and teaching. The individual awards aim to raise the profile of learning and teaching; recognise and celebrate individuals who make an outstanding impact on the student learning experience; and provide a national focus for institutional teaching and learning excellence schemes. The project strand aims to develop and disseminate good practice across the higher education sector. At the time of writing, project teams will be able to bid for funds of up to £200,000. Applications need to align themselves with one or more of the Higher Education Academy's four institutional themes, namely: innovations in the curriculum and student support; quality management; student assessment; and academic leadership. Interestingly all bidding teams must include a National Teaching Fellow (see www.heacademy.ac.uk/NTFS.htm).

The new NTFS: implications of the changes

Earlier in this chapter I argued that the radical potential of the NTFS flowed from its ambitious design. Unlike the majority of award schemes that focus on giving prizes, it sought to integrate three different types of award within one initiative, namely a traditional prize, a fellowship scheme and a development grant. The scope of the award was therefore very wide. It sought to reward high quality teaching performance, create a fellowship through collective activities and support teaching fellows carrying out systematic projects to improve educational practice. The emphasis was on recognising individual excellence and promoting teaching and learning more generally in the sector.

The recent 'decoupling' of the individual award from the project (with little mention of what happens to the 'Fellowship') therefore promises to have significant implications. In this section I want to explore two very different ways of interpreting the changes – one that sees them eroding the radical potential of the scheme and a second which regards them as being a progressive force. It is my hope that setting out these different perspectives will clarify my own and other people's thinking about recent changes to the NTFS and what they imply for our understanding of teaching excellence.

Decoupling as an erosion of the radical potential of the NTFS

One way of looking at the recent changes is that they significantly erode the radical potential of the original NTFS. From this perspective, the changes have effectively turned the NTFS into a *traditional prize* thereby losing its former distinctiveness. It has become more focused on conferring rewards on individual excellent teachers and releasing them from the pressure to undertake a project. In this way, it has become more like other award schemes both nationally and internationally. Of course it is possible for teachers to apply to both the individual and project strands of the new NTFS, but this is not a requirement. The decoupling of the individual award from the project strand therefore implies that teaching excellence is primarily about recognised performance rather than systematic inquiry into one's own practice.

Through the requirement of undertaking a systematic project, the NTFS originally supported the notion of teachers as 'knowledge producers' – that they had both the right and capability to contribute to the developing knowledge base about teaching and learning in higher education. With the recent changes to the scheme, applicants to the individual strand are no longer required to undertake systematic inquiry. Furthermore, those that apply to the project strand will not necessarily be developing *their own* practice. They will be part of a larger project team who will be 'developing and disseminating innovations' based on work undertaken across a range of institutions. Projects also need to focus on one of four HEFCE-determined priorities whereas originally NTFS project work could be guided more by individual interests and concerns. Given these changes, the radical potential of the NTFS as a focus for practitioner-led systematic inquiry into one's own practice has clearly been reduced.

As mentioned earlier, with the emphasis on 'de-*coupling*' in recent changes to the NTFS, there has been little consideration given to its original conception as a 'fellowship'. This fundamental aspect appears to have been overlooked which suggests a loosening of support which is perhaps not surprising given the findings of evaluation reports mentioned earlier. The demise of the fellowship again erodes the radical potential of the scheme in its ability to have broader impact on the sector, since there is less expectation that the teaching fellows will contribute to any collective activities. The notion of a fellowship provided an important space within which the NTFs could potentially collaborate with each other and develop an independent and distinctive voice on teaching and learning matters in higher education. Through expert guidance and the interdisciplinary sharing of project plans, the fellowship might have also offered a space for the development of hybrid methodologies for pedagogical research.

The decision to decouple the individual award from the project strand may also intensify the split between teaching and research in higher education. The individual strand is associated with recognised *teaching* performance whereas the project strand is associated with undertaking a pedagogical *research* project. The radical design of the original NTFS – with its potential to bring teaching and (pedagogical) research together – has therefore been severed.

On the other hand, the presence of teaching fellows on bidding teams for high status pedagogical research (grants of up to £200,000) might suggest that the new NTFS is fostering a stronger connection between teaching and research. The project strand may provide the opportunity for people recognised for their teaching excellence in the past to become a significant player in the future development of pedagogical research in higher education. The NTFs who will participate in the project strand may join that select group of people who conduct RAE-able pedagogical research. The positive aspects of this development need to be set against the detrimental impact of the new NTFS on practitioner research. The decoupling of the individual award from the project may well contribute to the downgrading of practitioner research since the emphasis has shifted away from NTFS undertaking enquiries into *their own* practice. The emphasis in the new NTFS is on larger, more generalisable studies. Teams of researchers from a range of institutions are to be entrusted with developing and disseminating innovations and 'good practice' to colleagues.

Decoupling as a progressive force

It is possible to see 'decoupling' in a different way – as a positive and progressive force for future development. According to this view, the separation of the individual award from the project is likely to ensure that the main thrust of the scheme is successful – that it genuinely rewards individuals and promotes teaching and learning at departmental and institutional level. Increasing the number of awards is also likely to increase the visibility and impact of the scheme.

Changes to the project strand can also be viewed as positive and radical. For example, requiring a NTF to be a part of a larger bidding team may mean that they get greater support for their development work. The quality of this work may therefore be enhanced which is likely to improve its chances of being take up by colleagues in the sector. The status of the NTFs may also be enhanced and opportunities for the development of hybrid pedagogical research methodologies could increase, as cross-institutional and/or interdisciplinary sharing of research plans take place in project teams. If NTFs become centrally positioned in bidding teams and displace the 'usual suspects' who apply for pedagogical development and research funding, this would radically shake up powerful constituencies. The increased presence of former NTFs in pedagogical research may also help them to develop an independent and distinctive 'voice' on teaching and learning matters in higher education.

Concluding remarks

Recent changes to the NTFS and their potential implications have to be considered in the light of broader changes that are taking place with respect to higher education pedagogy. Given the critique of educational research and the shift towards 'evidence-based practice' (see Skelton, 2005: 155–166), the HEA have recently outlined a framework for research to improve the student learning experience. Drawing on the work of Ernest Boyer (Boyer, 1990), this framework claims to offer a broad conception of evidence-informed approaches. It seeks to support scholarly work of different kinds notably: RAE-able pedagogic research (focus on theory and conceptual understanding); investigations and evaluations of local problems or issues; literature reviews (leading to recommendations for practice); scholarship of teaching and learning (evidence-based critical reflection on practice leading to improvement); and surveys of academic staff and student experiences of teaching and learning.

At the time of writing (June 2006) it is difficult to anticipate where the new NTFS projects fit into this framework. They are meant to develop and disseminate innovations and good practice in learning and teaching which does not map on clearly to any of the categories above. The HEA framework is an inclusive one which has the potential to foster a mature and effervescent higher education research community. However, important issues are not addressed, for example: the status differential between different types of evidence-informed work; the funding streams available to support them; who conducts different types of work and what is their presumed legitimacy?; paradigmatic differences in the constituencies that might undertake scholarship into the student learning experience; and how these might be resolved.

The new NTFS projects could be viewed as either 'research' or the 'scholarship of teaching and learning'. If they are meant to be 'research', then this opens up some of the progressive possibilities referred to in the previous section. However, it does raise the issue of whether a relatively small number of past NTFs will become part of an elite group of RAE-able researchers at the expense of practitioner research which will be downgraded. If the new NTFS projects are meant to contribute to the scholarship of teaching and learning (SoTL), then this raises questions about the *ownership* of SoTL. Historically – with the support of key organisations such as the Carnegie Foundation in the US – SoTL has tended to focus on practitioners pursuing enquiries into their own teaching with a view to improving that teaching. The new NTFS departs from this in requiring people to pursue themes predetermined by HEFCE and to work in teams that will foster 'good practice' for the sector.

Whatever our future hopes for the project strand, one thing about the scheme as a whole is clear. The radical design and potential of the old NTFS has been significantly eroded. Its implicit view of an excellent teacher – someone who consistently teaches to high standards, who undertakes systematic inquiry into their own practice and who is willing to engage in collective activities and share their work with other colleagues in the sector – has been replaced by a vision which appears much more conservative. As the main thrust of the NTFS retreats back into the giving of traditional prizes, it is hard not to conclude that there has been a failure of leadership and conviction. Recent changes to the NTFS have made no reference to the notion of a fellowship and there is no longer any requirement that NTFs engage in collective activities (although there are, of course, plenty of opportunities to contribute *voluntarily* to a range of networks, including the Association of National Teaching Fellows).

In retrospect it seems strange that the summative evaluation of the NTFS concluded that it was inevitable, given the scheme's difficulties, that the award for excellence should be decoupled from the requirement to undertake a project. An alternative response would have been to identify the reasons for the difficulties and take concerted 'remedial' action. In my own view the changes that have been made reflect an unwillingness to address the underlying tensions in the scheme (between recognising existing achievement and promoting future development) and their implications for how we understand teaching excellence. In my own research into the NTFS I became aware that both the HEFCE and ILTHE viewed the NTFS as an initiative to promote *teaching* and put it on a par with research. However understandable and laudable this aim was – given the research-intensive culture of higher education – it reflects dualistic thinking. The individual award of the NTFS has an obvious connection with teaching whereas the identity of the project – with its potential associations with (pedagogical) research – has always been problematic (see Skelton, 2005: 72). Decoupling these two is therefore a logical and inevitable strategy within a dualistic framework and it makes the scheme easier to administer and manage. It is a shame, however, that we have not been able to transcend this framework to give the NTFS – with all its radical potential – an opportunity to shine.

Chapter 15

Exploring teaching excellence in Canada

An interrogation of common practices and policies

Carolin Kreber
(University of Edinburgh, UK; University of Alberta, Canada)

Introduction

I propose in this chapter that Canada has not experienced the colonization of daily academic discourse by the worldwide teaching excellence movement to quite the same extent as has the UK or Australia and perhaps to a lesser degree the US. To situate the chapter, I first briefly summarize the higher education system in Canada to provide a sense of how quality assurance systems with respect to higher education function in that country. I then discuss the various traditional and more recent initiatives in place in Canada that are seeking to promote 'teaching excellence'. As part of this discussion, I will also explore whether the absence of certain initiatives (as found within the UK context, for example) can be seen as having positive or negative implications for the enhancement of teaching and learning in Canada. While the first part of the chapter is primarily descriptive and comparative in nature, the second part is more analytical and attempts to explore the notion of teaching excellence from two theoretical viewpoints: Canadian philosopher Charles Taylor's (1991) work on the ethics of authenticity and Jürgen Habermas's (1971) distinction between technical, practical and emancipatory interests.

Describing the Canadian context

Unlike the UK, Canada, to date, has experienced relatively little government interference with regards to teaching. Education, including higher education, falls within the realm of provincial rather than federal legislation and responsibility. Although all universities need to be officially recognized or accredited at the federal level, namely by the Association of Universities and Colleges of Canada (AUCC), degree accreditation is a provincial responsibility, and Canada's provinces and territories have so far resisted further involvement by the federal government in educational decisions (Marshall, 2004). While the federal government can be seen to fund higher education through transfer payments for health and education to the provinces, it is important to realize that it is up to the provinces to decide how they wish to allocate these funds. The federal government, therefore, supports higher education primarily through the major research councils and through support for students.

Generally, higher education in Canada is divided into university and college sectors, though each province has its own higher education system with different forms of transfer agreements between colleges and universities. Canada has 91 universities (and university colleges) and there are more than 200 community colleges (these latter institutions do not grant degrees and are more vocationally oriented); however, two of the community colleges provide higher education in the Yukon and Northwest Territories. Not surprisingly, most universities (45) are found in the most populated provinces of Ontario and Quebec. The number of universities (and university colleges) in the other eight provinces ranges from 11 in the province of British Columbia to one each in the provinces of Prince Edward Island and Newfoundland (Donald, 2006).

Although each institution is required to be officially recognized by AUCC, the provinces have their own unique procedures for quality control and approval of new programmes and institutions. Donald observes: 'Across the country, quality assurance occurs at three levels: the individual institution's program review process, some form of provincial or inter-provincial accreditation process, and membership in AUCC' (Donald, 2006: 27). For a more detailed description of quality assurance procedures in each province I recommend consulting Donald's (2006) chapter directly. Here it may suffice to say that while provincial undergraduate and postgraduate programme reviews are common practice in the province of Ontario, for example, the province of Alberta at present relies primarily on internal reviews but requires external accreditation of new programmes. Canada has not experienced the same degree of government control in relation to higher education as exercised by the QAA in the UK, although some provinces, for example Ontario, have seen greater government control than Alberta. There is in Canada no national Teaching Quality Website and, to date, no National Student Survey. Though Canada has witnessed the annual ranking of its universities for many years (published by the Maclean's weekly news magazine), the criteria tend to focus more on research than teaching, and the results are not linked to funding, which is in direct contrast to Australia, for example, where several performance criteria in relation to teaching and learning are used to determine future funding of institutions. Generally, universities in Canada enjoy a high degree of institutional autonomy balanced by accountability as exercised through internal reviews and procedures required by provincial governments.

Promoting 'teaching excellence' in Canada

In describing the initiatives in place in Canada that are aimed at promoting teaching excellence it is important to make reference to initiatives that are not in place. While there is no intent to provide a comprehensive comparative analysis, this section, therefore, will draw some comparisons between Canada and other countries, primarily the UK.

Despite some noteworthy developments over the years that suggest that teaching does enjoy greater recognition today than ten years ago, there are in Canada not the same pressures, but also not the same opportunities, associated with university teaching as exist in countries with established performance indicators for teaching excellence. There is in Canada no Learning and Teaching Performance Fund (Australian Government, 2006), no national QAA, and no Higher Education Academy that lobbies for teaching excellence with the government and provides nationwide support for 'the student learning experience' via subject-specific centres, generic work, accreditation of professional development programmes and funds for research and evaluation on teaching and learning. By extension, Canada has no national agenda with regards to supporting student learning (e.g. Smith, 1997). Compared to its neighbour to the South, Canada also has not benefited from major private foundations that fund pedagogical research and although there is some engagement with the scholarship of teaching and learning, Canada has no organization comparable to the Carnegie Foundation's CASTL programme in the US whose role is to prepare and support academics for this important aspect of scholarship. The Canadian Society for the Study of Higher Education (CSSHE) has not provided leadership for engaging with the question of what constitutes scholarly practice or meaningful synergies between teaching and research.

Canadian academics seeking financial support for pedagogical work notice quickly that such support is limited in Canada. Unlike the Higher Education Funding Council for England (HEFCE), Canadian governments, federal or provincial, have not launched initiatives aimed at enhancing teaching and learning at the university level (though a potentially promising initiative will be discussed below). For example, there are no Centres for Excellence in Teaching and Learning that provide substantial funds for research and development work on teaching. There is also no initiative comparable to the Teaching Quality Enhancement Fund (TQEF), which was aimed at enhancing teaching and learning at the level of institutions, subjects and individuals. By extension, Canadian universities have not been required to develop institutional 'Learning and Teaching Strategies' to demonstrate a strategic vision of how they will address learning and teaching issues they identified as critical and, consequently, there are no resources made available to support institutions in implementing their vision. As well, there is no National Teaching Fellowship Scheme which, as of 2006, provides not only substantial Awards for individual National Teaching Fellows but also for collaborative projects. There are virtually no funds available for the pursuit of pedagogical inquiry and innovations, except for small internal institutional grants (that typically range from 2,000 to 5,000 Canadian dollars).

Canadian academics seeking serious funding for pedagogical research would need to approach the Social Sciences and Humanities Research Council (SSHRC) yet few academics from disciplines other than education have the necessary skills and desirable track record to be successful in such a competition. SSHRC does not explicitly encourage innovation in teaching or context-specific forms of inquiry. Projects funded by the Council are typically those proposed by experts in the field of education rather than by academics from other disciplines who are motivated to experiment with educational innovations with the goal of improving teaching and learning within their given contexts. Chances of obtaining funds from SSHRC for educational research are roughly equivalent to chances of obtaining funding from the Economic and Social Research Council in the UK.

This rather bleak introduction to the general context in which teaching excellence is enhanced, promoted or discussed in Canada begs the question: so what, if any, initiatives are in place?

Institutional initiatives

In contrast to the UK, formal educational development initiatives in Canada have been geared primarily towards postgraduate students in their role as 'teaching assistants' rather than towards regular academic staff. Although different institutions organise such educational development for postgraduate students differently (typically referred to as 'Teaching Assistant', or simply 'TA training'), postgraduate students wishing to gain teaching experience while pursuing their degree have the opportunity to participate in generic programmes designed to prepare them for their teaching roles. While such preparation is a requirement in order to secure a teaching appointment in some departments, others do not require it and/or offer shorter subject-specific training delivered directly by the department or course organizer. Like most universities in the country, the University of Alberta, for example, offers a centralized TA programme through its educational development unit. TAs (tutors or lab demonstrators) have the opportunity to participate in a series of seminars and workshops as well as engage in a videotaped teaching practice for which they obtain feedback from an experienced staff member. Once the postgraduate student has attended a certain number of seminars offered throughout the year (and there is a considerable amount of choice built into the process) he or she is issued with a certificate. The programme is not formally accredited (there is no Higher Education Academy or similar central agency in Canada), and yet, when applying for positions, evidence of participation in such programmes is viewed very favourably.

The vast majority of Canadian universities have special units, sometimes centres, whose mandate is to support teaching and learning at the institution. Few if any have an explicit research remit but are service units, though a few of them engage in and also promote small-scale research. Some of these latter units offer a teaching grant competition that is aimed at encouraging pedagogical inquiry among staff. The money for this comes out of the university's operating budget and consequently the amount allocated to this purpose depends greatly on how sympathetic senior administration is towards such a scheme. Typically these educational development units also offer workshops on how to design a teaching portfolio (e.g. Knapper, 1995). TAs as well as academic staff can participate in this. These workshops tend to be offered frequently and are usually well attended as submission of teaching portfolios is increasingly expected by departments (though certainly not by all of them and not at all institutions) when applying for new positions, tenure and/or promotion.

Many universities also offer an orientation for new academic staff that focuses on the essentials of teaching and is skills-oriented. Some offer an entire semester-long theory-based course (module) on teaching and learning in higher education that staff and students can take for credit, and regular seminars, workshops, institutional conferences, discussion groups and reading circles are common practices throughout the year. Some universities have a peer observation of teaching scheme in place, typically facilitated by the educational development unit. Staff participating in the scheme are usually prepared for their roles through workshops and debriefing sessions. Importantly, uptake of any of these initiatives, including the orientation for new staff, is voluntary. It is essential to recognize that Canada has not yet witnessed anything like the UK White Paper (DfES, 2003) suggesting that all new academic staff need to receive preparation for their role as teachers. Most academics, and institutions, would consider such a move on the part of government a serious infringement on their autonomy.

Evaluating teaching via so-called 'universal student ratings of instruction' is common practice at most universities in the country. The questionnaires differ from institution to institution and some universities do not have a single form but allow individual faculties to develop their own. Most forms allow the students to add comments. The results of the evaluation are fed back to the staff member at the end of the course and are usually seen by the chair of the department. Student ratings of instruction (of individual semester-long courses) are considered in annual reviews of staff and in decisions with regards to tenure and promotion. Student ratings of instruction are complemented by peer reviews of teaching, self-evaluation of teaching, and as stated, increasingly a comprehensive teaching portfolio (which includes both of these sources of evidence plus a teaching philosophy statement and various other information [see for example Shore et al., 1986]). The extent to which evaluations of teaching carry weight differs across institutions. It is fair to say, however, that consistently poor ratings from students over the course of several semesters or years would thwart prospects for obtaining tenure at most, if not all, Canadian universities regardless of field or discipline.

In summary, Canadian universities have sought to enhance teaching excellence through educational development units offering an orientation programme for new staff, workshops, seminars and at times a peer observation scheme for new and experienced staff, formal TA training programmes, the widespread and fairly consistent use of student ratings of instruction of all courses taught and, more recently, at an increasing number of institutions including research-intensive ones, through teaching portfolios that are considered in decisions of appointment, tenure and promotion.

Initiatives outside of individual institutions

The Society for Teaching and Learning in Higher Education (STLHE) has been active for well over two decades and provides an important forum in Canada for academic staff to share ideas, educational innovations and increasingly insights gained from pedagogical inquiry (typically conducted on a small scale and without external funding but at times supported through internal institutional grants). The Society supports itself through membership fees and has now over 700 members. These include regular academic staff from a broad spectrum of disciplines but also educational developers. The society sustains a successful nationwide electronic discussion forum managed by the University of New Brunswick (the 'STLHE listserv', which also has subscribers from the US and a few from the UK) and meets once a year at a different university in the country for a five-day conference. In 2006 the conference took place at the University of Toronto and in 2007 it will be hosted by the University of Alberta, both leading research-intensive institutions. In 1986 the Society introduced a National Teaching Award (known as the 3M Award), which is held in high regard. However, the Award rewards past excellence of staff, does not explicitly support further inquiry into teaching and learning or educational innovation, and is associated with no funding comparable to that of the National Teaching Fellowship Scheme in the UK. Up to ten 3M fellowships are awarded each year. The selection criteria include 'excellence in teaching' over a number of years, principally (but not exclusively) at the undergraduate level and 'commitment' to the improvement of university teaching with particular emphasis on contributions beyond the nominee's discipline or profession to as broad an audience as possible (see 3M Teaching Fellowship Program, 2006). The award includes lifetime membership in STLHE, a citation and an invitation to participate in a three-day retreat at Chateau Montebello in Quebec. This retreat provides the winners with an opportunity to share past teaching experiences and discuss fresh ideas (see Skelton, 2005: 143–154). In 2006 there were 208 3M teaching fellows at Canadian universities representing a broad range of academic disciplines. As fellows, they work towards enhancing teaching and learning at their own institutions and through larger collaborative initiatives supported by STLHE.

Another important teaching award in Canada is the Alan Blizzard Award. Unlike the 3M Award, this award recognizes explicitly collaborative inquiry focused on active student learning. The website states 'Preference will be given to projects that involve active learning (e.g. simulations, inquiry, self-directed learning, or project work) and have a potential impact beyond the originating department(s) or institution(s)' (STLHE, 2006a). The funds for the project are carried by the individuals or institutions involved. The Alan Blizzard Award can also be classified as recognizing past excellence and is not meant to support future projects (although the assumption of course is that those who are rewarded for their important work will feel motivated to carry on).

A third very recent Award sponsored by STLHE is the Chris Knapper

Lifetime Achievement Award which seeks to recognize substantial contributions to educational development, teaching and learning in Canadian higher education. The successful nominee is invited to give a talk at the STLHE annual meeting with all expenses covered. To date, there are only two recipients of this award.

Next to these three main awards sponsored by STLHE, several of Canada's ten provinces (and three territories) recognize university teaching through a prestigious provincial award (for example, the Ontario Confederation of University Faculty Associations Awards) and institution-wide teaching awards are common in Canadian universities. Do these awards come with tangible benefits as do the CETLs in England that reward staff, for example, through enhanced pay or promotion to senior positions or even professorships (B. Smith, 2006)? The Canadian 3M, Alan Blizzard and Chris Knapper Awards do not carry the same significance in terms of institutional pay-off; however, they do carry some prestige even at research-intensive universities and there have been occasions when academic staff were promoted on the basis of having received the 3M Award.

In summary, Canadian initiatives aimed at enhancing teaching excellence generated from outside individual institutions have included the STLHE discussion forum, the annual conference of the STLHE and relatively prestigious teaching awards, which, however, do not come with any funding attached to them.

Recent initiatives

A recent Canadian initiative deserving mention is the Institute for the Advancement of Teaching in Higher Education (IATHE). The Institute was founded only a few years ago and has at present about 80 members from 30 institutions (including community colleges). The Institute invites both individual and institutional membership and appears to be most active in the province of Ontario. It is not a government initiative and there is consequently no expectation or pressure for staff or institutions to join. In addition to making available online resources on educational staff development and serving as a clearinghouse, the Institute offers workshops, seminars and summer institutes. It also provides an online course on Teaching and Learning in Higher Education. The website explains its mission this way:

> The Institute for the Advancement of Teaching in Higher Education (IATHE or 'the Institute') is a strategic alliance of educational development experts, award winning teachers, educational associations and institutions and corporations who are actively engaged in the scholarship of teaching and learning through the design and the delivery of professional development resources, programs and events to foster teaching excellence in higher education.
>
> (IATHE, 2006a)

The Institute to date has not had much impact across Canada and, importantly, it is unclear to what extent it serves the college (non-degree granting) or university sector. The Institute is perceived rather sceptically in some quarters given what appears to be a strong steering by business; yet, others see it as a promising mechanism to support teaching and learning in higher education. It should be stressed that the Institute is neither a research centre nor an agency like the Higher Education Academy that organizes a subject network, accredits educational development programmes, or provides funds for pedagogical inquiry.

A second recent initiative is the attempt to arrive at a deeper understanding (and better coordination) of the teaching and research relationship. The University of Alberta hosted two annual national conferences on the integration of teaching and research (University of Alberta, 2006) and there is in Canada an emergent interest in this theme especially now that a growing number of former colleges are receiving degree–granting powers for some undergraduate programmes ('university-colleges'). Institutions like the University of Alberta (or any of the other traditional universities in the country) are under increasing pressure to show that the high tuition fees they charge are justified. One subtheme of the conference on the integration of teaching and research is the role of pedagogical inquiry within the disciplines and whether, and if so how, such work may enhance student learning (see Kreber, 2006); however, the primary issue explored at these meetings is whether in an era of mass higher education, the Humboldtian notion of inquiry-based teaching can still be realized and, if not, what might be the alternatives. No provincial, let alone federal, policies have resulted from these discussions to date (though several universities have drafted such documents as part of their strategic plan). While an important underlying theme in these discussions is evidently the level of future funding for universities (which is based on tuition fees as well as direct provincial budget allocations based on student enrolment), there is a sense that the quality of teaching is enhanced if offered within a research-intensive environment.

A government initiative that could potentially have implications for the enhancement of teaching excellence in Canada is the Canada Research Chairs initiative. In 2000, the Government of Canada, through its Funding Councils, created a new permanent programme with the goal to establish 2000 research professorships – so-called Canada Research Chairs – in universities across the country by 2008. The Canada Research Chairs (CRC) Programme invests $300 million a year to attract and retain some of the world's best researchers. Of 1,632 CRCs filled by July 2006, 364 were funded by SSHRC (the others by either the Medical or the Natural Science and Engineering Research Councils), and only 34 were in education. Of those 34, five, perhaps not surprisingly, were in the area of new instructional technologies and distance education, one in pedagogy and instruction, one in self-regulated learning, one in lifelong learning and work and one in science education (including university science education). The others were very eclectic, ranging from globalization and internationalization to teacher training in grade school, but could not be linked to college or university education. On the whole one observes that the CRC initiative, at least to date, has paid only little attention to the study of higher education let alone the university curriculum and pedagogy.

Recently the president of the Society for Teaching and Learning in Higher Education reported that discussions are now underway between representatives of STLHE, the Social Sciences and Humanities Research Council, and Human Resources and Skills Development Canada to develop a national framework for supporting the Scholarship of Teaching and Learning (SoTL) in Canada. One proposed strategy is to extend the CRC Programme to include chairs in SoTL and to make available one CRC in SoTL per interested university across the country (Christensen Hughes, 2006). Surely, if approved, this would be the most profound investment into the enhancement of teaching and learning the Canadian government has made to date. For this reason, I would like to raise some unresolved issues with respect to this proposed CRC initiative.

Launching a Canada Research Chair in the scholarship of teaching and learning is perceived to have positive influences on teaching and learning at the institution where such a chair would be implemented as well as more widely within the entire university sector. It should be noted that a CRC comes with relatively little money attached to the position compared to the extent of funding that went into the CETLs in England, for example. In fact, holders of such chairs would be given a considerable start up grant but the basic award is that a CRC's salary is paid for by the Research Council (so securing a CRC is a great advantage for institutions as they, in essence, obtain a free staff member). In order to build research capacity, the holder of such a chair is required to apply to the SSHRC for funds for specific projects. These proposals are then subjected to a rigorous review process and it is by no means guaranteed that the application will be successful (but of course, CRCs become CRCs because they have an excellent track record with regards to research funding). There is also no additional money set aside for applications by CRCs but they compete with all other applicants for funding (SSHRC funds about 35 per cent of applications that are submitted to the Council as part of the standard research programme). A CRC is also expected to disseminate findings through traditional venues (academic conferences, journals or books) and although dissemination to the community of practice is encouraged, it is unclear what form this would take in the case of SoTL. Clearly, this dissemination would need to be well organized to have the desired impact on teaching and learning in Canadian universities. The other important issue to consider is the extent to which the initiative actually encourages institutions to pay greater attention to teaching. As mentioned, a CRC comes for free and does not rely on any institutional funds or commitments. It seems obvious that a single CRC at an institution of the size of, for example, the University of Toronto, would have very limited opportunity to make a difference in the teaching and learning environment of individual departments. A CRC in SoTL could be successful only if individual departments were to support or join the CRC in his or her mandate of enhancing research capacity on university pedagogy. This then raises the question of incentives and rewards. To what extent are academic staff in the various departments of the university rewarded for putting efforts into this initiative? This is precisely the question that remains unresolved in Canada.

The proposed CRC initiative would be at a great risk of failure unless institutions receiving such a chair are required to make a serious commitment to supporting their staff to engage in the work that the CRC would coordinate. If the CRC in SoTL is organized just like any other CRC in a traditional field, and the person works more or less independently perhaps with a few more researchers and postgraduate students from the home faculty (in this case likely education), the main purpose of the initiative gets lost. The main purpose of a CRC in SoTL, one would surmise, is to stimulate and promote reflection and coordinate inquiry into teaching and learning within and across disciplinary communities represented within the university, with the goal of enhancing understanding and practice in teaching and learning at the CRC's own institution as well as more broadly. A CRC working without support from subject areas or departments would have great difficulty fulfilling this role. As well, once the funding period for the CRC has come to an end, typically after five years, the achievements by the CRC may not be sustained unless the SoTL has been embedded within departments. For the scheme to work staff from other departments would need to bring in funds for pedagogical inquiry and should not be penalized in annual reviews for not having attracted a major grant for traditional research in their disciplinary field (*The Scholarship of Discovery*).

In summary, recent initiatives aimed at enhancing teaching excellence in Canada involve discussions of the relationships between teaching, learning and research, attempts to promote the scholarship of teaching and learning within institutions, the launch of the Institute for the Advancement of Teaching in Higher Education, and negotiations with the federal government over a proposal to create a Canada Research Chair in the scholarship of teaching and learning within each interested university in the country.

Analysing Canadian initiatives from two theoretical viewpoints

How might one characterize the 'discourse on teaching excellence' underlying these Canadian initiatives aimed at assuring, enhancing and/or promoting the quality of university teaching and learning? Drawing on two different theoretical frameworks, namely Charles Taylor's notion of authenticity as self-definition in dialogue around horizons of significance and Jürgen Habermas' distinction between technical, practical and emancipatory human interests, I intend to explore this question somewhat further. Rather than revisiting each of the initiatives described, my focus will be on the proposed CRC in SoTL, and SoTL in general, as parallels can be detected between these initiatives and some of those already operating within the UK context.

Discussing the nature of 'authenticity' Canadian philosopher Charles Taylor (1991: 66) remarked that:

> Briefly we can say that authenticity (A) involves (i) creation and construction as well as discovery, (ii) originality, and frequently (iii) opposition to the rules of society and even potentially to what we recognize as morality. But it is also true ... that it (B) requires (i) openness to horizons of significance (for otherwise the creation loses the background that can save it from insignificance) and (ii) self-definition in dialogue.

Grimmet and Neufeld (1994) applied Taylor's definition of authenticity directly to teachers, concluding that 'to be professional' (or here excellent) teachers need to 'possess an authentic identity' (p. 208). Connecting Taylor's ideal of authenticity also with Sergiovanni's (1992) moral leadership theory, they distinguish three motivations of teachers – the traditional, the alternative and the authentic.

The traditional motivation is to do what *is rewarded*. In the context of the previous discussion this would mean to approach teaching in such a way that it meets certain requirements as set, for example, by quality assurance agencies, funding councils, associations issuing teaching awards, the institution or department (e.g. ensuring that one does well on those items that appear on the student ratings of instruction questionnaire, etc.).

The alternative motivation is to do what *is rewarding*. What is personally rewarding can be understood within the context of some of the recent literature on teaching emphasizing the importance of 'knowing yourself' and acting accordingly (e.g. Palmer, 1998; Cranton, 2001). Applied to the previous discussion of teaching excellence this form of motivation can be observed when teachers, departments or institutions engage in activities that they find satisfying, fulfilling or rewarding for themselves. Surely, this could take on many different forms and, certainly, at times what is *rewarded* may also be perceived as *rewarding*. For example, a department undergoing an academic programme review may do so because it is rewarded (or required) but may actually find that going through the process was rewarding, useful or valuable. Alternatively, a department may expect its staff to engage in peer evaluation of teaching but some teachers may find the process very rewarding, while others do it solely because they have to. A better example, therefore, might be participation in a society like STLHE, which would involve contributing to the annual conference as well as being an ardent participant in discussions on the listserv. Most STLHE members chose to join the society not because it is rewarded (one earns few brownie points for doing this) but because there is a sense that exchange with colleagues is valuable. A further example for this second motivation can be found with staff choosing to engage in the scholarship of teaching and learning (SoTL). There are in Canada, to date, not many external incentives for such work. Institutions, at least the research-intensive ones, on the whole have not yet encouraged their staff to pursue pedagogical inquiry within their disciplines.

Hence, to suggest that staff engage in SoTL based on any external motivation (a sense that such efforts are *rewarded*) would seem, at least at present, rather counterintuitive (though such a motive, of course, cannot be ruled out entirely). It seems more likely that the few who choose to engage in SoTL do so because they find it intrinsically *rewarding*; that many of them would like to see their efforts also being rewarded is a different issue. I note here in passing that I see both a potential and a real danger for SoTL to be used as a way of engaging less research-productive staff in pedagogical research. As I will discuss below, it is not the idea of pedagogical inquiry that I am critical of; I am critical of delimiting the meaning of pedagogical inquiry to the parameters set by policy frameworks such as the Research Assessment Exercise.

The third motivation, the moral one, is to do what *is good*. Inspired by Taylor (1991), Grimmet and Neufeld (1994: 5) suggest that 'authentic motivation is … caught up in a struggle to do what is necessary and of value, not just for the organization nor just for oneself, *but ultimately in the important interests of learners*' (emphasis added). Teaching excellence in higher education can be conceptualized in the same way. Taylor (1991) emphasizes that authenticity involves self-definition in dialogue around horizons of significance. The horizon of significance within which to make decisions about how to assure and enhance teaching excellence in higher education is to do what is in the best interest of learners. What is *good* then may or may not be what is presently *rewarded*, nor is it necessarily what some of us consider most *rewarding* at this point. External rewards with respect to teaching excellence are necessary, but by themselves they are insufficient to enhance teaching and learning. Likewise, while I am sympathetic to the idea of doing what is rewarding in academic work aimed at teaching or supporting student learning, I suppose that exclusively doing what one finds rewarding involves the risk of becoming too self-indulgent.

The proposed Canada Research Chairs programme in SoTL serves as a good example to illustrate the three possible forms of underlying motivation just described. I might find it personally *rewarding* to hold such a chair (after all, a CRC is very prestigious) and I might be externally *rewarded* for it through substantial research grants from the research councils and invitations from other campuses to disseminate 'my' work. The university where I hold a CRC in SoTL may find it '*rewarding*' also because, most certainly, the fact that such a chair was launched there is one that the institution wishes to mention in public documents that speak to the extent to which it values teaching. It is not unlikely that the university may even get '*rewarded*' for this as more and more students choose to study there because a university with a CRC in SoTL surely does take teaching seriously! This is to say that the CRC in SoTL is based on a motivation that such efforts are to some extent *rewarded*. The other motivation at work here is that it is very *rewarding*. But how about the third motivation, to do what is *good*, or what is best for learners? It strikes me that we typically take the latter for granted, in fact the entire SoTL initiative (to take this as an example, and many initiatives from the UK context could be used instead) seems to be informed by the belief that ultimately this will benefit the students' learning experience. But how do we come to understand, or determine, what is best for learners? Habermas' (1971) distinction between technical, practical and emancipatory interests is helpful in addressing this issue.

In brief, Habermas (1971) suggests that the technical interest is to control and predict one's environment, the practical interest is to communicate openly with one another, to understand one another and negotiate social norms, and the emancipatory interest is to grow and develop by freeing oneself from internalized constraints. Importantly, what is not addressed when either technical or practical interests prevail, in the context of teaching excellence, is the question of how certain policies, institutional structures and established ways of supporting teaching and learning have become accepted ways of doing things. In other words, neither the technical nor the practical interest in teaching excellence, one may argue, contributes much by way of generating knowledge that would critically engage with dominant agendas.

The technical interest, one may argue, can be observed in discourses on teaching excellence that are prescriptive and regulatory in nature, but I suggest that relatively little of this can yet be observed in Canada (compared to some other countries). Since there are few grants or rewards for those institutions that do well on certain teaching quality indices, there is little indirect control either. If SoTL were suddenly given greater external credit, there might be a risk for the technical interest to emerge more strongly. Individual staff behaviour could then be seen as 'controlled' as institutions would reward publications in the area of university pedagogy. At present, I suggest that the main interest in Canada surrounding SoTL is still a communicative one. The goal is to better understand students and also to communicate more clearly with colleagues from within and beyond disciplinary boundaries about teaching and learning. The emancipatory interest comes into play as we explore why we tend to think of SoTL in certain ways, for example, primarily as research and as publications in peer-reviewed journals. Perhaps the moment we seek 'authenticity' as proponents of SoTL, and aim to go about our practice in ways that are in the best interest of students (as Taylor's and Grimmet and Neufeld's work would encourage us to do), we are provoked to engage in reflective critique of how we conceptualize SoTL itself. As part of this reflective critique, we would explore what is good for students and how this is reflected in present SoTL work. I suggest that scholarship which seeks to gain a deeper understanding of the needs, interests and ways of meaning-making of today's learners will benefit those learners (the usual rhetoric for this is 'understanding student learning'). Likewise, teachers gaining a deeper understanding of issues of diversity and inclusion and of what students need to learn in order to participate effectively, confidently and democratically in today's world, is likely to be in the best interest of students. In other words, SoTL involves asking what it is we hope students will learn or experience while engaged in higher education and deciding on what learning opportunities to provide to bring about desired learning outcomes.

It is widely recognized these days that the goals of undergraduate education need to transcend discipline-specific learning outcomes and include more generic ones. In this context there is a lot of talk about employability (e.g. Dearing Report, 1997; DfES, 2003) but also, at least within some quarters and particularly in North America, of the importance of universities and colleges to also educate citizens who have the Socratic capacity to engage in critical discourse on issues that matter to the our (global) society (e.g. Nussbaum, 1997; Axelrod, 2003). American philosopher Martha Nussbaum, especially, argues for the need of students to learn, as part of their university education, how to communicate across cultures. She would likely associate the notion of 'teaching excellence' less with instructional technique, perhaps also less with understanding how students learn, but primarily with thoughtful curriculum design that pays attention to questions such as whether undergraduates have exposure to courses that deal with issues of intercultural understanding, diversity and inclusion. Several scholars contend that the skills and attitudes critical for social responsibility and democratic citizenship are also relevant for success at work and other areas of lifelong learning (Baxter Magolda, 1999; Baxter Magolda and Terenzini, 1999; Yorke and Knight, 2003). While most academics would agree, to varying degrees, that university education should promote students' capacity to think critically (about social, political and environmental issues), solve problems and direct their own learning, it is less clear where, within a student's programme of study, the responsibility for these outcomes lie.

Barnett and Coate (2005) recently asked whether a new form of scholarship was needed; one that focused on 'curriculum'. I suggest that a problem with SoTL is precisely that it is not linked sufficiently to questions of curriculum. Perhaps rather than creating a separate 'scholarship of curriculum' our learners might be served better if the scholarship of curriculum were integrated explicitly into the scholarship of teaching and learning. Without doing so, SoTL could easily deprive itself of its main purpose, which is to enhance the student learning experience.

Essentially the point of the above discussion is this: SoTL may be informed by all three motivations outlined by Grimmet and Neufeld: doing what is *rewarded*, doing what is *rewarding* and doing what is *good*. Ideally, doing what is good would be the same as doing what is also rewarded and, ideally, doing what is good would be the same as that which we consider intrinsically rewarding. At the same time there is a real risk of SoTL being informed primarily by the first or second motivation. In both cases, as I tried to imply above, critical questions regarding the purpose of SoTL may not be asked and the achievements by those who engage in SoTL may meet certain criteria (as set by funding councils) but may contribute little to the enhancement of the student learning experience. Elsewhere I have proposed that the scholarship of teaching and learning encompasses more than traditional ways of engaging in, peer-reviewing and disseminating pedagogical research. I also argued for an approach to SoTL that, next to seeking a better understanding of how students learn, includes an engagement with the broader questions of what constitutes broader goals and purposes of Higher Education, or, put differently, engagement with the 'curriculum' (Kreber and Cranton, 2000; Kreber, 2005).

The Scholarship of Teaching and Learning might rise to the challenge of becoming an 'authentic practice', and perhaps it is this already, but it could also drift into little more than a way of meeting requirements to publish just a few more articles or obtain just a few more grants, with little real concern for the student learning experience. What direction it is going to take in Canada remains to be seen.

Chapter 16

Exploring and developing excellence

Towards a community of praxis

Philippa Levy
(University of Sheffield, UK)

Introduction

The ubiquity of teaching excellence in the discourse of UK higher education was further reinforced in April 2005, when a major new initiative was launched by the Higher Education Funding Council for England (HEFCE) to reward and further promote excellence in learning and teaching in the institutions it funds. This, the Council's largest ever single investment in learning and teaching development, was the establishment of 74 Centres for Excellence in Teaching and Learning (CETLs) across the sector. The competitive bidding process had invited institutions to make a case for existing excellence in teaching in subject or pedagogical areas of their choice, to demonstrate strategic commitment to reward and further develop and innovate in these areas, and to put forward business plans for sustainable development programmes. The result is a widely diverse range of CETLs that have been resourced over a five-year period, with funds of up to £4.5 million available in each case for reward and development activity and capital investment (new buildings and equipment).

At the University of Sheffield, the Centre for Inquiry-based Learning in the Arts and Social Sciences (CILASS) was created on the basis of a joint bid from the Faculties of Arts, Social Sciences and Law. The two-stage bid had been developed through the activity of a group of academic and learning services staff, working intensively over an eight-month period and undertaking a series of wider consultations with staff and students. 'Inquiry' emerged as the core pedagogical and developmental concept around which the proposal would be developed. The term 'inquiry-based learning' was not then in widespread usage within the University but seemed to offer a broad, umbrella concept that articulated well with what was valued by students and staff in learning and teaching, was a distinctive feature of practice identified as excellent in the Faculties, and chimed with the strategic goals of the University in relation to research-led teaching. The proposal that emerged was for an initiative that would be premised on a dual commitment to inquiry as the foundation for both student learning and for the development of pedagogical understanding and practice. A further key aspect of the conceptualisation of CILASS was a commitment to a strongly participatory approach to pedagogical development and knowledge-building, arising in part out of experiences of the new cross-disciplinary and inter-professional interactions that had taken place within the development group, and informed by the 'communities of practice' perspective on practitioner learning (Wenger, 1998).

CILASS occupies a unique position, structurally, within the University. An academically-led unit with a small core team of educational developers/researchers, programme management and administration, it sits operationally in a new space 'in-between' the academic service departments and faculties with which it works in close partnership. Links with departments are fostered by a network of student 'ambassadors' and academic staff 'champions'. The CETL is steered by a group including senior academic and academic services staff and the student coordinator of the student ambassador network, plus staff who are involved as departmental programme leaders and champions; its direction is also informed by an advisory group that includes members from outside the institution. Its programme encompasses strands focusing on educational development and innovation, evaluation and research, reward and recognition, enhancement of the University's physical estate for learning and teaching, and dissemination. The University's strategic commitment to inquiry-based learning is now articulated explicitly in the institutional Learning, Teaching and Assessment Strategy (2005–2010) and the intention is to extend the initial, faculty-based focus of CILASS to the wider University over time. In common with all CETLs, the role of CILASS also extends beyond the institution to engage with the wider sector.

This chapter approaches the idea of excellence in learning and teaching from a perspective that situates this in the practices of critical inquiry. My aim is to offer a reflection on what such a view means, in relation to the approach that CILASS is taking to exploring and developing inquiry-based learning, and to highlight some of the issues that arise in this context. The conceptual framework that is developed identifies critical inquiry as an integrating concept that offers the potential to connect students and teachers in new forms and relationships of learning and teaching, and that also provides the basis for a view of teaching excellence as praxis – that is, as a fundamentally open-ended, developmental form of engagement that generates both enhanced educational practice and new educational theory. The concept of critical inquiry is also offered as a point of departure for thinking about the developmental dimension of a CETL, not in terms of the traditional service provider model of educational development, but as a resource with which to open up new, reflexive spaces within an institution, in which there are opportunities for practitioners and students to participate collectively in educational innovation and knowledge-building. Some key aspects of the CILASS programme are highlighted in this chapter, in order to give a sense of the way in which this CETL is engaging with the notion of teaching excellence. However, my intention is not to give a full overview; further information is available at www.shef.ac.uk/cilass.

Teaching excellence

Any serious examination of the meaning of teaching excellence quickly raises fundamental questions about the purposes of higher education. Three broadly distinct perspectives are identifiable in current educational discourse. The first of these promotes the values and practices of academic learning: the purpose of higher education is that of enabling students to become competent in practicing an academic discipline, acquiring its conceptual knowledge and its analytical and representational techniques. A second perspective promotes higher education as a means of producing a skilled workforce, equipping students for roles in society and the economy through the development of generic, 'transferable' capabilities and skills in areas such as literacy, numeracy, communication, information-handling, new technology and collaborative working. The third, 'critical' perspective views the purpose and responsibility of higher education in terms of the goals of social empowerment and justice, and of engagement with what Barnett calls the inherent 'supercomplexity' of the contemporary world – that is, a world in which 'every framework, every value, and every action is contestable' (Barnett, 2005b: 793). In this conception, the role of higher education is to empower students not just to cope with the uncertainties and challenges of such a world, but to actively and critically engage with these in ways that enable their full participation in supercomplexity and its continuing evolution. There is an invitation here to look beyond instrumentalism, and the same time to see 'higher' learning less as a matter of the acquisition of discipline-based knowledge (though that clearly remains important) than of the development of a way of being that is characterised by dispositions and capabilities – such as critical reflexivity, autonomy and social responsibility – that enable this quality of participation. Barnett argues that in the context of supercomplexity, teaching has to take an ontological turn, from knowledge to being: 'Instead of knowing the world, being-in-the-world has to take primary place in the conceptualisations that inform university teaching' (Barnett, 2005b: 795).

Skelton's (2005) recent analysis of teaching excellence in higher education, referred to in the introduction to this book, identifies two dominant, mainstream perspectives which he characterises, respectively, as a 'performative' version, and a 'psychologised' version. The former reflects managerial concerns associated with maximising the efficiency of higher education in relation to socio-economic goals, and is promoted systemically through the production of external standards and criteria against which teachers' practice is controlled and measured. The psychologised version, widely espoused amongst practitioners, tends to situate excellence in the quality of the interactions between students and teachers, and students and students, both in relation to discipline-based learning and the development of generic competencies intended to enhance students' opportunities for employability and lifelong learning. Typically, this view is informed by a commitment to educational values and practices associated with 'student-centredness' and what Skelton characterises as 'progressive instrumentalism'; it is often underpinned at a theoretical level by constructivist, socio-cultural or relational perspectives on learning. It also typically accords a key role to reflective practice in the development of teaching excellence. However, from a critical perspective, this view often fails to engage with the implications of structural conditions that influence and constrain relations in the learning environment and the reflective practice of individuals, together with a tendency, as a consequence, to focus narrowly on technical questions about the 'what' and 'how' of higher education teaching to the exclusion of questions of its wider social purposes and value.

At a national level, HEFCE's CETL programme can, as Skelton (2005) suggests, readily be seen as both an expression of, and lever for, performativity in higher education. Through the programme, the discourse of excellence works (even if this is not the intention) to promote the idea of a gold standard against which professional practice can be controlled and measured, and upon which institutional claims to quality in the global higher education marketplace can be based. The programme clearly also accommodates and further circulates the psychologised view of excellence, as reflected in CETL commitments to learning understood as an active and social process, and to reflective practice. How far it embraces critical perspectives and pedagogies remains to be seen. But, as shown by Gosling and Hannan's analysis of the evolution of the thinking behind the CETL initiative (Chapter 10, this volume), HEFCE ultimately adopted a strongly developmental conception of CETLs that was not prescriptive of any one perspective on learning and teaching excellence. At the same time, there are possibilities, within institutional structures and cultures, to create spaces in which critical perspectives and practices may be explored and developed. In this way, opportunities may be created for CETLs to make a powerful contribution to challenging and providing alternatives to mainstream educational discourse and practices at the level of disciplines, institutions and indeed the sector as a whole.

Student inquiry

Inquiry-based learning is the term adopted by CILASS (and others) to refer to a spectrum of pedagogical approaches that are based on student-led inquiry or research (e.g. Healey, 2005; Khan and O'Rourke, 2005; Brew, 2006a). Students learn through engaging with the questions and problems of their discipline, and with the intellectual and creative works that constitute its focus or evidence base, in ways that mirror the scholarly and research processes of that discipline. CILASS aims to convey this by signalling a commitment to 'modelling the process of research within the student learning experience'. Different pedagogical approaches include case-study, problem-based and experiential learning methods, as well as small- and large-scale investigations and projects that enable students to engage fully with the inquiry practices of their disciplinary research communities. While the benefits are likely to be greater when student inquiry is placed at the centre of the learning experience at the level of whole programmes or modules, inquiry activities can also be incorporated productively in smaller-scale ways into more conventional curriculum designs, for example as part of seminar, laboratory or fieldwork activities.

The question of the value of student-led inquiry as the basis for pedagogy – or, to put it another way, the link between student inquiry and teaching excellence – can be approached from different angles. A persuasive body of research has demonstrated the benefits of student-focused, rather than teacher-focused, pedagogies for discipline-based learning: students are more likely to adopt 'deep' learning strategies, and to be motivated and enthusiastic, when they have opportunities to engage actively with intellectual and creative challenges that are authentic to their discipline (e.g. Brew and Boud, 1995; Prosser and Trigwell, 1999; Brew, 2001a; Biggs, 2003; Jenkins *et al.*, 2003). Student-led inquiry represents a powerful form of active learning and, as such, a progressive alternative to 'transmission' conceptions of, and approaches to, the teaching-learning relationship in the disciplines (e.g. Blackmore and Cousin, 2003). It also supports the development of capabilities and skills that will be of use to students in the workplace and other contexts outside the academy. More than these, however, pedagogies that place inquiry and research at the centre of learning in higher education offer the possibility for students to experience the uncertainties, conflicting ideas and open-ended problems of supercomplexity. Barnett (2000a) has argued that the notion of teaching as a means of disseminating information, research findings and scholarly understandings has to be abandoned, because this will not prepare students adequately for the challenges they will face in their lives. Instead, teaching must empower students to develop as creative, autonomous, 'critical beings' who understand the contested and fluid nature of knowledge and possess those skills of inquiry – such as gathering evidence, analysis, coming to judgements and reflecting critically on what they are doing and why – that are essential to full and engaged participation in a supercomplex society. 'Criticality', over and above 'activity', is at the heart of this conception of inquiry-based learning, and the pedagogy of inquiry represents not just a desirable, but arguably a defining, characteristic of what constitutes 'higher' education. Writing from this perspective, Brew (2006a: 14) says:

> The purpose of teaching thus becomes to induct students into various forms of inquiry so that individuals are able to live in a complex, uncertain world where knowing how to inquire is a key to survival. We are looking towards a higher education where inquiry can become centre stage for both academics and students.

There is a radical challenge here to the conventionally dichotomous relationship between teaching and research in universities. When inquiry is seen as the common link between what students do as learners and what teachers do as scholars and researchers, the distinction between learning and teaching begins to blur and possibilities for more integrated pedagogical approaches to higher learning emerge (Rowland, 2005). Through inquiry-based learning, students can be brought into fuller participation in the scholarly and research communities of their discipline, and into identities as co-learners, not only with peers but with more experienced scholars and researchers in the discipline. Brew (2006a: 3) articulates a vision of universities as:

> Places where academics work collaboratively in partnership with students as members of inclusive scholarly knowledge-building communities; where teaching and research are integrated, and where both students and academics are engaged in the challenging process of coming to understand the world through systematic investigation and collaborative decision-making in the light of evidence.

Of course, as Brew (2006a) notes, approaches to inquiry-based pedagogy vary widely and many do not extend to this vision of higher learning as an experience of partnership and collaboration within disciplinary communities of practice. Like excellence, inquiry-based learning is a concept that carries multiple meanings, accommodating diverse beliefs and value-positions about the enterprise of higher education. Disciplinary epistemologies, as well as the individual perspectives of teachers and the structural conditions of institutions and the sector, are all factors in the different ways in which teaching is understood and carried out in specific contexts of practice; the domain of inquiry-based learning is no exception here. The initiatives that are being developed through CILASS in the first phase of its programme are richly diverse in character and scale. So while broad consensus emerged rapidly within the CILASS development group around the concept of inquiry-based learning as the overarching pedagogical focus for our CETL, this is not to imply a unitary perspective on what this might look like or mean in different contexts of practice, and notions of difference and contestability must be set alongside that of consensus. A fundamental purpose of the CETL is to provide an opportunity for staff and students to explore this diversity of meaning and possibility through its development and research activities.

A feature of the CILASS approach is its work at departmental and school level, with the aim of encouraging further embedding of inquiry-based learning strategically, and in an integrated way, across degree programmes from the first year of undergraduate study upwards. Departments and schools in the core faculties have an opportunity to apply for funding for two successive inquiry-based learning initiatives within the five-year period. Healey (2005: 77) recommends 'modest shifts in practice' as a sensible way to start exploring inquiry-based learning at this level. Departmental programmes supported thus far by CILASS typically are focusing on the redesign, along inquiry-based lines, of specific modules or parts of modules; some also include preliminary projects in which staff are exploring current practice and issues in inquiry-based learning within their discipline, to inform their development activity. A smaller funding stream is available to enable staff to take forward projects outside of departmental programmes.

Building on existing practice and interest across the Faculties, the CETL has chosen to explore four particular themes in the pedagogy of inquiry-based learning. The theme of community and collaboration is one of these, with the aim of involving students in closer and richer interactions with peers and more experienced scholars and researchers, and of providing experiences of working practices that are of relevance to social and professional contexts beyond the academic world. The programme has also adopted a special focus on information literacy, on the premise that this area of capability is fundamental to creative and generative inquiry. Broadly defined as the capacity to find and use information effectively in any given context, through any medium (whether digital or other), the CILASS approach is informed by a view of information literacy as an inherently situated social practice rather than a set of generic skills, with a key role to play in the development of criticality, social responsibility and the creation and sharing of knowledge, as well as information seeking and processing (see, for example, Johnston and Webber 2003; Williams, 2005). CILASS projects are developing embedded, discipline-sensitive approaches to the development of students' information literacy within specific contexts of inquiry-based learning.

The digital environment offers an ever-widening range of creative possibilities for supporting and mediating student inquiry and research, including for the purposes of reflection and interaction within groups and communities of learners as well as for dissemination of, and access to, digital content. In a third thematic strand, CILASS is exploring and developing the use of learning technologies, including the University's virtual learning environment, social software such as weblogs and new digital tools for activity-focused pedagogical design. Finally, the CETL aims to encourage the development of more opportunities for students to engage in interdisciplinary inquiry, as a means of exploring beyond the practices and assumptions their own disciplinary paradigms, and of contributing to the learning of their peers in other disciplines.

Practitioner inquiry

The idea of teaching excellence that I am exploring in this chapter is based on the premise that critical practitioner inquiry into learning and teaching is fundamental to its development. This position rests on a number of foundational propositions about the nature of professional action and knowledge in teaching. Principal among these is the view that teaching is an intellectual and moral enterprise that calls upon teachers to exercise professional judgements flexibly in response to situations that are highly situated, constrained and dynamic, and that open up very real questions about how education should be thought about and approached. In such a context, the Aristotelian concept of *praxis* offers a way of conceptualising excellence in terms of 'informed, committed action' –

informed, that is, by practitioners' critical engagement with the questions and problems that arise in the lived context of their practice. We can recognise praxis as having a moral dimension in being an expression of the values that are brought to bear on action, and to be generative of both effective action and new practitioner knowledge (Carr and Kemmis, 1986).

Seen through the lens of praxis, teaching excellence emerges both as a quality or disposition of professional engagement (inquiring) and as a fundamentally situated and ongoing developmental process. Understood in this way, criteria and standards for excellence can never be rigidly or comprehensively pre-specified and can only be evidenced and evaluated qualitatively in terms of practical judgements, action and impact in specific educational contexts. Inquiring teachers reflect critically and explore questions about educational content, processes and impact as a means of improving what they do. They are willing to look afresh at the assumptions and beliefs that provide the basis for their educational thinking in the light of alternative perspectives and to engage explicitly with standards of judgement for the quality of their inquiries, and of their educational understandings and practices, from the wider field. As a CETL, CILASS has a role in the further development of recognition and reward for 'inquiring' teaching excellence at an institutional level, including through the CETL's award scheme for teaching excellence.

'Inquiry' in its broadest sense underpins a wide range of forms of active, critical practitioner engagement, from reflection on practice to in-depth research. Teaching excellence as 'informed, committed action' may, for example, arise out of ongoing engagement with current ideas about teaching in the field, peer review and student feedback. For CILASS, the idea of scholarship is central to the CETL's aim to build knowledge about inquiry-based learning collectively within our institutional context, and to contribute to the knowledge-base of the wider sector. A broad operational definition of the scholarship of teaching and learning is offered by the Carnegie Foundation for the Advancement of Teaching. Four core practices are identified: 'framing questions, gathering and exploring evidence, trying out and refining new insights in the classroom, and going public with what is learned in ways that others can build on' (Huber and Hutchings, 2006: 20). These authors advocate an inclusive definition of scholarship, encompassing small-scale efforts to examine and document teaching and share what has been learned at one end of the spectrum and, at the other, large-scale studies using complex research designs. Through the scholarship of teaching and learning, teachers who are committed to improving and innovating in their practice have opportunities to explore questions that are important in their own contexts and to contribute to the enhancement of practice in the wider community through sharing the outcomes of their work. It is argued that what distinguishes scholarship from experimentation and critical reflection on experience, is that scholars of teaching go further than these to engage with the scholarly literature of teaching and learning, and open up the educational understandings that arise out of their work to critical scrutiny through peer review, thereby contributing to the body of knowledge of the field. In a similar formulation, Trigwell *et al.* (2000) have suggested that 'higher-order' forms of the scholarship of teaching and learning are characterised by holding student-focused conceptions of teaching, reflecting on specific problems related to personal practice, consulting discipline-specific literature on teaching and learning, and communicating the results through peer-reviewed media. Inquiry approaches used in the scholarship of teaching and learning include, but are not limited to, educational action research; there is increasing interest in applying research approaches associated with a given discipline to exploring learning and teaching in that discipline, and it is recognised that what the scholarship of teaching and learning looks like may be different in different disciplines. From a strategic, institutional perspective, the scholarship of learning and teaching is as important at institutional level as at the level of individual staff, as a means of developing the university's knowledge base about teaching and its distinctive forms of teaching excellence.

Kreber (2005) has recently called for a more critical turn in the scholarship of learning and teaching, such that the work of scholars moves beyond asking how students learn in different circumstances to engage with the goals of educating for empowerment and social responsibility, and further develop the 'emancipatory knowledge' of the sector about student learning and educational practice. For an initiative such as CILASS, this means including in our inquiries exploration of tensions and conflicts arising out of the structural conditions of learning and teaching, at the levels of individual and disciplinary practice but also the institution and the wider sector. Fundamental questions and challenges arise at all these levels in relation to the role of power and organisational/sectoral processes and policies, in the practical development of inquiry-based pedagogy.

The notion of scholarly, practitioner-led inquiry clearly challenges the distinction that is often made between those who produce educational theory (researchers) and those who apply it (practitioners). Practitioner knowledge is – and has to be – context-sensitive and evolving. It does not make claims to universality in the way that scientific knowledge does. But this is not to suggest that practitioner inquiry does not have theoretical purposes or outcomes – rather, that the theory produced in this context might be thought of as a form of theory-in-process, a dynamic, 'living' theory that is always open to refinement and elaboration through further iterations of purposeful inquiry carried out within the context of practice. Living theory may well be informed by theory that has been produced outside of the context of practice, but as the outcome and expression of praxis it becomes particularised (Usher *et al.*, 1997). Borrowed from the literature of action research (McNiff *et al.*, 1996), the concept of living theory seems to capture well the nature of the knowledge that arises out of scholarly, practice-based pedagogical inquiry of any kind, whether that is action research or other forms of inquiry, including evaluation or research undertaken using the methods of the practitioner's academic discipline. It also offers a way of conceptualising the contribution that CILASS aims to make to the development of theory as well as practice in the wider educational community. From an epistemological perspective, this view begins to break down the distinction that is sometimes made between the production of 'discovery' knowledge *about* teaching through 'pedagogical research' and practitioner knowledge *in* teaching through 'scholarship' (e.g. Trigwell and Shale, 2004).

Arguably, it is through scholarship that practitioner inquiry truly becomes generative of 'living' theory. Scholarship adds a deeper dimension to praxis, extending and validating the pedagogical knowledge that is produced through engagement with other relevant work in the field and peer-review of the inquiry's outcomes. As is increasingly suggested, peer-reviewed course portfolios and case studies may be as or more appropriate to the dissemination of excellence as the scholarly journal article, since these forms of representation allow for better representation of the lived quality of praxis alongside the practitioner's educational understandings. Digital media offer new possibilities for capturing and sharing the texture of rich and productive educational situations, for example through case studies that incorporate video-clips of practice and reflections upon them by students and staff (Trigwell and Shale, 2004) or through 'reusable' designs for technology-supported learning. The CILASS collaboratory spaces are equipped with video-streaming technology which will enable staff to record their activities and use the clips for personal review and reflection, and the dissemination of their practice. The CETL is also leading a project funded by the Joint Information Systems Committee of HEFCE, to explore the use of an e-learning tool for sharing sequences of technology-mediated inquiry activity (see www.shef.ac.uk/desila).

Alongside and closely linked with its development activities, CILASS aims to add to the existing opportunities within the institution for practitioners to explore questions arising from their practice. The aim is to provide a framework in which critically reflective and scholarly approaches to inquiry-based learning may flourish – opportunities for inquiring teachers, in partnership with students, to develop the practice and living theory of inquiry-based learning from 'inside-out', by critically and reflexively exploring the educational questions that matter to them. Of course, in practice we can expect individuals to adopt widely differing levels and forms of engagement in this enterprise; the aim is provide a variety of 'ways in' to participation in the work of the CETL as a community of practice, and scope for different levels and forms of engagement over time.

Community

CILASS is strongly committed as a CETL to participatory ways of working, as a framework for both its governance and its support for developmental and scholarly practice. The idea of the CETL as a 'community' is not just important because of the general desirability of professional values such as collegiality, partnership and collaborative working. Inquiring practitioners need opportunities to discover what others are doing, to exchange practices and feedback, and to engage in critical, reflexive dialogues with those who bring different perspectives and approaches.

CILASS seeks to create the conditions within the institution to engage the participation of students, academic staff, and learning support and development professionals such as librarians, learning technologists and educational developers in a community of practice for inquiry-based learning that is also a community of inquiry – or, as we might perhaps think of it, a 'community of praxis'.

We are guided in this project by the theoretical framework offered by the communities of practice literature, in which learning is understood as an act of participation and identification: becoming knowledgeable or skilful, and developing an identity as a member of a community, are taken to be part and parcel of the same social process. As Wenger (1998: 4) puts it: 'participation refers here not just to local events of engagement in certain activities with certain people, but to a more encompassing process of being active participants in the *practices* of social communities and constructing *identities* in relation to these communities' [original emphasis]. At one level, communities of practice are understood as groups of practitioners who share a practice, a set of problems, a range of resources and an environment within which to interact and learn with and from each other. At another level, they are understood as groups of people who share a way of thinking and being. The capacity to move over time from the novice's position of 'legitimate peripheral participation' to the status of full membership of a community of practice depends upon gaining access to participation in the common practices of the community, to its range of members – peers and more experienced – and to its other sources of information and resource.

Wenger (1998) makes it clear that the conception of community that underpins these ideas arises out of a perspective on the social conditions for negotiating and creating meaning rather than out of an idealised view of what a community should be (Cousin and Deepwell, 2005). A community of practice, he notes:

> is neither a haven of togetherness nor an island of intimacy insulated from political and social relations. Disagreement, challenges, and competition are all forms of participation. As a form of participation, rebellion often reveals greater commitment than does passive conformity.
>
> (Wenger, 1998: 77)

Opportunities for dialogical interaction are central in the negotiation of meaning, and for the development of what Wenger calls the 'shared repertoires' – routines, ways of doing things, stories, actions and concepts – which define and produce a community of practice. A danger in this context is that shared repertoires solidify into fixed rules and orthodoxies about the ways in which things should be done and thought about, and that overemphasis on the values of consensus (or the perspectives and practices of more powerful community members) close down possibilities for critique and creative innovation. For a development initiative that holds inquiry as its central principle, the challenge must then be that the spaces it creates – events, workshops, research interactions

– offer possibilities for critical dialogue around the themes of the CETL's peda-gogical activities, and in which the voices of less as well as more powerful members can be heard. In relation to this point, CILASS is beginning to explore ways in which to engage students in fuller forms of participation in pedagogical change, not just through evaluation activities but through involvement in the development of new learning and teaching initiatives, and conducting and dis-seminating inquiries into their own experiences and the experiences of other stu-dents as learners. For example, at the time of writing, members of the student ambassador network are embarking on making a short film on the topic of inquiry-based learning, from the student perspective.

As a cross-disciplinary and inter-professional initiative, staff and students bring a range of disciplinary and professional identities to their interactions within CILASS contexts. Recognition of the importance of specific disciplinary epistemologies and practices in shaping understandings of teaching and learning has led to a growing interest in discipline-based educational development and inquiry in recent years. Disciplines have been seen as 'ready-made' communit-ies for scholarly educational development (Healey and Jenkins, 2003). Similarly, the Carnegie Foundation advocates grounding support for the scholarship of teaching and learning 'where faculty already are' (Huber and Hutchings, 2006: 63), that is, in their experience of, and commitment to, practice and discourse in their local discipline – for example, by setting up discipline-based special inter-est groups, and supporting modes of scholarship that reflect the values and prac-tices of intellectual inquiry within discipline-based communities of practice. At the same time, an equally important role is envisaged for cross-disciplinary engagement; indeed, it has been suggested that cross-disciplinary dialogue may be essential for true critique to emerge, through opportunities for staff to engage with alternatives to the cultural assumptions, concerns and practices of their own disciplines (e.g. Rowland, 2003; Skelton, 2005). The Carnegie vision of a 'teaching commons' – an 'intellectual space' in which ideas, practices and resources are made available, shared and built upon – encompasses both discipline-based neighbourhoods and cross-disciplinary networks or communit-ies. This offers a useful model for CILASS in informing our strategy to engage our community through both discipline-based and cross-disciplinary and inter-professional channels.

A framework for evaluation, scholarship and research

This chapter is putting forward a view of teaching excellence as praxis, with practitioner reflection and inquiry taken to be a fundamental dimension of this. From this premise, CILASS has developed a framework for inquiry-based prac-tice within our CETL that aims to offer staff and students a range of possibilities for reflection and inquiry on inquiry-based learning, through involvement in impact evaluation and different forms of scholarship and research. Activities associated with educational inquiry tend to be conceived as overlapping along a continuum (e.g. Healey, 2000). We might, for example, think in terms of reflection on personal experience as being situated at one end of such a spectrum and 'full-blown' pedagogical research at the other, with a variety of forms of evaluation and practice-led scholarship somewhere in-between. Approaches to evaluation, scholarship and research can, of course, be differentiated in terms of purpose, scope and method. However, the boundaries between these three broad categories of inquiry are blurred; for example, some forms of evaluation have much in common with practitioner-led scholarship. Nor is the relationship between them straightforwardly hierarchical as is sometimes implied – depending on one's epistemological stance, some forms of scholarship might, as suggested earlier, be thought of in much the same way, in terms of status, as 'discovery' research. The CILASS framework therefore conceptualises the relationship not as a series of overlapping points along a continuum but as a Venn diagram (Figure 16.1) in which inquiry is the central, integrating link. This reflects the aspiration to foster a close, dynamic relationship between these forms of inquiry in the CETL, by focusing on the productive inter-connections that can be made between them. From the different angles afforded by practitioner-led scholarship, participatory approaches to evaluation, and pedagogical research, the CETL aims to explore the educational purposes, understandings, practices and experiences of its academic community in the arts and social sciences in relation to its thematic foci, and understand the impact of its initiatives.

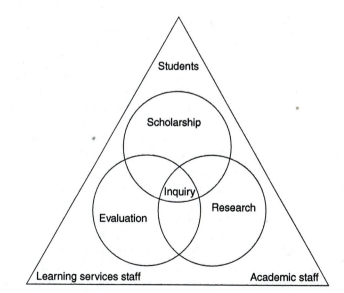

Figure 16.1 Towards an integrated view of evaluation, research and scholarship within a 'community of praxis'.

Evaluation can be seen as the central inquiry practice for the CETL – playing, from a communities of practice perspective, a key role in the development of shared repertoire and in the contribution of practitioners to collectively developing a body of knowledge. CILASS's approach to evaluation aligns with the new approach to evaluating learning and teaching development that is being applied more generally at the university from 2006 (Diercks-O'Brien and Powell, 2006). The approach is an adaptation of *Theories of Change* programme evaluation (Connell and Kubisch, 1996) combined with the use of *EPO (Enabling, Process and Outcome) Performance Indicators* (Helsby and Saunders, 1993). It is promising in providing a common framework for reflective, critical inquiry into pedagogical understandings, practice and impact within the CETL, and for collaborative exploration of commonalities and differences in the practices and understandings of diverse development initiatives and their relationship with overall programme-level activity. At programme level, the evaluation strategy aims to explore and assess the impact of the CETL as a change programme. The impact evaluation strategy includes an element of baseline inquiry and longitudinal follow-up, focusing on the student experience in core Faculties through an annual questionnaire survey combined with qualitative approaches.

The tensions between performative and critical perspectives on teaching excellence are perhaps particularly evident in the domain of evaluation; certainly the language of performance indicators more readily evokes the idea of measurement against system standards than reflexive critique. In the case of CILASS, we are exploring the use of the ToC and EPO approach as a way of facilitating ongoing reflection on practice in inquiry-based learning, and of recording the learning that arises from the process, thereby generating data that will inform discussions within the CETL and be of value from a range of different stakeholder perspectives. Normally employed at the level of complex social programmes, within CILASS the ToC approach is being applied both at overall programme level and at the level of departmental/school programmes and individual inquiry-based learning projects. At the level of learning and teaching initiatives supported by the CETL, practitioners are invited to reflect on the purposes and strategies of their strategic programmes/projects and to develop poster-style representations of their 'theories of change'. This leads into the establishment of indicators and evaluation plans. This is followed by six-monthly reflective cycles focusing on the way in which programmes and projects are developing over time, and feeding into iterative review of the wider programme and its activities so that learning can be shared across the community. Reflective conversations, facilitated by members of the CETL's core team, are complemented by formative evaluation of projects when they are first implemented with students, and then two years later by summative evaluation when there has been time to embed projects into the curriculum. CILASS makes available research and evaluation tools that can be customised, and ideas for creative approaches to collection of formative student feedback, such as student video diaries of field-trips, photographic journals of inquiry-based learning activity, and so on. Evaluation outcomes will include case studies, workshop events, journal papers and 'reusable' designs for learning.

The evaluation approach is, as a matter of principle, participatory in character, aiming to engage processes of evaluative inquiry that are stakeholder-owned. To this end, we are developing ways of involving students as well as staff, not just in terms of opportunities to provide feedback on new approaches to learning that they experience, but also in terms of participation in the ToC and EPO process, in developing the evaluation plans for initiatives in which they are involved, collecting evaluation data (with appropriate training, for example through student focus groups) and interpreting and discussing the findings.

CILASS aims to encourage and support different forms of scholarship in teaching and learning within the CETL, including action research and approaches that use the practitioners' discipline-based methods of inquiry. Academic fellowships provide opportunities for staff to take forward scholarly projects in their own discipline areas, and it is envisaged that fellows will contribute to supporting the development of scholarship within the wider community. A special interest group for scholarship has recently been established, and some collaborative project-work between academic staff in the Faculties and research staff in the CETL's core team has been initiated. A specific funding stream for 'scholarship' projects has been created, alongside those for development projects, and the student ambassador network has set up a student (online) journal for student contributions on inquiry-based learning and teaching. The 'scholarship' focus of CILASS's work articulates with other initiatives that aim to support and facilitate the scholarship of teaching and learning in the university, and serves to further champion it at institutional level.

The third strand of the CETL's inquiry programme aims to complement its evaluation and scholarship activities through a programme of pedagogical research. At the time of writing, a longitudinal study is commencing to explore arts and social sciences students' understandings and experiences of inquiry in the wider context of their engagement with higher education. This will be conducted alongside, and in connection with, a similarly longitudinal study of teachers' understandings of, and pedagogies for, inquiry-based learning in the same disciplines. In the light of research indicating that discipline context and staff conceptions of teaching, learning and research and the relations between them are critical in the development of inquiry-based pedagogies (e.g. Brew and Boud, 1995; Brew, 1999; Huber and Morreale, 2002), we are especially interested in investigating issues of disciplinarity, perceptions of the research–teaching nexus, and the impact of these on pedagogical practice and the learning experience. This research will include an explicitly participatory and action-oriented dimension, by using cycles of dialogical interaction amongst participants in a way that facilitates exploration of consensus and differences in understandings and the evolution of these over time.

Conclusion

In this chapter I have offered a view of both learning and teaching 'excellences' as inquiry-based practice. I have situated the development of teaching excellence within the context of critically reflexive, community-focused interaction in which teaching enhancement and innovation, and educational theory-building, go hand-in-hand. This is an ambitious vision and there are very real challenges for its realisation within the context of the CETL programme. The history of large-scale teaching enhancement programmes demonstrates the fragility of their impact when funding is short-term and when, systemically, discipline research is privileged over teaching and its scholarship. Gosling and Hannan (Chapter 10, this volume) highlight ideological tensions and ambiguities in the CETL programme that call into question its potential to significantly enhance the status of teaching both within institutions and across the sector. There are clear constraints on widespread engagement with the scholarship of teaching and learning in both research-intensive and teaching-intensive institutions; pressures on staff in terms of time and resource in all institutions are further exacerbated in those that are mostly impacted by a national Research Assessment Exercise that, historically, has accorded little recognition to this form of scholarship and pedagogical research. Critical understandings of learning and teaching are always at risk of marginalisation in the context of the 'performative university'. Nevertheless, I believe there is cause for optimism in the potential for CETLs, working strategically as individual units and as networks, to invigorate critical engagement with learning and teaching in institutions and across the sector, based on a teaching excellence that is, as Skelton envisages, meaningful in being 'dynamic, enquiring and reflexive' (2005: 174).

Acknowledgements

I would like to thank my colleague Andrew Cox, who coined the phrase 'community of praxis' during a discussion about CILASS and related ideas.

Conclusion

Alan Skelton
(University of Sheffield, UK)

A critical debate about teaching excellence

In a previous publication I stated how important it was for teaching excellence to be subjected to serious intellectual debate (Skelton, 2005: 167–170). This was partly because, at that time, initiatives to recognise and reward teaching excellence had gathered pace yet there was an absence of in-depth discussion about these initiatives, their unintended effects and how they related to broader understandings about the nature and purpose of higher education. The NTFS for teachers in England and Northern Ireland typified the overall trend: here was a national scheme with high material and cultural significance (each of the award winners received £50,000; institutions increasingly began to run award schemes based on NTFS criteria) and yet there was little deliberation about the meaning of 'teaching excellence' in the planning meetings of the National Advisory Panel that devised the criteria for the scheme (Skelton, 2005: 49–51). I also noted in the same publication (ibid.: 161) that much of the existing research into teaching excellence was of an *operational* kind – focusing on the extent to which schemes to promote teaching excellence had been successful within their own terms of reference. This approach to research failed to engage with the underlying assumptions of schemes, their implicit understandings of excellence and the values informing judgements about quality.

This current volume has set out to contribute to a debate about teaching excellence and to push that debate beyond the confines of the operational. The position taken by a critical approach to teaching excellence (see Skelton, 2005: 10–14) is that it is insufficient to make judgements about teaching excellence purely from an operational framework; one also has to scrutinise the framework itself and ask questions about the broader aims and purposes the framework intends to serve. Given the intellectual culture of higher education, it is important that there is a commitment to engaging critically with teaching excellence. This is because excellence speaks to fundamental ontological and epistemological projects: it is at the heart of debates about what the contemporary university stands for and what it is attempting to achieve. If teaching excellence is to get a foothold in higher education, therefore, and to be the catalyst for positive change, then we need to be intellectually curious about it and consider its different possibilities: this will ensure its fitness for purpose in the long term.

A range of international perspectives have been included in the book to strengthen its criticality. Some chapters have explicitly focused on developments (conceptual and practical) in a particular country (for example, Australia, Canada, Japan, New Zealand, South Africa, the US) whilst others have drawn on examples from different locations around the world. An important aspect of a critical approach is to make use of comparative perspectives and practices when examining teaching excellence in higher education. This helps to: 'contextualize, "locate" and "situate" our existing understanding.... Comparative perspectives offer an opportunity to see the world anew, to consider alternatives, to shake up taken-for-granted ideas' (Skelton, 2005: 13). An international collection also allows us to question the idea of a monolithic 'worldwide excellence movement': to discern the impact of globalising tendencies (such as teaching excellence discourses and practices) at the 'local' level.

Questioning the taken-for-granted

In the introduction to this volume, I outlined a number of commonly-held assumptions about teaching excellence that need to be subjected to public scrutiny. I want to now revisit these assumptions and consider them in the light of contributions made to this book.

Teaching excellence is a 'good thing'

Whilst the chapters in this book have reported many good things about teaching excellence and recognised its potential for positive change, they have also highlighted its limitations and the different ways in which it is impacting negatively on the sector. In Chapter 1, for example, Nixon challenges the view that contemporary higher education can offer students an excellence of their choice given the deep structural inequalities within the system. Within a stratified higher education which is resourced unevenly, he argues that students do not have access to equal forms of provision. The discourse of teaching excellence glosses over these deep structural inequalities enticing us into thinking that they can be overcome by the heroic efforts of individual teachers and/or the strategic planning of 'efficient' institutions. Furthermore, the teaching excellence 'movement' as a whole has tended to individualise teaching excellence and to deflect attention away from broader 'macro' questions relating to the quality of teaching and learning in higher education (e.g. institutional inequalities; reduced funding; high student-teacher ratios, etc.).

Teaching excellence initiatives have ostensibly been introduced to raise the status of teaching and learning and to recognise and reward the distinctive contribution of teaching-intensive institutions. An overt or covert association is often made, therefore, between teaching excellence and a process of *redistribution* in higher education – there is a view that it is only right that teaching-intensive institutions should receive a high proportion of the material rewards from schemes to recognise and promote teaching excellence. This is seen as good and socially just given that research-intensive institutions receive higher proportions of funding from research assessment exercises. Chapters in this book (e.g. Gosling and Hannan, Chapter 10; Jesson and Smith, Chapter 9) have shown, however, that teaching excellence initiatives tend not to be redistributive: 'research-intensive' institutions have been just as successful as their teaching-intensive counterparts in winning awards and being the recipients of funds for pedagogical development. Although governments may recognise that teaching excellence could serve a redistributive function and that this would be a good thing, they face the dilemma of wanting to encourage research-intensive institutions to devote more time to the quality of their teaching. This may help to explain why such institutions have been successful in teaching excellence initiatives.

Various chapters in the book also question the *fairness* of teaching excellence schemes. There is often an assumption that award schemes simply reward the excellence that naturally resides in those teachers or institutions that have been selected for recognition. Different chapters in this book, however, have shown that those that have been awarded the title of excellence are not always regarded by others as leaders in their pedagogical field and there are critical questions to be asked about the legitimacy of the evidence-base upon which claims to excellence are based (see Chapter 3 by Macfarlane).

Teaching excellence is value free and non-ideological

As many of the contributions to this volume show, teaching excellence is a contested concept which is underpinned by educational values and ideological positions. For example, Chapter 7 by Searle and McKenna demonstrates that teaching excellence is at the heart of struggles around the nature and purpose of higher education in a transforming South Africa. The country is involved in forming a new self-identity, and tensions around teaching excellence speak to larger questions about the relative importance of, and relationship between, socially transformative and economic agendas.

In writing about the CETL programme specifically, Gosling and Hannan (Chapter 10) expose the dominant neo-liberal ideology which underpins many contemporary excellence initiatives. They state:

> Although there are many variants within the broad concept of neo-liberalism, a common feature is the assumption that by encouraging enterprise, private endeavour and entrepreneurialism, public sector institutions will rise to greater achievements. The pursuit of self-interest is assumed to be the dominant human motivation. Success therefore needs to be rewarded even if this increases inequalities.... Not surprisingly this ideology has been

promoted by those who stand to gain most from it, the capitalist corporations, but successive governments, which have become increasingly dependent on these corporations, have been willing allies in its pursuit.

Whilst teaching excellence is often presented, therefore, as a neutral construct which is simply concerned with recognising and rewarding the efforts of hard working individuals and institutions, its ideological underpinning is much more suspect: as the authors point out above, rewarding success comes at the price of increasing inequality.

In Chapter 9, Jesson and Smith highlight the covert battles that are taking place in the development of a National Centre for Tertiary Teaching Excellence in New Zealand. They express concerns about whether high status institutions will 'colonise' what counts as excellence, since a traditional university model of teaching has already been valorised in award schemes. Kreber (Chapter 15) also holds up very different possibilities for an emergent teaching excellence in Canada. She shows that there are clear value-related questions involved in how teaching excellence is constructed in the future and advocates one that is for the public good.

All teachers and institutions can become excellent through continuous improvement

Various chapters in the book have shown that this assumption is problematic given the structural inequalities evident in most systems of higher education. Clearly, therefore, individuals and institutions do not start from a level 'playing field' and awards for excellence may reinforce and intensify inequality by responding to 'reputational' standings (see Chapter 12 by Dobson and Mori).

Some higher educators may work in settings with a high proportion of 'non-traditional' learners who have a wide range of support needs. They also may teach in contexts with a very high student-teacher ratio. Given such constraints, it may be difficult for such teachers to sign up to the excellence agenda even when we know that excellence often takes place – in terms of 'value added' to the learner – at the margins, in physical spaces and circumstances very different to those presented in glossy publicity material. Other higher educators may have little time and opportunity to inform their teaching with disciplinary research and the resources and infrastructure to support high quality teaching may simply not be available. Chapter 10 by Gosling and Hannan points out that although national teaching excellence initiatives are often meant to produce benefits for the whole sector, the CETL programme in the UK may experience difficulties in this respect, since some of the innovations will require expensive equipment and 'state of the art' physical spaces in order to be transferred.

Students want a teaching excellence that is responsive to their needs

We are led to believe that in recent years students have begun to take more of an active interest in the quality of teaching they experience in higher education. A Japanese student (reported in Chapter 12 by Dobson and Mori) made the following comments about the current situation: 'Since students are spending a lot of money as well as time, I think that teachers should try to improve their skills in teaching. I think there are many teachers who do not make an effort to improve the way they teach although they are spending time on their own research'. Such comments may seem unremarkable yet the consumer power of students could have significant repercussions for the way in which 'student need' is expressed and interpreted in the future. For example, it would be tempting to equate 'meeting student needs' with 'giving them what they want'. This might then get reduced down, within the busyness of new academic cultures, into an instrumental focus on what is required for the student to do well in formal assessment or the employment market. Or, alternatively, what higher educators may need to do to ensure high evaluation scores and 'customer delight' (McNay, 2003).

Various authors in this book have argued that this is not a sufficient response to 'student need' and changing material circumstances within which these needs are experienced and expressed (for example: students paying fees; having to take on paid work to finance their studies and cope with the impact this has on their study habits). The emphasis on inquiry in some of the accounts attempts to fundamentally shift the experience of the student in higher education and to reposition them, alongside their teachers, in a mutual quest to understand the world. This is not, therefore, about giving students what they want or using employability as the sole criteria to measure educational quality. Neither does it mean losing sight of the power relationship between teachers and students and the existing knowledge that academics have within their own areas of expertise. Positional power and vested authority can be exercised in principled ways (see Chapter 1 by Nixon) whilst recognising that people bring different resources to the process of inquiry. This means recognising that academic 'treatments' of subject matter and contemporary concerns (which valorise reason and rationality) have strengths and weaknesses. The recent emphasis on 'vocationalizing' the curriculum and championing knowledge that is of value to commerce and industry (see Symes and McIntyre, 2000) has shaken up the epistemology of higher education. A positive outcome of this has been a sensitivity to competing knowledge claims and the voices of different communities, including those of students.

Teaching excellence is necessary for economic competitiveness

At first sight, a teaching that is more responsive to the needs of the economy and commerce may be seen to be part of a broader 'democratisation' of knowledge within the academy. However, as many of the contributors to this volume have argued, simply 'vocationalising' higher education and its curriculum is not a sufficient epistemological and ontological response to conditions of 'supercomplexity' (Barnett, 2000a).

There is also a sense from some of the chapters in this volume that economic concerns are overshadowing other important issues that higher education needs to address. We have seen, for example, how teaching excellence discourses in South Africa (Chapter 7 by Searle and McKenna) reveal fundamental tensions between economic and social goals. Of course, an assumption is often made that the economic and social can come together and be directed towards the achievement of social justice. Searle and McKenna argue, however, that higher education is primarily being seen as a vehicle for positioning South Africa competitively within the global market economy and this is eclipsing the crucial project of social transformation.

Other chapters in the book have questioned whether performative approaches to teaching excellence will actually deliver the economic returns that are expected. For example, D'Andrea (Chapter 11) raises critical questions about national recognition and reward schemes, showing how they are often inadequately thought-through and conceptualised. This has meant that such schemes have had less impact on the overall quality of teaching in higher education than was expected given the substantial funds invested in them. A number of other contributors have shown that performative frameworks can induce a passive compliance in both students and teachers to teaching and learning situations – this stifles innovation and creativity. Those contributors who have advocated inquiry as a basis for teaching excellence identify the sorts of understanding, process knowledge and personal qualities that will be conferred through such inquiry – these are the very things that are likely to be most consistent with high productivity and 'competitive edge' in the new global economy.

Teaching excellence helps to promote teaching generally and lessens the teaching/research divide

Various chapters in this book (e.g. D'Andrea, Chapter 11; Fanghanel, Chapter 13; Skelton, Chapter 14; Zukas and Malcolm, Chapter 4) have cast doubt on whether teaching excellence initiatives have raised the general quality of teaching and learning in higher education. Sector-wide impact of national level schemes to recognise and promote teaching excellence has been disappointing and this can largely be attributed to inadequate understandings of educational change.

Chapter 8 by Jenkins and Healey demonstrates that higher education policies devoted to teaching and research have tended to intensify the separation between the two activities. They also show that policy on teaching excellence specifically has been based on at best a misreading of research into the teaching–research nexus. In the light of this, they advocate ways in which both 'teaching-intensive' and 'research-intensive' institutions can build upon this nexus in distinctive and positive ways. Various chapters in this book have sought to overcome the teaching–research divide in foregrounding inquiry at the centre of the work of contemporary higher education institutions.

Teaching can only be excellent if it serves learning

The view that teaching can only be excellent if it leads to predetermined and high quality learning outcomes is challenged by various contributors to this book. For example, Clegg (Chapter 6) sees the teacher-student relationship as a partnership rather than one between a service provider and a customer. She maintains that teachers and students enter into an unspoken contract: one which involves rights and responsibilities on both sides. Part of the student contract is that they have to commit to learning and take responsibility for putting time and effort into their studies. Teaching and learning situations are highly complex and can evoke all sorts of emotional response: pleasure, pain and struggle are all part of the pedagogical journey. Given this it is difficult if not impossible to anticipate what a particular student will learn and a teaching excellence that is too fixated on measuring outcomes will lose its dynamic quality. So although it is reasonable to be concerned with student learning and move away from a view of teaching excellence that is narcissistic (in terms of an obsessive preoccupation with the act of teaching and technical aspects of its procedure), it is limiting to try and predetermine and control that learning too far.

Some teaching is provocative and can disturb the very way in which students see the world. Learning, in some cases, may be a very gradual process and teachers often remark that some of their 'best' students are not the ones that necessarily do best in formal assessments. Macfarlane (Chapter 3) also notes that higher education teachers often set assignments, tests and examination questions for their students which raises ethical dilemmas in a performative culture (related to the vested interest of ensuring that the students one teaches perform well). For all these reasons, therefore, we should be wary of simply equating teaching excellence with 'successful' learning measured by demonstrable outcomes or formal assessment scores.

Emergent themes

Each of the chapters in this book have sought to question 'common sense' understandings about teaching excellence and to move debates about it into more critical directions. Some of the presented work has attempted to 're-appropriate' teaching excellence for the good of higher education; contributing to a 'reverse discourse' that is more meaningful and positive. Four main themes have emerged out of this critical engagement which are discussed below.

Reconceptualising teaching excellence

This book has shown that teaching excellence is often conceptualised in narrow reductive terms and separated off from other aspects of academic practice. This has led many of the contributing authors to offer a *reconceptualisation* of teaching excellence, locating it within a broader frame of reference and re-imagining it as part of a more ambitious project. For example, Zukas and Malcolm (Chapter 4) maintain that we should situate *teaching* excellence within a broader notion of *pedagogy* and Macfarlane (Chapter 3) states that the teaching that is often recognised in excellence initiatives are the performance elements that take place 'onstage' (such as 'delivering' a lecture). This renders invisible wider aspects of teaching that occur beyond the radar of mechanisms for measuring performance – for example, activities such as ongoing tutorial support for students.

Various authors (Jenkins and Healey, Chapter 7; Levy, Chapter 16) recognise the importance of theorising teaching excellence and relating it to changing social and epistemological circumstances. These authors draw on the work of Barnett and his notion of 'supercomplexity' (Barnett, 2000a) to propose a view of teaching excellence founded on inquiry. Gale and Skelton both argue that teaching excellence cannot be understood simply as established teaching performance. In order for teaching excellence to be dynamic and responsive to changing circumstances (different students, different teaching contexts), there must be a coming together of experience and ongoing scholarship.

Finally various contributors (e.g. chapters by Nixon, Chapter 1; Kreber, Chapter 15; Jenkins and Healey, Chapter 8; Fanghanel, Chapter 13) remind us of the importance of locating teaching excellence within a *holistic* view of academic practice. Nixon and Kreber suggest the need for overarching moral principles to unify academic practice so that practitioners think not simply about 'what works' but what contributes to the public good. Jenkins and Healey situate teaching excellence within debates about the research-teaching nexus and, like Fanghanel, they demonstrate that contemporary higher education policy not only separates teaching and research but also actively undermines teaching through initiatives and funding regimes that privilege research. Through these broader conceptualisations, the authors in this volume suggest different ways in which teaching excellence might shake off its low-status shackles. In other words, for teaching excellence to take up its rightful place within the academy it needs a thorough 'make-over'. To do this it needs to cast off the reductive and operational logic that has kept it in its place and become part of a 'joined-up' and more ambitious project.

Democratising teaching excellence

The chapters in this volume show how in recent years teaching excellence has successfully thrown off its elitist connotations. However, we have now moved to a situation where relativism appears to rule. The CETL programme in the UK demonstrates this very clearly (see Chapter 10 by Gosling and Hannan). Different versions and forms of teaching excellence are being proclaimed with little sense of how we might make judgements about their relative worth and potential contribution to the higher education sector. Many governments seem to take the view that the meaning of excellence is secondary to the performative impact of excellence initiatives. Why worry about what excellence means when we can use it to drive up general standards of teaching and learning?

The proliferation of different understandings of excellence may seem, at first glance, to be a *democratic* impulse, shifting excellence away from its 'traditional' bearings (see Skelton, 2005: 26–29) and any universal 'idea of the university' (Barnett, 1990). What we have in practice, however, is a sense that anything can be excellent ('excellence comes as standard' – see Clegg, Chapter 6) which means that we fall into relativism and excellence fails to have any meaning at all (Readings, 1996).

If teaching excellence is really to become a democratic force then we need two things. First, some rigorous sense of what universal standards of judgement might apply to it or to competing versions of teaching excellence (in other words what might be 'universal' standards of judgement for different understandings of teaching excellence – see Skelton, 2005: 21–37). This would prevent the performative 'anything goes' attitude and climate that currently prevails in higher education. What we then need is material and cultural change to ensure that different forms of teaching excellence are equally valued and resourced. In systems of higher education that are stratified and characterised by clear inequalities (in terms of resources available for students and teachers; in terms of the life chances that are bestowed on people who attend different universities etc.), this is a huge hurdle to overcome, requiring political will and changes in funding regimes (see Chapter 1 by Nixon for detailed suggestions on how this might be done). Cultural change also needs to occur if there is to be a real acceptance and valuing of different forms of excellence based on institutional identity and mission. Paradoxically what may be required to support such cultural change is the establishment of a unifying set of *core* principles for *all* higher education institutions and an entitlement to a level of resourcing that would allow these principles to be realised. It is only through such changes that we can overcome the limitations of relativism and move towards a situation where different expressions of excellence have meaning and carry equal status and weight.

Realising teaching excellence

The accounts in this volume demonstrate that, in order to realise teaching excellence, we need to adopt more sophisticated approaches to educational change at institutional and system levels. There are already too many examples of cost-intensive, major initiatives failing to deliver on what they set out to achieve (for example, the TQEF) and this is often due to inadequate understandings of the dynamics of change. It is also important to give due consideration to the 'meso' level of the department or discipline (Fanghanel, Chapter 13) when seeking to promote teaching excellence since it has been clearly shown in this book that this level has a significant impact on change as most academics identify with their departments more than their institution.

Sue Clegg (Chapter 6) argues persuasively that teaching excellence cannot be achieved by fiat, however dynamic, well-intentioned and committed change agents are to educational developments. This is because the 'brute sanity' (Fullan, 1982) of policymakers will always come up against the complexities and realities of practice. Clegg identifies a clear mismatch between the imposed standards of the quality movement (of which excellence is the latest expression) and those interiorised standards of judgement used by practitioners in craft-like activities such as teaching. To ignore such a mismatch is folly and undermines the potential of excellence initiatives to achieve any lasting change. A further problem with overly rational approaches to educational change imposed on higher education teachers is that even if these are successful they can encourage compliant and unimaginative responses to teaching and learning situations which is damaging to quality and professional standards in the long run. This is of particular concern in a country like South Africa (see Searle and McKenna, Chapter 7) where pedagogy is key to social transformation.

Zukas and Malcolm (Chapter 4) observe what happens when teaching excellence initiatives pay insufficient attention to existing higher education networks – including disciplinary communities. Whilst such initiatives may set out to improve the quality of teaching and raise overall standards, they are likely to meet with limited success if the creation of new communities (that are linked to the 'excellence movement' – involving award-winners, people responsible for teaching enhancement etc.) fail to interact positively with those already established. Fanghanel makes a similar point in drawing our attention to the lack of 'joined-up' policy making in higher education and its impact on teaching excellence. What emerges from this account is the recognition that policy has to be ambitious and follow a holistic conceptualisation of our work together in higher education. In order for teaching excellence to be realised, therefore, we need research and teaching to be brought together in a close relationship; unfortunately, as many of the accounts in this volume note, current policy and funding regimes that flow from this often support and further intensify the separation of teaching from research.

Radicalising teaching excellence

Many of the contributors to this volume show how limited performative and psychologised understandings are in capturing teaching excellence and identifying its part in the ontological and epistemological project of higher education. They have shown how the imposition of external measures of performance, drawn from the world of business and commerce, have made it very difficult for higher education teachers to 'write themselves in' to pedagogical practice (see Chapter 6 by Clegg), which encourages passivity, compliance and a reluctance to innovate. Not withstanding the impact of this on individuals – in terms of their emotional and psychological wellbeing – such a climate has significant implications for the future of higher education, since it is difficult to see how it can foster a fresh and radical teaching excellence that is required to inspire new generations of students.

Some of the chapters in the book offer us a new language to think about teaching excellence beyond the '3Es' of economy, efficiency and effectiveness. Nixon, for example, encourages to think about an academic practice built on truthfulness, respect and authenticity. Other chapters recognise the importance of opening up 'critical spaces' for teaching excellence, and show how schemes to promote excellence, such as the CETL programme, can be creatively interpreted within institutions (see Gosling and Hannan, Chapter 10) and shaped in the light of broader social transformatory goals (see Chapter 16 by Levy). In reflecting on the situation in Canada, where discourses of teaching excellence have yet to emerge to the same degree as in the UK and US, Kreber envisages three very different future scenarios: one where a performative teaching excellence takes hold; one where individual teachers develop their own understanding of teaching excellence; and a third, more radical conception of an excellence that serves the public good.

There are several chapters in the book which focus on the importance of inquiry in any contemporary understanding of teaching excellence. Inquiry has radical implications for the teacher-student relationship in higher education since it can be undertaken by all, building on the unique resources each person brings to the process (see Chapter 5 by Brew). What is important here is the development of an engagement with knowledge and the world which helps everyone manage conditions of supercomplexity. The chapters by Gale (Chapter 2) and Skelton (Chapter 14) focus on the importance of teacher inquiry in any understanding of teaching excellence. Here there is a fruitful coming together of disciplinary knowledge, established pedagogical expertise and the willingness to explore one's own practice. Skelton shows how recent changes to the NTFS have undermined its radical potential in separating out experienced performance from ongoing inquiry. The chapter concludes that any radical notion of teaching excellence would involve teachers themselves contributing to the production of pedagogical knowledge rather than leaving this to so-called 'experts'.

The end of excellence?

Given that teaching excellence is often understood in simply performative and/or psychologised terms, there have been moments in this book where contributors have suggested that we should have nothing to do with it – we should distance ourselves from excellence and wish for its demise. There has also been some recognition that the excellence movement is an expression of a particular historical moment – the latest in a series of organisational change management strategies to sweep public institutions. In the light of this, it is tempting to think that teaching excellence will only have a limited shelf-life and may soon disappear from our discursive and material existence. One way of thinking about the future of excellence, therefore, is to play a waiting game and hope that it will gradually whither away and die.

Some contributors have suggested that the term 'good' may be preferable to excellence since the former implies a moral quality rather than a scale. Doubts have been expressed as to whether excellence will ever be able to shake off its elitist connotations and be a force for positive change within mass systems of provision. Concerns have also been raised about whether a performative understanding of excellence provides an adequate language and set of underlying values for our work – using the term 'good' takes the mind much more effectively back to first principles.

Despite these understandable concerns, the overriding response in this book has been to view teaching excellence as an important concept and to consider ways in which it might be reappropriated for positive ends. Excellence is such a crucial concept because it gets to the heart of what we are trying to achieve in higher education – it takes us back to fundamental questions about aims and purposes and the role of higher education in a changing society. It can also bring us together, requiring us to think about what is distinct about higher learning in these times of turbulent change. This book maintains that in order for teaching excellence to move beyond elitist and relativistic notions and play a meaningful part in our lives, it needs to be reconceptualised, democratised, more effectively realised and radicalised in intent. This is not a book, therefore, about the end of excellence; rather it is an appeal to what excellence could be, if we breathe new life into it.

Bibliography

Academic Ranking of World Universities (ARWU) (2005) *Top World 500 Universities* (ed.sjtu.edu.cn/rank/2005/ARWU2005.xls – accessed 19 July 2006).

Akabayashi, H. (2006) 'Private universities and government policy in Japan', *International Higher Education*, 42: 17—19.

Allen, W.B. and Allen, C.M. (2003) *Habits of Mind: Fostering Access and Excellence in Higher Education*. New Brunswick and London: Transaction Publishers.

Altbach, P.G. and Ogawa, Y. (2002) 'Introduction', *Higher Education*, 43: 1—6.

Alvesson, M. (2002) *Understanding Organisational Culture*. London: Sage.

Amano, I. (1997) 'Structural changes in Japan's higher education system – from planning to a market model', *Higher Education*, 34: 125–139.

Andrews, J., Garrison, D.R. and Magnusson, K. (1996) 'The teaching and learning transaction in higher education: a study of excellent professors and their students', *Teaching in Higher Education*, 1: 81–103.

Apodaca, P. and Grad, H. (2006) 'The dimensionality of student ratings of teaching: integration of uni- and multi-dimensional models', *Studies in Higher Education*, 30: 723–748.

Apple, M.W. (2004) 'Creating difference: Neo-Liberalism, Neo-Conservatism and the politics of educational reform', *Educational Policy*, 18: 12–44.

Apter, M. (1989) 'Negativism and the sense of identity', in G. Breakwell (ed.) *Threatened Identities*. London: Wiley.

Archer, L. (2003) 'The "value" of higher education', in L. Archer, M. Hutchings and A. Ross (eds) *Higher Education and Social Class: Issues of Exclusion and Social Class*. Abingdon and New York: RoutledgeFalmer.

Arena (2001) 'Why are there so many award ceremonies?' BBC2, 11.20pm on 13 May.

Arendt, H. (1998) *The Human Condition*. Chicago: University of Chicago Press.

Arimoto, A. (1997) 'Market and higher education in Japan', *Higher Education Policy*, 10: 199—210.

Aristotle (1955) *The Ethics of Aristotle: The Nicomachean Ethics*. Translated by J.A.K. Thompson and revised by H. Tredennick. London: Penguin Books.

Armstrong, P. (2003) 'Teaching as stand-up comedy: the metaphor of scripted and improvised performance of teaching', paper presented at SCUTREA annual conference, Bangor, July.

Aron, D.C., Aucott, J.N. and Papp, K.K. (2000) 'Teaching awards and reduced departmental longevity: kiss of death or kiss goodbye. What happens to excellent clinical teachers?', *Medical Educ Online*, 5:3 (www.med-ed-online.org).

Ashcroft, C. (2005) 'Performance-Based Research Funding: a mechanism to allocate funds or a tool for academic promotion?', *New Zealand Journal of Educational Studies*, 40: 113–130.

Ashcroft, C. and Nairn, K. (2004) 'Critiquing the tertiary education's role in New Zealand's tertiary education system: policy, practice and panopticism', *ACCESS: Critical Perspectives on Communication, Cultural and Policy Studies*, 23: 43–55.

Ashwin, P. and McLean, M. (2005) 'Towards a reconciliation of phenomenographic and critical pedagogy perspectives in higher education through a focus on academic engagement', in C. Rust (ed.) *Improving Student Learning 12 – Diversity and Inclusivity*. Oxford: The Oxford Centre for Staff and Learning Development.

Asiaweek (2000) *Asia's Best Universities 2000* (www.asiaweek.com/asiaweek/features/universities2000/index.html – accessed 19 July 2006).

Asonuma, A. (2002) 'Finance reform in Japanese higher education', *Higher Education*, 43: 109–126.

Astin, A.W. (1993a) *What Matters in College: Four Critical Years Revisited*. San Francisco: Jossey-Bass.

Astin, A.W. (1993b) *Assessment for Excellence: The Philosophy and Practice of Assessment and Evaluation in Higher Education*. Phoenix: Oryx Press.

Astin, A.W. (2000) 'Competition or cooperation? Teaching teamwork as a basic skill', in D. Dezure (ed.) *Learning From Change, Landmarks in Teaching and Learning in Higher Education from Change Magazine*. London: Kogan Page.

Australian Government (2006) *Learning and Teaching Performance Fund* (www.dest.gov.au/sectors/higher_education/policy_issues_reviews/key_issues/learning_teaching/ltpf/ – accessed 19 September 2006).

Avis, J. (2000) 'Policing the subject: learning outcomes, managerialism and research in PCET', *British Journal of Educational Studies*, 48: 38–57.

Avis, J. (2003) 'Re-thinking trust in a performative culture: the case of education', *Journal of Education Policy*, 18: 315–332.

Axelrod, P. (2003) *Values in Conflict: The University, the Marketplace, and the Trials of Liberal Education*. Montreal: McGill-Queen's University Press.

Bakhtin, M. (1973) *Problems of Dostoevsky's Poetics*. Translated by R. Rotsch. Ann Arbor: Ardis.

Ball, S.J. (2003) 'The teacher's soul and the terrors of performativity', *Journal of Education Policy*, 18: 215–228.

Ball, S.J., Davies, J., David, M.E. and Reay, D. (2002) '"Classification" and "judgment": social class and the "cognitive structures" of choice of higher education', *British Journal of Sociology of Education*, 23: 51–72.

Ballantyne, R., Bain, J. and Packer, J. (1999) 'Researching university teaching in Australia: themes and issues in academics' reflections', *Studies in Higher Education*, 24: 237–257.

Barefoot, B.O. (2004) 'Higher education's revolving door: confronting the problem of student drop out in US colleges and universities', *Open Learning*, 19: 9–18.

Barnett, R. (1990) *The Idea of Higher Education*. Buckingham: The Society for Research into Higher Education (SRHE)/Open University Press.

Barnett, R. (1997) *Higher Education: A Critical Business*. Buckingham: Open University Press.

Barnett, R. (2000a) *Realizing the University in an Age of Supercomplexity*. Buckingham and Philadelphia: SRHE/Open University Press.

Barnett, R. (2000b) 'Supercomplexity and the curriculum', *Studies in Higher Education*, 25: 256–265.

Barnett, R. (2003) *Beyond All Reason. Living with Ideology in the University*. Buckingham: SRHE/Open University Press.

Barnett, R. (2004) 'Learning for an unknown future', *Higher Education Research and Development*, 23 (3): 247–260.

Barnett, R. (ed.) (2005a) *Reshaping the University: New Relationships Between Research, Scholarship and Teaching*. Maidenhead: Open University Press.

Barnett, R. (2005b) 'Recapturing the universal in the University', *Educational Philosophy and Theory*, 37: 785–797.

Barnett, R. and Coate, K. (2005) *Engaging the Curriculum in Higher Education*. Maidenhead, Berkshire: SRHE/Open University Press.

Barr, R.B. and Tagg, J. (1995) 'From teaching to learning – a new paradigm for undergraduate education', *Change*, 27: 12–25.

Barrett, R. (2006) *Building a Values-Driven Organization: A Whole System Approach to Cultural Transformation*. Oxford: Butterworth-Heinemann.

Bartlett, T. (2003) 'What makes a teacher great?', *Chronicle of Higher Education*, 50: A8–A9.

Baxter-Magolda, M. (1999) *Creating Contexts for Learning and Self-authorship. Constructive-developmental Pedagogy*. Nashville, TN: Vanderbilt University Press.

Baxter-Magolda, M. and Terenzini, P.T. (1999) *Learning and Teaching in the 21st Century: Trends and Implications for Practice* (www.acpa.nche.edu/srsch/magolda_terenzini.html).

Beaudry, M. and Bruce, A. (2003) *A Campus-Wide Mission: The Scholarship of Teaching*. Lowell, Massachusetts: American Association for Higher Education and University of Massachusetts.

Becher, T. and Trowler, P.R. (2001). *Academic Tribes and Territories*. Buckingham: SRHE/Open University Press.

Becker, W. and Andrews, M. (2004) *The Scholarship of Teaching and Learning in Higher Education: The Contribution of the Research Universities*. Bloomington: Indiana University Press.

Bereiter, C. (2002) *Education and the Mind in the Knowledge Age*. Mahwah: Lawrence Erlbaum Associates.

Bernstein, B. (1996) *Pedagogy, Symbolic Control, and Identity: Theory, Research, Critique*. London: Taylor and Francis.

Biggs, J. (1987) *Student Approaches to Learning and Study*. Melbourne: Australian Council for Educational Research.

Biggs, J.B. (2003) *Teaching for Quality Learning at University: What the Student does* (2nd edition). Maidenhead: SRHE/Open University Press.

Billett, S. (2004) 'Learning through work: workplace participatory practices', in H. Rainbird, A. Fuller and A. Munro (eds) *Workplace Learning in Context*. London: Routledge.

Bishop, R. and Glynn, T. (1999) *Culture Counts: Changing Power Relations in Education*. Palmerston North: Dunmore.

Blackmore, J. and Sachs, J. (2000) 'The "accidental" manager and the enterprise of the self. Gender, identity and a crisis of motivation in leadership?', paper presented at the Australian Association for Research in Education Conference, Sydney, December.

Blackmore, P. and Cousin, G. (2003) 'Linking teaching and research through research-based learning', *Educational Developments*, 4: 24–27.

Blackmore, P. and Wilson, A. (2005) 'Problems in staff and educational development leadership: solving, framing and avoiding', *International Journal of Academic Development*, 10: 107–123.

Boud, D. (1990) 'HERDSA checklist on valuing teaching', in *Priorities for Reform in Higher Education*, Report by the Senate Standing Committee on Employment, Education and Training, Canberra: Australian Government Publishing Service.

Boud, D. (1995) 'Assessment and learning: contradictory or complementary?' in P. Knight (ed.) *Assessment for Learning in Higher Education*. London: Kogan Page.

Bourdieu, P. (1988) *Homo Academicus*. Translated from the French by P. Collier. Cambridge: Polity Press.

Bourdieu, P. and Passeron, J. (1973) 'Cultural reproduction and social reproduction', in R. Brown (ed.) *Knowledge, Education and Cultural Change*. London: Tavistock.

Bowen, W.G. (2004) *Lecture I: In Pursuit of Excellence*. The Thomas Jefferson Foundation Distinguished Lecture Series: University of Virginia (www.mellon.org/pursuitofexcellence.pdf).

Boyer Commission on Educating Undergraduates in the Research University (1998) *Reinventing Undergraduate Education: A Blueprint for America's Research Universities*, Stony Brook: State University of New York at Stony Brook (available at: naples.cc.sunysb.edu/Pres/boyer.nsf/).

Boyer, E. (1987) *College: The Undergraduate Experience in America, the Carnegie Foundation for the Advancement of Teaching*. New York: Harper & Row.

Boyer, E. (1990) *Scholarship Reconsidered: Priorities of the Professoriate*. San Francisco: Jossey-Bass.

Bradford, S. (2006) 'Open plan work'. Email (10 May 2006).

Brennan, J. and Williams, R. (2004) *Collecting and Using Student Feedback – A Guide to Good Practice*. Higher Education Academy, Learning and Teaching Support Network (www.heacademy.ac.uk/snasdatabase.asp, accessed 15 April 2006).

Brew, A. (1999) 'Research and teaching: *changing* relations in a changing context', *Studies in Higher Education*, 24: 291–301.

Brew, A. (2001a) *The Nature of Research: Inquiry in Academic Contexts*. London: RoutledgeFalmer.

Brew, A. (2001b) 'Conceptions of research: a phenomenographic study', *Studies in Higher Education*, 26: 271–285.

Brew, A. (2006a) *Research and Teaching: Beyond the Divide*. London: Palgrave Macmillan.

Brew, A. (2006b) 'Going beyond the gaps: merging teaching, scholarship and research to transform academic practice', keynote paper presented at the Conference of the Australian and New Zealand Association for Medical Education, Gold Coast, Australia.

Brew, A. and Boud, D. (1995) 'Teaching and research: establishing the vital link with learning', *Higher Education*, 29: 261–273.

Brookfield, S. and Preskill, S. (1999) *Discussion as a Way of Teaching: Tools and Techniques for University Teachers*. Buckingham: SRHE/Open University Press.

Brown, P. and Lauder, H. (1997) 'Education, globalisation and economic development', in A.H. Halsey, P. Lauder, P. Brown and S. Wells (eds) *Education, Culture, Economy, Society*. Oxford: Oxford University Press.

Brown, P. and Lauder, H. (2001) *Capitalism and Social Progress: The Future of Society in a Global Economy*. Palgrave: Basingstoke.

Brown, R. (2003) 'Linking teaching and research', paper presented at University of Gloucestershire, May (www.glos.ac.uk/adu/clt/resteach/).

Brown, R. (2006) 'League tables – do we have to live with them?', *Perspectives*, 10: 33–38.

Brown, S. (2002) 'Student counselling and students' failure', in M. Peelo and T. Wareham (eds) *Failing Students in Higher Education*. Buckingham: SRHE/Open University Press.

Bruner, J. (1996) *The Culture of Education*. Harvard: Harvard University Press.

Bundy, C. (2004) 'Global patterns, local options? Changes in higher education', paper presented at Colloquium on 'Ten years of Democracy in Higher Education', Pretoria.

Butterworth, G. and Butterworth, S. (1998) *Reforming Education: The New Zealand Experience 1984–96*. Palmerston North: The Dunmore Press.

Butterworth, R. and Tarling, N. (1994) *A Shakeup Anyway: Government and the Universities in New Zealand in a Decade of Reform*. Auckland: Auckland University Press.

Callender, C. (2006) 'Access to higher education in Britain: the impact of tuition fees and financial assistance', in P.N. Texeira, D.B. Johnstone, M.J. Rosa and H. Vossensteyn (eds) *Cost-Sharing and Accessibility in Higher Education: A Fairer Deal?* The Netherlands: Springer.

Callon, M. (1986) 'Some elements of a sociology of translation: domestication of the scallops and the fishermen of St. Brieuc Bay', in J. Law (ed.) *Power, Action, Belief: A New Sociology of Knowledge?* London: Routledge.

Cambridge, B. (2004) *Campus Progress: Supporting the Scholarship of Teaching and Learning*. Washington, DC: American Association for Higher Education.

Carnegie Foundation for the Advancement of Teaching (2006) *Carnegie Scholars Program* (www.carnegiefoundation.org/programs/sub.asp?key=21&subkey=63&topkey=21 – accessed 29 May 2006).

Carnegie Foundation for the Advancement of Teaching (2006) *The Carnegie Academy for the Scholarship of Teaching and Learning (CASTL)* (www.carnegiefoundation.org/programs/index.asp?key=21 – accessed 29 May 2006).

Carr, W. and Kemmis, S. (1986) *Becoming Critical: Knowing Through Action Research*. London: Falmer.

Carrick Institute for Learning and Teaching in Higher Education (2006) *Carrick Awards for Australian University Teaching: Guidelines and Nomination Instructions 2006* (www.carrickinstitute.ed.au/carrick/go/op/preview/pid/97 – accessed on 16 March, 2006).

Carspecken, P.F. (1996) *Critical Ethnography in Educational Research: A Theoretical and Practical Guide*. London: Routledge.

Chang, H. (2006) 'Turning an undergraduate class into a professional research community', *Teaching in Higher Education*, 10: 387–394.

Chapman, B. (2006) 'Income related student loans: concepts, international reforms and administrative challenges', in P.N. Texeira, D.B. Johnstone, M.J. Rosa and H. Vossensteyn (eds) *Cost-Sharing and Accessibility in Higher Education: A Fairer Deal?* The Netherlands: Springer.

Chappell, C., Rhodes, C., Solomon, N., Tennant, M. and Yates, L. (2003) *Reconstructing the Lifelong Learner: Pedagogy and Identity in Individual, Organisational and Social Change*. London: RoutledgeFalmer.

Cheetham, G. and Chivers, G. (2001) 'How professionals learn in practice: an investigation of informal learning amongst people working in professions', *Journal of European Industrial Training*, 25: 248–292.

CHEMS Consulting/Critical Change Consultants (2001) *Formative Evaluation of the Teaching Quality Enhancement Fund*, a report to HEFCE.

CHEMS Consulting/Higher Education Consultancy Group (2005) *Summative Evaluation of the Teaching Quality Enhancement Fund*, a report to HEFCE.

Chickering, A.W. and Gamson, Z.F. (1991) *Applying the Seven Principles of Good Practice in Undergraduate Education*. San Francisco: Jossey-Bass.

Christensen Hughes, J. (2006) *The Scholarship of Teaching and Learning: A Canadian Perspective* (www.mcmaster.ca/stlhe/documents/SoTLCanadianPerspectiveJan06.pdf – accessed 3 August 2006).

Christie, H., Munro, M. and Fisher, T. (2004) 'Leaving university early: exploring the differences between continuing and non-continuing students', *Studies in Higher Education*, 29: 617–636.

Clarke, J. (2002) 'A new kind of symmetry: actor-network theories and the new literacy studies', *Studies in the Education of Adults*, 34: 107–122.

Clegg, S. (1999) 'Professional education, reflective practice and feminism', *International Journal of Inclusive Education*, 3: 167–179.

Clegg, S. (2004) 'Critical readings: progress files and the production of the autonomous learner', *Teaching in Higher Education*, 9: 287–298.

Clegg, S. (2005) 'Evidence-based practice in educational research: a critical realist critique of systematic review', *Sociology of Education*, 26: 415–428.

Clegg, S. (2007) 'The possibilities of sustaining critical intellectual work under regimes of evidence, audit, and ethical governance', *Journal of Curriculum Theorizing* (forthcoming).

Clegg, S. and Ashworth, P. (2004) 'Contested practices: learning outcomes and disciplinary understandings', in J. Satterthwaite, E. Atkinson, W. Martin (eds) *The Disciplining of Education; New Languages of Power and Resistance*. Stoke-on-Trent: Trentham Books.

Clegg. S. and David, M. (2006) 'Passion, pedagogies and the project of the personal in higher education', *Twenty-first Century Society*, 1, 2: 149–165.

Clegg, S. and Smith, K. (2006) 'The positioning of academics in learning, teaching and assessment strategy discourses in higher education', paper given at *ICED* conference, Sheffield Hallam University, June.

Clouder, L. (1998) 'Getting the "right answers": student evaluation as a reflection of intellectual development', *Teaching in Higher Education*, 3: 185–195.

Codd, J. (2002) 'The third way for tertiary education policy: TEAC and beyond', in I. Livingstone (ed.) *New Zealand Annual Review of Education*. Wellington: Victoria University.

Codd, J. (2005) 'The PBRF as ideology: lessons from the British RAE', in R. Smith and J. Jesson (eds) *Punishing the Discipline – the PBRF Regime: Evaluating the Position of Education – Where to from here?* Auckland: AUT University/University of Auckland, Faculty of Education.

Coffield, F., Moseley, D., Hall, E. and Ecclestone, K. (2004) *Should We Be Using Learning Styles? What Research Has to Say to Practice*. London: Learning and Skills Research Centre.

Colbeck, C. (1998) 'Merging in a seamless blend: how faculty integrate teaching and research', *The Journal of Higher Education*, 69: 647–671.

Colbeck, C. (2002) 'Balancing teaching with other responsibilities: integrating roles or feeding alligators', paper presented at the annual meeting of the American Educational Research Association, Penn State University.

Collier, A. (1997) 'Unhewn demonstrations', *Radical Philosophy*, 81: 22–26.

Collingwood, R.G. (1939) *An Autobiography*. Oxford: Clarendon Press.

Collini, S. (2003) 'HiEdBiz', *London Review of Books*, 25: 3–9.

Committee on Higher Education (The Robbins Report) (1963) *Higher Education*. London: HMSO.

Connell, J.P. and Kubisch, A.C. (1996) *Applying a theories of change approach to the evaluation of comprehensive community initiatives*. New York: Aspen Institute.

Considine, M. (2006) 'Theorizing the university as a cultural system: distinctions, identities, emergencies', *Educational Theory*, 56: 255–270.

Consortium of Excellence in Higher Education (2003) *Organisational Learning and the Future of Higher Education*. Sheffield: Sheffield Hallam University

Contu, A. and Willmott, H. (2003) 'Re-embedding situatedness: the importance of power relations in learning theory', *Organization Science*, 14: 283–296.

Cooper, D. and Subotzky, G. (2001) *The Skewed Revolution: Trends in South African Higher Education: 1988–1998*. Cape Town: EPU, UWC.

Council for Advancement and Support of Education (CASE) (2004) *1999 Professor of the Year National Winners* (www.case.org/Content/POY/Display.cfm?CONTENTITEMID=4677 – accessed 29 May 2006).

Council for Advancement and Support of Education (CASE) (2006) *U.S. Professors of the Year* (www.case.org/Container.cfm?CONTAINERID=184&NAVID=67 – accessed 29 May 2006).

Council for Advancement and Support of Education (CASE) (2007) *U.S. Professors of the Year* (www.usprofessorsoftheyear.org/default.cfm?pid=Home – accessed 3 May 2007).

Council on Higher Education (CHE) (2000) *Towards a new Higher Education Institutional Landscape: Meeting the Equity, Quality and Social Development Imperatives of the Twenty-First Century*. Report of the Size and Shape Task Team, Pretoria: CHE.

Council on Higher Education (CHE) (2001a) *Higher Education Quality Committee: Founding document*. Pretoria: CHE.

Council on Higher Education (CHE) (2001b) *A Framework for Improving Teaching and Learning Project*. Pretoria: CHE.

Council on Higher Education (CHE) (2001c) *Annual Report of the Council on Higher Education 2000/2001: The State of Higher Education in South Africa*. Pretoria: CHE.

Council on Higher Education (CHE) (2002a) *HEQC Programme Accreditation Framework*. Pretoria: CHE.

Council on Higher Education (CHE) (2002b) *Proceedings of the CHE colloquium*: 27–28 June. Pretoria: CHE.

Council on Higher Education (CHE) (2004a) *Criteria for Institutional Audits*. Pretoria: CHE (www.che.ac.za/documents/d000087/index.php – accessed April 2006).

Council on Higher Education (CHE) (2004b) *Framework for Institutional Audits*. Pretoria: CHE.

Council on Higher Education (CHE) (2004c) *Improving Teaching and Learning Project*. Pretoria: CHE (www.che.ac.za/documents/d000087/index.php – accessed April 2006).

Cousin, G. and Deepwell, F. (2005) 'Designs for network learning: a communities of practice perspective', *Studies in Higher Education*, 30: 57–66.

Cranton, P.A. (2001) *Becoming an Authentic Teacher in Higher Education*. Malabar: Krieger.

Cross, K.P. (2001) 'Leading edge efforts to improve teaching and learning; the Hesburgh Awards', *Change*, July–August (www.aahe.org/change/AUG2001.pdf).

Cullen, M. (2006) 'Address to University Chancellors', Tertiary Advisory and Monitoring Unit Workshop, 11 April (www.scoop.co.nz/stories/PA0604/S00202.htm).

D'Andrea, V. (2003) 'NTFS issues to consider', personal email to Joint Task Group on Rewarding Excellence in Teaching, 3 April.

D'Andrea, V. (2007) 'Comments on: A. Skelton's "Understanding teaching excellence in higher education"', *Teaching in Higher Education*, 12, 1: 141–144.

D'Andrea, V. and Gosling, D. (2001) 'Joining the dots: reconceptualising educational development', *Active Learning*, 2: 65–81.

D'Andrea, V. and Gosling, D. (2005) *Improving Teaching and Learning in Higher Education: A Whole Institution Approach*. Maidenhead: McGraw Hill, SRHE/Open University Press.

Darder, A. (2002) 'Teaching as an act of love: reflections on Paulo Freire and his contribution to our lives and our work', in A. Darder and R.D. Torres (eds) *The Critical Pedagogy Reader*. London: Routledge.

Darder, A. (2005) 'Unfettered bodies: forging a pedagogy for a new struggle', paper presented at the C-*SAP* Conference, Birmingham, November.

Davies, B. (1994) 'On the neglect of pedagogy in educational studies and its consequences', *British Journal of In-service Education*, 20: 17–34.

Deem, R. (1998) 'New managerialism in higher education – the management of performances and cultures in university', *International Studies in the Sociology of Education*, 8: 47–70.

Deem, R. (2004) 'Globalisation, new managerialism, academic capitalism and entrepreneurialism in universities', in M. Tight (ed.) *The Routledge Falmer Reader in Higher Education*. London: RoutledgeFalmer.

Deem, R. and Brehony, K.J. (2005) 'Management as ideology; the case of "new managerialism" in Higher Education', *Oxford Review of Higher Education*, 31, 2: 213–231.

Delanty, G. (2001) *Challenging Knowledge: The University in the Knowledge Society*. Buckinghamshire: Open University Press.

Department for Education and Skills (DfES) (2003) *The Future of Higher Education*. London: HMSO.

Department for Education and Skills (DfES) (2006) *Reform of Higher Education Research Assessment and Funding* (www.dfes.gov.uk/consultations/conDetails. cfm?consultationId=1404).

Department of Education (DoE) (1997) *White Paper 3. A Programme for the Transformation of Higher Education*. Pretoria: DoE.

Department of Education (DoE) (2001) *National Plan for Higher Education*. Pretoria: DoE

Department of Education (DoE) (2004) *A New Funding Framework: How Government Grants are allocated to Public Higher Education Institutions*. Pretoria: DoE.

Department of Education, Science and Training (DEST) (2006) *Research Quality Framework: Assessing the quality and impact of research in Australia, RQF Development 2006*. Australian Government, DEST: Canberra (www.dest.gov.au/sectors/research_sector/policies_issues_reviews/key_issues/research_quality_framework/rqf_development_2006.htm – accessed 13 November 2006).

de Winter Hebron, C. (2001) 'Conflicts of excellence in higher education', paper presented at the SRHE annual conference, Cambridge, England, December.

Diercks-O'Brien, G. and Powell, A. (2006) *An Impact Evaluation Framework for Learning and Teaching Activity*. Sheffield: Learning Development and Media Unit, University of Sheffield [internal consultation paper].

Dinham, S. and Scott, C. (2002) 'Awards for teaching excellence: intentions and realities', *Australian Association for Research in Education*, Brisbane, Australia, December.

Donald, J.G. (2002) *Learning to Think: Disciplinary Perspectives*. San Fransisco: Jossey-Bass.

Donald, J.G. (2006) 'Enhancing the Quality of Teaching in Canada', in C. Kreber (ed.) *International Policy Perspectives on Improving Learning with Limited Resources*, *New Directions for Higher Education*. San Francisco: Jossey-Bass/Wiley.

Doyon, P. (2001) 'A review of higher education reform in modern Japan', *Higher Education*, 41: 443–470.

Dunkin, M.J. (1995) 'Concepts of teaching and teaching excellence in higher education', *Higher Education Research and Development*, 14: 21–31.

Dunkin, M.J. and Precians, R.P. (1992) 'Award-winning university teachers' concepts of teaching', *Higher Education*, 24: 483–502.

Dweck, C.S. (1999) *Self-Theories: Their Role in Motivation, Personality, and Development*. Philadelphia: Psychology Press.

Eades, J.S. (2005) 'The Japanese 21st century of excellence program: internationalisation in action?', in J.S. Eades, R. Goodman and Y. Hada (eds) *The 'Big Bang' in Japanese Higher Education: The 2004 Reforms and the Dynamics of Change*. Melbourne: Trans Pacific Press.

Earl, S. and Mcarthur, J. (2003) 'Promoting excellence – the Scottish experience', *Exchange*, Autumn, 5: 17–18.

Edgerton, R. (1993) 'The re-examination of faculty priorities', *Change*, July/August: 10–25.

Edgerton, R. (1994) 'A national market for excellence in teaching', *Change*, Sep/Oct, 26: 4–6.

Edith Cowan University (2005) *Academic Staff Promotion Policy 2005* (www.ecu.edu.au/GPPS/policies_db/tmp/hr124.pdf – accessed 25 October 2005).

Edwards, R. (2003) 'Ordering subjects: actor-networks and intellectual technologies in lifelong learning', *Studies in the Education of Adults*, 35: 54–67.

Edwards, R. and Nicoll, K. (2004) 'Mobilizing workplaces: actors, discipline and governmentality', *Studies in Continuing Education*, 26: 159–173.

Ellis, A.B. (2006) 'Creating a culture for innovation', *The Chronicle in Higher Education*, 52, B20 (14 April).

Ellis, R. (1993) *Quality Assurance for University Teaching*. Buckingham: SRHE/Open University Press.

Elton, L. (1984) 'Evaluating teaching and assessing teachers in universities', *Assessment and Evaluation in Higher Education*, 9, 2: 97–115.

Elton, L. (1987) *Teaching in Higher Education: Appraisal and Training*. London: Kogan Page.

Elton, L. (1991) 'Teaching excellence and quality assurance', *Zeitschrift für Hochschuldidaktik*, 15: 102–115.

Elton, L. (1992) 'Quality enhancement and academic professionalism', *The New Academic*, 1: 3–5.

Elton, L. (2001) 'Training for a craft or a profession?', *Teaching in Higher Education*, 6: 421–422.

Elton, L. (2005) 'Scholarship and the research and teaching nexus', in R. Barnett (ed.) *Reshaping the University: New Relationships between Research, Scholarship and Teaching*. Maidenhead: McGraw-Hill/Open University Press: 108–118.

Elton, L. and Partington, P. (1993) *Teaching Standards and Excellence in Higher Education: Developing a Culture for Quality*. (2nd edn) Sheffield: CVCP.

Engeström, Y. (1987) *Learning by Expanding: An Activity-Theoretical Approach to Developmental Research.* Helsinki: Orienta-Konsultit.

Engeström, Y. (1999) 'Activity theory and individual and social transformation', in Y. Engestrom, R. Miettinen and R.L. Punamaki (eds) *Perspectives on Activity Theory.* Cambridge: Cambridge University Press.

Entwistle, N. (1992) *The Impact of Teaching on Learning Outcomes in Higher Education: a Literature Review.* Sheffield: Committee of Vice-Chancellors and Principals of the Universities of the United Kingdom, Universities' Staff Development Unit.

Entwistle, N. and Walker, P. (2002) 'Strategic alertness and expanded awareness within sophisticated conceptions of teaching', in N. Hativa and P. Goodyear (eds) *Teacher Thinking, Beliefs and Knowledge in Higher Education.* Dortrecht: Kluwer Academic Publishers.

Entwistle, N., Skinner, D., Entwistle, D. and Orr, S. (2000) 'Conceptions and beliefs about "good teaching": an integration of contrasting research areas', *Higher Education Research and Development,* 19: 5–26.

Entwistle, N.J. and Ramsden, P. (1983) *Understanding Student Learning.* London and Canberra: Croom Helm.

Evans, M. (2004) *Killing Thinking: The Death of Universities.* London: Continuum.

Fairclough, N. (1989) *Language and Power.* London: Longman.

Fanghanel, J. (2004) 'Capturing dissonance in university teacher education environments', *Studies in Higher Education,* 29: 575–590.

Fanghanel, J. (forthcoming) 'Enhancing educational development practices through a socio-cultural understanding of university teaching', *International Journal of Educational Research,* (Special Issue, forthcoming).

Fataar, A. (2003) 'Higher education policy discourse in South Africa', *South African Journal of Higher Education,* 17: 31–39.

Field, J. (2005) 'Widening access and diversity of provision: the expansion of short-cycle higher education in non-university settings', in G. Glaser (ed.) *Closing the Gap: the Impact of Widening Participation Strategies in the UK and the USA.* Leicester: National Institute of Adult and Continuing Education (NIACE).

Floyd, D.H. (2002) *Project Summary,* Carnegie Foundation for the Advancement of Teaching (www.carnegiefoundation.org/programs/sub.asp?key=21&subkey=63& topkey=21 – accessed 29 May 2006).

Fook, J. (2006) 'Beyond reflective practice: reworking the "critical" in critical reflection', keynote paper presented at Professional Lifelong Learning: Beyond Reflective Practice Conference, University of Leeds, July (www.leeds.ac.uk/medicine/meu/ lifelong06/papers.html – accessed July 2006).

Foucault, M. (1980) *Power/Knowledge: Selected Interviews and other Writings 1972–1977.* Edited and translated by C. Gordon. New York: Pantheon.

Frame, P., Johnson, M. and Rosie, A. (2003) 'How does it feel to be top of the class? Reflections on being a National Teaching Fellow', paper presented at the Third Annual US/UK Scholarship of Teaching and Learning Conference, University of East London, City University and the Carnegie Academy for the Scholarship of Teaching and Learning, London.

Frame, P., Johnson, M. and Rosie, A. (2006) 'Reward or award? Reflections on the initial experiences of winners of a national teaching fellowship', *Innovations in Education and Teaching International,* 43:4: 409–419.

Freire, P. (1970) *Pedagogy of the Oppressed.* New York: Continuum.

Fritzberg, G.J. (2000) 'Escaping the shadow of excellence', *Multicultural Education*, 8: 37–40.

Frost, S.H. and Teodorescu, D. (2001) 'Teaching excellence: how faculty guided change a research university', *The Review of Higher Education*, 24: 397–415.

Fullan, M. (1982) *The Meaning of Educational Change*. Toronto: Ontario Institute for Studies in Education Press.

Furedi, F. (2004) *Where Have all the Intellectuals Gone?* London: Continuum.

Gale, R. (forthcoming 2008) *Points Without Limits: Individual Inquiry, Collaborative Investigation, Collective Scholarship*, in D.R. Robertson and L.B. Nilson (eds) *To Improve the Academy*, Vol. 26, San Francisco: Jossey-Bass.

Gale, R. (2001) *Portfolio Assessment and Student Empowerment*. Carnegie Foundation for the Advancement of Teaching (www.cfkeep.org/html/snapshot.php?id= 2478563 – accessed 29 May 2006).

Gale, R. and Golde, C. (2004) 'Doctoral education and the scholarship of teaching and learning', *Peer Review*, Spring 2004, 6:3.

Gamson, Z.F. (1998) 'The stratification of the academy', in R. Martin (ed.) *Chalk Lines: the Politics of Work in the Managed University*. Durham and London: Duke University Press: 103–111.

Gibbs, G. (2004) 'Editorial', *Open Learning*, 19: 30–37.

Gibbs, G. (2005) 'Being strategic about improving teaching and learning', keynote address to Higher Education Research and Development Conference, Sydney, July (conference.herdsa.org.au/2005/gibbs.cfm – accessed 2 October 2006).

Gibbs, G. and Habeshaw, T. (2002) *Recognising and Rewarding Excellent Teaching – A Guide to Good Practice*. Milton Keynes: Centre for Higher Education Practice.

Gibbons, M., Limoges, C., Nowotny, H., Schwartzman, S., Scott, P. and Trow, M. (1994) *The New Production of Knowledge: The Dynamics of Science and Research in Contemporary Societies*. London: Sage.

Giddens, A. (1984) *The Constitution of Society: Outline of the Theory of Structuration*. Cambridge: Polity Press.

Giddens, A. (2002) *Runaway World: How Globalisation is Reshaping Our Lives*. London: Profile Books.

Giroux, H. (1997) 'Crossing the boundaries of educational discourse: modernism, postmodernism and feminism', in A.H. Halsey, H. Lauder, P. Brown and A. Stuart Wells (eds) *Education: Culture, Economy, and Society*. Oxford: Oxford University Press.

Glassick, C., Huber, M. and Maeroff, G. (1997) *Scholarship Assessed: A Special Report on Faculty Evaluation*. San Francisco: Jossey-Bass.

Goff, P. (1990) *Learning for Life*. Wellington: Office of Minister of Education.

Goldsmid, C.A., Gruber, J.E. and Willson, E.K. (1977) 'Perceived attributes of superior teachers (PAST): an inquiry into the giving of teacher awards', *American Educational Research Journal*, 14: 423–440.

Goodman, R. (2005) 'W(h)ither the Japanese university? An introduction to the 2004 higher education reforms in Japan', in J.S. Eades, R. Goodman and Y. Hada (eds) *The 'Big Bang' in Japanese Higher Education: The 2004 Reforms and the Dynamics of Change*. Melbourne: Trans Pacific Press.

Goodman, R., Hatakenaka, S. and Kim, T. (2007) 'The changing status of vocational higher education in contemporary Japan and South Korea', in D. Wilson and R. McLean (eds) *International Handbook of Technical and Vocational Education and Training*. UNEVOC: Bonn.

Gosling, D. (2002) *Models of Peer Observation of Teaching.* Learning and Teaching Support Network Generic Centre (www.heacademy.ac.uk/resources. htm – accessed 9 April 2006).

Gosling, D. (2005) *Peer Observation of Teaching*, SEDA paper 118. London: Staff and Educational Development Association.

Gosling, D. and Hannan, A. (2006) 'Theoretical underpinnings: an analysis of Centres for Excellence in Teaching and Learning', paper presented to the Improving Student Learning Conference, Bath, September.

Gosling, D. and Hannan, A. (2007) 'Responses to a policy initiative: the case of the Centres for Excellence in Teaching and Learning', *Studies in Higher Education* (forthcoming).

Grimmet, P. and Neufeld, J. (ed.) (1994) *Teacher Development and the Struggle for Authenticity. Professional Growth and Restructuring in the Context of Change.* New York: Teachers College Press.

Habermas, J. (1971) *Knowledge and Human Interests.* Boston: Beacon Press.

Hada, Y. (2005) 'Postgraduate and professional training in Japanese universities: causes and directions of change', in J.S. Eades, R. Goodman and Y. Hada (eds) *The 'Big Bang' in Japanese Higher Education: The 2004 Reforms and the Dynamics of Change.* Melbourne: Trans Pacific Press.

Haggis, T. (2003) 'Constructing images of ourselves? A critical investigation into "approaches to learning" research in higher education', *British Educational Research Journal*, 29: 89–104.

Hall, C., Morris Matthews, K. and Sawicka, T. (2004) 'Performance-Based Research Fund (PBRF): policy and practice', in I. Livingstone (ed.) *New Zealand Annual Review of Education*, 13: 79–104, Wellington: School of Education, Victoria University.

Hall, M., Symes, A. and Thierry M.L. (2002) *Governance in South African Higher Education.* Research report prepared for the Council on Higher Education. Pretoria: CHE.

Hall, S. (2003) 'New Labour's double-shuffle', *Soundings*, 10–24.

Hamilton, D. (1999) 'The pedagogic paradox (or why no didactics in England?)', *Pedagogy, Culture and Society*, 7: 135–152.

Hamilton, M. (2001) 'Privileged literacies: policy, institutional process and the life of the IALS', *Language and Education*, 15: 178–196.

Hannan, A. and Silver, H. (2000) *Innovating in Higher Education: Teaching, Learning and Institutional Cultures.* Buckingham: Open University Press.

Hargreaves, A. (1994) *Changing Teachers, Changing Times: Teachers' Work and Culture in the Postmodern Age.* London: Cassell.

Harré, R. (1998) *The Singular Self: An Introduction to the Psychology of Personhood.* London: Sage.

Harris, S. (2005) 'Rethinking academic identities in neo-liberal times', *Teaching in Higher Education*, 10: 421–434.

Hartley, D. (2006) 'Excellence and enjoyment: the logic of a "contradiction"', *British Journal of Educational Studies*, 54: 3–14.

Harvey, L. (2002) 'Evaluation for what?', *Teaching in Higher Education*, 7: 245–264.

Hatakenaka, S. (2005) 'The incorporation of national universities: the role of missing hybrids', in J.S. Eades, R. Goodman and Y. Hada (eds) *The 'Big Bang' in Japanese Higher Education: The 2004 Reforms and the Dynamics of Change.* Melbourne: Trans Pacific Press.

Hativa, N. (2000) *Teaching for Effective Learning in Higher Education*. London: Kluwer.

Hativa, N., Barak, R. and Simhi, E. (2001) 'Exemplary university teachers: knowledge and beliefs regarding effective teaching dimensions and strategies', *Journal of Higher Education*, 72: 699–729.

Hattie, J. and Marsh, H.W. (1996) 'The relationship between research and teaching: a meta-analysis', *Review of Educational Research*, 66: 507–542.

Hattie, J. and Marsh, H.W. (2004) 'One journey to unravel the relationship between research and teaching', *Research and Teaching: Closing the Divide? An International Colloquium*, Winchester, March (www.solent.ac.uk/ExternalUP/318/hattie_and_marsh_paper.doc).

Hayes, L.D. (1998) 'Higher education in Japan', in E.R. Beauchamp (ed.) *Education and Schooling in Japan since 1945*. New York: Garland.

Healey, M. (2000) 'Developing the scholarship of teaching in higher education: a discipline-based approach', *Higher Education Research and Development*, 19: 169–189.

Healey, M. (2005) 'Linking research and teaching: exploring disciplinary spaces and the role of inquiry-based learning', in R. Barnett (ed.) *Reshaping the University: New Relationships between Research, Scholarship and Teaching*. Maidenhead: McGraw-Hill/Open University Press.

Healey, M. and Jenkins, A. (2003) 'Discipline-based educational development', in H. Eggins and R. MacDonald (eds) *The Scholarship of Academic Development*. Buckingham: SRHE/Open University Press.

Healey, M. and Jenkins, A. (2006) 'Strengthening the teaching-research linkage in undergraduate courses and programmes', in C. Kreber (ed.) *Exploring Research-Based Teaching, New Directions in Teaching and Learning*, San Francisco: Jossey Bass/Wiley.

Helsby, G. and Saunders, M. (1993) 'Taylorism, Tylerism and performance indicators: defending the indefensible', *Educational Studies*, 19: 55–77.

Henkel, M. (2000) *Academic Identities and Policy Change in Higher Education*. London: Jessica Kingsley.

Hersh, H. and Merrow, J. (2005) *Declining by Degrees: Higher Education at Risk*. New York: Palgrave and Macmillan.

Higher Education Academy (2006) *Guidance for Nominees and Institutions*. (www.heacademy.ac.uk/4016.htm – accessed 5 April 2006).

Higher Education Funding Council for England (HEFCE) (1998) *Learning and Teaching: Strategy and Funding Proposals*. Bristol: HEFCE, Ref: 98/40.

HEFCE (1999) *Teaching Quality Enhancement Fund*. Bristol: HEFCE.

HEFCE (2000) *Review of Research*. Bristol: HEFCE, Ref: 00/37.

HEFCE (2001) *Risk Management: A Guide to Good Practice for Higher Education Institutions* (www.hefce.ac.uk/pubs/HEFCE/2001/01_28.htm – accessed 26 June 2006).

HEFCE (2002) *Teaching Quality Enhancement Fund: Funding Arrangements 2002–03 to 2004–05*. Bristol: HEFCE, Ref: 02/24.

HEFCE (2003) *Centres for Excellence in Teaching and Learning: Formal Consultation (2003/36)*. Bristol: HEFCE.

HEFCE (2004) *Centres for Excellence in Teaching and Learning: Invitation to Bid for Funds (2004/05)*. Bristol: HEFCE.

HEFCE (2005) *Centres for Excellence in Teaching and Learning*. Bristol: HEFCE.

HEFCE (2006) *Teaching Quality Enhancement Fund: Funding arrangements 2006–07 to 2008–09*. (www.hefce.ac.uk/pubs/HEFCE/2006/06_11/).

HEFCE National Student Survey (2005, 2006) (www.hefce.ac.uk/learning/nss/ – accessed 27 June 2006).

Hill, S. (2003) 'Royal Holloway confirms major new investment in research', College news, 10 December (www.rhul.ac.uk/Whats-New/news2003/research-posts.html).

Hillier, Y. and Vielba, C. (2001) 'Perceptions of excellence: personal constructs of excellence in teaching and learning', paper presented at the Institute for Learning and Teaching Annual Conference, York.

Hinchcliffe, G. (2006) 'Rethinking lifelong learning', *Studies in Philosophy and Education*, 25: 93–109.

Hollway, W. (1989) *Subjectivity and Method in Psychology: Gender, Meaning and Science*. London: Sage.

Honey, P. and Mumford, A. (1982) *The Manual of Learning Styles*. Maidenhead: Peter Honey.

Horie, M. (2002) 'The internationalization of higher education in Japan in the 1990s: a reconsideration', *Higher Education*, 43: 65–84.

Huber, M.T. (2000) Outreach, *'Evaluating Outreach: Scholarship Assessed Approach'* (www.outreach.psu.edu/News/Pubs/Monograph/eval.html).

Huber, M.T. (2004) *Balancing Acts: The Scholarship of Teaching and Learning in Academic Careers*. Washington, DC: The American Association for Higher Education (AAHE) and The Carnegie Foundation for the Advancement of Teaching.

Huber, M.T. and Hutchings, P. (2005) *The Advancement of Learning: Building the Teaching Commons*. San Francisco: Jossey-Bass.

Huber, M.T. and Hutchings, P. (2006) *The Advancement of Learning: Building the Teaching Commons. A Carnegie Foundation Report on the Scholarship of Teaching and Learning in Higher Education*. Stanford: Jossey-Bass.

Huber, M.T. and Morreale, S.P. (eds) (2002) *Disciplinary Styles in the Scholarship of Teaching and Learning: Exploring Common Ground*. Washington, DC: AAHE and Carnegie Foundation.

Hussey, T. and Smith, P. (2002) 'The trouble with learning outcomes', *Active Learning in Higher Education*, 3: 220–233.

Hutchings, P. (1995) *From Idea to Prototype: The Peer Review of Teaching – A Project Workbook*. Washington, DC: AAHE.

Hutchings, P. (2000) *Opening Lines: Approaches to the Scholarship of Teaching and Learning*. Menlo Park, CA: The Carnegie Foundation for the Advancement of Teaching.

Hutchings, P. and Shulman, L. (1999) 'The scholarship of teaching: new elaborations, new developments', *Change*, 31: 10–15.

Iannaccone, L. (1989) 'From equity to excellence: political context and dynamics', in W. Boyd and C. Kerchner (eds) *The Politics of Excellence and Choice in Education*. New York: The Falmer Press.

Inglis, F. (2004) 'A malediction upon managerialism', in F. Inglis (ed.) *Education and the Good Society*. Basingstoke: Palgrave.

Inoshita, O. (2003) 'FD no jissen', *Aera Mook*, 93: 30–32.

Institute for Learning and Teaching (2000) *Launch of the National Teaching Fellowship Scheme: Scheme Structure* (www.ilt.ac.uk/news/ntfs_structure.html).

Institute for the Advancement of Teaching in Higher Education (IATHE) (2006a) *The Mission of the Institute* (www.iathe.org/eng/about.asp – accessed 3 August 2006).

IATHE (2006b) *The History of the Institute* (www.iathe.org/eng/about.asp – accessed 3 August 2006).

Jackson, N. (2000) 'Programme specification and its role in promoting an outcomes model of learning', *Active Learning in Higher Education*, 1: 132–151.

Jansen, J. (1999) 'Why OBE will fail', in J. Jansen and P. Christie (eds) *Changing Curriculum: Studies on Outcomes-based Education in South Africa*. Cape Town: Juta.

Jaschik, S. (2006) 'A new Carnegie classification arrives', *Inside Higher Education*, April 4 (insidehighered.com/news/2006/04/04/carnegie).

Jenkins, A. (2004) *A Guide to the Research Evidence on Teaching-Research Relationships*. York: Higher Education Academy (www.heacademy.ac.uk/embedded_object.asp?id=21570&file).

Jenkins, A. and Healey, M. (2005) *Institutional Strategies to Link Teaching and Research*. York: The Higher Education Academy.

Jenkins, A., Blackman, T., Lindsay, R. and Paton-Saltzberg, R. (1998) 'Teaching and research: student perspectives and policy implications', *Studies in Higher Education*, 23: 127–141.

Jenkins, A., Breen, R., Lindsay, R. and Brew, A. (2003) *Re-shaping Higher Education: Linking Teaching and Research*. London: RoutledgeFalmer.

Jesson, J. (2005) 'The PBRF and Education: a state created standards body for governmentality of our own', in R. Smith and J. Jesson (eds) *Punishing the Discipline – the PBRF Regime: Evaluating the Position of Education – Where to from Here?* Auckland: AUT University/University of Auckland, Faculty of Education.

Johnston, B. and Webber, S. (2003) 'Information literacy in higher education: a review and case study', *Studies in Higher Education*, 28: 335–352.

Kapp, C. (2002) 'Promoting excellence in teaching in higher education: reflections of the recipients of the Vice-Chancellor's award for excellence in teaching', paper presented at *World Conference of the International Consortium for Educational Development in Higher Education*, Perth, July.

Kaufman, L.R. and Stock, E. (eds) (2004) *Reinvigorating the Undergraduate Experience: Successful Models Supported by NSF's AIRE/RAIRE Program*. Washington: Centre for Undergraduate Research (www.cur.org/publications/AIRE_RAIRE/ toc.asp).

Kemmis, K. (1998) 'System and lifeworld and the conditions of learning in late Modernity', paper presented at the Sixth International Conference on Experiential Learning, Tampere, Finland, July.

Kerr, C. (2001) *The Uses of the University* (5th edition). Cambridge and London: Harvard University Press.

Khan, P. and O'Rourke, K. (2005) *Guide to Curriculum Design: Enquiry-based Learning*. Higher Education Academy (www.heacademy.ac.uk/resources – accessed 25 September 2006).

Kinkead, J. (ed.) (2003) *Valuing and Supporting Undergraduate Research, New Directions for Teaching and Learning 93*. San Francisco: Jossey-Bass.

Kinman, G. and Jones, F. (2004) *Working to the Limit*. Report commissioned by the AUT.

Kinman, G., Jones, F. and Kinman, R. (2006) 'The well-being of the UK Academy, 1998–2004', *Quality in Higher Education*, 12: 15–27.

Kinmonth, E.H. (2005) 'From selection to seduction: the impact of demographic change on private higher education in Japan', in J.S. Eades, R. Goodman and Y. Hada (eds) *The 'Big Bang' in Japanese Higher Education: The 2004 Reforms and the Dynamics of Change*. Melbourne: Trans Pacific Press.

Kinser, K. (1998) 'Faculty at private for-profit universities: the University of Phoenix as a new model?', *International Higher Education*, 13: 13–14.

Kirov, S.M. (2003) 'Teaching and research: impossible or essential link?', *Microbiology Australia*, 24: 12–13.

Knapper, C.K. (1995) 'The origins of teaching portfolios', *Journal of Excellence in College Teaching*, 6: 45–56.

Knapper, C. (1997) 'Rewards for teaching', in P. Cranton (ed.) *University Challenges in Faculty Work: Fresh Perspectives from Around the World*. New Directions for Teaching and Learning, no. 65. San Francisco: Jossey-Bass.

Knight, P. (2002) *Being a Teacher in Higher Education*. Buckingham: SRHE/Open University Press.

Knight, P.T. and Trowler, P.R. (2001) *Departmental Leadership in Higher Education*, Buckingham: SRHE/Open University Press.

Kogan, M., Moses, I. and El-Khawas, E. (1994) *Staffing Higher Education: Meeting New Challenges*. London: Jessica Kingsley.

Kraak, A. (2001) 'Policy ambiguity and slippage: higher education under the new state 1994–2001', in A. Kraak and M. Young, M. (eds) *Education in Retrospect: Policy and Implementation since 1990*. Pretoria: Human Sciences Research Council.

Kreber, C. (2003) 'The scholarship of teaching: a comparison of conceptions held by experts and regular academic staff', *Higher Education*, 46: 93–121.

Kreber, C. (2005) 'Charting a critical course on the scholarship of university teaching movement', *Studies in Higher Education* 30: 389–407.

Kreber, C. (2006) *Why create synergies between teaching and research?* (www.uofaweb.ualberta.ca/researchandstudents/nav04.cfm?nav04=45312&nav03=45 152&nav02=32253&nav01=32191 – accessed 15 September 2006).

Kreber, C. and Cranton, P.A. (2000) 'Exploring the scholarship of teaching', *Journal of Higher Education*, 71: 476–495.

Kuh, G.D. and Pascarella, E.T. (2004) 'What does institutional selectivity tell us about educational quality?', *Change*, 36: 52–58.

Kulski, M. and Groombridge, B. (2004) 'Aligning teaching quality indicators with university reward mechanisms', *Tertiary Education and Management*, 10: 45–59.

Latour, B. (1987) *Science in Action*. Cambridge: Harvard University Press.

Latour, B. (1996) 'On actor-network theory: a few clarifications' ('*Sur la théorie acteur-réseau: quelques clarifications*'), *Soziale Welt*, 47: 369–381.

Latour, B. (2005) *Reassembling the Social: An Introduction to Actor-Network- Theory*. Oxford: Oxford University Press.

Lave, J. and Wenger, E. (1991) *Situated Learning: Legitimate Peripheral Participation*. Cambridge: Cambridge University Press.

Law, J. (2004) *After Method: Mess in Social Science Research*. Abingdon: Routledge.

Lea, M.R. and Nicoll, K. (2002) *Distributed Learning: Social and Cultural Approaches to Practice*. London: RoutledgeFalmer.

Lee-Cunin, M. (2005) 'The Japanese student perspective on universities', in J.S. Eades, R. Goodman and Y. Hada (eds) *The 'Big Bang' in Japanese Higher Education: The 2004 Reforms and the Dynamics of Change*. Melbourne: Trans Pacific Press.

Leon, P. (2002) 'Chameleon finds quality colours', *The Times Higher Educational Supplement*, 25 January.

Leontev, A.N. (1981) *Problems of the Development of the Mind*. Moscow: Progress Publishers.

Luckett, K. and Luckett, S. (1999) 'Implementing outcomes-based education in a South African University', *Academic Development*, 4: 125–154.

Luckett, K. and Webbstock, D. (1999) 'Tensions between system and lifeworld: the imposition of a National Qualifications Framework on the humanities in South Africa', *International Journal: Continuous Improvement Monitor*, 1 (4) (www.llanes.panam.edu/journal/library/Vol1No4/luckett.html – accessed June 2006).

Lundh, A. (2006) personal email communication.

Lyall, K. (2006) 'Sensible change in a confusing policy environment', keynote address to the CASTL Colloquium on the Scholarship of Teaching and Learning, 1 April 2006, Madison (www.carnegiefoundation.org/files/elibrary/Lyall_Sensible_Change.pdf – accessed 29 May 2006).

Lyon, P.M. and Hendry, G.D. (2002) 'The use of the Course Experience Questionnaire as a monitoring evaluation tool in a problem-based medical programme', *Assessment and Evaluation in Higher Education*, 27: 339–352.

Maassen, P. and Cloete, N. (2002) 'The limits of policy', in N. Cloete, R. Fehnel, P. Maassen, T. Moja and P. Gibbon (eds) *Transformation in Higher Education: Global Pressures and Local Realities in South Africa*. Cape Town: Juta.

McAlpine, L. and Weston, C. (2000) 'Reflection: issues related to improving professors' teaching and students' learning', *Instructional Science*, 28: 363–385.

McCormick, A.C. (2000) 'Bringing the Carnegie classification into the 21st century', *American Association for Higher Education Bulletin*, 52: 3–15.

McDonald, G. (1990) 'Excellence, promotion policies, and educational standards', in S. Middleton, J. Codd and J. Jones (eds) *New Zealand Education Policy Today: Critical Perspectives*. Wellington: Allen and Unwin.

MacDonald-Ross, G. (2005) 'Research into teaching philosophy', *Academy Exchange*, 2: 16–18.

Macfarlane, B. (2004) *Teaching with Integrity: The Ethics of Higher Education Practice*. London: RoutledgeFalmer.

Macfarlane, B. (2007) *The Academic Citizen: The Virtue of Service in University Life*. Oxford: Routledge.

MacIntyre, A. (1985) *After Virtue: A Study in Moral Theory* (2nd edition). London: Duckworth.

McKenna, S. and Sutherland, L. (2006) 'Balancing knowledge construction and skills training in universities of technology', *Perspectives in Education*, 24, 3: 15–24.

McKibbin, R. (2006) 'The destruction of the public sphere', *London Review of Books*, 28 (5 January): 3–6.

McLean, M. (2001) 'Rewarding teaching excellence. Can we measure teaching "excellence"? Who should be the judge?' *Medical Teacher*, 23: 6–11.

McMurtry, J. (1991) 'Education and the market model', *Journal of Philosophy of Education*, 25: 209–217.

McNaught, C. and Anwyl, J. (1993) 'Awards for "teaching excellence" at Australian Universities', *Higher Education Review*, 25: 31–44.

McNay, I. (1999) 'The paradoxes of research assessment and funding', in M. Henkel and B. Little (eds) *Changing Relations between Higher Education and the State*. London: Jessica Kingsley.

McNay, I. (2003) 'The e-factors and organization cultures in British universities', in G. Williams (ed.) *The Enterprising University: Reform, Excellence and Equity*. Buckingham: SRHE/Open University Press.

McNiff, J., Lomax, P. and Whitehead, J. (1996) *You and Your Action Research Project.* London: Routledge.

McVeigh, B.J. (2002) *Japanese Higher Education as Myth.* New York: M.E. Sharpe.

McWilliam, E. (1996) 'Touchy Subjects: a risky inquiry into pedagogic pleasure', *British Educational Research Journal,* 22: 305–317.

McWilliam, E. (2002). 'Against professional development', *Educational Philosophy and Theory,* 34: 289–299.

McWilliam, E. (2004) 'Changing the academic subject', *Studies in Higher Education,* 29: 151–163.

Maier, M. (2002) *Project Summary.* Carnegie Foundation for the Advancement of Teaching (www.carnegiefoundation.org/programs/sub.asp?key=21&subkey=63&topkey=21 – accessed 29 May 2006).

Malcolm, J. and Zukas, M. (1999) 'Models of the educator in higher education: perspectives and problems', paper presented at Society for Teaching and Learning in Higher Education Conference (Collaborative Learning for the 21st Century), University of Calgary, June.

Malcolm, J. and Zukas, M. (2000) 'Becoming an educator: communities of practice in higher education', in I. McNay (ed.) *Higher Education and its Communities.* Buckingham: SRHE/Open University Press.

Malcolm, J. and Zukas, M. (2001) 'Bridging pedagogic gaps: conceptual discontinuities in higher education', *Teaching in Higher Education,* 6: 33–42.

Malcolm, J. and Zukas, M. (2005a) 'Poor relations: exploring discipline, research and pedagogy in academic identity', in J. Caldwell (ed.) *What a Difference a Pedagogy Makes: Researching Lifelong Learning and Teaching.* University of Stirling: Centre for Research in Lifelong Learning.

Malcolm, J. and Zukas, M. (2005b) 'The imaginary workplace: academics as workplace learners', paper presented at the fourth International Conference on Researching Work and Learning, University of Technology Sydney, December.

Malcolm, J. and Zukas, M. (2006) 'Pedagogic learning in the pedagogic workplace', in R. Edwards, J. Gallagher and S. Whittaker (eds) *Learning Outside the Academy: International Research Perspectives.* Abingdon: RoutledgeFalmer.

Marquand, D. (2006) 'Brave new dawn', *New Statesman,* 24 April: 46–47.

Marshall, D. (2004) 'Degree accreditation in Canada', *Canadian Journal of Higher Education,* 34: 69–96.

Marton, F. and Säljö, R. (1976) 'On qualitative differences in learning II – Outcome as a function of the learner's conception of the task', *British Journal of Educational Psychology,* 46: 115–127.

Maslen, G. (1997) 'Teachers take Ozcars', *Times Higher Education Supplement,* 5 December: 13.

Mazelan, N.A., Harnevie, M. and Valida, A.C. (1999) *Multimedia Super Corridor: A Journey to Excellence in Institutions of Higher Learning.* London: ASEAN Academic Press.

Menges, R.J. (1996) 'Awards to Individuals', in M.D. Svinicki and R.J. Menges (eds) *Honoring Exemplary Teaching.* New Directions for Teaching and Learning, no. 65. San Francisco: Jossey-Bass.

Meyer, J.H.P. and Land, R. (2005) 'Threshold concepts and troublesome knowledge (2): epistemological considerations and a conceptual framework for teaching and learning', *Higher Education,* 49: 373–388.

Ministry of Education, Culture, Sports, Science and Technology (MEXT) (2005) *Japan's Education at a Glance, 2005*. Tokyo: Kokuritsu Insatsukyoku (www.mext.go.jp/english/statist/05101901/005.pdf – accessed 19 July 2006).

Middleton, S. (2005a) 'One flew over the PBRF: disciplining the subject of Education', in R. Smith and J. Jesson (eds) *Punishing the Discipline – the PBRF Regime: Evaluating the Position of Education – Where to from Here?* Auckland: AUT University/University of Auckland, Faculty of Education.

Middleton, S. (2005b) 'Disciplining the subject: the impact of PBRF on Education academics', *New Zealand Journal of Educational Studies*, 40: 131–156.

Milton, P. (2002) *The QAA Subject Review Experience of Peer Observation of Teaching*. Learning and Teaching Support Network Generic Centre (www.heacademy.ac.uk/resources. htm – accessed on 9 April 2006).

Mock, J. (2005) 'American universities in Japan', in J.S. Eades, R. Goodman and Y. Hada (eds) *The 'Big Bang' in Japanese Higher Education: The 2004 Reforms and the Dynamics of Change*. Melbourne: Trans Pacific Press.

Moore, R. and Lewis, K. (2002). *Curriculum Responsiveness: The Implications for Curriculum Management*. Pretoria: South African Universities Vice-Chancellors Association.

Mori, R. (2002) 'Entrance examinations and remedial education in Japanese higher education', *Higher Education*, 43: 27–42.

Morley, L. (1997) 'Change and equity in higher education', *British Journal of Sociology of Education*, 18: 231–242.

Morley, L. (2003) *Quality and Power in Higher Education*. Buckingham: SRHE/Open University Press.

Morris Matthews, K. and Hall, C. (2006) 'The impact of the Performance-Based Research Fund on teaching and the research-teaching balance: survey of a New Zealand university', paper presented at the Symposium on the Evaluation of the PBRF, Wellington: Ministry of Education, Tertiary Education Commission and the Victoria University of Wellington, Institute of Policy Studies, February.

Mulcahy, D. (2006) 'The salience of space for pedagogy and identity in teacher education: problem-based learning as a case in point', *Pedagogy, Culture and Society*, 14: 55–69.

Murphy, P. (1996) 'Defining pedagogy', in P. Murphy and C. Gipps (eds) *Equity in the Classroom*. London: Falmer Press.

Murtonen, M. (2005) 'University students' research orientations: do negative attitudes exist toward quantitative methods?', *Scandinavian Journal of Educational Research*, 49: 263–280.

Naidoo, P. (2005) Keynote address given at the SAADA conference Port Elizabeth, South Africa.

Naidoo, R. and Jamieson, I. (2005) 'Empowering participants or corroding learning? Towards a research agenda on the impact of consumerism on higher education', *Journal of Educational Policy*, 20: 267–281.

Nakayama, S. and Low, M.F. (1997) 'The research function of universities in Japan', *Higher Education*, 34: 245–258.

National Committee of Inquiry into Higher Education (NCIHE) (1997) *Higher Education in the Learning Society: Report of the National Committee* (The Dearing Report). London: The Stationery Office.

National Science Foundation (NSF) (2000) *NSF GPRA Strategic Plan for FY 2001–2006*. Arlington, Virginia: NSF (www.nsf.gov/pubs/2001/nsf0104/nsf0104.txt).

NSF (2006) *Undergraduate Research Collaboratives (URC) Program Solicitation*. NSF 06–521 (www.nsf.gov/pubs/2006/nsf06521/nsf06521.htm).

National Survey of Student Engagement (2006) *National Survey of Student Engagement* (nsse.iub.edu/index.cfm – accessed 2 October 2006).

Neave, G. (1988) 'The evaluative state reconsidered', *European Journal of Education*, 33, 3: 265–284.

Neave, G. (2005) 'The supermarketed university: reform, vision and ambiguity in British Higher Education', *Perspective*, 9: 17–22.

Nelson, B. (2005) 'Science meets Parliament', National Press Club Speech, 8 March (www.dest.gov.au/Ministers/Media/Nelson/2005/03/ntran080305.asp).

Nespor, J. (1994) *Knowledge in Motion: Space, Time and Curriculum in Undergraduate Physics and Management*. London: Falmer Press.

Neumann, R. (1992) 'Perceptions of the teaching-research nexus: a framework for analysis', *Higher Education*, 23: 159–171.

Neumann, R. (1994) 'The teaching–research nexus: applying a framework to university students' learning experiences', *European Journal of Education*, 29: 323–339.

Newble, D. and Cannon, R. (1995) *A Handbook for Teachers in Universities and Colleges: A Guide to Improving Teaching Methods*. London: Kogan Page.

Newby, H. (2003) Answers to questions, The United Kingdom Parliament, Select Committee on Education and Skills, Examination of Witness (www.publications.parliament.uk/pa/cm200203/cmselect/cmeduski/425/3030504.htm).

Newton, J. (2001) 'Views from below: academics coping with quality', *Quality in Higher Education*, 8: 39–61.

New Zealand Government (1990) *Education Amendment Act*. Wellington, New Zealand.

New Zealand Qualifications Authority (NZQA) (2001) *Tertiary Teaching Awards*. Wellington: NZQA (www.nzqa.govt.nz/for-providers/awards/ttea/index.html – accessed 15 May 2006).

Nicoll, K. and Harrison, R. (2003) 'Constructing the good teacher in higher education: the discursive work of standards', *Studies in Continuing Education*, 25: 23–35.

Nixon, J. (2004a) 'Learning the language of deliberative democracy', in M. Walker and J. Nixon (eds) *Reclaiming Universities from a Runaway World*. Maidenhead and New York: Open University Press/McGraw-Hill Education.

Nixon, J. (2004b) 'Education for the good society: the integrity of academic practice', *London Review of Education* [Special Issue: D. Halpin, J. Nixon, S. Ranson and T. Seddon (eds) 'Renewing Education for Civic Society'] 2: 245–252.

Nixon, J. (2006a) 'Towards a hermeneutics of hope: the legacy of Edward W. Said', *Discourse: Studies in the Cultural Politics of Education*, 27: 341–356.

Nixon, J. (2006b) 'Relationships of virtue: rethinking the goods of civil association', *Ethics and Education*, 1–2: 149–161.

Nixon, J. and Ranson, S. (1997) 'Theorising "agreement": the bases of a new professional ethic', *Discourse: Studies in the Cultural Politics of Education*, 18: 197–214.

Nixon, J., Marks, A., Rowland, S. and Walker, M. (2001) 'Towards a new academic professionalism: a manifesto of hope', *British Journal of Sociology of Education*, 22: 227–244.

Nixon, J., Martin, J., McKeown, P. and Ranson, S. (1997) 'Confronting "failure": towards a pedagogy of recognition', *International Journal of Inclusive Education*, 1: 121–141.

Nkoane, M. (2005) 'African Universities: evolving self', paper presented at the South

African Association for Research and Development in Higher Education conference, University of KwaZulu-Natal, Durban, South Africa.

Nowotny, H., Scott, P. and Gibbons, M. (2001) *Re-thinking Science: Knowledge and the Public in an Age of Uncertainty*. Cambridge: Polity Press.

Nussbaum, M. (1997) *Cultivating Humanity: A Classical Defense of Reform in Liberal Education*. Cambridge: Harvard University, Cahners Publishing.

Nussbaum, M.C. (2001) *The Fragility of Goodness: Luck and Ethics in Greek Tragedy and Philosophy* (revised edition). Cambridge: Cambridge University Press.

Ogasawara, M. (2002) 'Strategic planning of the graduate and undergraduate education in a research university in Japan', *Higher Education Policy*, 15: 55—60.

Ogawa, Y. (1999) 'Japanese higher education reform: the University Council report', *International Higher Education*, 18: 22–23.

Ogawa, Y. (2002) 'Challenging the traditional organization of Japanese universities', *Higher Education*, 43: 85—108.

Olssen, M. (2002) 'The neo-liberal appropriation of tertiary education policy in New Zealand: accountability, research and academic freedom', *State-of-the-Art, Monograph No. 8, (October 2001)*, Wellington: New Zealand Association for Research in Education.

Olssen, M., Codd, J. and O'Neill, A.M. (2004) *Education Policy: Globalization, Citizenship and Democracy*. London: Sage.

O'Neill, O. (2002) *A Question of Trust* (The BBC Reith Lectures 2002). Cambridge: Cambridge University Press.

Orrell, J. (2006) 'Feedback on learning achievement: rhetoric and reality', *Teaching in Higher Education*, 11: 441–446.

Ottewill, R. and Macfarlane, B. (2004) 'Quality and the Scholarship of Teaching and Learning: learning from subject review', *Quality in Higher Education*, 10: 231–241.

Pahl, R. (1995) *After Success: 'Fin-de-Siecle' Anxiety and Identity*. Cambridge: Polity Press.

Pahl, R. (2000) *On Friendship*. Cambridge: Polity Press.

Palmer, P. (1998) *The Courage to Teach. Exploring the Inner Landscape of a Teacher's Life*. San Francisco: Jossey-Bass.

Park, C. and Ramos, M. (2002) 'The donkey in the department? Insights into the Graduate Teaching Assistant (GTA) experience in the UK', *Journal of Graduate Education*, 3: 47–53.

Parker, J. (2002) 'A new disciplinarity: communities of knowledge, learning and practice', *Teaching in Higher Education*, 7: 373–386.

Parry, G. (2005) 'English higher education and near universal access: the college Contribution', in G. Glaser (ed.) *Closing the Gap: the Impact of Widening Participation Strategies in the UK and the USA*. Leicester: National Institute of Adult and Continuing Education (NIACE).

Pashley, B.W. (1974) 'Pastoral support for university students – in loco parentis or functional necessity?', *Universities Quarterly*, 28: 178–196.

Patterson, G. (2001) 'The applicability of institutional goals to the university organisation', *Journal of Higher Education Policy and Management*, 23: 159–169.

Peer Review of Teaching Project (2006) *Peer Review of Teaching Project*, Lincoln: University of Nebraska Lincoln (www.courseportfolio.org/peer/pages/index.jsp – accessed 29 May 2006).

Percy, K.A and Salter, F.W. (1976) 'Student and staff perceptions and "the pursuit of excellence" in British higher education', *Higher Education*, 5: 457–473.

Peters, M. (1990) *Performance and Aaccountability: A Critical Approach to the Issues in New Zealand Higher Education.* Auckland: Northern Region Tutor Training Centre at the Auckland Institute of Technology.

Peters, M. (ed.) (1997) *Cultural Politics and the University in Aotearoa/New Zealand.* Palmerston North: The Dunmore Press.

Peters, M. and Roberts, P. (1998) 'Agendas for change: universities in the 21st century', in I. Livingstone (ed.) *New Zealand Annual Review of Education: 7, 1997.* Wellington: School of Education, Victoria University.

Phillips, D. (2003) 'Postscript, reflections on British interest in education in Japan', in R. Goodman and D. Phillips (eds) *Can the Japanese Change their Education System?* Oxford: Symposium.

Piercy, N.F., Lane, N. and Peters, L.D. (1997) 'The validity and reliability of student evaluations of courses and Faculty in British Business Schools', *Journal of European Business Education*, 6: 72–84.

Pillar, P.R. (2006) 'Intelligence, policy, and the war in Iraq', *Foreign Affairs*, 85:2 (March/April): 15–27.

Pocklington, T. and Tupper, A. (2002) *No Place to Learn: Why Universities aren't Working.* Vancouver: University of British Columbia Press.

Poole, G.S. (2005) 'Reform of the university English language teaching curriculum in Japan: a cast study', in J.S. Eades, R. Goodman and Y. Hada (eds) *The 'Big Bang' in Japanese Higher Education: The 2004 Reforms and the Dynamics of Change.* Melbourne: Trans Pacific Press.

Poole, G.S. and Amano I. (2003) 'Higher education reform in Japan: Amano Ikuo on "the university in crisis"', *International Education Journal*, 4: 149–176.

Power, M. (1997) *The Audit Society: Rituals of Verification.* Oxford: Oxford University Press.

Prebble, T., Hargraves, H., Leach, L., Naidoo, K., Suddaby, G. and Zepke, N. (2004) *Supporting Students in Tertiary Study: A Summary of a Synthesis of Research on the Impact of Student Support Services on Student Outcomes in Undergraduate Tertiary Study.* Wellington: Ministry of Education (www.minedu.govt.nz/index.cfm – accessed 15 May 2006).

Pring, R. (2003) 'The virtues and vices of an educational researcher', in P. Sikes, J. Nixon, and W. Carr (eds) *The Moral Foundations of Educational Research: Knowledge, Inquiry and Values.* Maidenhead and Philadelphia: Open University Press/McGraw-Hill Education.

Prosser, M. and Trigwell, K. (1999) *Understanding Learning and Teaching: The Experience in Higher Education.* Buckingham: SRHE/Open University Press.

Quality Assurance Agency for Higher Education (2000) *Subject Review Handbook: September 2000 to December 2001.* Gloucester: QAA.

Ramsden, P. (1992) *Learning to Teach in Higher Education.* London: Routledge.

Ramsden, P. (2003). *Learning to Teach in Higher Education* (2nd edition). London: RoutledgeFalmer.

Ramsden, P. and Martin, E. (1996) 'Recognition of good university teaching; policies from an Australian study', *Studies in Higher Education*, 32: 299–316.

Ranson, S. and Stewart, J. (1994) *Management for the Public Domain: Enabling the Learning Society.* Basingstoke: Macmillan/St Martin's Press.

Readings, B. (1996) *The University in Ruins.* Cambridge: Harvard University Press.

Rees-Mogg, W. (2002) 'The economics of idiocy: a degree-level introduction', *The Times*, 2 December: 18.

Reichard, D. (2004) *Project Summary*, Carnegie Foundation for the Advancement of Teaching (www.carnegiefoundation.org/programs/sub.asp?key=21&subkey=63& topkey=21 – accessed 29 May 2006).

Republic of South Africa (1997) *Higher Education Act of 1997.* Government Gazette, Pretoria: Department of Education.

Republic of South Africa (1998) *Skills Development Act no 97 of 1998.* Government Gazette, Pretoria: Department of Labour.

Research Forum (2004) *The Relationship between Research and Teaching in Institutions of Higher Education* (www.dfes.gov.uk/hegateway/uploads/Forum's_advice_to_ Ministers_on_Teaching_and_Research[1].pdf).

Rhoades, G. and Slaughter, S. (1998) 'Academic capitalism, managed professionals, and supply-side higher education', in R. Martin (ed.) *Chalk Lines: the Politics of Work in the Managed University.* Durham and London: Duke University Press.

Rhodes, D.M. (1976) 'Achieving teaching excellence: some misconceptions and a proposal', *Higher Education Bulletin*, 4: 105–121.

Rhodes, F.H.T. (2001) *The Creation of the Future: The Role of the American University.* Ithaca and London: Cornell University Press.

Ritzer, G. (1998) *The McDonalization Thesis.* London: Sage.

Rivers, J. (2005) Edited version of Prebble, T., Hargraves, H., Leach, L., Naidoo, K., Suddaby, G. and Zepke, N. (2004) *Supporting Students in Tertiary Study: A Summary of a Synthesis of Research on the Impact of Student Support Services on Student Outcomes in Undergraduate Tertiary Study.* Wellington: Ministry of Education.

Robbins Report (1963) *Higher Education: Report of the committee appointed by the Prime Minister under the chairmanship of Lord Robbins 1961–1963.* London: The Stationery Office.

Roberts, C., Hanstock, J. and Oakey, D. (2003) 'Developing an environment which rewards and recognises teaching: a case study in a pre-1992 university', paper presented to the 3rd Annual International Conference on the Scholarship of Teaching and Learning (SoTL), London, England (June).

Roberts, P. (2006) 'Performativity, measurement and research: a critique of New Zealand PBRF scheme', in J. Ozga, T. Seddon and T. Popkewitz (eds) *World Yearbook of Education 2006: Evaluation Research and Policy.* London: RoutledgeFalmer.

Robson, J. (2006) *Teacher Professionalism in Further and Higher Education: Challenges to Culture and Practice.* London: Routledge.

Rowland, S. (2000) *The Enquiring University Teacher.* Buckingham: Open University Press/SRHE.

Rowland, S. (2001) 'Surface learning about teaching in higher education: the need for more critical conversations', *International Journal of Academic Development*, 6: 162–167.

Rowland, S. (2003) 'Academic development: a practical or theoretical business?', in H. Eggins and R. MacDonald (eds) *The Scholarship of Academic Development.* Buckingham: SRHE/Open University Press.

Rowland, S. (2005) 'Intellectual love and the link between teaching and research', in R. Barnett (ed.) *Reshaping the University: New Relationships between Research, Scholarship and Teaching.* Buckingham: SRHE/Open University Press.

Roxá, T. (2003) 'The Swedish experience', *Exchange*, autumn (5): 21.

Ruben, B.D. (2004) *Pursing Excellence in Higher Education: Eight Fundamental Challenges.* San Francisco: Jossey-Bass.

Sacks, J. (2000) *The Politics of Hope*. London: Vintage.

Said, E.W. (2004) *Humanism and Democratic Criticism*. New York: Columbia University Press.

Schlegel, W. (2004) *Project Summary*. Carnegie Foundation for the Advancement of Teaching (www.carnegiefoundation.org/programs/sub.asp?key=21&subkey=63&topkey=21 – accessed 29 May 2006).

Scott, P. (1995) *The Meaning of Mass Higher Education*. Buckingham: Open University Press.

Seely Brown, J. and Duguid, P. (1996) 'Organisational learning and communities-of-Practice: towards a unified view of working, learning and innovation'. in M.D. Cohen and L.S. Sproull (eds) *Organisational Learning*. London: Sage Publications.

Seki, M. (1995) *21 Seiki no Daigakuzo: Rekishiteki, Kokusaiteki Shiten kara no Kento*. Tokyo: Tamagawa Daigaku Shuppanbu.

Sennett, R. (1999) *The Corrosion of Character: the Personal Consequences of Work in the New Capitalism*. New York and London: W.W. Norton and Company.

Sennett, R. (2003) *Respect: the Formation of Character in an Age of Inequality*. London: Allen Lane The Penguin Press.

Sennett, R. (2006) *The Culture of the New Capitalism*. New Haven and London: Yale University Press.

Sergiovanni, T.J. (1992) *Moral Leadership: Getting to the Heart of School Leadership*. San Francisco: Jossey-Bass.

Sfard, A. (1998) 'On two metaphors for learning and the dangers of choosing just one', *Educational Researcher*, 27: 4–13.

Shannon, D.M., Twale, D.J. and Moore, M.S. (1998) 'TA teaching effectiveness', *The Journal of Higher Education*, 69: 440–466.

Shils, E. (1997) *The Calling of Education: The Academic Ethic and Other Essays on Higher Education*. Chicago: University of Chicago Press.

Shore, B.M., Foster, S.F., Knapper, C.K., Nadeau, G.G., Neill, N. and Sim, V. (1986) *The Teaching Dossier: A Guide to its Preparation and Use*. Montreal, Canada: Canadian Association for University Teachers.

Shulman, L.S. (1993) 'Teaching as community property', *Change*, 25: 6–7.

Shulman L.S. (2001) Foreword, *The Carnegie Classification of Institutions of Higher Education*. Stanford: Carnegie Foundation (www.carnegiefoundation.org/dynamic/downloads/file_1_341.pdf).

Shulman, L.S. (2004) 'Those who understand: knowledge growth in teaching', in S. Wilson (ed.) *The Wisdom of Practice: Essays on Teaching, Learning and Learning to Teach*. San Francisco: Jossey-Bass.

Shulman, L.S. (2005) 'Pedagogies of uncertainty', *Liberal Education*, Spring 2005, 91: 2 (www.aacu.org/liberaleducation/le-sp05/le- – accessed 29 May 2006).

Shulman, L.S. (2006) *Sustaining Momentum*, unpublished keynote address to the CASTL Colloquium on the Scholarship of Teaching and Learning, Madison, April.

Simon, B. (1981) 'Why no pedagogy in England?', in B. Simon and W. Taylor (eds) *Education in the Eighties*. London: Batsford.

Singh, M. (2001) 'Re-inserting the "public good" into Higher Education Transformation', *Kagisano* (www.che.ac.za/publications/kagisano.php).

Skelton, A. (2002) 'Understanding "teaching excellence" in higher education: a critical evaluation of the National Teaching Fellowship Scheme'. Final Report to the Economic and Social Research Council, July (award no: R000 22 3509).

Skelton, A. (2003) 'Promoting "teaching excellence" through fellowship schemes: three important issues to consider', *Medical Education*, 37: 188–189.

Skelton, A. (2004) 'Understanding "teaching excellence" in higher education: a critical evaluation of the National Teaching Fellowship Scheme', *Studies in Higher Education*, 29: 451–468.

Skelton, A. (2005) *Understanding Teaching Excellence in Higher Education: Towards a Critical Approach*. London: Routledge.

Smeby, J.C. (1998) 'Knowledge production and knowledge transmission. The interaction between research and teaching at universities', *Teaching in Higher Education*, 3: 5–20.

Smith, B. (2006) 'Quest for quality: the UK experience', in C. Kreber (ed.) *International Policy Perspectives on Improving Learning with Limited Resources*, New Directions for Higher Education. San Francisco: Jossey-Bass/Wiley.

Smith, L. (2006) 'Fourteen lessons of resistance to exclusion: learning from the Māori experience in New Zealand over the last two decades of neo-liberal reform', in M. Mulholland (ed.), *State of Māori Nation: Twenty-First-Century Issues in Aotearoa*. Auckland: Reed Publishers.

Smith, R. (1997) 'Making teaching count in Canadian higher education: developing a national agenda', Newsletter of the Society of Teaching and Learning in Higher Education 21.

Smith, R. (2005) 'Counting research in education: what counts under the Sherriff of Nottingham-style funding redistribution?', in R. Smith and J. Jesson (eds) *Punishing the Discipline – the PBRF Regime: Evaluating the position of Education – Where to from here?* Auckland: AUT University/University of Auckland, Faculty of Education.

Smith, R. and Jesson, J. (2005a) 'Shaping academic identity: the politics and "performativity" of research under government accountability frameworks: lessons from New Zealand', in J. Barbara, M. Leach and L. Walsh (eds) *Refereed Conference Proceedings of the Politics of Recognition: Identity, Respect and Justice*. Melbourne: Deakin University Press.

Smith, R. and Jesson, J. (eds) (2005b) *Punishing the Discipline – the PBRF Regime: Evaluating the position of Education – Where to from here?* Auckland: AUT University/University of Auckland, Faculty of Education.

Society for Teaching and Learning in Canada (2006a) (www.mcmaster.ca/stlhe/awards/alan.blizzard.award.html – accessed 3 August 2006).

Society for Teaching and Learning in Canada (2006b) *3M Teaching Fellowship Program* (www.mcmaster.ca.3Mteachingfellowships/nom_info.html – accessed 16 March 2006).

Sommerlad, E. (2003) 'Theory, research and practice – the problematic appearance of 'pedagogy' in post-compulsory education', *Journal of Adult and Continuing Education*, 8: 147–164.

Spady, W. (1995) *Outcomes-Based Education: Critical Issues*. American Association of School Administration: Breakthrough Systems.

Staffordshire University (2000) *Guidelines on the Peer Observation of Teaching* (www.staffs.ac.uk/services/qis/surf/append/app.13.doc – accessed 2 April 2006).

Stierer, B. and Antoniou, M. (2004) 'Are there distinctive methodologies for pedagogic research in higher education?', *Teaching in Higher Education*, 9: 275–285.

Sullivan, K. (1997) 'What should count as work in the Ivory Tower?: Determining academic workloads in tertiary institutions, A university case study', *State-of-the-Art,*

Monograph No. 6, (June). Wellington: New Zealand Association for Research in Education.

Sullivan, W.M. (2001) *What is Practical Reason*, Carnegie Foundation for the Advancement of Teaching (www.carnegiefoundation.org/dynamic/downloads/file_1_ 189.pdf – accessed 29 May 2006).

Sustaining Student Voices in the Scholarship of Teaching CASTL Program Leadership Cluster (2005) *Sustaining Student Voices in the Scholarship of Teaching and Learning*. Carnegie Foundation for the Advancement of Teaching (www.cfkeep.org/html/snapshot.php?id=9843158 – accessed 29 May 2006).

Swain, H. (1997) 'New learning and teaching body set to reward excellence', *Times Higher Education Supplement*, 21 November: 3.

Symes, C. and McIntyre, J. (2000) *Working Knowledge: The New Vocationalism and Higher Education*. Buckingham: SRHE/Open University Press.

Takeuchi, Y. (1997) 'The self-activating entrance examination system – its hidden agenda and its correspondence with the Japanese "salary man"', Higher Education, 34: 183–198.

Tanaka, T. (2003) 'Kyoto daigaku ni okeru FD', *IDE Gendai no Koto Kyoiku*, 447, March: 16–20.

Taylor, C. (1991) *The Ethics of Authenticity*. Cambridge and London: Harvard University Press.

Taylor, C. and Green, B. (2006) 'The Sydney Basin Aerobiology Survey: incorporating students into a current research program as part of the first year Biology curriculum', poster presented at the University of Sydney College of Science and Technology Teaching and Learning Showcase, Sydney NSW, November 2006 (science.uniserve.edu.au/courses/showcase/showcase2006/ – accessed 13 November 2006).

Teaching Matters Forum (2005a) *Teaching for Learning: Proposals for a National Centre for Tertiary Teaching Excellence*. A discussion document issued by the Teaching Matters Forum, April, Wellington: Tertiary Education Commission.

Teaching Matters Forum (2005b) *The Consultation Report*. Report on Submissions to the Teaching Matters Forum Discussion Paper and the Consultations Undertaken, July, Wellington: Tertiary Education Commission.

Teaching Matters Forum (2005c) *Report and Recommendations on Proposals for a National Centre for Tertiary Teaching Excellence*. July, Wellington: Tertiary Education Commission.

Teaching Matters Working Group (2005) *Report to the Sector on Governance and Management*. December, Wellington: Tertiary Education Commission.

Tertiary Education Advisory Committee (2001) *Collaborating For Efficiency*. Wellington: Steering Group Report on Staffing.

Tertiary Education Commission (2005) *Statement of Tertiary Education Priorities 2005–2007*. Wellington: Tertiary Education Commission.

Tertiary Education Commission (2006) *Invitation for a Proposal*. Wellington: Tertiary Education Commission.

Texeira, P.N., Johnstone, D.B., Rosa, M.J. and Vossensteyn, H. (eds) (2006) *Cost-Sharing and Accessibility in Higher Education: A Fairer Deal?* The Netherlands: Springer.

3M Teaching Fellowship Program (2006) (www.mcmaster.ca/3Mteachingfellowships/nom_info.html#4 – accessed 3 August 2006).

Times Higher Education Supplement (2000) *Blackstone Criticises Teaching Awards*, 21 July: 2.

Times Higher Education Supplement (THES) (2005) *World University Rankings* (www.thes.co.uk/statistics/international_comparisons/2005/top_unis.aspx?window_ty pe=popup – accessed 19 July 2006).

Tinto, V. (1993) *Leaving College: Rethinking the Causes and Cures of Student Attrition* (2nd edition). Chicago: Chicago University Press.

Trigwell, K. and Shale, S. (2004) 'Student learning and the scholarship of university teaching', *Studies in Higher Education*, 29: 266–275.

Trigwell, K. Martin, E., Benjamin, J. and Prosser, M. (2000) 'Scholarship of teaching: a model', *Higher Education Research and Development*, 19: 155–168.

Trowler, P. (1998) *Academics Responding to Change: New Higher Education Frameworks and Academic Cultures.* Buckingham: SRHE/Open University Press.

Trowler, P. (2002) *Higher Education Policy and Institutional Change: Intentions and Outcomes in Turbulent Environments.* Buckingham: SRHE/Open University Press.

Trowler, P. (2005) 'A sociology of teaching, learning and enhancement: improving practices in higher education', *Revista de Sociologia*, Papers 76: 13–32.

Trowler, P. and Bamber, R. (2005) 'Compulsory higher education teacher training: Joined-up policies, institutional architectures and enhancement cultures', *International Journal for Academic Development*, 10: 79–93.

Trowler, P. and Cooper, A. (2002) 'Teaching and learning regimes, implicit theories and recurrent practices in the enhancement of teaching and learning through educational development programmes', *Higher Education Research and Development*, 21: 221–240.

Trowler, P., Fanghanel, J. and Wareham, T. (2005) 'Freeing the chi of change: the Higher Education Academy and enhancing teaching and learning in higher education', *Studies in Higher Education*, 30: 427–444.

Tsuruta, Y. (2003) 'Globalisation and the recent reforms in Japanese higher education', in R. Goodman and D. Phillips (eds) *Can the Japanese Change their Education System?* Oxford: Symposium.

Umakoshi, T. (1997) 'Internationalization of Japanese higher education in the 1980s and early 1990s', *Higher Education*, 34: 259–273.

UNITEC Institute of Technology (1993) *Students Flyer.* Auckland: Unitec Institute of Technology (www.unitec.ac.nz – accessed 15 May 2006).

University of Alberta (2006) (www.uofaweb.ualberta.ca/researchandstudents/nav01. cfm?nav01=32191& – accessed 15 September 2006).

University of Arizona (n.d.) *The Honors College University of Arizona* (www.honors.arizona.edu/ProspectiveStudents/benefits.htm).

University of Sydney (2006) 'Scholarship Index' (www.usyd.edu.au/learning/quality/ si.shtml#faq – accessed 13 September 2006).

University of Warwick (2002) *Teaching Profile Preparation: Guidance Notes* (www2. warwick.ac.uk/services/cap/profdev/career/promotion/teachexcell.doc – accessed 4 April 2006).

Urry, J. (2002) 'Globalizing the academy', in K. Robins and F. Webster (eds) *The Virtual University?: Knowledge, Markets, and Management.* Oxford: Oxford University Press.

Usher, R. and Edwards, R.G. (2005) 'Subjects, networks and positions: thinking educational guidance differently', *British Journal of Guidance and Counselling*, 33: 397–410.

Usher, R., Bryant, I. and Johnston, R. (1997) *Adult Education and the Postmodern Challenge*. London: Routledge.

Ushiogi, M. (1997) 'Japanese graduate education and its problems', *Higher Education* 34: 237–244.

Verkleij, A.C. (1999) 'Different approaches to defining research quality', *Bulletin*, 2 March.

Vidovich, L. (2004) 'Global-national-local dynamics in policy processes: a case of "quality" policy in higher education', *British Journal of Sociology of Education*, 25: 341–354.

Walker, M. (2006) *Higher Education Pedagogies*. Maidenhead: Open University Press.

Warren, R. and Plumb, E. (1999) 'Survey of distinguished teacher award schemes in higher education', *Journal of Further and Higher Education*, 23: 245–255.

Webbstock, D. (1999) 'A proposed framework for a university response to external quality monitoring in South Africa', *Bulletin*, 13–17 March.

Weick, K.E. (1976) 'Educational organizations as loosely coupled systems', *Administrative Science Quarterly*, 21: 1–19.

Weimer, M.E. (1991) *Improving College Teaching*. San Francisco: Jossey-Bass.

Wenger, E. (1998) *Communities of Practice: Learning, Meaning and Identity*. Cambridge: Cambridge University Press.

Wenger, E., McDermott, R. and Snyder, W.M. (2002) *Cultivating Communities of Practice*. Boston: Harvard Business School Press.

Wentzel, H.K. (1987) 'Seminars in college teaching: an approach to faculty Development', *College Teaching*, 35: 70–71.

Werder, C. *et al.* (2005) *Sustaining Student Voices in the Scholarship of Teaching and Learning; A Carnegie Academy Campus Program Cluster*. The Carnegie Foundation for the Advancement of Teaching (www.cfkeep.org/html/snapshot.php?id=9843158 – accessed 29 May 2006).

Williams, B. (2002) *Truth and Truthfulness: An Essay in Genealogy*. Princeton and Oxford: Princeton University Press.

Williams, D. (2005) 'Literacies and learning', in P. Levy and S. Roberts (eds) *Developing the New Learning Environment: the Changing Role of the Academic Librarian*. London: Facet.

Woodhouse, D. (1998) 'Auditing research and the research/teaching nexus', *New Zealand Journal of Educational Studies*, 33: 39–53.

Yamada, R. (2001) 'University reform in the post-massification era in Japan: analysis of government education policy for the 21st century', *Higher Education Policy*, 14: 277–291.

Yamamoto, S. (2005) 'Government and the national universities: ministerial bureaucrats and dependent universities', in J.S. Eades, R. Goodman and Y. Hada (eds) *The 'Big Bang' in Japanese Higher Education: The 2004 Reforms and the Dynamics of Change*. Melbourne: Trans Pacific Press.

Yonezawa, A. (1998) 'Further privatization in Japanese higher education?', *International Higher Education*, 13: 20–22.

Yonezawa, A. (2002) 'The quality assurance system and market forces in Japanese higher education', *Higher Education*, 43: 127–139.

Yorke, M. (2001) 'Formative assessment and its relevance to retention', *Higher Education Research and Development*, 20: 115–126.

Yorke, M. (2004) 'Retention, persistence and success in on-campus higher education, and their enhancement in open and distance learning', *Open Learning*, 19: 19–32.

Yorke, M. and Knight, P. (2003) 'The undergraduate curriculum and employability', Enhancing Student Employability Co-ordination Team (ESECT) and Learning and Teaching Support Network (LTSN) Generic Centre.

Yorke, M. and Thomas, L. (2003) 'Improving student retention from lower socio- economic groups', *Journal of Higher Education Policy and Management*, 25: 63–74.

Yoshida, A. (2002) 'The curriculum reforms of the 1990s: what has changed?', *Higher Education*, 43: 43–63.

Young, M. (1961) *The Rise of the Meritocracy 1870–2033: An Essay on Education and Equality*. Harmondswoth: Penguin Books (first published 1958, Thames and Hudson).

Young, M.F.D (ed.) (1971) *Knowledge and Control: New Directions for the Sociology Of Education*. London: Collier-Macmillan.

Zamorski, B. (2002) 'Research-led teaching and learning in higher education: a case', *Teaching in Higher Education*, 7: 411–427.

Ze Amvela, E. (2000) 'Collaboration and partnership for excellence in higher education: a case study of the University of Douala in Cameroon', Towards the Global University II: redefining excellence in the Third Millennium conference, Stellenboch, South Africa, April.

Zukas, M. and Malcolm, J. (2002a) 'Pedagogies for lifelong learning: building bridges or building walls?', in R. Harrison, F. Reeve, A. Hanson and J. Clarke (eds) *Supporting Lifelong Learning: Volume 1 – Perspectives on Learning*. London: RoutledgeFalmer.

Zukas, M. and Malcolm, J. (2002b) 'Playing the game: regulation and scrutiny in academic identities', seminar paper presented at University of Sheffield, October.

Index